# The Vestry Book
OF
# Blisland (Blissland) Parish

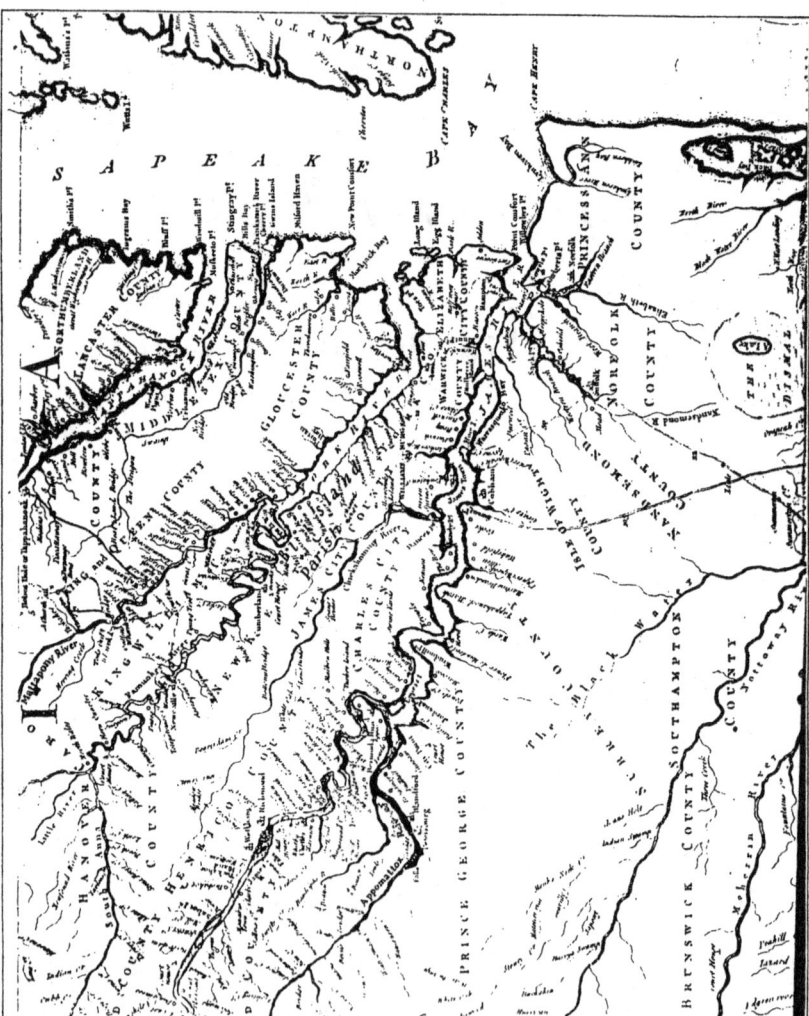

Section of a Map of the Most Inhabited Part of Virginia... By Joshua Fry and Peter Jefferson, 1775 Edition, to Which Have Been Added, at the Proper Places, the Names "Blisland Parish" and "Appomattox River."

# THE
# VESTRY BOOK

OF

## BLISLAND (BLISSLAND) PARISH

NEW KENT AND JAMES CITY COUNTIES, VIRGINIA

1721-1786

---

TRANSCRIBED AND EDITED BY

C. G. CHAMBERLAYNE

---

CLEARFIELD

Originally published
Richmond, Virginia, 1935

Reprinted for
Clearfield Company, Inc. by
Genealogical Publishing Co., Inc.
Baltimore, Maryland
1999

International Standard Book Number: 0-8063-4848-8

*Made in the United States of America*

# Prefatory Note

During the colonial period, not only was the Established Church, or Church of England, supreme in the religious life of Virginia but its parishes were also local governmental institutions which affected very closely the people in their secular affairs. Parish records are therefore, in a true sense, official, important and revealing. Extant vestry books and registers supplement the archives of local governments when they do not indeed supply the only existing records. For these reasons the Library Board has published from time to time certain original parish books, this being the fourth. It is hoped that this work may be continued for, although most of these original records have been lost or destroyed, there are still a number of them in existence, comparatively few of which have been published.

During almost the entire period covered by this vestry book (1721-1786) Blisland Parish was partly in the present New Kent County and partly in the present James City County, the records of both of which, prior to 1865, have been destroyed. This volume and two of those previously published by the Library Board ("The Vestry Book of Stratton Major Parish, King and Queen County, Virginia, 1729-1783" (1931) and "The Vestry Book of Petsworth Parish, Gloucester County, Virginia, 1677-1793" (1933) ) supply a record for a contiguous area of early Virginia whose local archives have been lost. This vestry book, therefore, enables us further to rescue from oblivion much of the life, customs and names of those who helped to create Virginia.

Dr. Churchill Gibson Chamberlayne, who has prepared the present volume, is the editor of the two other publications mentioned above. He had previously published at his own expense three other volumes of parish records. Actuated by love for his church and state, he has undertaken this exacting work without remuneration; qualified by scholarship and experience, he has thus made valuable contributions to the printed documents of Virginia. This volume maintains his high standards of editorship and historical research. Dr. Chamberlayne has the gratitude of the Library Board for this work as he will have that of the people of Virginia.

WILMER L. HALL,
*State Librarian.*

Richmond, May 8, 1935.

## List of Illustrations

Section of A Map of the Most Inhabited Part of Virginia, by Fry and Jefferson, 1775........Frontispiece

The Blisland Parish Grievances of 1677..........
　　　　　　　　　　Between pages xlii and xliii

Page 10 of the Manuscript.......Between pages 14 and 15

Hickory Neck Church, Blisland Parish, James City County, Virginia ...................Facing page 53

# Introduction

The manuscript volume hereinafter reproduced in print embodies the earliest consecutive records of Blisland (or Blissland) Parish, New Kent and James City counties, Virginia, known to be in existence. Doubtless there once were manuscript records of Blisland Parish antedating those here given to the public, but even before Bishop Meade's day all trace of them must have been lost, for the Bishop makes no reference to them. Indeed, when his *Old Churches, Ministers and Families of Virginia* was first published, in part and in tentative form in *The Protestant Episcopal Review, and Church Register* (beginning with the issue for April, 1855) and the *Southern Churchman* (beginning with the issue for April 26, 1855), Bishop Meade was apparently unaware of the existence of any parish record of Blisland; nor evidently did he learn that there was such a record until after the first volume of the *Old Churches* (1857) was in print, for on page 388 of that volume he says, referring to Blisland Parish, "No vestry-book remains to tells its history." However, before the second volume of the work was released from the press, a vestry-book of Blisland Parish came to light, and the Bishop refers to it in a note on the last page of his book.[1] The present publication now for the first time makes accessible to students of Colonial Virginia history these old and for many years lost and forgotten records of Blisland Parish.

The manuscript Vestry Book is a folio, 14⅛ by 9¼ inches in size, consisting of 77 leaves (154 pages) of heavy, unruled, laid paper, the water marks being two in number: The Roman numeral IV (½ inch by 1 inch); and a fleur-de-lis on a shield, surmounted by a crown, the whole over the monogram WR (5⅝ inches by 2¾ inches). Whether

---

[1] Meade, *Old Churches, Ministers and Families of Virginia*, Vol. II, page 496.

or not the volume ever contained more leaves than at present, the editor does not know, but he thinks not; certainly no leaves are missing at the back, and there is little or no indication that any have been torn out in front. The record as it now stands covers the period from the autumn of 1721 to October 11, 1786, or 65 years. This old manuscript volume is one of twenty-five or more Colonial Virginia parish record books belonging to the Protestant Episcopal Church in Virginia, which were formerly kept in the Library of the Theological Seminary at Alexandria, and are now in the custody of the Virginia State Library, in Richmond.

With regard to the origin of the name Blisland given to this old Colonial Virginia parish, the present editor is unhappily entirely ignorant. Under the circumstances, therefore, he can do no better than quote the opinion of the late Hon. Hugh Blair Grigsby, of Norfolk, as given to Bishop Meade in 1857. Mr. Grigsby wrote: "Blisland.—This is a common name in England, and is synonymous with 'happy land'. It is evidently applied from some local incident long lost, or from some place in England connected with some of its parishioners. The word was originally Bliss-land."[2]

## 1. Establishment and Territorial Changes

While the only manuscript vestry book of Blisland Parish known to be in existence begins in the year 1721, the parish itself can be traced back to a date much earlier, namely, to the year 1653, at which period the territory involved was included in York County.[3] Of course, in the absence of positive proof to the contrary, it may be that the parish was established some years prior to 1653; however, all the evidence on the subject discovered by the present editor, while

---
[2] Meade, *Old Churches*, Vol. II, page 426.
[3] See page xi.

entirely negative in character, points, as will be seen, to the three and a half months between July 1, 1653, and October 13, 1653, as the period within which Blisland Parish was established.

That Blisland Parish was established prior to October 13, 1653, is evidenced by the following land patent issued on that date:

> "To all &c Whereas &c Now Know Yee, That I yᵉ ſaid Richard Bennet Esq. &c Give and Grant unto Thomas Dunketon fifty acres of land scituated in York County, in Bliſland pariſh, Beginning from Mr. Barnehouſe his mark'd maple tree in matchemeed ſwamp running up Eaſt South Eaſt by a branch of the ſaiᵈ Swamp to yᵉ top of yᵉ hill, thence weſt by north to yᵉ land of Mr. Barnehouſe, & north north Eaſt to yᵉ place where It began, bounded by mark'd trees on all ſides; The ſaid land being due unto yᵉ ſaid Thomas Dunketon by and for yᵉ tranſportation of one ⅌ſon &c To have and to hold &c Yeilding & Paying &c wᶜʰ payment &c Dated yᵉ 13:ᵗʰ of October 1653."[4]

It might of course be objected that one land patent, itself a copy made in 1694, or later, of the original record (and so containing possibly a copyist's error as to the name Blisland Parish), is insufficient evidence of the antiquity of the parish. However, there is additional evidence practically to the same effect in the same book, namely the following land patent, which bears a date less than eight months later than that of the patent above:

> "To all &c Whereas &c Now Know Yee That I yᵉ ſaid Richard Bennet Eſq &c Give & Grant unto John Pouncey fower hundred and fifty acres of land ſcituated on yᵉ ſouth ſide of yᵉ freſhes of Yorke river, in yᵉ pariſh of Bliſsland

---
[4] Virginia Land Office, *Patent Book* No. 3, page 5.

between Pounceys Creek & Tanks Creeke & joining to yᵉ land of yᵉ ſaid Pouncey by and for yᵉ tranſportation of nine perſons into this Colony &c To have and to hold &c Yeilding & Paying &c w:ᶜʰ payment is to be made &c Provided &c Dated yᵉ 7:ᵗʰ of June 1654."[5]

It may be noted here in passing that in the Patent Books in the Virginia Land Office there are to be found copies of five land patents (the two immediately above and three others) giving the location of the lands as in Blisland Parish and dated respectively Oct. 13, 1653, June 7, 1654, Oct. 12, 1657, Oct. 30, 1657, and Nov. 18, 1663.

So much for the positive evidence that Blisland Parish was in existence on October 13, 1653. The evidence that the parish was not established many months prior to that date is by no means so conclusive, for it is purely negative in character; however, while each bit of evidence taken by itself is perhaps negligible, the weight of all the evidence when taken together is cumulative and therefore considerable if not absolutely convincing. That evidence is as follows:

*Patent Book* No. 2 in the Virginia Land Office contains copies of twenty or more patents to land in York County (or "in York river" or "Up pamunkee river") granted by Governor Sir William Berkeley between 1644 and 1652; but while Hampton Parish[6] is mentioned several times, some-

---

[5] Virginia Land Office, *Patent Book* No. 3, page 13.

[6] Hampton was one of the very early Virginia parishes. It was established in 1640. Until March, 1643, when its name was changed to Hampton, it was known as Chescake (or Chiskiack, or Chickyack, or Kiskeake or Kiskiacke, or Kiskyacke, or Kiskyake) Parish. In 1680 it was one of four parishes lying wholly or—as in the case of one of them, Bruton or Brewton—partly in York County. Its eastern boundary was Townsend Creek (later known as Yorktown Creek). Being the farthest west parish of a county which until 1654, when New Kent County was established, extended indefinitely to the west, Hampton had probably no western boundary line until the year that Blisland Parish was established (probably 1653), when Scimino Creek became its western boundary. With the establishment of Marston Parish in 1654, Queen's Creek (between Scimino and Townsend creeks) became Hampton's western boundary.

times under its original name of Kiskeake (or Chickyack), sometimes as Hampton, its new name given in 1643, there is no mention whatever of Blisland Parish. In this connection it is, however, only fair to say that over half the patents in question fail to refer by name to any parish; therefore the absence of the name Blisland from the pages of *Patent Book* No. 2 is in itself not absolute proof that the parish was not in existence before Governor Berkeley left office.

*Patent Book* No. 3 begins with patents issued by Governor Richard Bennett, who took office April 30, 1652. In this volume there are copies of ten or more patents to land in York County (or "on york river" or "in york river") granted between November 12, 1652, and June 7, 1654. Of these land patents, five, the latest of which is dated July 1, 1653, are of particular interest. The first of these patents, which is dated Nov. 12, 1652, reads: "grant unto John Rogers Seven hundred and twenty Acres of Land lying on the South Side of york river Near Skimmino Creeke." Now it is to be noted that the patent does not say on which side of "Skimmino Creeke" the land lay, and as that creek was in 1654 made the boundary line of New Kent County and presumably (for reasons to be given later) had been made the eastern boundary line of Blisland Parish at its establishment, it is impossible to state with certainty that this land lay within the bounds of Blisland Parish when established. The second and third patents, dated respectively Feb. 10 and Feb. 12, 1652,[7] are to land granted to Mrs. Hannah Clarke situated "in the County of Yorke and upon the South Side and within the ffreshes of yorke river" (the wording being exactly the same in the two patents). Now it is to be noted above, in the patent to John Pouncey, dated June 7, 1654, that land situated "on yᵉ ſouth ſide of yᵉ freſhes of York river" was in the parish of Blisland; therefore if Blisland Parish was in existence on Feb. 10, 1653, the lands mentioned in these two patents to Mrs. Hannah

---

[7] i. e. 1653.

Clarke were in Blisland Parish. The fourth patent that is of special interest in connection with the fixing of the date of the establishment of Blisland Parish is that granted on April 14, 1653, to William Hoccaday. It reads: "...... that I the Said Richard Bennett Esq$^r$. &c give and grant unto m$^r$ William Hoccaday one Thousand Acres of Land head of a former devident Neer the head of Ware Creeke on the ...... Side of yorke river beginning in the County of yorke bounded Viz$^t$ Northweſt by North upon his former devident South Eaſt by South upon the ware Creeke and North weſt by North towards Waraney Creeke." This patent is interesting for three reasons: (1) its reference to Ware Creek, which is west of Scimino Creek and was therefore well within the bounds of New Kent County as established in 1654.[8]. Later, in 1767, the line of Ware Creek was made a part of the eastern boundary line of New Kent County;[9] (2) its reference to Waraney Creek, which was in Blisland Parish and from which one of the churches within the bounds of that parish later took its name; and (3) its reference to an earlier patent granted to the same patentee. Now in *Patent Book* No. 2, page 93, there is to be seen a patent—doubtless the one referred to above—granted Aug. 6, 1646, by Sir William Berkeley to "William Hockaday" for "five hundred Acres of Land and lyeing on the South ſide of Charles [10] river Neare the Narrowes being in the County of yorke bounded (Viz$^t$) North weſt by weſt upon Warrany Creeke North Eaſt by Eaſt upon the river South Eaſt by Eaſt toward the ware Creeke." The last of the patents to be noted as of special interest in this connection is that granted July 1, 1653, to Robert Priddy for 377 acres of land "scituated in York County in y$^e$ Narrows running South West by y$^e$ Land of George Chapman . . . East to y$^e$ Lands of W$^m$ Cox and the Land of Jo$^a$ Hope."

---

[8] *Hening, Statutes at Large . . . of Virginia*, Vol. I, page 388.
[9] *Hening*, Vol. VIII, page 209.
[10] i. e. York.

In this patent the word to be noted is "Narrows," which in the patent to William Hockaday immediately above is associated with Ware Creek, which is known to be within the bounds of Blisland Parish.

Here then are five land patents, all of them dated less than one year prior to Oct. 13, 1653 (when Blisland Parish is mentioned by name in a patent to Thomas Dunketon), four of which almost certainly, and the fifth one possibly, refer to land within the known bounds of Blisland Parish, but none of which mentions the parish by name. Under the circumstances it seems most reasonable to suppose that Blisland Parish was not established many months prior to Oct. 13, 1653. However, in view of the fact before stated, that by no means all patents to land within the bounds of a parish refer to the parish by name, it is entirely possible that Blisland Parish may some day be found to have been established a year, or even two or three years, prior to 1653.

In this connection it is of interest to note: (1) that on July 5, 1653, there was convened the third Grand Assembly held subsequent to the surrender of the Colony of Virginia (on March 12, 1652) to the Parliament of the Commonwealth, and (2) that at this Assembly Mr. Wm. Hockaday sat as one of the four Burgesses for York County. It is the belief of the present editor that it was at this session of the Grand Assembly that Blisland Parish was established, and he thinks it most probable that it was on the motion of Mr. Wm. Hockaday, who was a large landowner in that part of York County that subsequently was included in Blisland Parish[11] and who took a somewhat prominent part in the proceedings of this Assembly,[12] that the Act establishing Blisland Parish was passed.

[11] See page xiv. Note also that there was a Hockaday on the vestry of Blisland Parish in 1703 (page lii) and that the Hockaday family was prominent in the parish through the whole period covered by the extant Vestry Book.

[12] *Hening*, Vol. I, pages 378, 379, and 380.

If from the evidence at hand it is impossible to determine absolutely the year when Blisland Parish was established, it is equally as impossible from the known existing records to say with absolute certainty what was the territorial extent of the parish at the time of its establishment, or even what was its eastern boundary line in its entirety.

With regard to the eastern boundary line of Blisland Parish, it seems to the editor most reasonable to suppose that it was the same as that of the county of New Kent as established in 1654, i. e., on the south side of the York the line of Scimino Creek.[13] Whether or not the parish ever included land on the north side of York River is as yet somewhat of an open question; if it did, then most probably the parish line on that side was the line of Poropotank Creek.[14] That Scimino Creek constituted a part at least of the eastern boundary line of Blisland Parish at the time of its establishment is witnessed to by three facts: (1) In 1654 the parish of Marston was established, with limits "From the head of the north side of Queen's creeke as high as to the head of Scimino creeke."[15] Marston was originally a part of Hampton Parish,[16] one of the very early

---

[13] *Hening*, Vol. I, p. 388.
[14] *Hening*, Vol. I, p. 388.
[15] *Hening*, Vol. I, page 388.
[16] The editor's reasons for making this unqualified statement are as follows: 1. Previous to the establishment of New Kent County (Nov. 20, 1654) all the territory afterwards incorporated in that county was a part of York County. 2. From (and presumably for some months before) Oct. 13, 1653, until Nov. 20, 1654, York County contained (in whole or—as in the case of one parish, Bruton, or Brewton—in part) five parishes; namely, New Poquoson (afterwards Charles), York, Bruton, Hampton, and Blisland, of which Blisland lay farthest west, the next most westerly parish being Hampton. 3. If these five parishes covered the county—and arguing from historical analogy one is led to conclude that they must have done so—then at its establishment (in 1653 or earlier) Blisland must have been cut off from the parish which at the moment was the far-west parish; i. e., Hampton. 4. Now Blisland had as its eastern boundary Scimino Creek; therefore in 1653 (after the establishment of Blisland) Scimino Creek was the western boundary of Hampton—for otherwise there would have been an extra-parochial strip of territory extending from the western boundary of Hampton up to the eatsern boundary of

Virginia parishes, which until 1643 had been known as Chescake (or Chiskiack or Kiskeake) Parish.[17] After comparatively few years of separate existence, Marston must have been reunited to Hampton Parish, for in the 1680 list of the parishes in Virginia the parishes in York County are given as Brewton, Hampton, Yorke, and New Pocoson.[18] Later, in 1707, York and Hampton Parishes were "united and consolidated into one parish to be called and known by the name of Yorkhampton."[19] (2) When in 1724 Blisland Parish was divided up into four precincts for the purpose of facilitating the counting of tobacco plants, the first precinct was defined as "That from the head of the Northwest branch of Ware Creeke Down the Swamp to Holdcrofts Mill and from thence to the extent of the Parish Downwards";[20] in other words at least a fourth, and possibly more, of the parish as it existed in 1724 lay below Ware Creek, and so the parish must have extended down to about as far as Scimino Creek. (3) The mouth of Scimino Creek marks today the beginning of the line separating Blisland Parish (in the Diocese of Southern Virginia) from the parish of York Hampton.

What now was the original area and extent of Blisland Parish? To this interesting question there can be at present, in view of the lack of sufficient documentary evidence on the subject, no conclusive answer. As far as the records at hand show, Blisland Parish as originally established may have coincided in territory (1) with that part of the original New Kent County that lies south of the line of the York

Blisland, a thing unprecedented in the history of the Colony. Therefore, when on Nov. 20, 1654, both New Kent County and Marston Parish were established, the bounds of Marston being defined as "From the head of the north side of Queen's creeke as high as to the head of Scimino creeke," Marston Parish must have been taken from Hampton Parish.

[17] *Hening*, Vol. I, page 251.
[18] Public Record Office, London. C. O. 1, Vol. 45, No. 27.
[19] *Executive Journals of the Council of Colonial Virginia*, Vol. III, page 140.
[20] See page 10.

and the Pamunkey, or (2) with that part of the original New Kent County that lies south of the line of the York and the ridge between the Pamunkey and the Mattaponi, or (3) with New Kent County as a whole as established in 1654, i. e., the entire water-shed of the Pamunkey-Mattaponi-York River system from Poropotank Creek on the north side of the York, and Scimino Creek on the south side, westward to an indefinite extent.

In favor of the supposition that Blisland Parish was from the beginning confined in area to territory lying south of the York and the Pamunkey is the fact that no document has been found linking the name of Blisland Parish with any part of the territory to the north of the line of those two rivers. Moreover, had Blisland Parish originally included any territory between the Pamunkey and the Mattaponi (in early Colonial times called Pamunkey Neck) then when in 1678-9 St. Peter's Parish was established, the dividing line between the two parishes would have run across Pamunkey Neck as well as across that part of the original New Kent County that lies south of the York and the Pamunkey, roughly speaking the present New Kent County. However, whenever in the manuscript Vestry Book of St. Peter's Parish there is occasion to mention the starting point of the dividing line between St. Peter's and Blisland, the wording is "begin at ye mouth of a Creek Called Capᵗ: Baſsetts Landing"[21] or "Beginning at Pamunkey River side at a Small gutts mouth Known by the name of Baſsetts landing."[22] There is nowhere any reference to Pamunkey Neck by name or indeed any reference at all to territory north of the Pamunkey.

Opposed to the supposition that Blisland Parish was from the beginning confined in area to territory lying south of the York and the Pamunkey, and confirming the supposition that it did include also at least a part of the territory

---

[21] MS. Vestry Book of St. Peter's Parish, page 11.
[22] MS. Vestry Book of St. Peter's Parish, page 15.

between the Pamunkey and the Mattaponi, known as Pamunkey Neck, i. e., as far north as to the ridge between the two rivers, are the following facts and considerations:

(1) In the year 1680 St. Peter's Parish included territory in Pamunkey Neck, as is evidenced by the following:

> Att A Gen$^{rll}$ Assembly Begunne at *James City* June the 8th 1680 . . .
> The Petition of the Inhabitants of *Pamunkey* Neck praying that they may be made a Parifh and it being Averred to this Affembly that part of that Neck belongs to $S^t$ *Peters* parifh soe farre as *Johns* Creek and to the Ridge of the $f^d$ Neck, this Affembly doe declare and Order that they have liberty to make a Parifh downwards from the faid *Johns* Creek and Soe up the Ridge on Mattaponie Side, if they think Convenient.[23]

This territory in Pamunkey Neck was, it may be said in passing, retained by St. Peter's Parish until the year 1691, when it was annexed to St. John's Parish.[24] Now St. Peter's Parish had been established in 1678-9, the year that Blisland Parish was divided; all the territory therefore included in St. Peter's at its establishment had before that date presumably been included in Blisland Parish. In other words, that part of Pamunkey Neck which in 1680 (and until 1691) was a part of St. Peter's Parish must presumably have been prior to 1678-9 a part of Blisland Parish, for there is otherwise no logical way to account for its connection with St. Peter's. But if the Pamunkey Neck portion of St. Peter's Parish was originally, like the rest of St. Peter's, a part of Blisland, then originally Blisland

---

[23] *Journals of the House of Burgesses of Virginia 1659/60-1693*, page 150.

[24] *Hening*, Vol. III, p. 94. There are numerous references (direct as to the inhabitants, indirect as to the territory) to the Pamunkey Neck part of St. Peter's Parish in the MS. Vestry Book of St. Peter's Parish, between pages 2 and 17. Two very plain references occur on pages 11 (May 4, 1689) and 14 (Feb. 17, 1690).

Parish embraced at least all that part of Pamunkey Neck lying south of the ridge between the Mattaponi and the Pamunkey as well as the territory south of the line of the York and the Pamunkey.

(2) The absence of any reference to Pamunkey Neck in the wording of the entries in the manuscript Vestry Book of St. Peter's Parish referring to the dividing line between Blisland and St. Peter's parishes proves nothing, for the reason that those entries were made subsequent to the establishment (after June 8, 1680) of St. John's Parish, which at the date of its establishment embraced that part of Pamunkey Neck (later King William County) below John's (or Jack's) Creek, together with territory perhaps above the line of that creek on the Mattaponi side of the Neck.[25] But if Blisland Parish originally included a part of Pamunkey Neck as well as the territory south of the line of the York and the Pamunkey, then with the establishment of St. John's Parish (subsequent to June 8, 1680) Blisland, which had already by the establishment of St. Peter's Parish in 1678-9 suffered the loss of that portion of its territory in Pamunkey Neck that lies west of John's (or Jack's) Creek, was deprived of the remaining part of its Pamunkey Neck territory. Accordingly when in the year 1689, and again in the year 1690, there was talk of running the line between Blisland and St. Peter's parishes, there was naturally no reason to mention that part of the original dividing line that ran across the southern half of Pamunkey Neck, for after the establishment of St. John's Parish the dividing line between St. Peter's and Blisland, now confined in area to territory south of the York and the Pamunkey, did actually begin at a point on the south side of Pamunkey River.

(3) In the schedule of parishes in Virginia, in the Public Record Office in London, dated June 30, 1680, there are

---

[25] See page xix.

four parishes listed as being in New Kent County. Of these four, St. Stephen's (established prior to Feb. 18, 1674)[26] and Stratton Major (established in 1655)[27] are listed under the heading "North Side," and St. Peter's and Blisland are listed under the heading "South Side." The question then arises, what was the dividing line between New Kent County, North Side and New Kent County, South Side—was it the Pamunkey or the ridge between the Mattaponi and the Pamunkey? To this question the editor is obliged, in view of the absence of conclusive documentary proof, to answer that he does not know. However, he inclines to the belief that the ridge between the two rivers was the dividing line. His reasons for so thinking are as follows: (a) From 1654 until 1691 New Kent County extended north and south from the ridge north of the Mattaponi to the ridge south of the Pamunkey, therefore the ridge between these two rivers would be just about the half-way line. (b) In Virginia in the seventeenth century rivers were not commonly the dividing lines between counties or between parishes, but the ridges between rivers were. (c) Between the years 1680 and 1691 St. Peter's Parish, listed as a South Side parish, extended north across the Pamunkey (counted at that time as the upper part of the York and referred to in official documents as the York[28]) as far as to the ridge between it and the Mattaponi.[29] (d) The wording of the Act establishing Stratton Major Parish does not militate against the supposition that the parish at its establishment extended south across the Mattaponi as far as to the ridge between it and the Pamunkey, for in accordance with the practice of the period, under which counties and parishes occupied both sides of river valleys,

---

[26] Virginia Land Office, *Patent Book* No. 6, page 502.
[27] *Hening*, Vol. I, page 404.
[28] Virginia Land Office, *Patent Book* No. 3, p. 93 (patent to Capt. John West, dated July 3, 1652) and p. 290 (patent to Capt. John West, dated March 6, 1653).
[29] See page xix.

the words, "from Poropotank to Mattapony upward (vizt) on the north side of York river be a distinct parish by the name of Stratton Major," could properly have meant the land north of the present York River from Poropotank Creek up to the point where the Mattaponi and the Pamunkey come together, and, from that point, the land north of the ridge between the two rivers.[30] Now it is a fair inference that the four parishes listed covered the whole of New Kent County as far as it was inhabited, for in Colonial Virginia wherever there were inhabitants there there was a parish. If then the "North Side" of New Kent County was covered by St. Stephen's and Stratton Major parishes, and St. Peter's Parish covered the western portion of the "South Side," including that part of Pamunkey Neck lying west of John's (or Jack's) Creek and south of the ridge between the Mattaponi and the Pamunkey, then there was but one parish that could have included the eastern portion of Pamunkey Neck south of the ridge, and that was Blisland.

(4) There remains a fourth circumstance to be considered. In the year 1677 certain inhabitants of Blisland Parish presented to the Commissioners who had been sent over to Virginia to inquire into the causes of Bacon's Rebellion a list of "grievances." These "grievances" were signed by some eighty-seven persons, among the signatures being those of Robert Andersone and George Coxe. Now in this connection it is interesting to note (a) that in a patent granted April 22, 1670, to George Chapman for 4150 acres of land in "Pamunkey Necke," the name "Robt. Anderson" occurs in the list given of the names of persons on account of whose transportation into Virginia the tract

---

[30] It is to be noted here that as the earliest continuous records of Stratton Major Parish known to be in existence, the records of the vestry meetings, begin in 1721 (long after the establishment of Pamunkey Neck as a parish under the name of St. John's), it is not possible to substantiate by reference to the Stratton Major Parish Vestry Book the theory that that parish did at first actually include territory south of the Mattaponi.

had been granted,[31] and (b) in the list of "Processioners" for the Pamunkey Neck part of St. Peter's Parish in the year 1689 occurs the name of Geo: Cox.[32] If then in 1677 Robt. Andersone and George Coxe were inhabitants of Blisland Parish, and if also a "Robt. Anderson" in 1670 and a "Geo: Cox" in 1689 are found living in Pamunkey Neck, the supposition that Pamunkey Neck, or at least a part of it, was originally included in Blisland Parish is certainly strengthened.

Practically to clinch the matter that at least that part of Pamunkey Neck that lies south of the ridge was included in Blisland Parish at the date of its establishment two possible objections must be met. The first objection is that if there were no English settlers at all, or even if there were very few English settlers, in the eastern portion of Pamunkey Neck between 1653 and 1680, then there would have been no need of including that territory in any parish before that date. Now, as it happens, this is a very weighty objection, and it is so because of the fact that Pamunkey Neck was not open to settlement at all until about 1653, whereas at that date the land north of the Mattaponi and that south of the Pamunkey, in each case for some distance west of the fork of those two rivers, had already and for some years past been open to settlement. Moreover it is well known that whereas by the year 1678 (or 9) there were two parishes north of the Mattaponi, Stratton Major (est. 1655) and St. Stephen's (est. before Feb. 18, 1674), and two south of the Pamunkey, Blisland (est. 1653 or earlier) and St. Peter's (est. 1678 or 1679), it was not until 1680 or later that by the establishment of St. John's Parish the inhabitants of Pamunkey Neck were given independent parish life.[33]

---

[31] Virginia Land Office, *Patent Book* No. 6, page 78.
[32] MS. Vestry Book of St. Peter's Parish, page 11.
[33] The delay in the settlement of Pamunkey Neck and the thinness of the population of the "Neck" as compared with that of the lands north and south of it is well brought out by Dr. Malcolm H. Harris in his

However, granted the above are facts, as they undoubtedly are, and granted furthermore that a considerable portion of the land in the eastern part of Pamunkey Neck was in 1653, as it has been ever since, an Indian Reservation and as such closed to settlement, nevertheless there is another side to the story, and it is equally true: (1) that as early as 1653 the extreme eastern tip of the "Neck" was occupied by English settlers;[34] (2) that before 1680 there were at least so many settlers in that part of the "Neck" lying west of John's (or Jack's) Creek that there is particular mention of them in the records as being members of St. Peter's Parish; and (3) that in 1680 the inhabitants in the "Neck" living east, or below, John's Creek were numerous enough to obtain the consent of the General Assembly to the formation of a new parish for themselves.[35]

The other objection is one based on the wording of the Act of Assembly of 1691 establishing King and Queen County. In that Act occurs the following passage: "That the inhabitants of Pomunkey Necke, that now belong to St. Peters parish be restored and added to St. Johns parish, from which they formerly were taken."[36] Here the statement is plainly made that the Pamunkey Neck portion of St. Peter's Parish had formerly been a part of St. John's Parish. The answer is simply this, that that part of Pamunkey Neck that lies above (west of) John's (or Jack's) Creek had been a part of St. Peter's Parish before St.

article, *"Delaware Town" and "West Point" in King William County, Va. William and Mary College Quarterly Historical Magazine,* Second Series, Vol. XIV, No. 4, Oct. 1934, pp. 343-345.

[34] Virginia Land Office, *Patent Book* No. 3, p. 93 (Capt. John West, 850 acres, transportation of 17 persons, dated July 3, 1652), p. 291 (Capt. John West, 3,300 acres, transportation of 49 persons, dated March 6, 1653), p. 34 (Col. William Clayborne, 5,000 acres, transportation of 100 persons, dated Sep. 1, 1653).

[35] *Journals of the House of Burgesses of Virginia, 1659/60-1693,* page 150.

[36] *Hening,* Vol. III, page 94.

John's Parish was established.[37] Incidentally the apparent discrepancy in the records can be explained by understanding the words, "be restored and added to St. Johns parish, from which they formerly were taken" to mean "be annexed to St. John's Parish to which when the whole of Pamunkey Neck was a part of Blisland Parish (i. e., before 1678-9) they may be said formerly to have belonged." However, the best explanation of the wording of the Act of Assembly of 1691 is perhaps that the author of the bill was ignorant of the fact that part of Pamunkey Neck had been included in St. Peter's Parish as early as 1680 (i e., before the establishment of St. John's Parish) and gratuitously embodied in his bill, which in due course was enacted as drawn, a statement which was contrary to fact.

Summing up the matter thus far, the evidence seems to the editor fairly conclusive that Blisland Parish originally included not only all that part of the territory of New Kent County as established in 1654 that lies south of the line of the York and the Pamunkey, but at least the southern half of Pamunkey Neck (the present King William County) as well. There remains to be considered the question whether or not Blisland Parish originally included also all the territory included in New Kent County as established in 1654 that lies north of the line of the York and the ridge between the Pamunkey and the Mattaponi.

Opposed to the supposition that Blisland Parish originally included territory north of the York and the ridge between the Pamunkey and the Mattaponi is the reason advanced above[38] against the supposition that Blisland Parish originally included any of the territory between the Pamunkey and the Mattaponi, called Pamunkey Neck, namely the fact that no document has as yet been found linking the name of Blisland Parish with any part at all of

---

[37] *Journals of the House of Burgesses of Virginia 1659/60-1693*, page 150, quoted above on page xix.
[38] Page xviii.

the territory of New Kent County as established in 1654 that lies north of the line of the Pamunkey and the York.

In favor of the supposition that Blisland Parish originally (i. e., in 1653 or earlier) included territory north as well as south of the ridge between the Pamunkey and the Mattaponi, in other words that it included all the territory included in 1654 in the newly created county of New Kent (i. e., the whole water-shed of the Pamunkey-Mattaponi-York River system), are the following facts and considerations:

(1) That as a general rule the parishes in Virginia established during the period from 1643 to 1655 lay on both sides of a river and included from east to west all the territory drained by the river. Some of the parishes that illustrate this rule, with the dates of their establishment, are Bristol (1643), on the Appomattox; Westover (prior to 1652), on the James; Weyanoke (1643), on the James; Wallingford (prior to Oct. 2, 1640), on the Chickahominy; Wilmington (prior to 1680), on the Chickahominy; and Farnham (1654), on the Rappahannock.

(2) That when in the seventeenth and early part of the eighteenth centuries a new county in Virginia was established shortly after the establishment of a parish in the same general district, it was not unusual to make the county co-terminous with the parish in area. This was, for example, done in the case of (Old) Rappahannock County (est. 1656),[39] whose bounds coincided with those of Farnham Parish (est. 1654) and in the case of Middlesex County (est. 1669),[40] whose bounds to this day coincide with those of Christ Church Parish (est. 1666), and was probably done in the case of Hanover County (est. 1720),

---

[39] *Hening*, Vol. I, p. 427.
[40] *The Vestry Book of Christ Church Parish, Middlesex County, Virginia, 1663-1767*, p. XIII; *The Virginia Magazine of History and Biography*, Vol. XLII, January, 1934, p. 31—*Middlesex County, Virginia: The Date of Its Origin.*

whose northern, eastern, and southern boundaries coincide with those of St. Paul's Parish (est. 1704).

(3) Chescake (or Chiskiack or Kiskeake) Parish was one of the very early Colonial Virginia parishes, having been established in 1640. It was the most western of the parishes in Charles River County, the name of which was changed to York County in 1643, the same year that the name of the parish was changed from Chescake to Hampton.[41] Now just how far to the west Hampton Parish extended between 1650 and 1653 (the most probable date of the establishment of Blisland Parish) is not definitely known. However, since there is no documentary proof whatever that any parish lay between Hampton and Blisland at the time of the establishment of the latter, and since, as has been shown above,[42] the eastern boundary of Blisland at its establishment was Scimino Creek, the inference is clear (a) that Blisland was cut off from Hampton, and (b) that before the establishment of Blisland, Hampton Parish must have extended up York River to a point beyond (i. e., west of) Scimino Creek.

Now in 1654 New Kent County was established, and that same year the upper portion of Hampton Parish was erected into a new parish, Marston, whose eastern and western limits are given, in the order for its establishment, as Queen's Creek and Scimino Creek, respectively.[43] The very next year (1655) Stratton Major Parish was established. But if Blisland Parish at its establishment (prior to Oct. 13, 1653) had not included the territory afterwards included in Stratton Major Parish as established in 1655 (i. e., the present King and Queen County, roughly speaking) then all that territory incorporated in Stratton Major Parish in 1655 must between Oct. 13, 1653, and Nov. 20, 1654, (the date of the establishment of Marston Parish) have

---
[41] *Hening*, Vol. I, pages 249 and 251.
[42] Page xvi.
[43] *Hening*, Vol. I, page 388.

been separated from Hampton Parish (to which it must under those circumstances have belonged, as there was no other parish to which it could have belonged) by that part of Blisland Parish extending from Scimino Creek up to a point on the south side of the York opposite the mouth of Poropotank Creek; and between Nov. 20, 1654, and March 24, 1655, (the date of the establishment of Stratton Major Parish) it must have been separated from Hampton Parish not only by the part of Blisland Parish above referred to, but also by the whole extent of Marston Parish —a state of affairs that to any one having even the slightest acquaintance with Colonial Virginia parish history is inconceivable.

In view then of the above considerations, and in spite of the lack of any direct documentary proof that such was the case, the editor thinks it most probable that Blisland Parish as originally established included just the territory that was included in New Kent County at its establishment in 1654; i. e., the whole water-shed of the Pamunkey-Mattaponi-York River system from Poropotank Creek, on the north, and Scimino Creek, on the south, as far toward the west as there were inhabitants.

Assuming then that Blisland Parish at the date of its establishment included all the territory included in New Kent County in 1654, its first loss of territory was suffered when in 1655 Stratton Major Parish (including practically what is now King and Queen County and also most probably that part of Pamunkey Neck lying north of the ridge) was established. Its next loss of territory occurred when in 1678-9 St. Peter's Parish (including the upper half of the present New Kent County on the Pamunkey River side, the lower part of the present Hanover County, and that part of Pamunkey Neck (King William Couny) lying west of John's (or Jack's) Creek and south of the ridge between the Pamunkey and the Mattaponi) was established. It suffered its third and last loss of territory when shortly after

June 8, 1680, St. John's Parish (including all the lower part of Pamunkey Neck from John's (or Jack's) Creek downward, and the northern side of the upper part of the "Neck," between the ridge and Mattaponi River) was established.

In 1725[44] Blisland Parish underwent still another territorial change, this time a change by addition. In that year Wilmington Parish, which lay on both sides of the Chickahominy from near the mouth of the river to a point some thirty miles up stream (i. e., to the west) was dissolved, and that part of the parish lying south of the Chickahominy (i. e., in Charles City County) was added to Westover Parish, while the part lying north of the river (i. e., in James City County) was divided between James City, Blisland, and St. Peter's parishes, the middle section being annexed to Blisland. After March 1, 1725, then, Blisland Parish lay partly in New Kent County and partly in James City County, the larger portion of the parish being in New Kent.[45]

The complete wording of the Act for dissolving the parish of Wilmington, which has not, it is believed, heretofore appeared in print, is as follows:

> *An Act* for dissolving the parish of Wilmington in the Counties of James City and Charles City and adding the Same to other parishes.
>
> *Whereas* the parish of Wilmington lying in the Counties of James City and Charles City by reason of its Situation on both Sides of Chicohominy River and the great length thereof is very inconvenient to the far greater part of the parishoners thereof *Be it Enacted* by the Lieu$^t$ Gov$^r$. Coun-

---

[44] In the Act dissolving Wilmington Parish, the date when the provisions of the Act were to take effect is given as March 1, 1724. This date is evidently according to the "Old Style" reckoning, for it was not until April 24, 1725, that former vestrymen of Wilmington Parish were sworn in as vestrymen of Blisland Parish. (See page 15.)

[45] *Hening*, Vol. IV, page 141; *Journals of the House of Burgesses of Virginia, 1712-1726*, page 387.

cil and Burgesses of this present General Assembly and it is hereby Enacted by the Authority of the Same That from and after the first Day of March which shall be in the Year of our Lord One Thousand Seven hundred and Twenty ffour or within One Month after the Same shall become vacant by the death resignation or other disability of the present incumbent which-soever Shall first happen the Said parish of Wilmington and the Vestry of the Said Parish shall be and hereby are intirely dissolved. And that that part of the Said Parish of Wilmington lying below the Mouth of Coles Mill Creek running up the Said Creek and the Lowermost branch thereof to the Head of a Valley a little below the Dwelling House of one George Weldy Be added to the parish of James City And the Said added part & the parish of James City Shall be for Ever One intire parish and be called by the Name of James City Parish And that that part of the Said parish of Wilmington lying above the Mouth of the said Mill Creek to a Line to be run from Chicohominy River a little below the plantation of William Brown Gent running from thence in a direct Line to Diascun Swamp Just below the plantation of John Netherland Gent. from there up the Said Swamp to the Line now dividing the parish of Blisland from the parish of S$^t$. peter Be added to the Said Parish of Blisland in the County of New-Kent And that the Said added part and the parish of Blisland shall be for Ever One intire Parish and be called by the name of Blisland Parish And that all that remaining part of the Said Parish of Wilmington lying on the East side of Chicohominy River be added to the Said Parish of S$^t$. Peter in the County of New Kent And that the Said added part and the parish of S$^t$. peter shall be for ever One intire parish and be called by the Name of the parish of S$^t$. Peter And that the remaining part of the Said parish of Wilmington lying on the West side of Chicohominy River be added to parish of Westover in the County of Charles City and that the Said added part and the parish of Westover shall be for Ever One intire parish and be called by the Name of Westover parish All which Said parts of the Said parish of Wilmington so divided and added as aforesaid shall be liable to the respective dependencies Offices Charges Contributions and parochial Duties whatsoever payable by and incumbent on the other Inhabitants of the Said parishes to w$^{ch}$ they are So added and be capable to receive and enjoy all privileges and Advantages relating thereto *And Be it* further *Enacted* by the Authority aforesaid That from & after the Comencement of this Act the Vestry Men of the Said parish of Wilmington who shall reside and dwell in any part of that parish added to any other parish shall be and are by virtue of this Act added to the Vestry of the Parish to which they are so added and Shall and may have and exercise the like power & Authority for ordering and regulating the Affairs of the Said parish as the Vestry of Such parish to which they are hereby added now have and Exercise *Provided* That None of the Said parish's of James City Blisland S$^t$. Peter or Westover shall at any Time hereafter Elect or Choose any Vestry Man in either or any of the Said parishes until there shall be less in Number than Twelve persons in the Vestry of any of the said Parishes.[46]

In 1767 Blisland Parish experienced still one more change, this last being rather a change in geographical name than one of territory. In that year the lower end of New Kent County on the York River side (which was part of Blisland Parish), extending from Ware Creek down to Scimino Creek, was cut off from New Kent County and added to James City County, while at the same time the upper end of James City County on the Chickahominy River side,

---
[46] Public Record Office, London. C. O. 5, Vol. 1387.

i. e., all that part of the county lying above, or north-west, of Diascun Creek, was cut off from James City County and added to New Kent County.[47] But the Act which made this rearrangement of county boundaries left the parish boundaries unchanged, and the net result of the legislation as far as Blisland Parish was concerned was that thereafter the lower part of the York River side of the parish was in James City County instead of being in New Kent County as before, and that the lower part of the Chickahominy River side of the parish was in New Kent County instead of being in James City County as before.

The foregoing discussion of the establishment of Blisland Parish and of its territorial extent at various periods in its history makes it abundantly clear that Blisand not only was one of the early parishes of Colonial Virginia and the mother parish of St. Peter's, but was also in all probability the mother of two other parishes, Stratton-Major and St. John's, like St. Peter's more famous than itself. How it came about that the ancient origin and early history of Blisland Parish were so completely forgotten that in 1857 Bishop Meade could write, "About the year 1684 or 1685, a parish, east of St. Peter's, on Pamunkey and York Rivers, toward Williamsburg, was formed, by the name of Blisland," the present editor does not know. He does know, however, that the Bishop's incorrect assumption that St. Peter's Parish was established prior to the establishment of Blisland and that the latter was formed in 1684 or 1685[48] has been followed up to the present time by students of Colonial Virginia history generally. Bishop Meade's error is all the more remarkable for the reason that while writing his articles on the "Parishes in New Kent," he had before him the manuscript Vestry Book of St. Peter's, on page 7 of which occurs the following entry under the date March 31, 1688:

---

[47] *Hening*, Vol. VIII, p. 208.
[48] Meade, *Old Churches*, Vol. I, page 383.

It is ordered by this ₱'sent vestry y': M': Jn°: Roper and M': Will Baſse[tt] Church-wardens of this ₱'ish doe imploy a S'voyer to Runn a dividing Line between this ₱'ish of S': Peters and y° ₱arish of Bliſſland upon y° 30ᵗʰ: of May next according to an agreement of twelve men Choſen by Ord[er] of veſtry of Bliſsland p'ish in y°: year 1678 for y°: dividing of y°: Sam[e]

As a matter of fact the above entry in the Vestry Book of St. Peter's Parish would in itself alone be conclusive evidence of the fact that Blisland was the mother parish of St. Peter's, and that the latter was cut off from Blisland in 1678 or 1679. However, the manuscript Vestry Book of St. Peter's Parish contains still further evidence of the fact that Blisland was the mother parish of St. Peter's, for on page 11 occurs the following item:

At a Councell held at James City Octoᵣ y° 18 1689
Pres:ᵗ Nath: Bacon Esq:ᵣ Presi:ᵈᵗ & Councell
For Determination of y:° Difference between Bliſsland ₱arish & S:ᵗ Peters ₱arish in New Kent County it appearing y:ᵗ it was agreed on when Bliſsland Parish was to be Divided y:ᵗ y° Dividing line ſhou[ld] begin at y° mouth of a Creek Called Cap:ᵗ Baſsetts Landing etc.

Finally there is the testimony of the following item on page 11 of Vol. I of the *Calendar of Virginia State Papers and Other Manuscripts 1652-1781*—testimony that was not available to Bishop Meade but has been available to every student of Virginia history for the past fifty years and more:

At a Genˡ Court held at James City, April 29ᵗʰ, 1679, p'sent: the Deputy Gov' and Councell
The Pariſh of Bliſsland petitioning, yᵗ by unanimous consent of y° whole pariſh, a Diviſion by suffitient men by

them choſen is made of yᵉ sᵈ p'iſh, and praying that yᵉ Division be confirmed and ffoure of the Veſtry appearing, and affirming that yᵉ Division was made by consent of yᵉ pariſh. This Court therefore confirmed the sᵈ Division

Ver. Cop. Teſte: Roland Davis
W. P. Edwards, Clk
Gen¹ Coᵗ.

## 2. Further History

The insurrection known as Bacon's Rebellion broke out in the year 1676. Among the counties directly and deeply implicated in and affected by that rebellion was New Kent County, at that time embracing a territory including not only the greater part of the present county of New Kent but also practically the whole of the present counties of King and Queen, King William, and Hanover, and the upper part of the present county of James City. At that time there were in all that territory only two parishes of which there is any record discoverable—Stratton-Major (est. 1655), in what is now King and Queen County and Blisland (est. 1653, or earlier), which at that time included the upper end of the present James City County and the greater part of the present counties of New Kent and Hanover, as well as, probably the southern half of the present county of King William (called then Pamunkey Neck).

About the end of April, 1676, Nathaniel Bacon, commanding a force of some 300 men, of whom a number had been recruited in New Kent County,[49] set out upon his expedition against the Indians in the country between James River and Carolina. In June Bacon, after an unsuccessful attempt to induce Governor Berkeley to grant him a commission as General in the war against the Indians, having fled from Jamestown secretly, returned to Jamestown from the

---

[49] Andrews, *Narratives of the Insurrections, 1675-1690,—A True Narrative of the Late Rebellion in Virginia, By the Royal Commissioners, 1677*, p. 111.

up-country at the head of an armed force composed in part of men from New Kent County.[50] On June 26, Bacon left Jamestown at the head of his men and with his commission from Governor Berkeley in his possession.[51] On his second march on Jamestown, in September and after his expedition against the Pamunkey Indians, Bacon stopped again in New Kent to recruit his forces.[52]

Nathaniel Bacon the Rebel died on Oct. 26, 1676, but the rebellion was not entirely suppressed until about the middle of January following. Meanwhile the insurgents were divided into five chief groups. One, under Ingram, was at West Point, at the junction of the Pamunkey and Mattaponi rivers. A second group, under Captain Drew, was at "Green Spring", Governor Berkeley's residence, on James River a few miles above Jamestown. A third, under Maj. Whaley, was at the house of Nathaniel Bacon, Sr. (member of the Council and a partizan of Berkeley's, although an uncle of the Rebel) on King's Creek, York County. The fourth group, with which Drummond and Lawrence were associated, remained at the Brick House, in New Kent County, just across the Pamunkey from West Point, until Christmas time, when all who were there moved up the river to the house of Colonel Henry Gooch, where Whaley joined them. The fifth group, under Captain Catlin and Colonel Groves, was south of James River, in Nansemond

---

[50] *Calendar of State Papers, Colonial Series, America and West Indies, 1675-1676*, pp. 415-416. Letter of William Sherwood, a partizan of Berkeley's and a member of the Council, to Secretary Sir Joseph Williamson, dated June 28, 1676.

[51] Ibid.

[52] Andrews, *Narratives of the Insurrections, 1675-1690,—A True Narrative of the Late Rebellion in Virginia, By the Royal Commissioners, 1677*, pp. 129-130, where the account reads: "Bacon in most incens'd manner Threatens to be revenged on the Governor and his party, swearing his soldiers to give noe quarter and professing to scorne to take any themselves, and soe in a great fury marches on towards James Town, onely halting a while about New Kent to gain some fresh Forces, and sending to the upper parts of James River for what they could assist him with."

County, behind Warrascoyack bay.[53] Thus it will be seen that of the five main bodies in which the followers of Nathaniel Bacon the Rebel were grouped after his death, two —that under Ingram and the detachment at the Brick House—were in the single county of New Kent (then including King and Queen, King William, and Hanover) and one of those two, namely the detachment at the Brick House, was in Blisland Parish.

Ingram, at West Point, soon came to terms with Capt. Grantham, commander of an English merchant ship then lying in York River, who was acting for Berkeley, and his force was promptly disbanded. The force at the Brick House held out longer but to no purpose, as the event showed; finally it simply disintegrated. Whaley and Lawrence made their escape; Col. Gooch and several other leaders including Drummond were taken prisoner, and among those executed by Berkeley was "one Mr. H[all] Clarke of New Kent Court, a parson of Neate Ingenuo[us] parts, but adicted to a more than ordnary prying in [to] the Secrits of State affaires, which som yeares las[t pa]st wrought him into the Governours [dis]pleasure."[54]

But Thomas Hall was not the one and only person of prominence in New Kent County (and probably in Blisland Parish) that suffered at the hands of the government

---

[53] Andrews, *Narratives of the Insurrections, 1675-1690. The History of Bacon's and Ingram's Rebellion, 1676*, p. 85, note 3.

[54] Andrews, *Narratives of the Insurrections 1675-1690. The History of Bacon's and Ingram's Rebellion, 1676*, p. 97. See also *A List of Those That Have Been Executed for y⁰ Late Rebellion in Virginia, by Willm Berkeley*, p. 3. (in Force's Tracts, Vol. I, 1836), where this New Kent County victim is described in Berkeley's own words as "One Hall, a Clerk of a County but more useful to the rebels than 40 army men— that dyed very penitent confessing his rebellion against his King and his ingratitude to me." See also *Hening*, Vol. II, p. 546, where the record of Hall's trial by court martial on board Capt. Jno. Martin's ship in York River, Jan. 11, 1676/7, is to be found, and in which his first name, Thomas, is given. See also *Calendar of Virginia State Papers and Other Manuscripts 1652-1781*, Vol. I, p. 6, on which, under the date, Oct. 27, 1665, is given a copy of the petition of one Samuel Sutton to the Justices of New Kent signed "Thos. Hall, Clk &c."

on account of his participation in Bacon's Rebellion. Lt. Col. Henry Gooch, who had been with Drummond and Lawrence at the Brick House, and who later along with Drummond had been taken prisoner by Berkeley's forces, was brought before the Governor and Council at a court held at Green Spring on March 22, 1677, and was fined 6000 lb of pork, to be paid the following November "for the use of his majesties souldiers."[55]

Prominent people, however, were not the only inhabitants of New Kent County to suffer on account of their participation, actual or supposed, in Bacon's Rebellion. A recent search of the Public Record Office in London brought to light the following documents,[56] which amply prove that New Kent County—and in particular that part of the county that lay within the bounds of Blisland Parish—had more than its share of sufferers from among its planters of the moderately-well-to-do class:

1. To the R$^t$ Honb$^{le}$. Herbert Jeffreys Esq$^{re}$. Govern$^r$ & Capt$^n$. Gen$^l$. of Virginia; Sir John Berry K$^{nt}$. & Francis Moryson Esq$^{re}$. his Maj$^{ties}$: Com$^{rs}$. for the Affairs of Virginia.

The humble petition of Richard. Clarke of New Kent County—Sheweth

That yo$^r$ pet$^r$. with other the Inhabitants of this Colony hath been forced into the late unhappy Rebellion, but yo$^r$. pet$^r$ never took any man's goods or wronged any one, but endeavoured to continue quietly under his owne Roofe, But soe itt is may it please yo$^r$ Hon$^{rs}$ that on the ffirst day of January last past, att which time yo$^r$ Pet$^r$. was gon from home with his wife on a visitt, severall Armed men under y$^e$ Comand of one Roger

---
[55] *Hening*, Vol. II, p. 556.
[56] As far as the present editor knows, these documents are here published for the first time.

potter & M<sup>r</sup> Bryan Smith, came to yo<sup>r</sup> petr<sup>s</sup> howse where they togather with W<sup>m</sup> Hartwell, Richard Awborne & Sam<sup>ll</sup> Mathews, did take & carry away from of yo<sup>r</sup> pet<sup>rs</sup> plantation, fower English servants, seven Negroes, & all his howsehold goods, Bedds, Lining, & other estate, which by a reasonable value amounts to att least fower hundred pounds sterl. to the almost utter ruin of yo<sup>r</sup> pet<sup>r</sup>: Two of which English servants & the said seven Negroes are in possession of Maj<sup>r</sup> Robert Beverlye who utterly refuseth to deliver them to yo<sup>r</sup>. pet<sup>r</sup>. and one other of the said English servants is detayned by the said Bryan Smith

Yo<sup>r</sup>. Pet<sup>r</sup>. therefore humbly presents the premisses to yo<sup>r</sup>. Hon<sup>rs</sup>. serious consideration, praying that the said potter, Smith & Beverlye may appear before yo<sup>r</sup>. Hon<sup>s</sup>. to answere the same, & if upon Examination itt shall apeare to be a Grievance—that then yo<sup>r</sup> Hon<sup>rs</sup> will make such order here, & Report thereof to his Ma<sup>ty</sup>: as to yo<sup>r</sup>. Hon<sup>rs</sup>. shall seeme expedient.

And yo<sup>r</sup> pet<sup>r</sup>. shall ever pray etc. etc.

Virginia 19 die Maij 1677

It is hereby ordered that Roger Potter, Robert Beverley and Bryan Smith doe severally give in good securitie for such goods & servants of the Petitioner's (Richard Clarke) as are in their or any of their possession or Custody, together with a true Inventory of the same, to be Registered on Record in the Secretary's office, as also security against any wilfull wast or embezlement of the said Estate, or any part thereof, & to be accountable for the meane profitts till his Majesties Royall Pleasure be knowne, which Bond for performance hereof is to bee given in before the next Justice or Justices of the Peace where the partie lives in whose possession the said Goods & Servants or other Estate of the Said Clarke is or shall be found.

>Herb. Jeffreys
>Francis Moryson[57]

2. The case of M$^r$. Richard Clarke of New Kent County, humbly presented upon oath to the Hon$^{ble}$. Com$^r$. for the affairs of Virg$^{ia}$.

During the late unhappy times the complainant being under y$^e$ same force the whole country was, and haveing a small estate on which he hoped to live comfortably, and endeavouring the preservation thereof, the late Grand Rebell Nath$^{ll}$. Bacon Jun$^r$. when he laid seige to James Town & all the Neighbourhood under his absolute comand, the said Bacon sent six troopers to the Complainant with a Comission as Capt$^n$. upon which he confesseth being constrained thereunto, he came with Eight of his Neighbours where he staid two Days, in that time he acquainted Bacon of his unskillfulness in military affairs, and protested ag$^{te}$ Bacons plundering & fyreing, upon which the compl$^t$. returned home, & never bore Armes or associated with Bacon or (either before or after) taking any mans goods, or concerning himself in y$^e$ troubles but remained peaceably att his owne howse. That after Bacon dyed Ingram sent twice for the complainant & offered him the like Commission, but he would not otherwise accept it then by securing his owne family & estate for that he lay open to the River & soe lyable to be plundered by many that lay privily lurking & skulking to plunder, & the Complainant confesseth that seven of his Neighbours for their security came to the complainants howse where they continued fower days; & on the twenty fowerth day of December last, they went from

[57] Public Record Office, London. C. O. 1, Vol. 40, No. 5.

thence and the same day he with his wife went on a visitt to Mr. Wm. Beackey's att least twenty miles from his howse and in the time of his being there a party of men under the Command of Roger potter, with whome was Bryan Smith, Richd. Awborne, Wm. Hartwell, & Saml. Mathews, came to this deponant's howse (as he can well prove) & carryed away fower English servants, seven Negroes, and all his howsehold goods & other estate, which by a moderate computation amounteth to fower hundred pounds sterl. besides his payd bills, accompts for debts due to him amounting to att least twenty three thousand pounds of tobacco, Which Negroes & two of the English servants Majr Robert Beverlye hath in his custody & denys to deliver them to this deponant, pretending he bought them of the souldiers he being then their cheife Commander (as the dep{t}. is informed) And one other of ye Deponants English servants is detayned by the said Bryan Smith who also refuseth to redeliver him.

Richard Clarke

Jurat 19 die Maij 1677
    coram nobis
        Herb. Jeffreys
        Francis Moryson[58]

3. To the Honble Herbert Jeffreys Esqre: Sr John Berry K{nt} & Francis Moryson Esqr his most sacred Maties: Com{rs}: for Virginia

The humble petition & grievance of Robert Lowder, John Cocker & Robert porter planters of New Kent County Most humbly sheweth

That yor pet{rs}: Amongst other Inhab{ts}: of this late disloyall Colony have been seduced into & forced into the late unhappy Rebellion, for wch (out of a deepe sense of their guilt) they doe most heartily repent, and have laid holde of his Maties most gratious pardon, taken the oath of

---

[58] Public Record Office, London. C. O. I, Vol. 40, No. 6

obedience, & resolved to continue his most sacred Ma^{ties}: loyall subjects:

But soe itt is may itt please yo^r. Hon^o. that M^r. Bryan Smith hath lately by force & threats compelled yo^r. pet^rs: to give him bills for the sum of 4250 ^{lbs} of tobacco & Caske under pretence that yo^r. pet^{rs}. in the late Rebellion killed his hoggs, & threatnes that unless we would give our bill for y^t summe he would immediately comitt us to prison, soe yt. we being under that dures & feere, did pass our bills, but we having read yo^r Hon^o. declaration to the Inhab^{ts}. of this Colony to present their grievances do therefore:

Most humbly Complain of the said force & compulsion of the said M^r Smith, & humbly begg such releife therein as to yo^r. hon^o. in yo^r. mature Judgm^{ts}. shall be thought meete

And yo^r pet^{rs} shall ever pray for y^e kings Ma^{ty}: & yo^r. hon^{rs}. everlasting prosperity and the peace & wellfare of this poore Colony

    Robert Lowder
    John Cocker
    signed :
    Robert Porter

M^d. to send for Smith ℈ order of the Com^{rs}:[59]

4. To the Hon^{ble}. Herbert Jeffries Esq^r. S^r. John Berry Kn^t. & Francis Morison Esq^r. his most sacred Ma^{ties} Com^{rs}. for Virginia

The humble petition of Stephen Tarleton of New Kent County Most humbly sheweth

That yo^r pet^r being as he most penitently & sorrowfully acknowledgeth seduced into the late horrible Rebellion, & taken y^t unlawful oath imposed by the late grand Rebell Nathaniell Bacon Jun^r., & being conscious of his guilt

---

[59] Public Record Office, London. C. O. 1, Vol. 40, No. 25.

thereof, did upon the firste publishing his most sacred Ma^{ties}: gratious & surpassing Act of pardon, to his distressed subjects of this late disloyall Colony lay hold of the same, & take the oath of Allegiance & then was & still is ready to performe those other due & reasonable Conditions which by his Ma^{ties}: said pardon he is justly enioyned to doe, & being by the hon^{ble} Govern^{r}. proclamation of the 9^{th} of ffebruary last referred to the determination of yo^{r} hon^{rs}.

> Yo^{r} Pet^{r}. therefore in all humility beseecheth Mercy & pardon for his said Crimes, and humbly prayeth y^{t}. he may be admitted to the full benefit of his Ma^{ties} said Act of pardon
>
> And he as in duty bound, shall ever pray etc. etc.[60]

On January 29, 1677, the commissioners sent over by the English Government to inquire into and report upon the state of affairs in the colony arrived in Virginia. When they let it be known that they would receive and examine "grievances" that were duly signed and sworn to, many such "grievances," complaining of the oppressions whch had caused the Rebellion, were presented by the inhabitants of various counties and parishes—and among these documents was the following from Blisland Parish, which, it is believed, is here published for the first time:

> To the Honorable Herberte Jeffries Esq^{r}. S^{r} John Berrie Knighte ffrancis Morrison Esq^{r} his Maiesties Commissioners apointed to Enquire into, and to make reporte to his most Exelent Maiestie of the Grievances and pressur's of his Maiesties Subjects of this his Maiesties plantation of Virginia.
>
> We his Maiesties most obedient and Gratefull Subiects being Some of y^{e} Inhabitants of the parishe of Blisland,

---

[60] Public Record Office, London. C. O. 1, Vol. 40, No. 31.

The Blisland Parish Grievances of 1677

in the Countie of New Kent, in obedience to his Maiesties Condescention and ꝑmission, doe humbley present to you.ʳ honouʳ's these ffollowinge Greiveances and pressures.

Wee present as an insupportable Greiveance the greate taxes impos'd upon us yearely, especially the sixtie pounds ꝑ poll w<sup>ch</sup> for two years together was levied upon the Countrie, over and beside all ordenarie and Legall [    ] for the publique, Countie and parishe,

Wee present as a most Heavie Greivance the late frequent Horrid and barbarous Murthers Committed and ꝑpetuated upon our ffellow Subjects by the ꝑfidious Indians, the Manifould Rapins and depredations by them Committed upon our stocks and estates, and still Expectinge releife, but no order was taken but only that wee should drawe together at Least tenne able men to one house, Whereupon ensued the Lamentable burninge of Houses, and Severall Kild ꝑ the Indians, in adventuringe to goe to there plantation to make some Corne.

We present as a greivance the Greate exactions of shirriffes, althoughe the Compleate Sallarie of Tenn in the Hundred be raised w<sup>th</sup> y<sup>e</sup> Leavie, yet in Case a man hath not tobacco readie at his owne house, he will not receive it at any other place w'hout the alowance of Tenn pounds more for every hundred more

We present as a greivance, the sellinge of strong drinke at any place where the Countie Courte is kept during the Courte day or what time the Courte shall sitt or Continue, it breeding Matter of protraction in the Countie afayres, to the great expence and Losse of time to those that live remote

We present as a maniffest Greeance the ffort Duties Mentioned in the printed booke of Acts of Assemblie Levied upon the ships ffor and towards a Magazeene, it being as we Conceive for the use of the publique, notw'hstandinge when we are at any time Called fourth by publicke authorie upon any Millitarie occation, we are forced to find our selves Amunition upon our private Charge, nor canne we understand, who have, or to what use imployed the sayd Amunition soe raysed to soe Nessesarie and good intent

We present as a great greevance the imposition of two shillinges the Hogshead, we humbly Conceive if Narrowly Looked into, and imploy'd according to the true intent and Meaninge of the express words of the acte, it would Lessen the Leavie and give Mutch Creaditt to the publicke Dated the 2ᵗʰ day of Aprill 1677 we the subscribers have sett our names or Markes[61]

| | |
|---|---|
| Rees Hughes | [ ]sephe Pease |
| [ ]illiam Adkins | [ ]n Hill[67] |
| John Lucerie[62] [?] Jonioʳ | David Crafford[68] |
| James Blackwell[63] | George Phillips |
| Lewis Williams | John Longworthie |
| John Mackoy[64] | John Roe [?] |
| [ ]icholas Barnhouse[65] | Thomas Tilſley |
| [ ]obert Harman[66] | Peter Maſsie |
| [ ]eeffery Davis | Edward Gray |
| [ ]rancis Little | James Perrine |

[61] Public Record Office, London. C. O. 1, Vol. 39, No. 86.

[62] *John Lucerie Jonioʳ.* This name should possibly have been rendered "Ducerie." The editor is uncertain what the correct reading is.

[63] *James Blackwell.* A certain James Blackwell was a processioner in St. Peter's Parish in the year 1689. See MS. Vestry Book of St. Peter's Parish, p. 11.

[64] *John Mackoy.* A certain Jnº Mackoy was a processioner in St. Peter's Parish in the year 1689. See MS. Vestry Book of St. Peter's Parish, p. 11.

[65] [ ]*icholas Barnhouse.* See page xi.

[66] [ ]*obert Harman.* A certain Robt. Harman was a processioner in St. Peter's Parish in the year 1689. See MS. Vestry Book of St. Peter's Parish, p. 11.

[67] [ ]*n Hill.* See page 69, "To Sarah Haukins for Cureing John Hillˢ Legg—00500." Oct. 12, 1738.

[68] *David Crafford.* A certain David Craford Junʳ was a processioner in St. Peter's Parish in the year 1689. See MS. Vestry Book of St. Peter's Parish, p. 11.

Edward Burton
John ffleming[69]
Robert Andersone[70]
Thomas Gittins
Martin Mid[ ]lton
Thomas Glasse
John Dawes
Charles Lovall[71]
Giles Andrewes
Henry Snead
Robert Hughes[72]
Rch: Corley

Andrew Spraglinge
Charles Millsford[73] [ ?]
Thomas Page
Luke Haward
Charles Bostike[74]
Thomas Mooreman
James Garrett
Tho: Lownell
John Baughan[75]
James Niccoll [ ?]
Nichols Lawsone[76]
Edward Johnson
James Austin[77]

---

[69] *John ffleming.* A certain Chas. ffleming was a processioner in St. Peter's Parish in the year 1689. See MS. Vestry Book of St. Peter's Parish, p. 11.

[70] *Robert Andersone.* In a patent dated Apl. 22, 1670 (and recorded on p. 78 of *Patent Book* No. 6 in the Virginia Land Office) to 4150 acres in "Pamunkey Necke," there occurs, in the list of persons on account of whose transportation into Virginia the land was granted, the name of Robt. Anderson.

[71] *Charles Lovall.* A certain Chas. Lovell was a processioner in St. Peter's Parish in the year 1689. See MS. Vestry Book of St. Peter's Parish, p. 11.

[72] *Robert Hughes.* A certain Robt. Hughes was a processioner in St. Peter's Parish in the year 1689. See MS. Vestry Book of St. Peter's Parish, p. 11.

[73] *Charles Millsford.* This name should possibly have been rendered "Willsford" or "Hillsford." The editor is uncertain what the correct reading is.

[74] *Charles Bostike.* See page xlix, where, under date of May 19, 1682, Charles Bostwicke, of New Kent County, is ordered committed to the custody of the Sheriff of York County for, "words greatly encourageing the present distractions, by cutting up Tobacco plants." Note also that a certain Chas. Bostick was a processioner in St. Peter's Parish in the year 1689. See MS. Vestry Book of St. Peter's Parish, p. 11.

[75] *John Baughan.* A certain Jnº Baughan was a processioner in St. Peter's Parish in the year 1689. See MS. Vestry Book of St. Peter's Parish, p. 11.

[76] *Nichols Lawsone.* A certain Nick: Losʃen was a processioner in St. Peter's Parish in the year 1689. See MS. Vestry Book of St. Peter's Parish, p. 11.

[77] *James Austin.* In a patent dated May 15, 1670 (and recorded on p. 463 of *Patent Book* No. 6 in the Virginia Land Office) to a tract

Rowland Horsley[78]
William Daniell
Thomas Geeves [?]
James Moore
Richard Horsl[79]
will wrighte[80]
Edward Dorrell
Roger Pouncie[81]
James Smith
william Garnatis [?]
Edward Harrison
Thomas Mims
Richard Sidwell

Edward Morgan
Edmund Price
William Carter [?]
Henry Turner[82]
Will : Mosse[83]
John Wakefeild
Henry Strange
Josi Addison [?]
Roger Burgis
John Barnett[84]
John Vaughan[85]
Gregory barnatt[86]

of land on the south side of the Mattaponi occurs the name of Sam Oustin. Note also that a certain James Austin was a processioner in St. Peter's Parish in the year 1689. See MS. Vestry Book of St. Peter's Parish, p. 11.

[78] *Rowland Horsley.* A certain Rouland Horſley was a processioner in St. Peter's Parish in the year 1689. See MS. Vestry Book of St. Peter's Parish, p. 11.

[79] *Richard Horsl* . This signature was left unfinished and has evidently been scratched through with a pen.

[80] *will wrighte.* In a patent dated Apl. 22, 1670 (and recorded on p. 78 of *Patent Book* No. 6 in the Virginia Land Office) to 4150 acres in "Pamunkey Necke," there occurs, in the list of persons on account of whose transportation into Virginia the land was granted, the name of Arth. Wright.

[81] *Roger Pouncie.* See page xi.

[82] *Henry Turner.* A certain Hen: Turner was a processioner in St. Peter's Parish in the year 1689. See MS. Vestry Book of St. Peter's Parish, p. 11.

[83] *Will: Mosse.* A certain W$^m$ Moss was a processioner in St. Peter's Parish in the year 1689. See MS. Vestry Book of St. Peter's Parish, p. 11.

[84] *John Barnett.* In a patent dated Sep. 4, 1670 (and recorded on p. 77 of *Patent Book* No. 6 in the Virginia Land Office) to 1900 acres in "Pamunckey Necke," there occurs, in the list of persons on account of whose transportation into Virginia the land was granted, the name of W$^m$ Barnett.

[85] *John Vaughan.* A certain Jn° Vaughan was a processioner in St. Peter's Parish in the year 1689. See MS. Vestry Book of St. Peter's Parish, p. 10.

[86] *Gregory barnatt.* See note above on *John Barnett.*

INTRODUCTION                                          xlvii

Robert Speare[87]                Richmond Terrell[92]
Henry Greene[88]                John Blomefield
John Waddell[89]                W[m] [?] Plant
W[m] ffalconer                    John Bright
Andrew Sharp                    George Coxe[93]
Edward Walton                   Tho Stubs
Henry winifride                 Geo: Smith[94]
Sam : wrighte[90]               John Roper[95] [?]
Will : Rosse[91]                 John Lane

Within little more than five years after the suppression of Bacon's Rebellion, the Colony of Virginia was the scene of another uprising—the Tobacco Riots—and again New Kent was among the counties most deeply involved in the disturbance.

[87] *Robert Speare.* A certain Rob[t] Speare was a processioner in St. Peter's Parish in the year 1689. See MS. Vestry Book of St. Peter's Parish, p. 10.

[88] *Henry Greene.* A certain Hen: Green was a processioner in St. Peter's Parish in the year 1689. See MS. Vestry Book of St. Peter's Parish, p. 10.

[89] *John Waddell.* A certain John Waddell was a processioner in St. Peter's Parish in the year 1689. See MS. Vestry Book of St. Peter's Parish, p. 10.

[90] *Sam: wrighte.* See note above on *will wrighte.*

[91] *Will: Rosse.* A certain W[m] Ross was a processioner in St. Peter's Parish in the year 1689. See MS. Vestry Book of St. Peter's Parish, p. 10.

[92] *Richmond Terrell.* See within, pp. 75 to 179, where a certain Richmond Terrell appears continuously from 1740 to 1768 as a Vestryman of Blisland Parish.

[93] *George Coxe.* A certain Geo. Cox was a processioner in the Pamunkey Neck district of St. Peter's Parish in the year 1689. See MS. Vestry Book of St. Peter's Parish, p. 11.

[94] *Geo: Smith.* A certain Geo: Smith was a processioner in St. Peter's Parish in the year 1689. See MS. Vestry Book of St. Peter's Parish, p. 10.

[95] *John Roper.* See page xxxiii, where a certain John Roper is mentioned as being one of the church wardens of St. Peter's Parish in the year 1688. This John Roper was a vestryman of St. Peter's as early as 1686, and is listed in 1689 as a processioner. See MS. Vestry Book of St. Peter's Parish, pp. 7, 3, and 10.

During the session of the General Assembly that met at Jamestown June 8, 1680, it was enacted "that there be within two months next, and immediately after the publication hereof in every respective county within this his majesties colony ffifty acres of land purchased by the ffeoffees of the several counties at the rates hereafter sett downe and measured about, layd out and appointed for a town for storehouses, &c. for such county as is hereafter sett downe and expressed, that is to say, . . .
In New Kent county att the Brick house a long the high land from marsh to marsh"[96]

The underlying cause of the passage of the above Act was the low price of tobacco prevailing at the time, a price which the various provisions of the Act would, it was hoped, tend to raise. However, the Act had an effect directly opposite to the one intended, and in the event it was itself one of the main contributing causes of widespread tobacco riots, when groups of poor tobacco planters went about destroying tobacco plants in the beds before they could be transplanted. These riots began in Gloucester County, but soon spread to Middlesex and New Kent. The connection between Act V of the General Assembly of 1680 and the tobacco riots of May-August, 1682, in which many of the inhabitants of Blisland Parish must have been implicated, is well given in a report made on May 4, 1683, by the Council to Governor Culpeper.[97]

Among the existing records bearing witness to the fact that New Kent County and, by implication, Blisland Parish were involved in the Tobacco Riots of 1682 are the following:

1. A letter of the Secretary of Virginia, Nicholas Spencer, to Sir Leoline Jenkins, dated May 8, 1682, in which he

---

[96] *Hening*, Vol. II, pages 471-478.
[97] *Hening*, Vol. II, page 561.

writes that the tobacco riots in Gloucester are now spreading to New Kent;[98]

2. An Order, dated May 19, 1682, for the committal of Stephen Tarleton and Charles Bostwicke, of New Kent County, to the custody of the Sheriff of York County for "words greatly encourageing the present distractions; by cutting up Tobacco plants";[99]

3. An Order, dated May 23$^{rd}$, 1682, for the suspension of John Woodington, of New Kent County, from his office of Justice of the Peace, and for his committal to the custody of the Sheriff of York County for his failure to check "y$^e$ Plant Cutters" and for his encouraging them "to proceed in their riotous and tumultuous manners and to cut up other plants";[100]

4. A letter of Sir Henry Chicheley, Acting Governor, to Sir Leoline Jenkins, dated May 30, 1682, in which he writes: "Things are much improved, thank God, since my last, though the rioters persisted by day or night till they had destroyed the plants of near three parts of Gloucester, half New Kent, the lower part of Middlesex," etc.[101]

In connection with the order above for the committal to custody of Stephen Tarleton and Charles Bostwicke, it is of interest to note (1) that the former had been somewhat deeply implicated in Bacon's Rebellion, that in May 1682 he was under arrest for complicity in the Tobacco Riots, and that nevertheless within three and a half years thereafter he was holding the prominent position of vestryman

---

[98] *Calendar of State Papers, Colonial Series, America and West Indies, 1681-1685*, p. 228, No. 495.
[99] *Executive Journals of the Council of Colonial Virginia*, Vol. I (1680-1699), p. 21.
[100] Ibid, p. 22.
[101] *Calendar of State Papers, Colonial Series, America and West Indies, 1681-1685*, p. 241, No. 531.

in St. Peter's Parish¹⁰²; and that (2) a certain Charles Bosticke was one of the signers of the Blisland Parish Grievances of 1677¹⁰³ and that in the year 1689 Char: Bostick was appointed a processioner in St. Peter's Parish.¹⁰⁴

The uprising known as the Tobacco Riots of 1682 was the last disturbance of more than local importance that Blisland Parish figured in until the outbreak of the American Revolution. Meanwhile, however, a number of events took place that doubtless were of more or less interest to the people of the parish generally. Perhaps the first of these events— a mere incident except to the persons chiefly concerned in it—is the one graphically recorded in the following entry in the Executive Journals of the Council:

Fryday y® 30ᵗʰ of October 1696

Anne Grey of Blisland Parish in New Kent County convicted and condemned for y® murder of John Reynolds, presenting a petition sign'd by many of the principal Inhabitants of this Colony praying a repreive for her, & being rep'sented to his Excellency by y® Councill as an object of mercy his Exᶜʸ granted her a repreive till the fourth day of October Genˡˡ Court next that in the mean time she may apply for his Maˢ Grace and pardon.¹⁰⁵

In the year 1702 Blisland Parish, now much reduced in area since its first days, contained only 526 tithables.¹⁰⁶

On July 29, 1703, Sir Edward Northey, Knight, her Majesty's Attorney General, rendered his opinion upon the

---

¹⁰² MS. Vestry Book of St. Peter's Parish, page 2, under the date Nov. 16, 1685.
¹⁰³ See page xlv.
¹⁰⁴ MS. Vestry Book of St. Peter's Parish, page 11.
¹⁰⁵ *Executive Journals of the Council of Colonial Virginia*, Vol. I, page 359.
¹⁰⁶ Public Record Office, London. C. O. 5, Vol. 1312, No. 38¹¹. *List of the Parishes, Tythables, Ministers, etc. in Virginia in July 1702.*

Act of Assembly of the Colony of Virginia "relating to the Church and particularly Concerning Induction of Minist[rs]." On the 3$^{rd}$ of March following, this opinion was read at a Council held at Williamsburg, and the Governor, Francis Nicholson, in Council was pleased to order that a copy of it be sent "to the Churchwardens of each parish within this Colony Requiring them upon receipt thereof forthwith to Call a vestry, and there to cause the Same to be read and entered into the vestry book to the intent the S$^d$ vestry may offer to his Excellency what they think proper thereupon."[107]

In reply to the order contained in the Governor's letter, the vestry of Blisland Parish wrote as follows:

> To his Excell$^{cy}$ ffrancis Nicholson Esq$^r$ her Majestys Lieu$^t$ and Govern$^r$ Gen$^{ll}$ of Virginia
>
> We the Subscribers the Vestry for Blissland ℔ish in New Kent County humbly Acquaint your Excellency that the Rev$^d$ M$^r$ Daniel Taylor our present Minister hath hitherto Aproved himself a person Every way answerable to your Excellencys Charact:$^r$ We therefore think ourselves in Duty and Gratitude Obliged to ℔sent the Reverend M$^r$ Danil Taylor whome if yo$^r$ Excell.$^{cy}$ pleases to admit, We humbly desire may be Instituted & Inducted into our parish and we shall be Most thankfull who are
>
> Yo$^r$ Excell$^{cys}$ Most Dutyfull and
> Humble Servants to power
> W$^m$ Bassett
> Roger Thompson ⎱ Church ward$^s$
> John Vaughon ⎰

---

[107] *Vestry Book of Petsworth Parish, Gloucester County, Virginia, 1677-1793*, pp. 80-81. See also Ibid., pp. 78-79 for a copy of Sir Edward Northey's "opinion."

| | |
|---|---|
| Warick Mohun | Jnº Dibdall |
| Joell Croome | Tho Taylor |
| George Clough | Jnº Pettis |
| Rich Bamshaw | Jnº Hockaday |
| | George Keeling[108] |

It is to be noted that Blisland Parish, through its vestry, asked that its minister be inducted, as did also Christ Church Parish, Middlesex County[109]; while the vestry of St. Peter's Parish, New Kent County, wrote, "that they are not for Inducting the Miniſter not for any diſlike they have to him but that the whole ℔iſh in Gen" is ag' Induction"[110]; and the vestry of Petsworth Parish, Gloucester County, at first ignored the Governor's letter of March 3, 1704, but being admonished by the latter in a second communication written nearly seven weeks later (April 18), they submitted themselves and wrote to the Governor humbly praying his Excellency to grant their minister, the Rev. Emanuel Jones, institution and induction.[111]

On June 18, 1724, the Rev. John Brunskill, Minister of Wilmington Parish, wrote the following in reply to a letter from the Lord Bishop of London asking for information about the parish:

"It is about 30 miles in length and nine in breadth and contains about 180 Families, white, Christian people."[112]

In reply to a similar letter addressed to him, the Rev. Daniel Taylor, Minister of Blisland Parish, wrote that

---

[108] Public Record Office, London. C. O. 5, Vol. 1314, No. 63$^{xvii}$.

[109] *Vestry Book of Christ Church Parish, Middlesex County, Virginia, 1663-1767,* pp. 98-100.

[110] MS. Vestry Book of St. Peter's Parish, New Kent County, Virginia, 1684-1758, pp. 68-72.

[111] *Vestry Book of Petsworth Parish,* etc., pp. 79-81; also Public Record Office, London. C. O. 5, Vol. 1314, No. 63$^{xvii}$.

[112] Perry, *Historical Collections relating to the American Colonial Church,* Vol. 1—Virginia, pp. 277-279.

Blisland was thirty miles long and contained one hundred and thirty six families.[113]

In connection with the letter of the Rev. Mr. Brunskill above referred to, it is to be noted that in accordance with the provisions of Act XII of the General Assembly of May 9, 1723, the parish of Wilmington was due to be dissolved on March 1, 1725.[114]

That the Act of Assembly dissolving Wilmington Parish did not in all its provisions meet with the approval of all the inhabitants of the parish is evident from the following:

> Thursday, February 8, 1727
>
> Alſo a petition of ſundry Inhabitants of that part of the pariſh of *Bliſland* which was formerly a part of the s'd diſſolved pariſh of *Wilmington,* praying that that part of the pariſh may be united to the parish of the *St. Peters,* were ſeverally preſented to the Houſe & read
>
> Reſolved, that the ſaid petitions be Rejected.[115]

From a paper in the Public Record Office, London, dated 1729 and entitled "The present State of Virginia," it appears that at that date New Kent County was 97,325 acres in extent; that there were 1364 tithables in the county; that the Sheriff was W[m] Kenney; that the Coroners were John Scott and Rich[d] Richardson; that the Burgesses were Rich[d] Richardson and John Bacon; that the Justices of the Peace were John Scott, John Sclater, Charles Lewis, William Macon, Nich[s] Aldersey, William Kenney, Rich[d] Richardson, Thomas Bray, Ebenezer Adams, Thomas Massie, William Morris, Joseph ffoster, Robert Lewis, John Otey,

---

[113] Perry, *Historical Collections relating to the American Colonial Church,* Vol. 1—Virginia, pp. 279-281.

[114] *Hening,* Vol. IV, p. 141. See also within, pages xxix and xxx and page 15, where under the date April 24, 1725, it is recorded that three former vestrymen of Wilmington Parish were sworn in as vestrymen of the parish of Blisland.

[115] *Journals of the House of Burgesses of Virginia 1727-1740,* p. 13.

Charles Massie, and W^m Makain—of whom the last six constituted the "Quorum"; that the County Clerk was John Thornton; that there were two parishes, Blisland, with the Rev. Daniel Taylor as minister, and St. Peter's, with the Rev. Mr. Mossom as minister; that the Surveyor was John Syme; and that the County Lieutenant was John Carter, Esq^r.[116]

In the *Journals of the House of Burgesses of Virginia* there occurs the following item relative to the Rev. Chicheley Thacker, Minister of Blisland Parish:

> Monday, November 13, 1738.
>
> *Ordered,* That the Thanks of this Houſe be return'd to the Rev. M^r *Chichley Thacker,* for his excellent Sermon Yesterday, preach'd before this Houſe; And that M^r *Conway,* M^r *Fitzhugh,* M^r *Willis,* and M^r *Carter,* acquaint him therewith.
>
> *Ordered,* That One Thouſand Copies of the ſaid Sermon be printed, at the Public Charge, to be proportioned amongſt the ſeveral Counties in this Colony; to be diſtributed by the reſpective Courts of the ſaid Counties, in the beſt Manner, for the Comfort of Chriſtians, againſt the groundleſs Objections to the Divinity and Dignity of the Bleſſed Jesus.[117]

In 1738 a difference of opinion arose over the desirability of continuing the public warehouse at Taskanask, which was situated probably near the mouth of the creek of that name flowing into York River between Ware Creek and Scimino Creek,[118] and petitions pro and con were presented to the General Assembly. The following entry on page 336 of the *Journals of the House of Burgesses of Virginia, 1727-*

---
[116] Public Record Office, London. C. O. 5, Vol. 1322, pp. 235-254.
[117] *Journals of the House of Burgesses of Virginia, 1727-1734, 1736-1740,* p. 338.
[118] See Frontispiece Map.

*1740,* shows the interest of the people of Blisland Parish in the matter:

Wedneſday December 6, 1738

The Houſe proceeded to the Consideration of the Report from the Committee of Propoſitions and Grievances, upon the Petition of the Inhabitants of the Pariſh of *Bliſland,* in the County of *New Kent,* for repealing the Public Warehouſe at Taskanask . . .

Reſolved that the ſaid Warehouſe be diſcontinued, and another inſtead thereof, appointed at the *Brick-houſe*[119]

At some time during the year 1751, or possibly in January or February 1752, on three successive Sundays, those present at divine service in the parish church of Blisland were treated to what in those days was probably not an unusual interruption to the regular order of service, when there was read out a notice that application would be made to the next General Assembly for the passage of "An Act for docking the entail of certain lands in the county of James-City, and vesting the same in Thomas Chamberlayne, gentleman, in fee simple; and for settling other lands of greater value to the same uses."[120]

On page 124 of this volume is recorded an Order of Vestry, "that the Church Wardens of this Parish do Sell the Glebe Land in James City County, Purſuant to an Act of Aſsembly made in 1753." The preliminary legislative action which made that order possible was as follows:

Monday December 17ᵗʰ [1753]

The Bill intituled *An Act to enable the Vestry of the Pariſh of* Bliſland *in the Counties* of James City *&* New

---

[119] The Fry & Jefferson map locates the Brick-house near the point where the modern Richmond-West Point highway crosses the Pamunkey at West Point. (See Frontispiece Map.)

[120] *Hening,* Vol. VI, pp. 319-320. See also Ibid., pp. 321-324.

Kent *to ſell a Plantation and two Hundred Acres of Land in the ſaid Pariſh, and to buy Communion plate & Ornaments for the lower Church in that Parish with the Purchaſe Money.* was read the first Time . . . Read a Second Time . . . Read . . . a Third Time . . . *Reſolved* that the ſaid Bill be agreed to.[121]

Wedneſday December 19, 1753

The Blisland parish bill [to sell land and buy Church plate and ornaments] passed.[122]

It is a well-known fact that George Washington's wife, Martha (Dandridge) Custis, was a native of New Kent County, and that at the time of her marriage to Col. Washington she was the mistress of the White House plantation, on Pamunkey River, in St. Peter's Parish, New Kent. It is also well-known that Anna Maria Dandridge, Mrs. Washington's sister, was the wife of Col. Burwell Bassett, of "Eltham," in Blisland Parish, New Kent County. Under the circumstances it was natural that Washington stopped frequently and visited somewhat widely in New Kent when travelling through that county on his many trips from "Mt. Vernon" to Williamsburg and back again. Among the entries in Washington's diaries mentioning people, homes, and churches in New Kent County visited by him between May 7, 1768, and Nov. 16, 1773, are the following, which are taken from John C. Fitzpatrick's, *The Diaries of George Washington, 1748-1799:*

Vol. I, p. 268

1768, May 7. Came up to Colo. Bassett's to Dinner.

8. Went to Church and returned to Dinner.

11. Dined at the Glebe with Mr. Davis.

---

[121] *Legislative Journals of the Council of Colonial Virginia,* Vol. II, p. 112.

[122] *Journals of the House of Burgesses of Virginia, 1752-1758,* p. 170.

Vol. II, p. 18
1771, May 15. Dined at Mrs. Chamberlayne's with Mrs. Washington, and returned to Colo. Bassett's in the Eveng.

16. Dined at Mrs. Dangerfield's with Colo. Bassett's Family, and returned in the afternoon to Eltham.

18. Rid to the Brick House . . . and returned to Dinner, after which went to Mr. Davis's and Drank Tea.

19. Went to Church and returned to Colo. Bassett's to Dinner.

Vol. II, p. 59
1772, April 4. Took a Cold dinner at Mr. Southal's and came up to Eltham in the afternoon.

5. Went to see Mrs. Dandridge betwn. Breakfast and Dinner.

Vol. II, p. 86
1772, Nov. 8. At Colo. Bassett's all day.

10. Rid up with Mr. Hill to Rockahock, and Plantations in New Kent, and returned, after Dining with Mrs. Chamberlayne, to Colo. Bassett's at Night. Mr. Custis went with me.

Vol. II, p. 130
1773, Nov. 16. Went with Mrs. Washington and Mr. Custis to Mr. Burbidge's to see Mr. Bat Dandridge. Stayd all Night.

In commenting on several of the above entries, Mr. Fitzpatrick, largely following the late Dr. Joseph Meredith Toner, makes one or two mistakes. He says:

(1) That Mr. Davis was "The Rev. Thomas Davis later minister of Christ Church, Alexandria. He officiated at Washington's funeral (Toner)."

The Mr. Davis referred to here by Washington was without doubt the Rev. Price Davies, Rector of Blisland Parish, of which Col. Burwell Bassett was then (1768) a vestryman, and the Upper Church of which was within a few miles of "Eltham," Col. Bassett's home.

(2) That Mrs. Chamberlayne was "Mrs. William Chamberlayne, Williams' Ferry on the Pamunkey. According to tradition it was at Col. William Chamberlayne's house that Washington first met Mrs. Martha Custis, the widow of Daniel Parke Custis, and it was he who introduced Washington to his future wife."

The Mrs. Chamberlayne referred to here by Washington was most probably Mrs. Richard Chamberlayne, the daughter-in-law of William Chamberlayne, who died in 1736. William Chamberlayne's widow, Elizabeth (Littlepage) Chamberlayne remarried less than four years after her first husband's death. Her second husband was William Gray, of New Kent County.[123]

(3) That the church Washington says he attended on May 19, 1771, was "St. Peter's Episcopal Church, New Kent County."

It is most improbable that the church here referred to by Washington was St. Peter's Church. It was almost certainly the Upper Church of Blisland Parish, which Washington's brother-in-law and host, a vestryman of the parish, naturally attended. Incidentally, had Washington, who only the day before had visited the Rev. Mr. Price Davies at the latter's home, the Glebe, on this day attended service at St. Peter's Church, he would have been doing at one and the same time three somewhat peculiar things:

---

[123] *Hening*, Vol. V, pp. 117-119.

(a) passing by one Episcopal Church near at hand to attend another many miles farther away, (b) neglecting the church of the parish of which his host was vestryman and had frequently been church warden to attend a church in a neighboring parish, and (c) failing to attend the church of which his friend that he had gone to see the day before was the minister and, instead, going off to attend another church. Under the circumstances it is not too much to say that on Sunday, May 19, 1771, Washington attended service at the Upper Church of Blisland Parish. If it was not the Upper Church of Blisland Parish that Washington attended that day, then it was the Lower Church of Blisland, which while at a greater distance from "Eltham" than was the Upper Church, was nearer to "Eltham" than St. Peter's Church was.

The further history of Blisland Parish apart from what is given in the main body of this volume is soon told. Blisland was represented by its minister and a lay delegate in the Diocesan Convention of 1785,[124] and by lay delegates in the Conventions of 1787 and 1796 to 1799. In 1892 the Diocese of Southern Virginia was cut off from the Diocese of Virginia, the dividing line between New Kent and James City counties being part of the dividing line between the dioceses; therefore Blisland Parish in the Diocese of Virginia now lies wholly in New Kent County, while Blisland Parish in the Diocese of Southern Virginia lies wholly in James City County.

The four-line heading to page 1 of this volume is, of course not a transcript from the original record. The manuscript record begins with the words:

    At a Veſtry [          ] Bl[     ]d Pariſh at [    ]
    Brick Church [          ].

---

[124] See page 231.

The facsimile of the Blisland Parish "Grievances" of 1677, between pages xlii and xliii of this introduction, is from a photograph made in London especially for this work. The map which serves as a frontispiece to the volume is from a photostat of a part of the 1775 edition of the map of Virginia drawn by Joshua Fry and Peter Jefferson. At the proper places the names "Blisland Parish" and "Appomattox River," which do not appear on the Fry and Jefferson map, have been inserted with a view to making the map more useful as a guide to students not intimately acquainted wth the geography of Tide-Water Virginia.

Blanks in the manuscript which were left by the Clerk to be filled in later, but were never filled in, are indicated in the printed reproduction by blank spaces. Gaps in the manuscript resulting from tearing, rubbing, or other kinds of intentional or unintentional mutilation are indicated by blank spaces enclosed in brackets. Unintentional omissions in the manuscript and all other mistakes of whatever kind are, as far as it was found possible to do so, reproduced exactly. Pages in the manuscript are indicated in the printed reproduction by Arabic numerals enclosed in brackets. In the index the number of times an item occurs on a page is indicated by a small Arabic numeral above, and to the right of, the numeral indicating the number of the page.

It is to be noted that wherever in this preface a date in the Old Style (for example, March 2, 1642/3) occurs in a quoted passage, the date is reproduced as it appears in the original passage: where, however, reference merely is made to a date which in the document from which it is taken appears in the Old Style, it is given in the New Style; for example, the date above would appear as March 2, 1643. This change the editor thinks justified on the ground that it makes it easier for the general reader to follow the chronology.

The editor wishes here to make grateful acknowledgment of his indebtedness to Mr. Joseph W. Geddes, A.I.A., P.A.S.I., of Williamsburg, Va., for the photograph of Hickory Neck Church, which appears as one of the illustrations to this volume, as well as for certain data which served as the basis for the historical note appended to the photograph; to the Rev. Arthur P. Gray of West Point, Va., and to Mr. Rutherford Snell, of Richmond, for helpful suggestions made during the writing of this introduction; and to the Rev. G. MacLaren Brydon, D. D., Historiographer of the Diocese of Virginia, Mr. Morgan P. Robinson, Archivist of the Virginia State Library, and Mr. Wilmer L. Hall, State Librarian, for their courtesy in reading the introduction while in manuscript form. Although in frequent instances changes suggested by these gentlemen have been made, the editor wishes it to be understood that he alone is responsible for the theories and hypotheses advanced in this introduction. As to the main thesis embodied in these pages, that for about four months after the establishment of New Kent County that county and Blisland Parish were most probably coterminous in area, the editor thinks it only fair to himself to state that it is entirely his own, that it occurred to him only very gradually, and that it took final form only after months spent by him in laborious investigation of all the sources available to him.

The editor has read the proof sheets of the Vestry Book several times, and in cases of doubt has always referred to the original manuscript; but he is well aware of the fact that in work of this kind some mistakes are bound to occur, and he can only hope that the mistakes made, whether of judgment or of oversight, in this printed reproduction of the original are few in number. In this connection he would refer the reader to the list of errata—possible, probable, and certain—to be found inserted between the Appendix and the Index. Any one wishing to check up on the editor in his work can do so by comparing the printed Vestry Book with the original manuscript volume, which is now in the custody of the Archives Division of the Virginia State Library, in Richmond.

C. G. CHAMBERLAYNE.

Richmond, Va.,
May 1, 1935.

# The Vestry Book
...of...
# Blisland Parish
### New Kent County, Virginia, 1721-1786

---

At a Veſtry [     ] Bl[    ]d Pariſh at [    ] Brick Church [                       ]

P'ſent M' Daniel Taylor Miniſt' Cap': Nicholas Alderſey & Cap: [    ] Kenney Ch w

| Will^m Baſsett Eſq': <br> Majo': Jn°: Thornton <br> Cap': Jn°: Hockaday <br> Cap': Geo: Keeling | and | M': William Cox <br> M': William Morris <br> Cap': Jn°: Armistead <br> Hen: Holdcraft | Veſtrymen |

Whereas m' John Slaughter: is Come Again to Dwell in this Pariſh: he is Now Choſen A Veſtryman inſtead of Cap': John Stanup Deceaſed: and being p'ſent is Sworne accordingly before Cap': Will^m Ken[    ] a Majeſtrate of this County

P'ſent M' Jn° Slaughter

[ ]liſland Pariſh D' 1721:       this Veſtry proceeds to Lay [    ]

To: M': Daniel Taylor Miniſt' for a yeares Sall'y: 16000 ^lb ^Tobb: & Conveniency to Ditto: according to Law 800                                               16800

To: Caſke to Ditto: according to the Veſtryes Agreement for Deficiency of the Glebe 8 p: Cent is      01280

To: M' Francis: Cooke Cla'k of y° Pariſh for a yeares Sallary 1500 & Caſke to Ditto at 8 p' C' & Convenicy to di[    ]                              01695

## VESTRY BOOK OF BLISLAND PARISH

To: Henry Holdcraft Cle'k of the: Veſtry for a
years Sall'y 500 & Caſke to Ditto at 8 pʳ Cenᵗ  00540
To: Walter Wood Saxton of yᵉ Uppʳ Church: his
years Sall'y 500 & Caſk to Ditto 40  00540
To: Francis: Shoemaker: Saxton of the Lower
Church for a yeares Sall'y 500 & Caſke to Ditto
40  00540
To: Mʳ Daniell Taylor Miniſter for 2 delinquᵗˢ Re-
turned John Langford & Fras Harman  00156
To: Mʳ John Doran Sherif & Laſt yeares Collectʳ his
Accoᵗ Adjuſted & Allowed  00234
To: Majoʳ: John Thornetons: Fees allowed  00094
To: Capᵗ: John Hockaday his Charge for being An
Evidence for the Pariſh allowed  00223
To: Thomas Baker his Charge for being An Evi-
dence for the Pariſh allowed  [ * ]
To: Thomas Fiſher his Order for being An Evidence
for yᵉ Pariſh allowed  [ * ]
To: William Fiſher his Order for Attendᵗᵉ being An
Evidence for yᵉ Parriſh  00648
To: Richᵈ: Halfield for being An Evidence for yᵉ
Pariſh Ordʳ attendce  00228
To: John: Eaton Depᵗ Sherrf of James City County
his Fees allowed  [ * ]
To: Richᵈ: Baker Carpenter his account adjuſted and
allowed in all  [ * ]
To: Capᵗ: William Kenney Churchwarden his Accoᵗ
Allowed  [ * ]
To: Capᵗ: Nicholas Alderſey Churchwarden his ac-
counᵗ allowed  [ * ]
To: Nathaneˡˡ Norris for his Wifes yeares Maintain-
ance 800 & Caſke to Do 64  00864
To: Mʳ: David Holt for Keeping Tho Salmon a year
850 & Caſke to Ditto 68  00918

*Figures illegible.—C. G. C.

To: Bryan Henry for his yeares Maintainance 850
    & Caſke to Ditto 68                                    00918
To: Cap$^t$: Kenney Churchward$^n$ for paying W$^m$
    Brewin for Keeping Jn$^o$ Pethwood a year &
[ † ]                                                                           [ * ]
    To Sall'y to Receive 31070$^l$ Tobb at 5 p$^r$ Cent
    is                                                                              01553

                Totall Deb$^t$ is                 326[*]
Creditt ut Supra
By: One half of Francis Shoemakers bond for his
    Daughters fine                          250$^l$
By: 532 Titheables at 61$^l$ of Tobbacco p$^r$: pole   3270[ ]
    is                                          32452
By: 79$^l$ of Tobbacco the Surplus to be p$^d$ the
    Pariſh Next year                     79

Cap$^t$: Nicholas Alderſey & Cap$^t$: William Kenney: Churchwardens are hereby Diſcharged from their ſ$^d$ Off[ ] And M$^r$ William Cox & M$^r$ William Morris are appointed Churchwardens in their Stead and [     ] Sworne accordingly: before Cap$^t$ Will$^m$ Kenney a Majeſtrate of this County

It is Ordered by this P$^r$ſent Veſtry that the Churchwardens take C[   ] to Agree With Some perſ[
       ] & Maintain him for the [        ] and that what they shall agree for [
       ]

[2]
It is Ordered by this Preſent Veſtry that: the Pariſh Levy for this p$^r$ſent year be: Sixty One pou[   ] of Tobbaccoe p$^r$ pole and that: M$^r$ John Doran Depu$^ty$ Sheriff of this County Collect the Said su[  ] of Sixty & One poundes of Tobbaccoe from Every Individuall Titheable perſon Within

---
†Word illegible.—C. G. C.
*Figures illegible.—C. G. C.

[    ] Parifh and upon Refufall of Payment to Levy the Same by Diftrefs: The S⁴ Sherriff first Entring into Bond With Good & Sufficient Security to the pʳſent Churchwarde[ ] of this parifh for Payment of the Said Tobbaccoes to the Severall Refpective Parifh Creditors beforementioned to Whome it is Due: in hhᵈs of Such weightes and at Such times as the Sᵈ Churchwardens Shall Direct and appoint And that the Clark of the Veftry Take Bond as aforefaid before he Deliver Copies of the Parifh Charge and of this Order of Veftry to the Sᵈ Collector

Teſt: Henʳ: Holdcraft Clk Veftry

At: A: Veftry: held for Blifland Parifh: At the Brick Church: the: 10ᵗʰ: day of Octobʳ: 1722:

Pʳſent: Mʳ: Danˡ: Taylor: Miniſtʳ: Mˢ William: Cox: & Mʳ: Willᵐ: Morris: Churchwardens

William: Bafsett: Esqʳ:        Capᵗ: Richᵈ: Richardfon
Majoʳ: John: Thornton          Capᵗ: Nichõ: Alderfey
Mʳ: John Sclater               Cap: John Arimſtead
        & Henry Holdcraft
                                                Veftrymen

This Veftry Proceeds to Lay the Parifh Levy 1722 Blifland Parifh Dʳ:

| | |
|---|---:|
| To: Mʳ Danˡ: Taylor Miniſtʳ: for A yeares Sall'y: According to Law | 16000 |
| To: Cafke: to Ditto: Allowᵈ for the Deficiency of yᵉ Glebe: 1280: & Conveniency to ditt | 02080 |
| To: Francis Cooke Clarke of the Parifh for a yeares Sall'y: 1500 & Cafk & Conv to ditt: | 01695 |
| To: Henry: Holdcraft Clarke of the Veftry for a yeares Sall'y 500 & CC. to ditto | 00565 |
| To: Walter Wood Saxton for a years Sallry With Cafke 540 | 00540 |

To: Fras: Shoemaker Saxton: for a yeares Sallry
With Caſke 540                                                         00540
To: Mʳ: Danˡ Taylor for 4 Delinquᵗˢ Returned: Allowed                                                                 00324
To: Majoʳ Thorntons for Clerkes Fees Allowed     00080
To: Mʳ John Doran Late Collectʳ: for 2: delinqts Returned Allowed                                                 00162
To Capᵗ: Willᵐ: Kenney for Clerkes fees pᵈ by him in
James City Laſt year                                              00371
To Henry Holdcraft: for 219ˡ Tobbacco pᵈ Geoʳ:
Weldy: an Evidence laſt year                            00219
To: Bryan: Henry: for his yeares Maintainance 850
& Caſke to Ditto 68                                               00918
To: Mʳ: Willᵐ: Cox Churchwarden his account allowed: £ 1=0=8 Tobbacco                             00207
To: Quittrents for the Glebe land for yᵉ yeares 1721:
& 1722: to Mʳ Jnᵒ Doran                                   00048
To: Mʳ: Willᵐ: Morris Churchwarden his accoᵗ: Adjuſted & Allowed With Caſke                         01506
To: Bryan Henry for Keeping Tho: Salmon 6
moneths With Caſke Included                         00459
To: Bryan Henry for Charge & trouble Attending
The: Sᵈ Salmon in Sicknes & his buryall       00194
To: Nathaniel Norris: for his Wifes Maintaince &
for her buryall 432: With Caſke Included Ordered to be paid to Henry Holdcraft: for Neceſsaryes he: furniſhed yᵐ With                 00432
To: Richard Warren: for his Aſsiſtance Towards the
Cure of his Sore Legg & CC                         01130
To: Bryan Henry for Keeping Lucey Gilles his
Grandaughter a year                                       00300
To: Sall'y: for Receiveing 27770 pounds of Tobbaco
at 5 pʳ Cent 1388                                                 01388

                                                                              29158

[3]

Credit

| | |
|---|---|
| By: Pariſh Credit 79$^{lb}$ Tobbacco Left Laſt year in M$^{r}$: Dorans handes | 00079 |
| By: 546: Titheables at 53 poundes of Tobbacco p$^{r}$ pole is | 28938 |
| By: Tobbacco: Wanting to pay the Pariſh Debt to be Raiſed & paid to the Collecto$^{r}$ Nex$^{t}$ year | 141 |
| | 29158 |

It is Ordered by this p$^{r}$ſent Veſtry: that the Pariſh Levy for this preſent year be fifty & three poundes of Tobbacco: p$^{r}$ pole And that M$^{r}$: John Doran Dep$^{t}$ Sheriff of this County Collect the S$^{d}$ Summ̃ of Fifty & three poundes of Tobbaccoe from Every Individuall Titheable perſon Within this Pariſh And upon: Refuſall of Payment: to Levy the Same by Diſtreſs: The S$^{d}$ Sherrif firſt Entring into Bond: With Good & Sufficient Security to y$^{e}$ Preſent Churchwardens of this Pariſh for for payment of the S$^{d}$ Tobbaccoes: To the Severall Reſpective Pariſh Creditto$^{rs}$ before mentiooned To: Whome it is Due in hh$^{ds}$ of Such Waightes And at Such Times as the S$^{d}$ Churchwarden[ ] Shall Direct & Appoint: And that the Clerke of the Veſtry Take Bond as aforeſaid Before he Deliver Copys of the Pariſh Charge And this Order of Veſtry to y$^{e}$ S$^{d}$ Collector

Teſt Hen$^{r}$: Holdcraft Cl$^{r}$k of y$^{e}$ Veſtry

[4]

At: A: Veſtry held for Bliſland: Pariſh: At the Brick Church: October: y$^{e}$ 11$^{th}$: 1723

P$^{r}$ſent M$^{r}$ Daniel Taylor Miniſter: and: M$^{r}$ Will Morris Churchward

Majo': John: Thornton
Cap': Geo': Keeling
M': John: Sclater
Cap': Richard: Richardſon

Cap': Nicholas: Alderſey
Cap': John: Armiſtead
Henry: Holdcroft

and

Veſtrymen

Bliſlᵈ: Pariſh Dʳ: 1723
This: pʳſent Veſtry proceedes to Lay the Pariſh Levy. (Vizᵗ)

| | |
|---|---:|
| To: Mʳ Daniel Taylor Miniſteʳ for a years: Sall'y: | 16000 |
| To: Caſke to Ditto: inſtead of a Glebe by the Veſtrys agreemᵗ | 01280 |
| To: Conveniencey to Ditto According to Law | 00800 |
| To: Francis Cooke: Clkʳ: of yᵉ Pariſh for a yeares Sal'y 1500 & CC to ditto | 01695 |
| To Henry Holdcroft: Clʳk of Veſtry: for a yeares Sall'y 500 & CC to Dito | 00565 |
| To: Walter: Wood Saxton: his yeares Sall'y: 500 & Caſke to Do & a bruſh | 00560 |
| To: Francis Shoemaker: Saxton his yeares Sall'y 500 & Caſke 40 | 00540 |
| To: Mʳ Danˡ Taylor for 5 Delinqᵗˢ Returned Vizᵗ Gideon Cumbo: Thomas: Evans: William Dowde & Richᵈ Gilmett 2 | 00265 |
| To: Mʳ John Doran late Collectoʳ: for 4 delinqᵗˢ Returnd Vizᵗ John: Evans: William Filbeach: John Waſher & Negro: Alice: Liſted by him | 00212 |
| To: Majoʳ: John Thornton for Copy of Liſtes of Titheables | 40 |
| To: Bryan Henry for his years Maintainance: With Caſke | 918 |
| To: Mʳ: William Cox Churchwarden his Accoᵗ: Allowed at 12/6 pʳ | 312 |
| To: Mʳ William Morris Churchwarden his Account allowed | 325 |

| | |
|---|---:|
| To: M.' John Doran late Collector his accot & for Glebe laſt *[y's qtr'] | 104 |
| To: Bryan Henry for Keeping Lucey Gill | 400 |
| To: Rebecca farthing for Keeping John Pethwood a year: With Caſk | 756 |
| To: Docto': Rob': Burbidg: his acco': abou' Jone Corbett allowed | 640 |
| To: M'": Frances Langley for Keeping Jone Corbet: 4 Months & 3 Weeks | 760 |
| To: Richard Waren for: his yeares Maintainance | 400 |
| To: M.': Doran: for Keeping Reuben Laton & Endeavo' to Cure his Legg one year | 200 |
| To: Sall'y: for: 26772: pounds of Tobbaccoe at 5 p' Cent is | 1338 |
| To: M' Doran Collector for Tobbacco: Wanting Laſt year to pay y° Par Deb' | 141 |
| Totall is | 28251 |

Credit utt Supra

| | |
|---|---:|
| By: 542 Titheables at 52 pounds Tobb p' pole is | 28184 |
| By: Tobbacco: Wanting to pay the Pariſh Deb' to be Raiſed Next year | 00067 |
| | 28251 |

on the Other Side

[5]

M.': William Cox and M.': William Morris late Churchwardens are hereby Diſcharged: from their Said Office: And Cap': John Arimſtead & Henry Holdcroft are hereby Apointed Churchwardens for this pariſh and are Sworne accordingly before Cap': Richard Richardſon: a Majeſtrate of this County

---

*These two abbreviations were difficult to read. I may not have read them correctly.—C. G. C.

It is Ordered by this pʳſent Veſtry that the Pariſh Levy: for this preſent year be Fifty & Two: poundes of Tobbacco: pʳ: pole: And that Mʳ John Doran Deputy Sherrif of this County: Collect the Said Sum of fifty & two poundes Weight of Tobbbaccoe from Every Individuall: Titheable perſon Within this Pariſh: And upon Refuſall of Payment: to Levy the Same by Diſtreſs: according to Law: The Sᵈ Doran firſt Entring into Bond With Good & Sufficient Security to the preſent Churchwardens of this pariſh for the Uſe of the parriſh: for payment of the Said Summes of Tobbacco to the Severall Reſpective pariſh Creditors beforementioned to Whome it is Due: in hhogsheds — of Such Weightes & at Such times as the Said Churchwardens Shall Direct & Appoint: And alſoe Ordered that the Clerk of the Veſtry take Bond as aforeſaid before he Deliver a Copie of the pariſh Charge and Copy of this Order of Veſtry to the Said Collector
        Teſt: Henry: Holdcroft: Clʳk Veſtry

[6]
   At A Veſtry held for Bliſland Pariſh at yᵉ Brick Church: June: 12ᵗʰ: 1724

                   Pʳſent
Mʳ: Daniel Taylor Miniſtʳ   Capᵗ: John Arimſtead
                          and Henry Holdcroft
                                       Churchwardˢ

| | |
|---|---|
| Major John: Thornton | Mʳ John: Sclater |
| Capᵗ: George: Keeling | Mʳ: Will: Cox |
| Capᵗ: Richard: Richardſon | Mʳ: William Morris |
| Capᵗ: Wᵐ: Kenney | |

} Veſtrymen

   This pʳſent Veſtry proceeds to Lay out this Pariſh into pʳcincts: in Order to have the Tobbacco: plants Numbred According to yᵉ Late Law for the more Effectuall Improving the Staple of Tobacco.

It is Ordered by this preſent Veſtry That from the head of the Northweſt branch of Ware Creeke Down the Swamp to Holdcrofts Mill and from thence to the Extent of the Pariſh Downwards be One precinct: And from thence to: Mr Coxes Mill Creeke: Another p'cinct: And from Mr: Coxes Mill Creeke to the Main Road: that Leades from Christophr Barretts Landing to the Extent of the County Backwards Leaveing Lenleys Plantation in the Lower p'cinct Another: And from the Said Road to the Extent of the Said Pariſh Upwards Another p'cinct

Capt: Richard Richardſon And Mr William Morris are Apointed to Examine & Enquire of the Names and Number of the perſons (in the Lower precinct of of this County (Which are Allowed by the Sd Recited Act of Aſsembly) to tend Tobbacco). And the Cropps of the Severall Planters Within the Said precinct: And the Number of Plants Growing on any or Every plantation or Plantations Within the Same: Sometime in the Moneth of July yearly: And that the perſons hereby Appointed Doe take the Oath Appointed by the Sd Act of Aſsembly: before they proceed to Execute this Order

Mr Dan¹¹: Allen & Mr John Keen: Are hereby Appointed to Examine & Enquire of the Names & Number of the perſons: in their Precinct: which is Between Ware Creeke and Mr: Coxes Mill Creeke: (Which are Allowed by the Sd Recited Act of Aſsembly: to tend Tōbacco) And the Cropps of the Severall Planters Within the Said Precinct and the Number of Plants Growing on any or Every Plantation or Plantations Within the Same Some time in the Moneth of July yearly And that ye Perſons hereby appointed Doe take the Oath appointed by the Said Act of Aſsembly before the proceed to Execute this Order

[7]
Mr: Richard Clough and Mr Roger Williams are hereby Appointed to Examine & Enquire of the Names and Num-

ber: of the perſons in their Precinct wch is (between Mr Coxes Mill Creeke and the Main Road that Leades from Christopher Barretts Landing to the Extent of the County Backwards Leaving Lendleyes Plantation in the Lower Precinct) Which are Allowed by the Said Recited Act of Aſsembly: to tend Tobbaccoe And the Cropps: of the Severall Planters: Within the Said Precinct and the Number of Plants Growing on Any or Every Plantation or Plantations Within the Sam[ ] Sometime in the Moneth of July Yearly: And that the perſons hereby appointed doe take the Oath appointed by the Said Act of Aſsembly before they proceed to Execute this Order

Capt: John Foſter and Peter Carpenter are Appointed to Examine: & Enquire of the Names and Number of the perſons in their precinct (Which is from the Main Road Which Leades from Christopher Barretts Landing to the Extent of this parrish Upward) Which are Allowed by the Said Recited Act of Aſsembly to tend Tobbaccoe: And the Croppes of the Severall Planters Within their Said Precinct: And the Number of Plantes Growing on Any or Every Plantation or Plantations Within the Same Sometime in the Moneth of July Yearly: And that the Perſons hereby Appointed: Doe take the Oath Appointed by the Said Act of Aſsembly before they proceed to Execute this Order

Teſt: Henry Holdcroft Cl'k: Veſtry

[8]

At: A Veſtry held for Bliſland Pariſh: At the Lower Church: y°: 5th: day of October Annoque: Domini 1724

P'ſent

Mr: Daniel Taylor: Miniſter: Capt: John Arimſtead: & Henry Holdcroft: Churchwardens

Cap.ᵗ: John Hockaday  }
M.ʳ: William: Cox  }
Cap.ᵗ: Geo.ʳ: Keeling  }
M.ʳ: John: Sclater  }
M.ʳ: Will.ᵐ: Morris  }

Majo.ʳ John: Thornton  }
Cap.ᵗ: Rich.ᵈ: Richardſon  }
& Cap.ᵗ: William Kenney  } Veſtrymen
Cap.ᵗ: Nicholas Alderſey  }

This Preſent: Veſtry: Proceedes to Lay the Pariſh Levy Bliſl.ᵈ Pariſh 1724 D.ʳ  Tobbacco

To: M.ʳ Daniel Taylor Miniſter for A yeares Sall'y: 16000 ᵀᵒᵇᵇ: & Conveniency to ditto  16800
To: Caſke to Ditto inſtead of A Glebe by the Veſtrys Agreement at 8 p.ʳ Cent:  01280
To: Francis Cooke Cl'ke of the Pariſh for a yeares Sall'y 1500 & Caſke & Convency to ditto  01695
To: Henry: Holdcroft: Clerke of the Veſtry: for a yeares Sall'y 500: & Caſke & Convency to dito  00565
To: Francis Shoemaker Saxton of the Lower Church a yeares Sall'y 500 & Caſke to ditto 40  00540
To: Richard Waren: Saxton of the Upper Church for years Sall'y 500 & Caſke 40  00540
To: Majo.ʳ John Thornton for Copyes of the Liſtes of Titheables  00040
To: Bryan Henry for his yeares Maintainance & Caſke  00918
To: Bryan Henry for Keepeing Lucey Gill: A Year  00400
To: M.ʳ J.nᵒ Doran Late Pariſh Collector for Tobbacco: Wanting Laſt year 67 & Quitt.ʳ for Glebe  00091
To: Henry Holdcroft: Churchw.ᵈ: for 3 Comunions 300 & Repairing the Church finding Nailes Planck &.ᶜ as by his Account Allowed  00473
To: M.ʳ Tho: Ballard for John Pethwoods Coffin Allowed  00060
To: Rebecca: Farthing for Keeping John Pethwood 3 moneths & two Weekes  00216
To: Elizabeth: Walton for Keepeing Mary Ogleſby 3 Moneths: being a pariſh Child  00150

| | |
|---|---|
| To: Richard Jones for a Coffin for Widow Hazelwood | 00060 |
| To: Mr William Livingſtone for Phiſick & for Keepeing Mary Burke | 00200 |
| To: Mr John Doran: for: Cureing Suſanna Barker & her Board 3 moneths 1200 and: Caſke & Conveniency to Ditto 168 & for Salivateing William Jones 1000 With Caſke & Conveniency to Ditto: 140 as pr Churwadens agreemt & 6 Delinqts in | 02820 |
| To: Mrs Margrett Dibdall for Cureing Benjamin Baitch of a Scald: Head & Keeping him a year in Dyet & Cloathes | 00700 |
| To: Doctor William Levingſtone: for Keepeing Frances Haſewell a baſtard Child borne of: his Servant Mary Haſewell: he Giveing Bond to Save the Pariſh: Harmeles & Indemnified from any further Charge abot: the Sd Child | 00500 |
| To: Sallary to Receiveing: 28048ll of Tobbacc at 5 pr Cent is 1402 | 01402 |
| Totall Pariſh Debt is | 29450 |

Creditt Utt Supra
| | |
|---|---|
| By 604: Titheables at 49ll pounds of Tobbacco pr pole is 29596 | 29596 |
| Ballce Due to the Pariſh to be allowed by the Collector Next year | 146 |
| | 29450 |

[9]
It is Ordered by this Preſent Veſtry that the Pariſh Levy for this Preſent year be Forty and Nine Poundes of Tobbaccoe pr pole: And that Mr John Doran Deputy Sherriff of this County: Collect the Said: Summ of Forty and Nine

poundes of Tobbacco: from Every Individuall Titheable perſon: Within this Pariſh and Upon Refuſall of paymᵗ to Levy the Same by Diſtreſs According to Law: the Said John Doran firſt Entring into Bond With Good & Sufficient Security to Henry: Holdcroft: One of the preſen[ ] Churchwardens: for the Uſe of the Sᵈ Pariſh for the Payment of the Said Summs of Tobbacc[ ] to the Severall Reſpective Pariſh Creditors Above Mentioned to Whome it is due in hhds of Such Weightes and at Such times: as the Sᵈ Churchwarden Shall appoint And it is Alsoe Ordered that Henry Holdcroft Clerke of the Veſtry: and Churchwarden take Bond as aforeſaid before he Deliver a Copie of the Pariſh Charge and a Copie of this Order of Veſtry to the Said Collector

It: is Ordered by this preſent Veſtry that A Veſtryman be Choſen for this Pariſh in the Stead of Collonⁿ: William Baſsett Deceaſed And Mʳ John Doran being preſenᵗ is Choſen A Veſtryman: for this pariſh And is Sworne Accordingly before Mʳ John Sclater A Majeſtrate of this County

Capᵗ: John Arimſtead haveing served Laſt year: As Churchwarden of this Pariſh: And Refuſeing to Continue Any Longer in the Said Office: Mʳ John Doran is Appointed Churchwarden in his Stead and is Accordingly Sworne before Mʳ John Sclater A Majeſtrate of this County

Test: Henry Holdcroft Cl'k of the Veſtry

[10]

At: A: Veſtry held for Bliſland Pariſh: At the Brick Church: the 24ᵗʰ: day of Aprill: 1725:

P:'ſent:

Mʳ Daniell: Taylor: Miniſtʳ: Mʳ: John: Doran & Henry: Holdcroft: Churchwardens

At a Vestry held for ye Church of Wilmington the Brick Church the 29th day of Aprill 1725.

Psent: Mr Powell Taylor Mr [illegible] Doran & Henry Holding — Churchwardens —
Mr William Cox, Mr John [illegible] & Richard Richardson
Capt John Lewiston & Capt Nicholas Alderson — } Vestrymen

Mr George Woodward, Mr [illegible] & Mr Thomas Williams being added to this Vestry by Directions of the Late [illegible] for the Erecting of Wilmington Parish & for ye [illegible] are sworne Accordingly before Capt John Hainstead a Justice of this County ——

Psent: Mr George Woodward Mr Thomas Williams & Mr Lawrence Woodward } Vestrymen

Mr George Woodward & Mr Thomas Williams are appointed to View & Count the Tobacco plants in all the precincts which are lately Wilmington Parish and is now added to this parish. And it is Ordered by the sd Vestry that for the Viewing of Wilmington Parish the sd Williams and Woodward Doe take the Oath appointed by the said act of assembly Entituled an act for the More Effectuall improving the Staple of Tobacco, before they Enter upon the Execution of the sd Office.

Whereas Mr John Anston who was formerly appointed to Vue & Number the Tobacco plants with Peter Carpenter in the Uppermost precincts of this parish is Removed & Dwells now in King William County. Mr William Harman in his Motion is appointed in his stead with the said Carpenter to Vue and Number the Tobacco plants in that precinct the said William Harman first to take the Oath appointed by the act of Assembly Entituled An act for the More Effectuall improving the Staple of Tobacco before he Enter upon the Execution of his said Office.

Whereas there was five hundred pounds of Tobacco Raised at the Last Vestry & appointed to be disposed of to Mr William Livingstone Tobacco & finding out a bastard Child borne of the Body of Mary Halwell a Servant to the said William: the said Child being dead before it was brought out according to the said Servant it is therefore Ordered that the said Livingstone be paid only three hundred pounds of the said Tobacco for the Trouble & Charge in keeping the sd Child while it Lived and his trouble & Charge about burying it.

Elizabeth the Wife of Evan Jones Complaining to this Vestry for Relief & Shewing that her husband being of Sound Mind but of another Distracted with fitts of Lunacy & Distraction and that she hath three Small Children to Maintaine and hath not any known Estate nor hath no way to purchase any sustenance for her & husband Selfe & children. It is therefore Ordered by this psent Vestry that Mr John Doran the Late Parish Collector do pay the Sume of 151 pounds of Tobacco out of the Ballance of the Five hundred hogsheads of Tobacco: Raised Last year for putting out Mary Halwells Bastard Child: after the three hundred paid to Mr Livingstone; & some pt of Evan Jones debts, that was in being to paid. But all the sd 151 to paid towards the Relieving the sd Evan & Maintaining some. And it is further Ordered that the Churchwardens of this parish doe bind out the said Evan Jones Children as the Law Directs for poor parish Children &c to be provided for.

Mʳ William: Cox: Mʳ: John: Sclater: Capᵗ: Richard: Richardſon Capᵗ: John: Arimstead; & Capᵗ: Nicholas Alderſey—Veſtrymen

Mʳ: George: Woodward: Mʳ Lanceloᵗᵗ: Woodward & Mʳ: Thomas: Williams: being: Added: to this Veſtry by: Directions of the Late Law for the Diſsolving of Willmington Pariſh & Now Appearing: are Sworne Accordingly: before Capᵗ John Armistead A Juſtice of this County

Pʳſent: Mʳ George: Woodward: Mʳ: Thomas: Williams: & Mʳ Lancelott: Woodward—Veſtrymen

Mʳ Lancelott: Woodward: & Mʳ Thomas: Williams: are Appointed to View & Count the Tobbacco: plants in: all that precinct: Which: Was Lately: Wilmington Pariſh (and is Now Added to this pariſh) of Bliſland by the Sᵈ Recited Law for the Diſolving of Wilmington Pariſh and that the Sᵈ Williams and Woodward: Doe Take the Oaths appointed by the Said Act (of Aſsembly: Entitled an act for the More Effectuall: Improving the Staple of Tobacco): before: they: Enter Upon the Execution of that Office

Whereas: Mʳ John Foſter: Who: Was: formerly: Appointed to View & Number The Tobbaccoe plants: With Peter Carpenter in the Uppermoſt precincts of this pariſh: is Removed: & Dwelles Now in King William County: Mʳ William Harman: On his Motion is Appointed: in his Stead With the Said Carpenter To: View & Number the Tobbaccoe plants in that precinct the Said William Harman firſt Takeing the Oath: Appointed by the Act of Aſsembly: Entituled An Act for the More Effectuall Improveing the Staple of Tobbaccoe: before: he: Enter upon the Execution of his Said: Office

Whereas: There: Was five hundred: poundes of Tobbaccoe: Raiſed at the Laſt Veſtry: & Appointed to be diſpoſed of: for: Mʳ William Levingſtones Keepeing: & binding out: a baſtard Child: borne of the Body of Mary Haſwell: A Servant to the Said William: the Said Child being

Dead before it was bound out apprentice According to the Said Agreem$^t$: it is therefore Ordered that the Said Livingſtone be paid Only Three hundred poundes of the Said Tobbacco: for the Trouble & Charge in Keeping the S$^d$ Child Whileſt it Lived: and his trouble & Charge about burying it

Elizabeth The Wife of Evan Jones: Complaing to this Veſtry for Relief: & Shewing that her huſband: Nott being: of Sound Mind: but oftentimes: Diſturbed With fitts of Lunacy & Diſtraction: and that She hath three Small Children to Maintain: And hath Not any Bread Corne: Nor hath Noe Way to purchaſe Any Suſtenance: for her S$^d$ Huſband Self & Children: It is Therefore Ordered by this preſent Veſtry: that M$^r$: John Doran: the Late Pariſh Collector Doe pay the Summ of 151 poundes of Tobb being: the Ballance of the five hundred pounds of Tobbacco: Raiſed Laſt year: for putting out Mary Haſwells Baſtard Child: after the three hundred paid to M$^r$ Livingſtone: & Some part of Evan Joneses Levyes: Which Was in Arrear: be paid: that then the S$^d$ 151 be paid: towards the Relieving the Said Jones & family With Corne: And it is further Ordered that the Churchwardens of this pariſh Doe Bind Out the Said Evan Joneses Children: as the Law Directs: for Poor pariſh Children: &cr to be provided for

[11]

It: is Ordered: by this preſent Veſtry that: Anne Leaver: the baſe Daughter of Mary Leaver Deceaſed: being Now a Pariſh Charge: And Cannot as yett be Certainly Known Whether Shee the Said Baſtard Child be A Mullatto: or Not:) be: Bound Out: to M$^r$ Roger Williams to Serve him or his Aſsignes as the Law in that Caſe Directs: for Children in Such Caſes and under Such Circumſtances as that shall hereafter appear to be Lyable Unto: Whether it Shall prove hereafter to be a White Child or a Mulatto: And this Veſtry Agrees With the Said Roger Williams to Raiſe &

pay him for his Charge and trouble in Keepeing and Maintaining the Said Child: from being any further Chargeable to this pariſh Dureing the time of the Said Childs Service or Apprenticeſhip: the Summ̃ of Seven hundred pounds of Tobbacco & Caſke at the Laying of the Next Pariſh Levy—The Said Roger Williams Giveing Bond & Security: before he Receives the Said 700ˡˡ of Tobbacco & Caſke: for his performance of his Said Agreement: and this Veſtry further agrees With the Sᵈ Roger Williams that incaſe the Said baſtard Child Should Live Untill She attain to Lawfull age and Then: Shall be Lawfully Entituled to Demand & have Freedom Corne & Cloathes that then & In Such Caſe: that this Pariſh Shall & Will find & provide Corne & Cloathes for her according as the Law in that Caſe Directs

Martha: Goodin: A poor Woman: being Under a Deploreable Affliction: With A Sore Legg and is thereby uncapeable of Getting her Livelyhood: haveing Applyed her Self to yᵉ Churchwardens of this Pariſh for Relief: It is therefore Agreed: Between this Veſtry in behalf of this pariſh: and Mʳ John Doran: as Followes: Vizᵗ: The Said Doran hath this day Undertaken to Cure the Said Martha of her Ailement: & Sore Legg: And is To have for his trouble & Charge: about the Said Cure and for Maintaining the Said Martha at his Own Coſtes & Charge: Whileſt She is Under the Said Cure: the Summ̃ of Fifteen hundred poundes of Tobbacco & Caſke to be Raiſed & paid him at the Laying of the Next Pariſh Levy: But incaſe the Said Martha Should Dye before Shee be perfectly Cured: Then & in that Caſe the Said Doran: Agrees to have Only Six hundred po[ ]ndes of Tobbacco: & Caſke for his trouble & Charge about the Sᵈ Martha: to be Raiſed & paid as aforeſaid: And the Said Doran Agrees With this Veſtry: to Save this Pariſh harmeles: & Indemnified from any Further or Other Charges or Expence Whatſoever about the

Said Martha: for & dureing the term & Space of One year from the Date here of: and further that he the Said Doran before the Said fifteen hundred poundes of Tobbacco be Raiſed & paid to him he will Give Bond & Security to: the Churchwardens: that incase the Said Martha: be Not perfectly Cured & Well: at the End of the Said year Now Enſueing: And the Said fifteen hundred poundes of Tobbacco: beforementioned: is then all or the Moſt part thereof paid: to the Said Doran: that then & in that Caſe that he will Refund and Repay to the Veſtry for the Uſe of this Pariſh Nine hundred pounds of Tobbaccoe & Caſke or Soe Much as he Shall have Received: More then Six hundred & Caſke Which is Agreed he Shall have for his Charge & trouble: incase of her the Said Marthas death as aforsd or: being Endeavoured With: & Not Cured at the Expiracon of One year as aforeſaid

 Teſt: Henry: Holdcroft: Clk Veſtry Bliſlᵈ Pariſh

[12]

At: A: Veſtry: held: for Bliſland: Pariſh: yᵉ: thirteenth day of: October: At the Brick Church: 1725:

    Pʳſent:

Mʳ. Daniel: Taylor: Miniſtʳ: Henry: Holdcroft: & John Doran: Church: Wardens

Capᵗ: George: Keeling: Majoʳ John: Thornton: Capᵗ: Will Kenney: Mʳ William: Morriſs: Cap: John: Arimſtead: Mʳ: George: Woodward & Mʳ Lancelott Woodward—Veſtrymen

This: Preſent: Veſtry Proceedes to Lay the Pariſh Levy —Vizᵗ Bliſlᵈ: Pariſh Dʳ 1725

| | | |
|---|---:|---:|
| To: Mʳ Daniel Taylor: Miniſtʳ: for A yeares Sall'y | | |
|  16000 | 16000 | |
| To: Caſke to Ditto: as pʳ: Veſtrys agreement: for | | |
|  yᵉ Deficiency of yᵉ Glebe: 1200 | 01280 | |

To: Conveniency: to yᵉ Miniſters Sall'y according to Law at 5 pʳ Cᵗ: is    00800
To: Francis: Cooke: Clark of yᵉ Pariſh & yeares Sall'y 1500 & Caſke & Conveniency to ditto    01695
To: Henry Holdcroft Cleʳk of: this Veſtry for a years Sall'y: 500 ᵀᵒᵇᵇ & Caſke & Conv to ditto    00565
To: Richard Warren: for his Sall'y: being Saxton of the Uppʳ: Church: 500 ¹¹ ᵀᵒᵇᵇ & Caſk    00540
To: Francis Shoemaker: Deceaſed for 8 monthes being Saxton of yᵉ Lower Church & Caſk    00360
To: Evan Robards for being Saxton at yᵉ Loweʳ Church: 4 moneths & Caſke Included    00180
To: Bryan: Henry for his yeares Maintainence & Caſke allowed him to it in all    00918
To: Bryan Henry for Keeping Lucey Gill his Grandaughtʳ: 1 yeaʳ    00400
To: John Doran for Cureing Martha Goodings deceaſd of a Sore legg as: pʳ the Veſtrys agreement 1500 ᵀᵒᵇᵇ: & CC to ditto    01695
To: Majoʳ: Thornton Clerke of the Court: for: his Copyes Liſt Tithes & Fees: in Suit vs mary Field    00170
To: Henry Holdcroft: Churchwarden: his account: adjuſted & Allowed:    00610
To: Mʳ John Doran: Churchward: Late pariſh Collectoʳ: for 21 Titheables Delinquenᵗˢ Returned    01029
To: Mʳ Doran: For: 2 Sherriffs: Fees Verſus Field & Stranger at Gaddyes    00040
To: Doctoʳ: John Brody: for Phiſick & Attendance: for Jone Corbett: 700 ᵀᵒᵇᵇ: & Caſke    00756
To: Ditto Brody for Salavateing Richard Gillmett: & Emanˡˡ: Demetrius by The: Agreement of Mʳ John Doran: Churchwarden 1000: but: yᵉ later Not Cured    01000

To: Sarah Smallepage for her: Laſt yeares Maintainance 500 ᵀᵒᵇᵇ & Caſke                             00540
To: John: Laffoon: for: his Maintainance this Enſueing yeaʳ 300: & 74: Arrears Not paid in Willmington Pariſh Laſt Year allowed him      00374
To: Mʳ William: Browne Late Churchwarden of Willmington pʳſh his proporcon of arrears allowᵈ 00071
To: Ditto: for 2 delinqᵗˢ Returned. Vizᵗ: Peter Jennings & 1 Overcharged Len Henley                 0106
To: Mʳ Will: MᶜKain: for Arrears being Clark of Willming pʳſh Laſt year                             0248
To: Moſes Crawford for arreares: of his Sall'y: in Wilm̃ton pʳ:ſh Laſt year                         0074
To: Mʳ: Roger Williams: for: takeing: Anne Lever: Abaſtard Childe of Mary Lever: Deceaſed as by his agreement With the Veſtry to: Keep the Said Child from being a pariſh Charge    0756
To: Sall'y for Receiveing 30207 poundes of Tobbacco at 5 pʳ Cent for yᵉ Collector                   1510

      Pariſh Charge Totall: Sum̃                 31717

    Bliſland Pariſh Creditt Utt Supra
By Surplus Tobbacco in Mʳ Dorans yᵉ laſt Collectoʳˢ hands to be pᵈ Now this yeʳ            00146
By: 43ˡˡ: & ½ˡˡ of Tobbacco: pʳ pole on 726 Titheables amounᵗˢ to                          31581

                                                 31727

In yᵉ Collectors hands—By: 10ˡˡ of Tobb. Surplus to be pᵈ Nexᵗ year Reduct                10

                                                 31717

The Names of the Delinq`ts`: Returned by M`r`: John Doran late Collecto`r`: are as Followes Viz`t`

Francis Harman: 1: Edward Henry: 2: Richard Gillmett: 1: Rob`t`: Lockalere: 1: Owen Morris: 1: Edw`d` Merritt: 1: Joſeph Darling: 2: Henry Crutchley: 1: Matt Pond: 1: William: Jones: 1: Henry: Lindley: 1: Jn°: Holland 1: Charles: Ogleſby: 1: Franck Darling: 1: Sarah Yates: 1: Rob`t`: Clinch: 1: Jn°: Rountree: 1: John: James: 1: Suſanna Darling: 1:

[13]
Mary Shelbourn Petitioning this Veſtry: to allow her Some help towards paying her Cur[ ] It: is: Ordered: by this: P`r`ſent: Veſtry: that the Fine: Due from Doctor: William Livingſtone: by his Aſsumpſitt: in Court: for Mary Haſwell—his Servant: haveing a Baſtard Child being two pound[ ] And Tenn Shillings Current Money: and the Caſh: Received: from the: Strange Woman Which Was brought to: bed at: Richard Gaddeyes: being: Twenty: Five Shillings & five Shillings: M`r` Daniel Taylor: promiſed and five Shillings Cap`t`: Keeling: promised to: Give Towards: paying Docto`r`: John Scott being in all four pounds: five Shillings to be Collected by Henry Holdcroft: Churchwarden: & paid to: the S`d` Doctor: John Scott: for the Cure of Mary Shelbourns: Sore: Legg: he promiſeing: to Accept of the Same for the Diſchargeing of: her Debt: to him: for the S`d` Cure

On: the Petition of Moſes Crawford: for the Office of Saxton: of one Of the Churches in this Pariſh It: is: Conſidered: & Accordingly Ordered that the S`d` Moſes be Admitted Saxton of the Lower Church in this Pariſh & that he be Allowed: Annually the Summ̃ of three hundred poundes of Tobbaccoe and Caſke for the S`d` Service:

Joſeph: Linſey: Petitioning: this Veſtry: to Diſcharge: him from paying Levyes for his Lame Negroe Man Called:

Toby: It is Ordered that the Said Toby be: Diſcharged from Pariſh Levy dureing his: debility

Richard: Waren: on his Petition: Setting forth that he is Lame & Unable to Labour for his Liveing & only Deſireing to be Levy free: it is Ordered that he be Diſcharged from paying Pariſh Levyes Untill he Recovered of his S$^d$ Lamenes

Richard Hatfield Son of Richard Hatfield: a poor Diſseaſed perſon: on his petition is. is Diſcharged from Paying Pariſh Levys: Untill it Shall pleaſe God to Reſtore him to his health that he be able to Gett his living

It: is Ordered by this preſent Veſtry: that the: Rent of the Glebe: plantation Which Was Lately added to this Pariſh: be Collected by the Church wardens: and applyed: Towards the Maintainance: & Cure of Emanuel Demetrius a poor Diſseaſed Perſon belonging to this Pariſh

Whereas: there: appeares Due to the Pariſh: from M$^r$ John Doran: the Summ̃: of Twenty: Shillings On the Ballance of: his Caſh account: as being One of the Churchwardens of this pariſh: It is Ordered that the S$^d$ Twenty Shillings Caſh be paid to Henry Holdcroft: Churchwardn: for the Uſe & hurt done to a Small Feather bed he provided for Martha Goodin: While She was Under her Cure

It is: Ordered by this: p'ſent: Veſtry that the Pariſh Levy for this p'ſent year be Forty three & an half poundes Weight of Tobbaccoe p': pole: and that M$^r$ John James Deputy Sher'iff of this County: Collect: & Receive the S$^d$ Summ̃ of: Forty three and one half poundes Weight of Tobbacco: from Every Individuall: Titheable: perſon Within this Pariſh: and on Refuſall of payment To Levy the Same by diſtreſs according to Law: The S$^d$: John James first Entring in to bond with Good and Sufficient Security: to the preſent Churchwardens: for the Uſe of this Pariſh: for payment of the Said Severall Summes

of Tobbaccoe to the Severall Reſpective pariſh Creditors to
Whome it is Due: according as they are: above mentioned &
Expreſed in the: Pariſh: Charge: in hh$^{ds}$ of Such Weightes
and at Such Times as the S$^d$ Churchwardens Shall Direct & appoint: And it is alſoe Ordered that the Clerke of the Veſtry:
take bond as aforeſaid: before he Deliver a Copy of: the Pariſh
Charge and a Copie of this Order of Veſtry to the S$^d$ Collector

It is: Ordered: by this p'ſent: Veſtry that: Henry Holdcroft
& John Doran be Continued Church wardens for this Enſueing
year

Teſt: Henry: Holdcroft: Cl'k of y$^e$: Veſtry

[14]

At: A Veſtry held for: Bliſland: Pariſh: At the Lower
Church December y$^e$ 22$^d$: 1725:

P:'ſent:

M$^r$: Daniel Taylor Miniſte$^r$:   M$^r$. Henry Holdcroft & M$^r$
John Doran: Church wardens

Cap$^t$: George: Keeling:   ⎧Cap$^t$: William: Kenney⎫
M$^r$: William: Cox:   & ⎨Cap$^t$: John: Arimſtead⎬Veſtrymen
M$^r$: John: Sclater:   ⎩M$^r$: Thomas: Williams⎭

Whereas M$^r$: John: James: Who: was Appointed Collector
of the Pariſh Levy for this p'ſent Year is Lately Deceaſed:
And hath: done Very Little (:if any part) of the Pariſh Col-
lection: And M$^r$: John Doran: Acquainting this Veſtry that he:
hath Agreed With Cap$^t$: William Macon Sherriff of this
County: to Serve: as Deputy Sherriff of this Lower precincts:
thereof: and haveing applyed himſelf to this Veſtry for the
Pariſh Collection: And the Pariſh Levy Laid: at the Laſt
Veſtry held for this Pariſh: the thirteenth day of October
Laſt *and amou[ ] To: the Summ of Forty three poundes

―――――
*This word is scratched through in the MS but is still legible.—C. G. C.

and One half pound Waight of Tobbacco: pʳ: pole as by the Said Order May appear: It is therefore Ordered by this preſent Veſtry: That yᵉ Sᵈ Mʳ: John Doran Doe Collect & Receive the Sum̃ of Forty three & one half poundes: Waight of Tobbacco: from: Every Individuall Titheable perſon Within this Pariſh and Upon Refuſaall of payment to Levy the Same by Diſtreſs (according to Law): the Said Doran firſt Entring into bond With good and Sufficient: Security: to Henry Holdcroft: Church warden: For the Uſe of the Pariſh for the due Payment: of yᵉ Said Summ̃s of Tobbaccoe: to the Severall Reſpective Pariſh Creditors: to Whome it is due and: according: as it is: Ordered & Appointed to be paid: by the Sᵈ Recited Order of the Laſt Veſtry and to pay the Same in hhᵈˢ of Such Weightes and at Such times as the Said (Holdcroft) Church warden Shall: Direct & Appoint: And: the Sᵈ Holdcroft: Clerke of the Veſtry: Take bond and Security as aforeſaid before he Deliver a Copy of the Pariſh Charge & Copy of this Order of Veſtry to the Sᵈ Collector

Mʳ: William: Levingſtone Complaining to this Veſtry: That Whereas: the Veſtry of this Pariſh by their Order Dated the: fifth day of October 1724: did Order & Raiſe the Summ̃ of five hundred poundes of Tobbaccoe: for: Undertakeing to Keep: a baſtard Child of Mary Haſwells, and to Give Bond to Save the Pariſh Indemnified: from any further Charge about the Sᵈ Child: and the Sᵈ Child Dyeing before: the Sᵈ Bond was Given: the Said Liveingſtone Was only paid 300ˡ poundes of: the Sᵈ 500ˡ: pᵈs of Tobbacco: upon Conſideration thereof It is Ordered that the Sᵈ Levingſton be allowed & paid two hundred poundes of Tobbacco to be Raiſed and paid at the Laying of the Next pariſh Levys

Capᵗ: John Arimſtead: On his Motion: Offering to the Veſtry that: incaſe the Veſtry Wold: Grant him an Order. for a Pew in the: Brick Church of this pariſh for himſelf and: his familyes uſe: That himſelf and his Wife Wold: forthwith:

—— Make & Execute: Good authentique Deedes of Sale or any Legall Conveyances: To the Veſtry or Church wardens of the Pariſh: for the Pariſhes uſe: Two Acres of Land: Wheron the S$^d$ Brick Church Now Standes: And the Veſtry Conſidering thereof have thought fitt to Refferrit for a Fuller Veſtry: to: Reſolve about the Said: affair:

Copia: Teſt Henry: Holdcroft Clk Veſtry

[15]

At A Veſtry held for Bliſland Bliſland Pariſh at the Brick Church June 24$^{th}$: 1726

P'ſent:

M$^r$ Daniel Taylor Minister   Henry: Holdcroft  } Churchwardens
                               John: Doran

Cap$^t$: Geo$^r$: Keeling        } M$^r$: Geo$^r$: Woodward      }
Cap$^t$: Rich$^d$: Richardſon    } M$^r$: Thomas: Williams       } Veſtrymen
M$^r$: Will: Morris              } M$^r$: Lancell$^t$: Woodward  }

This Veſtry: proceedes to: Appoint Viewers & Tellers to Examine & Enquire of the Names & Number of Perſons in this Pariſh allowed by Law to plant & Tend Tobbacco: and Forasmuch as the Pariſh hath been already Laid out into Convenient precincts: and the Several Perſons Which have been already appointed & have Served are all Continued in their Sevuall precincts: Only M$^r$ John Keen Who is unwilling to Serve any long$^r$ in that: Office: Benjamin Richardſon therefore is appointed in his Stead in the Same p'cinct With M$^r$ Daniel Allen & Ordered that he be Sworne accordingly before he Enter upon the Execution of that Office

M$^r$ Richard Clough being Removed out of this Pariſh M$^r$ David Williams is appointed a teller in his Stead along With his Brother M$^r$ Roger Williams And it is Ordered that he be Sworn Accordingly before he Enter into the Said Office

Mr Peter Carpenter being Lately Deceaſed: Was a Teller of Tobbacco in the Upper p'cincts of this Pariſh: With Mr William Harman: Mr John Luck on his Motion is appointed a Teller in the Stead of the Said Peter Carpentr and it is Ordered that he be Sworne according to Law before he proceed in the Said Office

Teſt: Henry: Holdcroft

[16]

At: a Veſtry: held for Bliſland Pariſh: the 12th: day of October: 1726: At Mr Furneas Ordinary

P'ſent

Mr Daniel: Taylor: Miniſtr: Henry: Holdcroft & John Doran Church wardens

| | |
|---|---|
| Capt: George: Keeling: | Mr: John: Slater: |
| Capt: Richd: Richardſon: | Mr: William: Morris: |
| Capt: Will: Kenney: | Mr: George: Woodward |
| Capt: John: Arimſtead | Mr: Lancelt: Woodward |
| Mr: William: Cox: | Mr Thomas: Williams |

Vestrymen

This: Veſtry proceedes to Lay the Pariſh Levy     Tobbacco

| | |
|---|---:|
| To: Mr: Daniel: Taylor Miniſtr for a yeares Sall'y | 16000 |
| To: Caſke to Ditto: as pr: yͤ Veſtryes Agreement: for the deficiency of the Glebe | 01280 |
| To: Conveniency: to Ditto according to Law at 5 pr Cent | 0800 |
| To Mr Francis: Cooke: Clarke of the Pariſh for a yeares Sallr 1500 & C C to ditto | 1695 |
| To: Henry: Holdcroft: Clerke of the Veſtry for a yeares Sall'y 500: & Caske & Conveniency to do | 565 |
| To: Moſes Crafford Saxton of the Lower Church for his yeares: Sall'y: by agreemt | 300 |
| To: Richard: Waren: Saxton of yͤ Uppr Church: for a yeares Sall'y: 500 & Caske to ditto | 540 |

| | |
|---|---|
| To: Bryan: Henry for his yeares Maintain⁰⁰: and Caske & Conveniency to Ditto | 918 |
| To Bryan Henry: for: Keeping Lucey Gilles & his Grandaughter a year | 400 |
| To: Majoʳ John Thornton: his Clerkes Fees: in theſe Following Suites Vizᵗ: the Par vs Langly & Gaddy & Couſins: Mackormack: Jammeſon & for 2 Liſtes of Titheables | 208 |
| To: Mʳ John: Doran Late Collectoʳ: for: 16: delinquents: & an Order: for Mʳ: Levingſtones 200 & the Quittrents of the: Old Glebe Land: in all amounting to | 912 |
| To: Henry Holdcroft: Church warden his Accouᵗ: Adjuſted & Allowed | 639½ |
| To: John Laffoon: for his yeares Maintainance allowed by the Pariſh | 300 |
| To: Sarah: Smallpage Allowed for her yeares Maintaince 500: & Caſke to ditto 40 | 540 |
| To: Mʳ Daniel: Taylor: Miniſtʳ for 15: Delinquenᵗˢ Returned: Which yᵉ Sherrif pᵈ him | 652½ |
| To: Joſeph Hawkins for Keeping Hannah Hopkins: a lame Woman 6 monthes: pʳ ordʳ: | 300 |
| To: Mʳ Archer Clerke of James County Court: for Copie of Liſt tithes Laſt year & this year | 40 |
| To: Henry: Holdcroft Churchwarᵈ to pay Quittrents for 2 yeares for the Glebe land in Ja City County | 96 |
| To: Collon¹¹: John: Scott: in part of his Agreement: for yᵉ Cure of Eliza: Barker | 550 |
| To: Mary: Shelbourn: Allowed Towards Maintainance of her lame Daught Mary Shelbourn: Who is Soe afflicted She Cannot Gett her liveing: to be putt into the hands of Henry: Holdcroft to: lay out in Meat for her | 300 |

To: Sall<sup>r</sup>: for Receiveing 27036" Tobbacco: att 5 p<sup>r</sup>
Cent to be for Collecto<sup>r</sup>                          1351

        Totall Parifh Debt is                   28387

Creditt Utt Supra
    By: 40" Tobbacco: p<sup>r</sup>: p<sup>r</sup> pole on: 714
        Titheables:                                28560
    By: M<sup>r</sup> John Doran Late Collecto<sup>r</sup>: due
        Laft year                                    10

                                       28570
    By: 183": of Tobbacco: the Surplus
Now Levyed: the Collecto<sup>r</sup> to pay Next year

    Henry Holdcroft & John Doran late Church wardens are Difcharged from their Said Office: And Cap<sup>t</sup>: Rich<sup>d</sup>: Richardfon & M<sup>r</sup>. John Sclater: are Appointed Churchwardens: in their Stead: And Was Sworne accordingly: before M<sup>r</sup>: William Morris: A Majeftrate

    It: is Ordered by this prefent Veftry that Henry Holdcroft Gen<sup>t</sup>: Endeavour to Receive & Collect: What Tobbacco is Due to the parifh from the Sundry Delinquents Who did Not pay their Parifh Levyes Laft year or any year before that Can be Recovered  And be accountable to the Veftry for What Received

[17]

    It: is Ordered: by this p<sup>r</sup>fent Veftry: that the Parifh Levy for this p<sup>r</sup>fent year be: Fourty poundes Weigh<sup>t</sup> of Tobbaccoe: p<sup>r</sup>: pole: And M<sup>r</sup> John: Sclater Sherriff of this County: is Ordered to Collect: and Receive the Said Summ̃: of Fourty poundes Weight of Tobbaccoe: from Every Individuall: Titheable perfon Within this Parifh: and on default of payment to Make Diftrefs: for the Same according to: Law:  The Said Sclater: firft Entring into bond With Good & Sufficient

Securityes to the Other Churchwarden for the Uſe of the Said Pariſh: for payment of the Said: Tobbaccoes to the Severall Reſpective Pariſh Credito^(rs): above Mentioned: for Whome it is Raiſed as it is Appointed: & directed by the Pariſh Charge: In hh^(ds) of Such: Weightes and at Such times as the Said Church warden Shall Direct & appoint: And it is Ordered that the Clerke of the Veſtry Take: Bond & Security as aforeſ^d before: he deliver a Copy of this Order of Veſtry & a Copy of the Pariſh Charge to the Said Collecto^r:

Ordered by this Veſtry: that on the Complaint of Bryan Henryes Wife: for More allowance for: Keeping Lucey Gilles & being informed that the S^d Child Was More then Ordinary troubleſome: they are to be allowed Annually 200 poundes of Tobbaccoe: More then their former allowance

Samuel Curl appearing at this Veſtry Did Aſsume: to pay to M^r William Cox: for the Uſe of the pariſh five hundred poundes of Tobbaccoe: being for the Rent of the Glebe: Laſt year 400^(ll) and 100 in part for this preſent yeares Rent and haveing Given his bill: to the p^rſent Churchwardens: for three hundred poundes of Tobbaccoe to be Paid Next: year at the Laying of the Parriſh Levy being the Remainder of the Rent: for this: preſent year: it being: Lett at four hundred poundes Tobbacco p^r annum:

William Charleton: on his Motion to this Veſtry for pay for his trouble in tranſporting Elizabeth Barker to Collon^(ll) John Scottes: and for his trouble in Goeing: to Fetch the S^d Scott Down to See the S^d Ba^rker & to Undertake: her Cure: for Which Service the Veſtry: hath Ordered that he be allowed: one hundred poundes of Tobbaccoe: to be paid this year of the Tobbacco: Which Was: Now Levyed it Not being: Entred in the Pariſh Charge

   Teſt Henry: Holdcroft Clk: of y^e Veſtry

[18]
At: a: Veſtry held for Bliſland Pariſh: At the Lower: Church October: yᵉ 11ᵗʰ: anno Domini: 1727

Preſent:

Mʳ Daniel: Taylor: Miniſter:  Capᵗ: Richard: Richardſon: & Mʳ: Jnᵒ: Sclater: Church warden

| | |
|---|---|
| Mʳ: William Cox | Capᵗ: Jnᵒ: Arimſtead |
| Capᵗ: Geoʳ: Keeling | Mʳ Jnᵒ: Doran |
| Capᵗ: Will: Kenney | Mʳ: George Woodward |
| Mʳ: William Morris | Mʳ Lancellᵗ: Woodward |
| Mʳ: Henry: Holdcroft | Veſtrymen |

This pʳſent Veſtry: proceedes to Lay the Pariſh Levy Bliſland Pariſh Dʳ 1727

To: Mʳ: Danˡ: Taylor: Miniſter: for a yeares Sall'y according to Law  16000
To: Caſke to ditto: inſtead of a Glebe: by agreemᵗ:ᵃ 1280¹¹: Tobb: & Conveniency to ditto accordⁱⁿᵍ to law  02080
To: Francis Cooke Clke of the pariſh for a yeares Sall'y 1500 & Caſke & Conveniency to ditto  01695
To: Henry: Holdcroft: Clerke of the Veſtry for a yeares Sallʳʸ: 500 & Cask & Convenᶜʸ: 65  00565
To: Richard: Warren Saxton of the Uppʳ Church for a yeares Sallʳ: 500 & Caſke to ditto  00540
To: Moſes Crafford for a yeares Sall'y 500 & Caske 40:  00540
To: Dorothy: Henry for Keepeing Lucey Gilles a year by yᵉ Veſtrys agreemᵗ  00600
To: Dorothy: Henry: for her Keeping her huſband part of the year: 310: & for his buriall 150  00460
To: Mʳ Richard: Hickman Clerke of James City County Court: for Copy of a Liſt Titheables  00020

To: Majo': John: Thornton Cl'k: of the Court for: 2
Copies Liſtes of Titheables      00040
To: Collon'': John: Scott: the Remainder of the
Tobbacco: by y^e: Veſtrys agreem^t: for: his
Keepeing & Endeavouring to Cure Elizabeth
Barkers Sore Legg      00450
To: Thomas: Henderſon for Makeing two horſe-
blockes for y^e Upp^r Church: & find all things      00250
To: M^r: Townes for his trouble Keepeing a Strange
Woman traveller Sick at his q'ter      00200
To: Mary: Shelbourn: for help towards her Main-
tainance Allowed      00200
To: M^r John: Doran for his trouble & Charge about
the Cure of Eman^ll Demetrius according to the
Church wardens agreem^t in Writeing dated the
15^th of auguſt 1727: M^r Doran Giveing bond to
perform the Said agreemt 2000 & Caſk      02160
To: M^r Rich^d: Richardſon Churchwarden for 3 Com-
munions 300'': & Mending Windows      00355
To: Sall^r: to Collecting 26155'': of Tobb at 5 p^r Cent:
is      01308

         Totall Sum Pariſh Deb^t is      27463

Utt Supra C^r
By: M^r Henry Holdcroft Received 1 Pariſh
Levy: of John Jennett      043½
By: M^r John Doran 1 ditto for Edward Henry:      043½
By: Surplus Tobbacco: in M^r Sclaters the Col-
lectors hands laſt year      183
By: 751 Titheables at 36'' of Tobbacco p^r pole is      27036
By: The Surplus Tobbacco to be left in y^e Col-
lecto^rs hands Untill Next yea^r:      0157

     27463

It is Ordered by this: Prefent Veftry that the Parifh Levy for this Prefent year be Thirty & Six poundes of Tobbaccoe p' pole and that M' John Sclater Sheriff & Collecto' of Blifland Parrifh Collect the Said Sum̃ of thirty & Six poundes of Tobbacco from Every Individuall Titheable perfon Within this Parifh and that he Pay the S$^d$ Tobbaccoes to the Severall Refpective parifh Creditors above mentioned To Whome it is Due in hh$^{ds}$ of Such Weightes & at Such times as the Other Church-Warden Shall Direct & appoint: And on Default of payment to Levy the Same by Diftrefs: And that the Clerk of the Veftry take Bond With Good & Sufficient Security of the S$^d$ Sclater for Payment of the Said Tobbaccoes: before he Deliver to him a Copy of the Parifh Charge and Copy of this Order of Veftry

[19]

Henry: Holdcroft: formerly of the Churchwardens of thif Parifh this day Offering to pay fifty Shillings Current money: being a fine Due from: Elizabeth Jemmyfon for her haveing a baftard Child: and Was Due to this Parifh: by Law: Whilest the S$^d$ Holdcroft Was Church warden: and alfoe five Shillings: forfeited for: Prophane Swearing: Wherefore the Veftry Ordered: that the Said Holdcroft Should: Lay out the S$^d$ fifty five Shillings: in Necefsary Cloathing: Linnen & Woollen. & Other Necefsaries for Emanuel Demetrius a poor Lame perfon Which this parifh have put under the Care of M' John Doran for Cure of a Very Sore Legg: And the S$^d$ Holdcroft: Agreed to Lay out & Difpofe of the S$^d$ Money accordingly

Francis: Shoemaker: being in a Very Aileing Weak Condition: petitioned this Veftry to be free from paying Parifh Levy: On Confideration: Whereof this Veftry have thought fitt to Difcharge him from paying parifh Levys Untill he Shall: be: Capeable to Worke & labour for Maintainance

This Veftry have Thought: it Necefsary: by the Confent of M' Daniel Taylor Minift' of this Parifh that the Prefen$^t$:

Regiſter Booke of this Pariſh be Delivered into the handes & Charge of Francis Cooke Clerke of this Pariſh: And that he is hereby Admitted Clerk of the Regiſter and that he truely & Carefully & Set Down & Enter on the S⁴ Pariſh Regiſter all birthes & Deaths that he hath an account Given him of: and Make Such Returnes as the Law Directs: & it is Ordered that he be Sworne accordingly

Teſt Henry: Holdcroft: Clk Veſtry Bliſl⁴

[20]
At a veſtery held for Bliſland Parriſh at M' Henry Holdcroft⁰ y⁰ 15 day of June 1728—preſent

M' Daniell Taylor Mineſter

| | |
|---|---|
| Capᵗ George Keeling | Capᵗ: Rich⁴. Rich⁴ſon Church Warden |
| Capᵗ Wᵐ: Kenney | M' Henry Holdcroft |
| M' Wᵐ: Morris | M' George Woodward |
| Capᵗ Nicho: Alderſey | M' Tho: Williams |
| M' Wᵐ: Cox | M' Lanclet Woodward |
| M' John Doran | Major John Thornton |

This veſtery proceeds to Apoint viewers & Tellers to Examine and Inquire of the Names & Numbers of perſons in this Parriſh Alowed by Law to plant and Tend Tobacco and as the Parriſh is Already Laid oute into Conveneant precincts M' John Allen & M' John Hankins is Apointed as Tellers of tobb in the place of Capᵗ: Rich⁴: Rich⁴ſon & M' Wᵐ: Morris And Ordered that they bee Sworn Accordingly

John Rowntree is Apointed a Teler of Tobb with Benj: Rich⁴ſon in the place of M' Daniell Allen and Ordered that he be Sworn Accordingly

John Breeding is Apointed a teller of Tobb: with John Burnett in the place of David Williams and Orderd that he bee Sworn Accordingly

John Luck being removed out of the parriſh John Hogg is Apointed a teler of Tobb: in his Stead with Wᵐ: Harman and orderd he be Sworn Accordingly

Mʳ Lancᵗ. Woodard & Mʳ Tho: Williams Apointed Tobb: telers for All that part of the Pariſh which Lyes in James Citty County and Orderd that they be Sworn Accordingly

Teſt Francis Cooke Clerk Veſtry Bliſland Parriſh

Mʳ Henry Holdcroft haveing reſigned his being Clerk of the Veſtry Francis Cooke is Apointed Clerk of the Said Veſtry & Sworn Accordly

Teſt Francis Cooke Clerk Veſtry

[21]

At a Veſtry held for Bliſland Pariſh at yᵉ Brick Church yᵉ 13ᵗʰ of November 1728

Pſent

Mʳ Danˡˡ Taylor Mineſter

Capᵗ William Kenney  
Mʳ Georg Woodward  
Mʳ Lanclet Woodward  
Mʳ Thomas Williams  
Capᵗ John Armiſtead  
Mʳ John Doran  
Mʳ William Cox  
Majʳ: John Thornton  

This Veſtry proceeds to Lay the Pariſh Levie

| | |
|---|---|
| To Mʳ Daniell Taylor Mineſter & for this years Sallery | 16000 |
| To Caſke to Ditto by the Veſtry' Agrement for the defeciency of a Glebe | 01280 |
| To Fraˢ: Cooke Clerk of yᵉ Pariſh for a years Salery 1500 & Caſk | 01620 |
| To Mʳ Henry Holdcrafts years Salery for Clerk of the Veſtry C C | 00540 |
| To Moſes Croford Saxton at yᵉ Lower Church a years Salery & Caſk | 00540 |
| To Richᵈ Waren Saxton at yᵉ Uper Church a years Salery & Caſk | 00540 |
| To Sarah Smallpage for this years Maintanance 500 & Caſk | 00540 |

| | |
|---|---:|
| To M<sup>r</sup> Rich<sup>d</sup>: Hickman Clrk James Citty for a Coppie Lift of Tithables | 00020 |
| To Dorothy Henry for keeping Lucy Gills a yeare | 00600 |
| To Maj<sup>r</sup>: John Thornton his acco<sup>t</sup>: for Clerks fees | 00120 |
| To Docter Philip Jones his Acco<sup>t</sup>. for Joane Corbat Alowd by y<sup>e</sup> Veftry | 00576 |
| To Rice Downes for keeping James Cornute Eighteen Moneths @ 400 p<sup>r</sup> yeare | 00600 |
| To Sarah Smallpage for Laft years Maintainance forgot which M<sup>r</sup> Sclater p<sup>d</sup> & to be kept in y<sup>e</sup> Collecters hands | 00540 |
| To M<sup>r</sup> John Sclater for two Comuions | 00200 |
| To M<sup>r</sup> John Sclater for John Lafoone laft year w<sup>ch</sup>: y<sup>e</sup> Veftry beleves M<sup>r</sup> Sclater paid | 00300 |
| To M<sup>r</sup> William Cox his Acc<sup>t</sup> againft Joane Corbit | 00344 |
| To John Lafoon for this years Maintainance 500 & Cafke | 00540 |
| To Tho: Henderfon for makeing a horfe block | 00125 |
| To Edward Linfey for keeping Even Jones Child Mary Jones from any Charge to this Parifh Till Shee be of Age 900 & Cafk | 00972 |
| To Cap<sup>t</sup>: Rich<sup>d</sup>fon for two Communions | 00200 |
| To M<sup>r</sup> John Doran for Cureing Benja: Breeding & his Trouble from the 26<sup>th</sup> day of December Laft till this day 2100 & Cafk | 02268 |
| To M<sup>r</sup> Tho: Ballard for Makein one horfe block & Repairing another | 00080 |
| To M<sup>r</sup> John Doran for his acco<sup>t</sup>: againft Joane Corbat | 00120 |
| To M<sup>r</sup> Marks for his acco<sup>t</sup>: againft Joane Corbit for her buriall | 00100 |
| To M<sup>r</sup> Daniell Taylor<sup>s</sup> Cafk on 16000 at 8 ⅌ C<sup>t</sup> | 01280 |
| To Cap<sup>t</sup>: Richardfon his acco<sup>t</sup>. | 00250 |
| To Sallery on 30295 at 10 ⅌ C<sup>t</sup> | 03029 |
| | 33324 |

Ut Supra
By Mr John Sclater for tobacco he recd. of Samll Curll
for Rent  700
By 780 Tithables at 42 ℔ pole  32760

Ballanc due to the pariſh to be paid by the Collecter Next year   136

[22]
Brought over

It is ordered by this preſent Vestrey that the Pariſh Levy be fourty two pounds of Tobacco pr pole and that Capt: william Kenney High Sherif of this County is ordered to Collect and Receive the Same from Every Individuall Tithable person Within this Parish & one Default of payment to make Diſtreſs for the Same According to Law, the said Kenney first Entring into Bond with Good and Sufficient Security to the other Church Warden for the uſe of the said parish for Paymt. of the said Tobacco to the Several respective Creditors for Whom the Same is Raiſed  In hhds. of such weights & at Such Times As the said Church Warden Shall Derrect and Appoint and it is ordered that the Clerk of the vestrey take Bond and Seccurity As Aforsaid Befor he deliver a Coppy of this order of Vestry and a Copy of the pariſh Charge to the sd Collector

Teſt Francis Cooke Clerk Veſtry

[23]
At a Veſtry held for Bliſland Pariſh at Mr Stephen Fornea' on Monday the 16th day of June 1729

Preſent

The Reverd Mr Danl Taylor Minſtr

Major John Thornton ⎫
Capt Wm: Keney      ⎬ Churchwardens

Capt George Keeling           Mr George Woodward
Capt. Richd Richardſon        Mr Lanclett Woodward
Mr Wm: Cox                    Mr John Doran
Mr Wm: Morris                 Veſtry Men

The Veſtry being this day Mett purſuant to Law do proceed to Appoint and Conſtitute the following Perſons Vewers & telers of tob⁰⁰ plants planted in the Said Pariſh this preſent yeare to wit

John Allen & John Hankins are Continued  
Benjⁿ. Richᵈſon & John Rountree are Continued  
John Breeding & John Burnett Continued  
John Hogg & Wm: Harman Continued  
Mʳ Lanclet woodward & Mʳ Tho: Williams Continued  
} In there Reſpective preçincts

It is Ordered that they have Notice thereof that they May be Sworn Accordingly

It is Ordered by this Preſent Veſtry that Jefery a Negro Man belonging to David Pryor be Leavy free

Teſt Frances Cook Clerk Veſtry

[24]

At a Veſtry for Bliſland Pariſh at Mʳ Stephen Forneaˢ yᵉ 21ˢᵗ Day of July 1729

preſent

yᵉ Reverend Mʳ Daniall Taylor Mineſter

Mʳ Wm Cox          Capᵗ Wm: Kenney Churchwarden  
Mʳ John Doran      Mʳ Wm: Morris      } Veſtry Men  
Mʳ George Woodward Mʳ Tho: Williams

Mʳ John Hankins who was formerly Apointed one of the Counters of tobacco being diſabled from performing his duty this preſent Veſtry hath Mʳ Daniell Allen Junʳ to serve in his roome & that he be Sworn Accordingly

it is Ordered by this preſent Veſtry that Ann Evans a pore Widdow of this Pariſh have two hundred pounds of tobacco & Caſque paide to her or her Order towards yᵉ Suport of three Small Children

Teſt Frances Cook Clerk Veſtry

[25]
At a Veſtry held for Bliſland Parriſh at the Lower Church yᵉ 27 October 1729

Preſent

| | |
|---|---|
| Major John Thornton | Capᵗ William Kenney Church wardens |
| Mʳ William Cox | Capᵗ Richᵈ. Richᵈſon |
| Capᵗ Nicholas Alderſey | Mʳ John Sclater |
| Mʳ Georg Woodward | Mʳ Lancelett Woodward |
| Mʳ John Doran | Mʳ William Morris |
| Capᵗ George Keeling | |

This Veſtry proceeds to Lay the Parriſh Leavie

| | | |
|---|---:|---:|
| To the revernᵈ Mʳ Daniel Taylor Mineſter for ten Moneths Sallery | 13334 | |
| To Cask to Dᵒ: & Deficiency of pᵉ Gleeb | 2134 | 15468 |
| To Francis Cook Clark of the parrish & Vestry his Sallery | | 02160 |
| To moses Crarford Saxton at the Lower Church Dᵒ: | | 00540 |
| To Richᵈ: Warren Saxton at the upper Church Dᵒ: | | 00540 |
| To Sarah Smallpage for this years maintenance | | 00540 |
| To mʳ: John Doran for curing Thomas Shelbourn | | 01728 |
| To Doll Henry for Keeping Lucey Gill a year | | 00600 |
| To Majʳ. Thornton for a Copy of the Liſt of Tythables | | 00040 |
| To Richᵈ: Warren for three Comunions | | 00300 |
| To Rice Downs for Keeping of James Cornute a year | | 00400 |
| To Samuel Curl for work Done on yᵉ: Gleeb 400ˡ Tobᵒ | | |
| To Capᵗ: William Kenneys accᵗ: | | 00444 |
| To Mary Shelbourn for Keeping her Son in distreſs | | 00648 |
| To Robert Pennington for Returns | | 00500 |
| To mʳ: John Sclater for two Returns & Collecting 700ˡ Tobᵒ | | 00174 |
| To 1 Levie of Christopʳ: Charltons & Collecting of it | | 00046 |
| To 30ˡ Tobᶜᵒ pʳ: Tyth on 798 Tythables is | | 23940 |
| To Caſk to Dᵒ | | 01916 |
| To the Collectʳ for Receiving & making Convenent | | 04999 |

By 798 Tyths at 69ˡ Tob°: pʳ: Tythable is    55062
By Samuel Curls years Rent for yᵉ Gleep 400 pound of Tob°
Ball due to yᵉ: parish to be allowed by the Collector next year    79

It is ordered by this preſent Veſtry that yᵉ parish Leavie be 69 pound of Tob° pʳ: pole and that Capᵗ. William Kenney High Sherif of this *Said County is ordered to Collect and receive the same from Every individuall Tythable person within this parish and on default of paymen[t] To make Distreſs for the Same according to Law the Said Kenney firſt Entering into Bond with Good Sufficient Security to the other Churchwarden for the uſe of the Said parish Creditors for home yᵉ Same is raised in hh$^{d[s]}$ of Such weights & at Such time as the sᵈ: Churchwarden Shall direct and appoint and it is ordered that the Clark of the Vestry take bond & Security as aforesaid before he Deliver a Copy of this order of Vestry and a Copy of the parish charge to the Collector

Copy   Teſt Francis Cook Clark Veſtry

[26]
Turn Over

It is Ordered by this preſent Veſtry That James Curnute be put Benj Tyre at 400ˡ of Tobb pʳ yeare the Said Tyre promiſing to Learn yᵉ Sᵈ Curnut to Knit or weave

it is Alſo Ordered yᵗ Mary Whitehead° Neagro Man Jack be Leavy free

This Veſtry do agree with yᵉ Reverᵈ. Mʳ Moſom & yᵉ Revᵈ. Mʳ Leneve to preach yᵉ one at yᵉ Uper Church & yᵉ Other at yᵉ Lower Church Every Alternate Saterday & to alow to Each of them three hundred and Twenty pounds of Tobb: with Caſque & Conveneancy for Evry Sermon

Cop   Teſt Frances Cook Clerk Veſtry

---

*Scratched through in original, but still legible.—C. G. C.

Gentlemen

The Reverend Mʳ Thacker is so well known in This Country that it will be sufficient for me to signifie to you as I hereby do that I am well Satiſfied he is a perſon of good Life and Converſation and fully Quallified for Undertaking the Cure of youre Parriſh

                      I am Gentlemen Your
                      Affectionate Friend
Wmsburgh         and humble Service
  Feb: 6: 1729/30         William Gooch

                     Williamsburgh Feb: 6: 1729-30

Gentlemen

The Honourable the Governour having recommended the Reverend Bearer Mʳ Chichley Thacker to your Parriſh I thought it my duty to acquaint you that I have Seen his Orders and Licence from my Lord Biſhop of London and that he has so good a Character of his good behaviour in the University that I Can not in the Least doubt but that he will be very acceptable to you and so much the more as being a Virginian and having Laid the first foundation of Learning at the College in this Country I hope ye will be happy in Each other and am

                Gentlemen Yoʳ Moſt
                Humble Servant
                    James Blair

Teſt Frances Cook Clerk Veſtry

[27]

It is ordered by this preſent Veſtry that the Pariſh Levy for this preſent yeare be Seventy Nine pounds & half of tobacco pʳ pole and that Major Richard Richardſon Sheriff and Collector of Bliſland pariſh Collect the Said Sum of seventy Nine pounds and half of tobacco from Every Indeviduall Tithable perſon within this pariſh and that he pay the Sᵈ tobaccoes to yᵉ Severall Reſpective pariſh Creditors before Mentioned to whome it is due in hh$^{ds}$ of Such weight and at such times as the Churchwardens shall derect and apoint and on default of payment to Levy the Same by diſtreſs and that the Clerk of the veſtry take bond with good and Suficent Security of the S$^{d}$ Richardſon for payment of the S$^{d}$ tobaccoes before he deliver to him a Copy of the pariſh Charge and Copy of this Order of Veſtry

Anthony Allom and John Browing boath petitioned this Veſtry to be free from paying pariſh Levy being both very aged and not able to work for theire Living as formerly which is Granted

Cap$^{t}$ George Keeling deſiring to be Excuſed from being a veſtry man is diſchard from his Office and William Mackain Gen$^{t}$. is Choſen in his Steade and Sworn accordingly by M$^{r}$ John Sclater a Majeſtrate for this County

Major John Thornton & Cap$^{t}$ William Kenney Late Churchwardens are diſcharg$^{d}$ from theire ofice & Coll William Baſsett & M$^{r}$ William Morris are apointed Churchwardens in theire Steade & Sworn Accordingly by M$^{r}$ John Sclater a Majeſtrate for this County

This preſent Veſtry has agreed to alow Benj$^{a}$ Tyree for Keeping James Curnute after y$^{e}$ rate of 400$^{lt}$ of tobacco p$^{r}$ yeare dureing y$^{e}$ time y$^{e}$ S$^{d}$ James Shall be there

      Teſt Frances Cook Clerk Veſtry

[28]

At a Veſtry held for Bliſland Pariſh at the Brick Church y$^{e}$ 12 Auguſt 1730

      Preſent
   the Reverend M$^{r}$ Thacker Mineſter

| | |
|---|---|
| Major Rich$^{d}$: Richardſon | Cap$^{t}$ William Kenney Chu Warden |
| Cap$^{t}$ William Morris | M$^{r}$ Georg Woodward |
| M$^{r}$ William Cox | M$^{r}$ Lanclett Woodward |
| M$^{r}$ John Sclater | M$^{r}$ John Doran |
| Coll William Baſsett | Veſtry Men |

it is Ordered by this preſent Veſtry that a Veſtry Man be Choſen in the roome of Capᵗ Nicholas Alderſey Coll William Baſsett being preſent is Choſen a veſtry man for this pariſh and is Sworn Accordingly by Capᵗ William Morris a Majeſtrate for this County

it is Ordered Alſo by this preſent veſtry that Capᵗ William Kenney pay to Mʳˢ Armiſtead three and twenty Shillings for for boarding the Workman While repairing the Gleibe houſe

The Veſtry this day Agrees With Coll William Baſsett to build and Erect two Brick Chimneys to the Gleibe houſe and Underpin the Said houſe with Brick & to build a Cloſsett and to Cover yᵉ Kitchen & to paile in yᵉ Garden to the Sattiſfaction of the Mineſter in Conſideration the Veſtry to forty pounds Curant Money at the Laying the Next Levie

[29]

At a Veſtry held for Bliſland Pariſh at the Lower Church yᵉ 13 March 1730

Preſent yᵉ Reverend Mʳ Chichley Thacker Mineſter

| Major Richard Richardſon | Coll William Baſsett | Church |
| Capᵗ William Kenney | Capᵗ William Morris | wardens |
| Mʳ William Cox | Mʳ Lanclett Woodward | |
| Mʳ William Mackaine | Mʳ Tha. Williams | |
| Mʳ George Woodward | Veſtrymen | |

This Veſtry proceeds to Chuſe a Veſtryman in yᵉ Roome of Major John Thornton Deceaſt it is Ordered yᵗ Mʳ Georg Clough be Choſen a veſtryman for this Pariſh and is Sworn Accordingly by Mʳ Mʳ William Mackaine a Majestrate for this County

Coll Baſsettˢ Accᵗ which is as followeth Alowed by this Veſtry

| January yᵉ 3ᵈ 1730 | To pᵈ for Makeing a Caſement | £0= 3=0 |
| Bliſland Pariſh Dʳ | To Lead and Glaſs | 0= 8=0 |

|  |  |
|---|---|
| To Caſh pᵈ Cliff for altering Caſements | 0= 6=0 |
| To 2 pʳ of Large hooks and hinges for the Gleibe Gates | 0=13=5 |
|  | 1=10=5 |

Capᵗ Kenney his Accᵗ. alowed by this Veſtry which is as followeth

Bliſland Pariſh Dʳ March yᵉ 13: 1730

| | |
|---|---|
| To 6 yᵈˢ of Purple Cloath at 18ˢ pʳ yᵈ | £ 5= 8=0 |
| To 19¾ yᵈˢ purple Silk Lace at 8ᵈ | 13=2 |
| To 9 Ounces ⅛ Deep Silk fring at 3ˢ pʳ ounc | 1= 7=4½ |
| To 2 purple Silk Toſsels at 3ˢ | 6 |
| To 2 Skins Leather & 4 pᵈˢ feathers | 8=3 |
| To Making them | 10 |
| To 2 Common prayer Bookˢ | 1=10 |
| To 2 Surplices yᵗ 22 Ells of Gulick holᵈ 6/10 | 7=10=4 |
| To making them | 1 |
| To a Box | 3 |
| To prinage & all Charges till on board | 7 |
| To Com̄ on £ 19=3=1½ at 2½ p Cᵗ | 9=7½ |
| To 75 ℔ Cᵗ on £ 19=12=9 is | 14=14=6¾ |
| Caſh due ℔ʳ yᵉ pariſh | £ 4=12=5 |
|  | 38=19=8¾ |

[30]
Brought Over

Francis Shoemaker is Choſen Sexton y this Veſtry to Serve at yᵉ Lower Church after yᵉ rate of five hundred pounds of tobb & Caſque ℔ʳ yeare

it is Ordered by this preſent Veſtry that Coll William Baſett & Capᵗ William Morris do Sell yᵉ tobb Raiſed to pay the pariſh Debts as they Shall think

at the Motion of the Mineſter the Veſtry Conſents to build a quarter on yͤ Gleibe for his Neagroes 16 & 12 with a Shed on one Side Coll Baſsett has undertaken to build it Major Richardſon & Capᵗ Morris is apointed to vallue yͤ Sᵈ houſe

it is Ordered by this preſent Veſtry that William Hart be bound to John Bates to Lern yͤ trade of a Carpenter

This Day Benjamin Tyree Surendered James Curnute up to to the Pariſh & it is Ordered that yͤ Sᵈ Curnute be bound out by the pariſh which is accordingly done to Richᵈ Maples

       C. Thacker Mineſter
       William Baſsett
       William Morris

     Teſt Francis Cook Clerk Veſtry

[31]

This Indenture Made this 13ᵗʰ day of March Annoqᵘ Domini one Thouſand Seven hundred and thirty By and between Coˡˡ William Baſsett and Capᵗ William Morris Churchwardens of the Pariſh of Bliſland for the time being of the one part and Richard Maples of the Said Pariſh Taylor of the Other part Witneſseth that the Said Churchwardens for Several good Cauſes and Conſiderations hereafter Mentioned and Expreſsed doth hereby binde and put James Kernute a Servant and an aprentice Unto the Said Richard Maples to Serve him well and truly from the day and date hereof untill he Shall Come to the age of twenty one Years from the day of his Birth and that in all Lawfull Service and Imployment he Shall Excerciſe and Imploy himſelf about dureing the afore Said term and in Conſideration of the Said Service the Said Richard Maples doth hereby Covenant promiſe grant and agree to and with the Said Churchwardens to doe his true and utmoſt Endeavor to Learn and Teach his Said aprentic[e] the art and Miſtry of a Taylor and that in all things and that in all things relateing to the Said trade and to find and Maintaine his Said aprentice with all Neſeſar Cloathin Meate drink waſhing and Lodging and that dureing the whole time and Term aforeſaid and Shall allwaiſe

Endeavor to Inſtill piety and vertue into him and at the End and Expiration of his Said Apreniceſhip Shill give and alow to his Said aprentice one good Sute of aparell in Witneſs wereof all the above Named partyes have hereunto Set theire hands and Seales the day and yeare firſt above written

       William Baſsett ⎱ Churchward<sup>s</sup>
       William Morris ⎰

Signed Sealed
and in preſents of us
  Francis Cook
  Tho: Williams

     Copia Teſt Francis Cook Clerk Veſtry

[32]

At a Veſtry held for Bliſland Pariſh at y<sup>e</sup> Brick Church y<sup>e</sup> 23<sup>d</sup> of Auguſt 1731
      preſent
  the Reverend Chicheley Thacker Mineſter
Coll William Baſsett & Cap<sup>t</sup> William Morris Churchwardens
Major Rich<sup>d</sup>: Richardſon M<sup>r</sup> Georg Woodward
M<sup>r</sup> John Sclater    M<sup>r</sup> Lanclett Woodward ⎫ Veſtrymen
M<sup>r</sup> William Mackain  M<sup>r</sup> Georg Clough   ⎬
   M<sup>r</sup> John Doran          ⎭

This Veſtry agrees with Coll: William Baſsett to build a dary or Milkhouſe for the Miniſter to his Likeing & to bring his acc<sup>t</sup> to the Laying of the Next pariſh Levie to be paid According to the Vallue of the Work

William Son of Sarah Sawyer is diſcharged from paying Levie till the veſtry Shall think him Capable to pay it

This veſtry has alowed Mary Crook three hundred pounds of Tobb towards building her a dwelling houſe

       Chichley Thacker Miniſter
       William Baſsett ⎱ Churchwarden
       William Morris ⎰
    Teſt Fran Cook Clerk veſtry

[33]
At a Veſtry held for Bliſland Pariſh at yᵉ Lower Church yᵉ 9ᵗʰ day of Novebʳ 1731

Preſen yᵉ Reverent Mʳ Thacker Miniſter

Mʳ John Sclater ⎫
Maj Richᵈſon ⎪
Capᵗ William Kenney ⎬
Mʳ William Mackain ⎪
Mʳ Georg Woodward ⎭

Coll William Baſsett ⎫ Churchwardens
Capᵗ William Morris ⎭

Mʳ Georg Clough ⎫
Mʳ John Doran ⎬ Veſtry men
Mʳ Lanclett Woodward ⎭

This Veſtry proceeds to Lay yᵉ Pariſh Levie

| | |
|---|---:|
| To yᵉ Revᵈ. Mʳ Thacker Miniſter for one years Sallery | 16000 |
| To Caſque at 4 ℔ Cᵗ to Dᵒ. | 640 |
| To Francis Cook his years Sallery & Caſk alowd at 4 ℔ Cᵗ. | 2080 |
| To Francis Shoemaker Sexton Since the 13ᵗʰ of March Laſt | 334 |
| To Richard Warren Sexton at yᵉ upper Church | 520 |
| To Sarah Smallpage her Maintaineanc this year | 520 |
| To Mʳ Joh Dandridge for 2 Copies Liſts of Tithables | 40 |
| To Mʳ Mathew Kemp Clerk James Citty for one Copie Dᵒ. | 20 |
| To Jane Crafford a Ballance due to her houſband | 186 |
| To Capᵗ Morris Churchwarden for four Communions | 400 |
| To Dᵒ. his Accᵗ for Sundrys | 238 |
| To Mary Crook toward building her houſe | 300 |
| To Major Richardſon for Sallevateing Ann Evans & waranting yᵉ Cure till Novbʳ | 1040 |
| To Coll: William Baſsett his Accᵗ £11=13=8½ in Tobb at 11 S ℔ Cᵗ | 2126 |
| To John Richardſon his Accᵗ for delinquents | 732 |
| To Mʳ John Doran for Medicens for Eliz: Barker paſt & till Next veſtry | 520 |

| | |
|---|---:|
| To Benjⁿ. Tyree for Keeping James Curnute two Moneths | 67 |
| To Dorothy Henry for Keeping Lucy Gill | 832 |
| | 26595 |

### Ut Supra Cʳ

| | |
|---|---:|
| By Tobᵒ. due from the Collector Laſt yeare | 58 |
| By Dᵒ. Short paid yᵉ pariſh Tobᵒ £ | 1064 |
| By Samˡˡ Curll | 400 |
| | 1522 |
| The Pariſh Debt is | 25073 |
| | 26595 |
| To 14 ℔ Cᵗ on 25073 pounds of Tobᵒ | 3510 |
| To 15 ℔ polle for Tobᵒ. towards building a Church on 761 Tithes is | 11415 |
| To 18 ℔ Cᵗ on 11415 pounds of Tobacco | 2055 |
| | 42053 |

### Ut Supra Cʳ

| | |
|---|---:|
| By 761 Tithables at 55 ℔ polle is | 41856 |
| By Tobacco to be paid by the Collector & to be Levied for him Next year | 198 |
| | 42053 |

[34]

Joſeph Linsey upon his petetion to This Veſtry is diſcharged from paying his Pariſh Levie

It is Ordered by this preſent Veſtry that the Tobacco Levied Towards Building a New Church remaine in the Collectors hands till the Next Veſtry

It is Ordered by this preſent Veſtry that the Pariſh Levie for this preſent yeare be fifty five pounds of Tobacco ℔ pole and that Major Richard Richardſon Sherif and Collector of this Pariſh Collect the Said Summ of fifty five pounds of Tobaccoes from Every Indevdual Tithable perſon in this Pariſh and that he pay the ſaid Tobaccoes to the Severall Reſpective Pariſh Creditors by Inſpectors Notes before the tenth day of Aprill Next and that the Clerk of the veſtry tak Bond with good and Sufficient Security of the Said Richardſon for the payment of the Said Tobaccoes before he deliver him a Copie of this Order of Veſtry and of the Pariſh Charge

      Chicheley Thacker Miniſter
      William Baſsett
      William Morris

     Teſt Francis Cook Clerk veſtry

 at a Veſtry held for Bliſland Pariſh at yᵉ Brick Church yᵉ 26ᵗʰ: day of June 1732

    ℘reſent yᵉ Revnᵈ Mʳ Thacker Mineſter
    Coll. William Baſsett Churchwarden

| Major Richᵈ Richardſon | Mʳ Georg Woodward |
| Capᵗ William Kenney | Mʳ John Doran |
| Mʳ William Cox | Mʳ Lanclett Woodward |

 it is Ordered by this preſent veſtry that Coll. William Baſsett do Sell what Tobacco yᵉ Collector Can gett in of yᵉ Pariſh Tobacco by Next Newkent Court and that what money the Said Tobacco Sels for remaine in his hands till further Orders from the Veſtry

 Isaac Godin upon his petition to this Veſtry has his Neagro Man Harry diſcharged from paying Pariſh Levy

 John Williams at his requeſt is diſcharged from paying Pariſh Levy

     Teſt Francis Cook Clerk Veſtry

[35]
Att a veſtry held for Bliſland Pariſh at yᵉ Brick Church yᵉ 9ᵗʰ of October 1732

   Preſent the Revnᵈ. Mʳ Thacker Mineſter
   Coll William Baſsett ⎫
   Capᵗ William Morris ⎭ Churchwarden⁶

| Mʳ William Cox ⎫ | Mʳ Lanclett Woodward ⎫ |
| Mʳ John Doran ⎬ | Mʳ Tho: Williams ⎬ |
| Mʳ Georg Woodward ⎭ | Mʳ Georg Clough ⎭ |
|   Veſtry Men |   Veſtry Men |

This Veſtry Proceeds to Lay yᵉ Pariſh Levie

| | |
|---|---:|
| To the Revnd Mʳ Thacker Mineſter for a yeas Sallery | 16000 |
| To Caſque ⅌ʳ Dᵒ: at 4 ⅌ʳ Cᵗ | 640 |
| To Frañ. Cook Clerk for his Sallery this yeare with Caſque Included | 2080 |
| To Frañ Shoomaker Sexton for this years Sallery | 520 |
| To Richᵈ Warren Sexton for this years Sallery | 520 |
| To Sarah Smallpage for her years Maintainance | 520 |
| To Mʳ Matthew Kemp for a Copie of yᵉ Liſt of tiths | 20 |
| To Mʳ John Dandridge for two Copies of the Liſts of Tiths | 40 |
| To Capᵗ William Morris for four Communions | 400 |
| To Tho: Lyon for Keeping Mary Crook & her Child three Moneths | 400 |
| To Mʳ Tho: Williams for Keeping Jane Croford two Moneths | 100 |
| To Frañ: Cook for the Uſe of Evan Jones | 500 |
| To John Miller | 250 |
| To Rebeckah Merideth Toward building her a houſe | 300 |
| To Dorothy Henry for keeping Lucy Gills | 800 |
| To John Richardſon his Accompᵗ for delinquents | 1566 |

             24656

VESTRY BOOK OF BLISLAND PARISH

To Coll. William Baſsett £17=16=4 To Mʳ Thacker £1=6=0 for building a Smoak houſe on the Gliebe £1=15=0
Crᵈ by Samuell Curll                                      400

|  |  |
|---|---|
|  | 24256 |
| To 14 ℔ Cᵗ on 24256ˢ of Tob° | 3396¾ |
| To 10 pounds of Tobb ℔ pole Towards building a Church | 7700 |
| To 18 ℔ Cᵗ on 7700 | 1386 |
| Tobacco due from the Collector Next yeare | 222 |

Cʳ

by 770 Tiths at 48 ℔ pole                               36960

[36]        Brought Over

Mʳ William Cox Refuſing to Serve any Longer as a Veſtry Man in this Pariſh Mʳ Joſeph Allen is Choſen in his place and Sworn Accordingly by Mʳ John Sclater a Majeſtrate for this County

Mʳ Tho: Williams Agreed with This Veſtry to keepe Jane Croford for ffifty pounds of Tobb & Caſque ℔ʳ Moneth

It is Ordred by this preſent veſtry that Tho Garrot upon his ℔etetion be Aquited from paying Pariſh Levie

Mʳ William Mackain & Mʳ Georg Clough are Choſen Church wardens for this Pariſh in yᵉ roome of Coll: William Baſsett and Capᵗ: William Morris & were Accordingly Sworn by Mʳ John Sclater one of his Majeſtys Juſtices

It is Ordered by this preſent Veſtry that the pariſh Levie for this preſent yeare be forty Eight pounds of Tobbacco ℔ʳ pole and that Mʳ John Thornton Sub Sherif and Collector of this pariſh do Collect the Said Summ of forty Eight pounds of Tobacco from Every Indeviduall Tithable perſon within this pariſh Except the pole Abaitment and that hee pay the Said Tobbaccoes to the Severall reſpective pariſh Creditors to whome it is due by Inſpectors Notes before the Laſt day of Aprill Next and that the Clerk of the veſtry take Bond with good and Sufficient Security of the Said Collector for the payment of the Said Tobbaccoes before he deliver him a Copie of this Order of Veſtry and the pariſh Charge

C Thacker Miniſter<br>
W<sup>m</sup> Baſsett<br>
W<sup>m</sup> Morris

Teſt Frañ Cook Clerk Veſtry

[37]

At a Veſtry held for Bliſland Pariſh at y<sup>e</sup> Brick Church y<sup>e</sup> 13<sup>th</sup> day of June 1733

preſent y<sup>e</sup> Rev<sup>d</sup> Chichley Thacker Miniſter

Coll William Baſsett    M<sup>r</sup> William Mackaine ⎱ Church
Major Rich<sup>d</sup> Richardſon   M<sup>r</sup> Georg Clough     ⎰ warde[ns]
Cap<sup>t</sup> William Kenney    M<sup>r</sup> John Sclater
M<sup>r</sup> John Doran

This Veſtry Apoints Coll William Baſsett to Sell the tobb which was raiſed towards Building of a Church at publick Auction

Phillip Charles upon his Wifes petition to this Veſtry is Aquited from paying Pariſh Levie while he remaines in this Condition

Cornelious Jones on his pett<sup>n</sup> to this Veſtry has his Son Stephen Aquited from payin pariſh Levie this yeare

C Thacker Miniſter<br>
William Mackaine ⎱<br>
Georg Clough      ⎰ Church w

Teſt Frañ Cook Clerk of y<sup>e</sup> veſtry

[38]

At a Veſtry held for Bliſland Pariſh at the Lower Church y<sup>e</sup> 31 day of October 1733

## 52 VESTRY BOOK OF BLISLAND PARISH

   Prefent the Ren<sup>d</sup> M<sup>r</sup> Thacker Minefter
Cap<sup>t</sup> William Kenney    M<sup>r</sup> William Mackain ⎱ Church
M<sup>r</sup> Jofeph Allen      M<sup>r</sup> Georg Clough  ⎰ Wardens
Major Rich<sup>d</sup> Richardfon   M<sup>r</sup> John Sclater
Cap<sup>t</sup> William Morris    M<sup>r</sup> John Doran
M<sup>r</sup> Georg Woodward

 This Veftry proceeds to Lay the Parifh Levie

| | |
|---|---:|
| To the Ren<sup>d</sup> M<sup>r</sup> Thacker Minefter for a years Sallery | 16000 |
| To Cafque to D<sup>o</sup> at 4 ⅌ C<sup>t</sup> | 640 |
| To Frañ Cook Clerk for a years Sallery Cafque Included | 2080 |
| To Frañ Shoomaker Sexton for a years Sallery | 520 |
| To Rich<sup>d</sup> Warren Sexton for a years Sallery | 520 |
| To M<sup>r</sup> Matthew Kemp for a Copie of the Lift of tithes | 20 |
| To M<sup>r</sup> John Dandridge for 2 Copies of the Lift of tithes | 40 |
| To Cap<sup>t</sup> William Morrif for 3 Communions | 300 |
| To Dorothy Henry for Keeping Lucy Gills | 832 |
| To M<sup>r</sup> Tho Williams for keeping Jane Croford | 550 |
| To Cafque to D<sup>o</sup> | 22 |
| To John Miller toward his years Maintainanc | 300 |
| To Rich<sup>d</sup> Jones for keeping Mary Crook 4 Moneths | 400 |
| To M<sup>r</sup> Mackain for one Communion | 100 |
| To Ann Evans | 200 |
| To Jones Parifh for keeping Jane Croford | 34 |
| To Peter Ball for 2 horfe blocks & 6 benches finding Matearals | 150 |
| To Jane Croford for her Maintainance | 520 |
| | 23228 |
| To 14 p<sup>r</sup> C<sup>t</sup> on 23228 | 3251 |
| | 26479 |
| C<sup>r</sup> by Samuell Curl   400 | |
| C<sup>r</sup> in M<sup>r</sup> Thorntons hands   222 | 622 |
| | 25857 |

HICKORY NECK CHURCH, BLISLAND PARISH, JAMES CITY COUNTY, VIRGINIA

(*Courtesy of Mr. Joseph W. Geddes, A.I.A., P.A.S.I., Williamsburg, Virginia*)

The north, or rear, portion of this church is a part of the addition made in 1774-1776 on the north side of the Lower Church of Blisland Parish, which was erected in 1734-1738. Sometime during or subsequent to the Revolution, the whole church with the exception of most of the north wing was torn down, and the south, or front, portion of the present church building was erected, the bricks used being evidently some of those that had been in the walls of the original church.

| | |
|---|---:|
| Tobacco Levied toward a Church | 24000 |
| To 18 pʳ Cᵗ on 24000 pounds of Tobacco | 4320 |
| | 54177 |
| *Cʳ by 769 tithes at 71 pʳ pole | |
| Tobacco in yᵉ Colectors hands to be paid Next yeare | 422 |
| | 54599 |
| Mʳ William Mackain & Mʳ Georg Clough Continued Churchwardens | |
| by 769 tiths at 71 ℔ | 54599 |

[39]

It is Ordered by this preſent Veſtry that Mʳ Joſeph Allen and Mʳ John Doran Settle with Coll Baſsett the Pariſh Accᵗ

it is Ordered by this preſent Veſtry that a Church be built of Brick in the Lower part of this pariſh Sixty foot Long & 26 foot wide within the Walles the farther Dementions to be as the Veſtry Shall agree with the workmen

it is Ordered by this preſent veſtry that the Churchwardens Sell the goods belonging to Mary Crook

it is Ordered that the Churchwardens demand the Church plate which belonged to the Uper Church of the Late pariſh of Wilmington Now in the hands of Mʳ William Brown Genᵗ

it is Ordered by this preſent Veſtry that the pariſh Levie for this preſent yeare be Seventy one pounds of tobb pʳ pole and that Capᵗ William Morris high Sherif and Collector of this pariſh do Collect the Said Summ of Seventy one pounds of tobacco from Every Indevidual tithable perſon on this pariſh Except the pole abatemt and that he pay the Said Tobaccoes to the Severall reſpective pariſh Creditors to whome it is due by Inſpectors Notes before the Laſt day of Aprill Next and that the Clerk of the veſtry take bond with good Suficient Security of the Said Collector for the payment of the Said

---

*This line scratched through in original, but still legible.—C. G. C.

Tobb before he deliver him a Copie of this Order of Veſtry and the pariſh Charg

       Chichley Thacker Minſʳ
       William Mackaine
       Georg Clough

     Teſt Frañ Cook Clerk Veſtry

Memorandum Tobᵒ. due to the pariſh

| | |
|---|---:|
| To Tobacco In the Colectors han | 422 |
| To Tobacco Levied for Jane Craford not due Untill next Year | 520 |
| To 1 pariſh Levie paid by Mʳ Ballard not Levied | 71 |
| | 1013 |

     *Wᵐ Mackain C:W

[40]

At a Veſtry held for Bliſland Pariſh at the Lower Church the 11 day of December 1733

      Preſent

The Reverend Chichley Thacker Miniſter ⎫
Coll William Baſsett  Mʳ William Mackain ⎬ Church warden
Major Richᵈ. Richardſon  Mʳ Georg Clough
Capᵗ William Kenney  Capᵗ William Morris
Mʳ John Sclater  Mʳ John Doran
Mʳ Joſeph Allen  Mʳ Lanclett Woodward

 it is Ordered by this preſent Veſtry that a deviding line be run between this pariſh and Sᵗ peters pariſh Croſs the Late pariſh of Wilmington According to Law

 it is Ordered by this Preſent Veſtry that a Church be built of Brick for the Lower part of this Pariſh of Bliſland on Mʳˢ Holdcrofts Land on the Maine Roade below yᵉ Late plantation of Mʳˢ Weldey* on part of the Land where Mʳˢ Holdcroft Now

---
*This name was difficult to decipher.—C. G. C.

Lives being an Acre of Land given by Mʳˢ Holdcroft for that Uſe

it is Ordered by this preſent Veſtry that a Vſtry be held at Mʳ Stephen Forneaˢ yᵉ first day of febuary in Order to Lett the building of the Church to Such workmen as the Veſtry Shall agree with the Church to be Sixty foot Long and twenty six foot wide within the walls & fifteen foot pitch from the flooring of the pews to the Lower part of the plate and two foot from yᵉ top of the Earth to the top of the flower with a gallery & the Ile to be Laid with white Square Stone

> Chichley Thacker Minister
> William Mackain } Church war
> Georg Clough
>
> Teſt Fran Cook Clerk Veſtry

[41]

At a Veſtry held for Bliſland Pariſh at the houſe of Mʳ Stephen Furnea the first day of Febuary 1733⁴

Preſent

The Reverend Mʳ Thacker Miniſter

| | |
|---|---|
| Coll William Baſsett | Mʳ William Mackain } Church wardens |
| Mʳ Joſeph Allen | Mʳ Georg Clough |
| Major Richard Richardſon | Mʳ John Doran |
| Capᵗ William Kenney | Capᵗ William Morris |
| Mʳ John Sclater | Mʳ Lanclett Woodward |

This Veſtry this day agreed with Mʳ John Moore and Mʳ Lewis Deloney to build a Church in Bliſland Pariſh as followeth Sixty foot Long and Twenty six foot wide within the walls fifteen foot from the Flooring of the pews up to the plate yᵉ flooring of the pewes one foot from yᵉ hieſt part of the ground a Compas Seiling yᵉ Isle to be Laid with white Briſtol Stones the walls to be three bricks thick up to yᵉ water table & two bricks & half thick from yᵉ water table upwards a galery twelve foot Long Six windoors in yᵉ body of the Church & two in yͤ Eaſt End in proportion to the pitch of the walls yͤ Windoors to be Arched with Saſhes to be glaiſed with Saſh glaſs & to be hung with Leads & pulleys wainſcoate Shutters wainſcoate pews yͤ front of yͤ pews pulpit & deſk to be quarter Round & raiſed panells Mondillion Eave with plaine gable Endnds & Single Corniſh the Roofe to Covered with plank and Shingled on that yͤ Doores & dore Caſes & windoore frames to be twiſe primed first with Spaniſh brown then with white Lead & a Compaſs Alter with railes & baneſters & a table & Font as Uſeall to be a Compleat Finiſhed Church workman Like turn Key and goe & this Veſtry agrees to pay the Said Moore & Deloney as follows two hundred & fifty pounds yͤ 10$^{th}$ day of June Next & Eighty fivę pounds yͤ 10$^{th}$ day of June 1735 and the Laſt payment Eighty five pounds yͤ 10$^{th}$ of June 1736

This Veſtry has apointed Capᵗ Henry Powers togather with Mʳ William Mackain & Mʳ George Clough to take bond of John Moore & Lewis Delony for theire faithfull performance of the above Said work and Likewiſe as Superviſors to Overlook the Said Moore & Delony in theire proceedings

      Chichley Thacker Miniſter
      William Mackain
      George Clough

    Teſt Francis Cooke Clerk Veſtry

[42]

At a veſtry held for Bliſland Pariſh at yͤ Uper Church 17$^{th}$ day of October 1734

    ℘'eſent yͤ Renᵈ Mʳ Thacker Miniſter

| | |
|---|---|
| Coll William Baſsett | Mʳ William Mackain ⎱ Church- |
| Capᵗ William Kenney | Mʳ Georg Clough  ⎰ wardens |
| Capᵗ William Morris | Mʳ Joſeph Allen |
| Mʳ John Doran | Mʳ Lanclett Woodward |
| Mʳ William Hockaday | Major Richᵈ Richardſon |

This Veſtry proceeds to Lay yᵉ Pariſh Levie

| | |
|---|---:|
| To the Revirend Mʳ Thacker for a years Sallery | 16000 |
| To Caſk to Dᵒ at 4 ℔ʳ Cᵗ | 640 |
| To Francis Cook Cleark for a years Sallery | 2080 |
| To Francis Shomaker Sexton for a years Sallery | 520 |
| To Richard Waring Sexton for a years Sallery | 520 |
| To mʳ John Dandridge his account | 140 |
| To majʳ Kemp for of yᵉ Liſt of Tiths J Citty | 20 |
| To Dorithy Henry for Lucy Gills | 832 |
| To John miller for his Years maintainance | 300 |
| To mʳ mackain for four Communians | 400 |
| To ann Evans | 200 |
| To Ballard Dormer for Thomas Bates—8 months | 300 |
| To mʳ Hockaday a Ballance of an account | 355 |
| To mʳ John Thornton alloud in his account | 88 |
| To the Church Wardens for Evan Jones | 300 |
| To James Charles for Keeping his father | 400 |
| To mʳ John Markland for wrighting a deed for yᵉ Church Land | 100 |
| | 23195 |
| To 14 ℔ʳ Cᵗ on 23195ˡ of Tobbᵒ | 3247 |
| | 26442 |
| To 15 ℔ʳ pole toward the Church on 773 Tiths | 11595 |
| To 14 ℔ʳ Cᵗ on 11595ˡ Tobbᵒ | 1623 |
| | 39660 |
| By 773 Tithables at 51 ℔ʳ pole | 39433 |
| a Ballance dew to the Collecter for next year | 237 |
| | 39670 |

ordered that the Collecter Receive of Samuel Curll four hundred pounds of Tobbaco for his Rent and four hundred that is a bove Levied for James Charles not now due that he keep the Said 800 pounds of Tobbᵒ in his hands and account with the Veſtry for the Same

[43]
October the 17ᵗʰ 1734

Wheares John Sclater Genᵗˡ a late Veſtry man for this pariſh is dead this Veſtry has Chose mʳ William Hockaday to Serve in his Stead who was Sworn accordingly by mʳ Wᵐ mackain Geᵗ

Wᵐ mackain & Joſeph Allen & mʳ John Doran Genᵗˡ are appoynted to Settle with the Late Collecters & Retern an account to the Vestry

Joseph Allen Genᵗˡ & mʳ Wᵐ Hockaday are Chose Church Wardens in the Room of mʳ Wᵐ mackain & mʳ Georg Clough & ware Sworn accordingly by mʳ mʳ Wᵐ mackain

It is ordered by this preasant Veſtry that mʳ Lancelott Woodward Demand the Church plate plate belonging to the uper Church in the late Wilmanton pariſh now in the hands of mʳ Brown Genᵗˡ

This Veſtry has agreed with the minister to Build a new Glebe House on the Glebe Land as Soon as they have payd for all the Charges of the new Church now Building

Chichly Thacker ministr
Joſeph Allen
Wᵐ Hockaday

Teſt Francis Cook Cleark Vestry

it is Ordered by this preſent Veſtry that the pariſh Levie for this preſent yeare be fifty one pounds of Tobacco ℔r pole and that Capᵗ William Morris high Sherif of this County and Collector of this pariſh do Collect the Said Summ of fifty one pounds of Tobacco from Every Indeviduall Tithable perſon in this Pariſh Except the pole abatement and that he pay the Said Tobaccoes to the Severall reſpective Pariſh Creditors to whome it is due by Inſpectors Notes before the Laſt day of

Aprill Next and that the Clerk of the veſtry take bond with good Suficient Security of the Said Collector for the payment of the Said Tobacco before he deliver him a Copie of this Order of Veſtry and yͤ Pariſh Charg

Teſt Frañ Cooke Clerk Veſtry

[44]

at a Veſtry held for Bliſland Pariſh at the Lower Church the 14ᵗʰ day of October 1735

preſent<br>the Reverend Mʳ Thacker Miniſter

| | | |
|---|---|---|
| Major Richardſon | Mʳ Joſeph Allen | ⎫ Church |
| Capᵗ William Kenney | Mʳ William Hockaday | ⎬ wardens |
| Capᵗ William Morris | Mʳ William Mackain | |
| Mʳ John Doran | | |

This Veſtry proceeds to Lay the Pariſh Levie

| | |
|---|---:|
| To the Reverend Mʳ Thacker Miniſter for his years Sallery | 16000 |
| To Caſque to Dᵒ at 4 ℔ʳ Cᵗ | 640 |
| To Francis Cook Clerk of the uper Church for his years Sallery | 2080 |
| To Thomas Pettus Clerk of the Lower Church for his years Sall | 1040 |
| To Francis Shoomaker Sexton at the Lower Church | 520 |
| To Richard Warren Sexton at the uper Church | 520 |
| To Majoʳ Kemp for a Copie of the Liſt in James Citty | 20 |
| To Mʳ John Dandridge for a Copie of the Liſt of tiths | 40 |
| To Dorothy Henry for keeping Lucy Gills | 832 |
| To Mʳ William Hockaday for 4 Comunions | 400 |
| To John Miller for his years Maintainance | 300 |
| To Ann Evans toward her Maintainance | 200 |
| To Ballard Dormar for keeping Tho Bates | 450 |
| To Sarah Taylor toward her Suport | 300 |
| To Francis Day for Burying John Hall | 200 |

|  |  |  |
|---|---|---|
| To Charity Bracket for keeping Jane Crofford one yeare | | 600 |
| To Ballance due to Mʳ Hockaday Laſt yeare | | 237 |
| To Ballance his Accᵗ this yeare for Delinquents | | 120 |
| To Eliz Hurt toward Maintaing her Children | | 300 |
| | | 24799 |
| To 15 ℔ʳ pole on 775 Tithes is | | 11625 |
| | | 36424 |
| To 4 ℔ʳ Cᵗ on 36424 is | | 1457 |
| The whole pariſh Debt is | 37881 | 37881 |
| Ballance due from the Collector | 119 | 119 |
| By Mʳ Hockaday for Samˡˡ Curll his rent Laſt yeare | 400 Cʳ | *400 |
| By Samˡˡ Curll⁕ rent due this yeare | 400 | *400 |
| By 775 tithes at 48ˡˡ ℔ʳ pole is 37200 | *38800 | 37200 |
| | | 38000 |

[45]

It is Ordered by this preſent Veſtry that 600ˡˡ of Tobacco be Levied for the Suport or Maintainance of Jane Crofford this Enſuing yeare for who Soever will Keep her

It is Ordered by this preſent Veſtry that Edward Lively be Saxton at the Lower Church in the roome of Francis Shoomaker

Mʳ William Hockaday and Mʳ John Doran are Choſen Churchwardens for this Enſuing yeare and were Accordingly Sworn before Mʳ William Mackain a Majeſtrate for this County

It is Ordered by this preſent Veſtry that Julious Burbidge Collect the pariſh Tobacco this Enſuing yeare

It is Ordered by this preſent Veſtry that the Churchwardens Vew The Reverend Mʳ Thacker⁕ Barn and if they finde it

---

*Scratched through in original, but still legible.—C. G. C.

worthy of Repairing to Caufe it to be done otherwife to Build a New one

It is Ordered by this prefent Veftry that the Parifh Levie for this prefent yeare be forty Eight pounds of Tobacco ⅌ʳ pole and that Mʳ Julious Burbidge deputy Sheriff of this County and Collector of this Parifh do Collect the Said Summ of forty Eight pounds of Tobacco from Every Indeviduall tithable perfon in this parifh and upon Refufall of payment of Any part to make diftrefs According to Law and that he pay the Said Tobaccoes to the Several parifh Creditors to whome it is Exprefft to be due by Infpectors Notes before the Laft day of Aprill Next and that the Clerk of the Veftry Take Bond with good and Sufficient Security of the Said Collector for the payment of the Said Tobacco before he deliver him a Copie of this Order of Veftry and the parifh Charge

      C Thacker Minifter
      John Doran
      William Hockaday

[46]

At a Vestry held for Blisland Parifh at yᵉ Uper Church the 21ˢᵗ day of June 1736

      ⅌reasant
   the Revirend mʳ Thacker minifter

| Coll William Bafsett | Mʳ John Doran | } Church |
| Mʳ William Mackain | Mʳ William Hockaday | } wardˢ |
| Mʳ Lancelott Woodward | Mʳ Thomas Williams | |
| Mʳ George Woodward | Mʳ George Clough | |
| Capᵗ William Morris | Mʳ John Richardfon | |
| | Majʳ Richard Richardfon | |

Mʳ John Richardfon being Elected a vestry man for this ⅌arish & having Taken the Oath appoyinted for a vestry man is admitted one for the future

This vestry hath agreed to Levy the Sum of tenn Thousand ℔ounds of Tobacco upon the Tithable Persons of this Pariſh Every year untill they have paid the Sum of two Hundred pounds Corant money for Building a Gleb house upon the glebe of this ℔ariſh the S⁴ house to be Built according to the Dementions and Directions of Coll° William Baſsett and the Revirend m' Chichly Thacker, the Tobacco to be Sold by the Church wardens Every year to the beſt markitt they can gett untill the Said Summ is comply'de with

M' Jeremiah Stanup is Elected a Vestry man for this ℔ariſh and ordered that he be Sworn the firſt oppertunity

      C Thacker Minist'
      John Doran Chur⁴
      William Hockaday: Ch'

   Teſt Francis Cook Cler: Ves'

[47]

At a vestry held for Bliſland Parish at the Uper Church the 18ᵗʰ day of october 1736

      Preasant

| | |
|---|---|
| the Revirand m' Thacker minister | M' John Doran |
| Maj' Richard Richardson | M' william Hockaday |
| Cap' william Morris | M' George woodward |
| M' william Mackain | M' George Clough |
| Coll william Baſsett | M' John Richardſon |
| M' Lancᵗᵗ Woodward | M' Jeremiah Stanup |

This Vestry Proceeds to Lay the Parish Levie

| | |
|---|---|
| To the Revi'd m' Thacker minister for his years Sallery | 16000 |
| To Caſk to Do at 4 ℔' Cᵗ | 00640 |
| To Fran Cook Clerk at the uper Church his years Sallary | 02080 |
| To Thoˢ Pettus Clerk at the Lower Church his years Sallary | 01040 |

| | |
|---|---|
| To Richard Warrin Sexton at the uper Church | 00520 |
| To Edward Lively Sexton at the Lower Church | 00520 |
| To Dorothy Henry for years maintainance Lycy Gills | 00832 |
| To John Miller | 00300 |
| To ann Evans | 00200 |
| To David Pryer for keeping Thoˢ Bates laſt year | 00450 |
| To Eliza Hurt toward maintaining her children | 00300 |
| To mʳ William Hockaday for fore communians | 00400 |
| To Sarah Taylor | 00300 |
| To Majʳ Kemp for James citty list of Tiths | 00020 |
| To Majʳ Dandridge his account | 00141 |
| To John Evans for Keeping Jane Crofford laſt year | 00700 |
| To Tobbᵒ Levie'd towards a Glebe House | 10000 |
| To Julias K Birbidge Collecter his Ballˢ | 00069 |
| | 34512 |
| To 6 ℔ Cᵗ for Collecting 34512¹¹ Tobᵒ | 02071 |
| | 36583 |
| Due from the collecter to be paid next year | 101 |
| | 36684 |
| By Samˡ Curls Rent | 400 |
| By 772 Tiths at 47 ℔ʳ Poll | 36284 |
| | 36684 |

Ordered that majʳ Richard Richardſon mʳ willᵐ mackain and mʳ william Hockaday meet and Settle the account of the Late mʳ Joseph Allen & Mʳ John Doran for Tobbo Bought of yᵉ Parish

Mʳ John Richardſon is Choosen Church warden in yᵉ room of mʳ william Hockaday & was Sworn accordingly upon the Petetion of william mackain Gen^t his negro boy Jemmey being a crippel, & a naturall fool is discharg'd from paying Parish Levies

[48]
Ordered that the Church wardens Gett the County Surveyer and run the dividing line Between the parish of S^t Peters and the Parish of Blisland & that they give the Church Wardens of S^t Peters Parish notice thereof

orderd that M^r John Doran church Warden Pay Thomas maples four pounds tenn Shill^s for keeping anderson Odals Child                                                4=10=—
Do to Richard Waring Washing the y^e Surplis —= 5=—
Do Leonard Henley his acc^t                     1= 3=—
and the ball^e of m^r Hockaday's acc^t

Ordered that Julias King Burbidge is the Collecter of the Parish Tobb^o this Year he giving Bond & Security as usual

                     C Thacker min^r
                     John Doran: Chur^n
                     John Richardson

         Teſt Fran Cook Clerk of the Vestry

At a veſtry held for Bliſland Pariſh at the Lower Church y^e 10^th day of october 1737

          Preſent the Reverend M^r Thacker Miniſter

| Coll William Baſsett | M^r John Doran | ⎱ Church |
| Major Richard Richardſon | M^r Jn^o Richardſon | ⎰ wardens |
| Major William Morris | Cap^t Lanclot Woodward | |
| M^r William Mackain | M^r Georg Woodward | |
| M^r Georg Clough | M^r William Hockaday | |
| M^r Jeremiah Stanup | M^r Leonard Henley | |

M^r Leonard Henley Choſen a veſtryman in y^e roome of M^r Th^o Williams dec^d having this day taken all the oaths apointed to be Taken to his Majeſty King Georg the Second are thereby Continued veſtry men for the future

Ordered that his *Honrs Letter Sent to this Veſtry be Recorded which is as followeth

Gentlemen

Being informed that Some Scruple hath ariſen among you whether one who hath taken the Oaths to the Government as a Juſtice of peace ought to Take them againe on his Admition in to the Veſtry I am to acquaint you the Oaths Ought to be taken in Every different Capaſity one Acts in though Never So often taken before and that without doing it no man Can be a Veſtry man I am Gent your Moſt humble Sert

William Gooch

[49]

This Veſtry proceeds to Lay the Pariſh Levie

| | |
|---|---|
| To the Reverend Mr Thacker Miniſter for his years Sallery | 16000 |
| To Caſque to Do at 4 ℔r Ct | 00640 |
| To Francis Cook Clerk at the uper Church his years Sallery | 02080 |
| To Tho: Pettus Clerk at the Lower Church his years Sallery | 01040 |
| To Richard Warren Sexton at the uper Church | 00520 |
| To Edward Lively Sexton at the Lower Church | 00520 |
| To the Maintainance of Lucy Gills | 00624 |
| To Mr John Dandridg for two Copies of the Liſts of tithes | 00040 |
| To Mr Matthew Kemp for the Liſt in James Citty | 00020 |
| To John Miller for his years Suport | 00300 |
| To Mr John Richardſon for four Communs 400 to paying Mr Eatons Acct | 00700 |
| To John Pigg for a dyall poſt | 00050 |

*Written above another word, probably "Excelencie's," which has been scratched through and is illegible.—C. G. C.

| | |
|---|---:|
| To Robert Taylor towards his Maintainance | 00300 |
| To Tobb towards a Gleibe houſe | 10000 |
| To David Pryer for Keeping Tho: Bates laſt yeare | 00450 |
| To Tho: Maples for keeping Anderſon Odalls Child | 00750 |
| To William Farthing for keeping Tho: Linſey | 00700 |
| To William Hatfeild for keeping Jane Croford | 00350 |
| To Sarah Taylor towards her Maintainance | 00300 |
| To Eliz: Hurt towards her Maintainance | 00300 |
| To M'ʳ Edmᵈ Walker for Seates & harbour | 00050 |
| To Daniell Allen Junʳ | 00060 |
| To Mʳ Ruſsell a Levie over Charged Laſt yeare | 00047 |
| To pay the Ballance of Mʳ Burbidg his Accᵗ | 00460 |
| To Samˡˡ Curll for Burying Rebeckah Smith | 00100 |
| To Mʳ John Richᵈſon for burying Evan Jones | 00120 |
| To Samˡˡ Curll for Cureing Sarah Phips | 00180 |
| To Mʳ Henley his Accᵗ | 00086 |
| To Richᵈ Haiſelwood for two horſe blocks | 00250 |
| To Prudence Fiſhers Son Cleaning the Church yard | 00050 |
| | 37087 |
| To Sallery on 37087 is | 2225 |
| | 39312 |
| Cʳ By Samˡˡ Curll his Rent | 400 |
| | 38912 |

It is Ordered by this preſent vſtry yᵗ Lewis Deloney be alowᵈ forty Shill for yᵉ two Windows in yᵉ Gallery & yᵗ he be pᵈ no more money till he hath finiſhed yᵉ Church According to Agreemᵗ

Coll William Baſsett Elected Churchwarden in yᵉ roome of Mʳ John Doran & Sworn with Mʳ John Richᵈſon Accordingly

Ordered yᵗ the Governers Letter be recorded in yᵉ Veſtry Book

This day the Veſtry do hereby Agree yᵗ all the former Orders by them made before they took the Oaths be good and in force

Ordered that Mʳ Burbidg Collect the pariſh Tobacco giving Bond with Sufficient Security

      C Thacker Miniſter
      William Baſsett ⎱ Ch Wardens
      John Richardſon ⎰

     Teſt Frañ Cook Clerk Veſtry

[50]

At a veſtry held for Bliſland Pariſh at the uper Church yᵉ 12ᵗʰ day of July 1738

     ₱reſent
   The Reverend Mʳ Thacker Miniſter

| Mʳ Wᵐ Mackain | Mʳ John Richᵈſon Church warden |
| Capᵗ John Doran | Mʳ George Woodward |
| Capᵗ Lanclett Woodward | Capᵗ Wᵐ Hockaday |
| Mʳ Leonard Henley | Mʳ Jeremiah Stanup |

It is Ordered by this preſent Veſtry that Mʳ Wᵐ Mackain Capᵗ Wᵐ Hockaday and Mʳ Leonard Henley do Settle all the pariſh Accᵗˢ the day after Auguſt Court Next if faire if not the Next faire day at Coll Wᵐ Baſsettˢ and Make a return of theire proceedings to the Next veſtry

it is Ordered by this preſent Veſtry that Mʳ Lewiſ Deloney and Mʳ John Moore do finiſh theire work at the Lower Church According to agreement by the tenth day of October Next and upon theire failure Ordered that the Churchwardens Imploy workmen to finiſh the Sᵈ Church According to agreement

it is Ordered by this preſent Veſtry that Coll William Baſsett one of the preſent Churchwardens agree with Some Maſter of a Ship to Carry Honour Moore to Briſtoll and alſo to alow her Something to beare her Charges from Briſtoll to Irland and bring his Charge to the veſtry and it Shall be alowed him

James Brown petitioned this Veſtry to be Levy free and he apearing a Criple & very Unable to Labour it is Ordered that he be diſcharged from paying pariſh Levies for the future and alſo diſcharged from all arears of pariſh Levies Now due

C Thacker Min<sup>r</sup>
John Rich<sup>d</sup>ſon Churchwarden

Teſt Frañ. Cook Clerk veſtry

[51]

At a Veſtry held for Bliſland Pariſh at the Uper Church Octobe<sup>r</sup> y<sup>e</sup> 12<sup>th</sup> 1738

preſent The Reverend M<sup>r</sup> Thacker Miniſter

Coll W<sup>m</sup> Baſsett }
M<sup>r</sup> John Rich<sup>d</sup>ſon } Churchwardens

| | |
|---|---|
| Major Rich<sup>d</sup> Rich<sup>d</sup>ſon | M<sup>r</sup> George Woodward |
| M<sup>r</sup> W<sup>m</sup> Mackain | M<sup>r</sup> Lancl<sup>t</sup> Woodward |
| Cap<sup>t</sup> John Doran | M<sup>r</sup> Jeremyah Stanup |
| Cap<sup>t</sup> W<sup>m</sup> Hockaday | M<sup>r</sup> Georg Clough |
| Majo<sup>r</sup> W<sup>m</sup> Morris | Veſtrymen |

This Veſtry proceeds to Lay the pariſh Levie

| | |
|---|---:|
| To the Rever<sup>d</sup>. M<sup>r</sup> Thacker Miniſt<sup>r</sup> for his years Sallery | 16000 |
| To Caſque to D<sup>o</sup> at 4 p<sup>r</sup> C<sup>t</sup> | 00640 |
| To Frañ Cook Clerk at the uper Church | 02080 |
| To Tho: Pettus Clerk at the Lower Church | 01248 |
| To Rich<sup>d</sup> Warren Sexton at the uper Church | 00520 |
| To Ed: Lively Sexton at the Lower Church | 00520 |
| To Rich<sup>d</sup> Warren for waſhing y<sup>e</sup> Surplus two years | 00100 |
| To Ed: Lively for waſhing the Surplus two years | 00100 |
| To the Maintainance of Lucy Gills | 00624 |
| To John Miller toward his Maintainance | 00300 |
| To M<sup>r</sup> John Rich<sup>d</sup>ſon for four Communions | 00400 |

| | |
|---|---:|
| To Ballard Dormar for keeping Tho: Bates | 00119 |
| To Ann Glaſbrook for keeing Samˡˡ Pauley | 00462 |
| To Mʳ John Richardſon for planting trees at the Lower Church | 00050 |
| To Robert Taylor toward his Maintainance | 00300 |
| To Mʳ Mackain being Over Chargᵈ Laſt year 3 tithes | 00144 |
| To Mˢ John Dandridg his Accᵗ | 00081 |
| To Mʳ Kemp for a Copie of the Liſt of Tiths | 00018 |
| To Sarah Haukins for Cureing John Hillˢ Legg | 00500 |
| To Eliz: Hurt towards her Maintainance | 00300 |
| To Tho: Maples for keeping Anderſon Odals Child | 00750 |
| To Wᵐ Shelbourn for Cleaning yᵉ yard at yᵉ Lower Church | 00048 |
| To Sarah Taylor toward her Maintainance | 00300 |
| To Ballard Dormar for burying Tho: Bates | 00075 |
| To Mʳ Julious King Burbidge his Accᵗ. | 00400 |
| To Capᵗ Doran for Salevateing Eliz: Philbates | 01000 |
| To tobb: Levied toward the Gleibe houſe | 10000 |
| | 37079 |
| To Salery @ 6 ℔ Cᵗ on 37079 | 2225 |
| | 39304 |
| By Samˡˡ Curls Rent | 400 |
| | 38904 |
| By 809 Tiths @ 48 ℔ pol | 38832 |
| Bal due to yᵉ Collector | 72 |
| | 38904 |

Turn Over

[52]

Turn over

it is Ordered by this preſent that yᵉ Churchwardens Agree with Charles Rawson to keep Honour Moore for five hundred pounds of tobb & Caſque till October Next

it is Ordered that Coll William Baſsett do Build a Brick Chimney & other Neſesaryes to Mʳ Thackers kitchin

it is Ordered that the Churchwardens do pay Mʳ Penningtonˢ Accᵗ of thirty Shillings

it is Ordered that the Churchwardens do lett Sarah Hatfeild have two barells of Corn & Cotten to her a pettycoate

it is Ordered that Joyce Odall do keep Anderſon Odals Child for five hundred pounds of tobb & Caſque a yeare

Coll William Baſsett & Capᵗ William Hockaday are Choſen Church wardens for this preſent yeare & Sworn Accordingly

it is Ordered by this preſent Veſtry that the pariſh Levie for this preſent yeare be forty Eight pounds of Tobb: pʳ pole & Coll William Baſsett & Capᵗ Wm: Hockaday Churchwardens for the Said pariſh are apointed to Collect & receive the Said Sumᵐ of forty Eight pounds of tobacco from Every Indeviduall tithable perſon within this pariſh & in Caſe of refuſall of payment of any part thereof to Levie the Same by diſtreſs According to Law the Said Coll: Baſsett & Capᵗ Hockaday firſt Entering into bond with good & Suficient Security to the Veſtry for the Uſe of this pariſh for the payment of the Said Severall Sums of tobacco to the Severall reſpective pariſh Creditors to whome it is due According as they are Mentioned & Expreſt in the pariſh Charg and it is alſo Ordered that the Clerk of the Veſtry take Bond as aforeſaid before he deliver a Copie of the pariſh Charg and of this Order of Veſtry to the Collectors

    C Thacker Minʳ
    Wᵐ Baſsett
    Wᵐ Hockaday   Churchwardens

[53]
At a Veſtry held for Bliſland Pariſh at the Lower Church yᵉ 8ᵗʰ day of October 1739

preſent<br>
the Reverend Mʳ Thacker Miniſter<br>
Capᵗ William Hockaday Church Warden

| | |
|---|---|
| Major William Morris | Capᵗ John Doran |
| Mʳ William Mackain | Mʳ Lanclot Woodward |
| Mʳ Georg Woodward | Mʳ Jeremiah Stanup |
| Mʳ Georg Clough | Mʳ Leonard Henley |

This preſent Veſtry proceeds to Lay the pariſh Levie<br>
Bliſland pariſh Dʳ

| | |
|---|---|
| To the Reverᵈ Mʳ Thacker Miniſter Caſque Included | 16640 |
| To Frañ Cook Clerk at the uper Church Caſque Included | 2080 |
| To Mʳ Tho: Pettus Clerk at the Lower Church Caſque Included | 1248 |
| To Richard Warren Sexton at yᵉ Uper Church Caſque Included | 520 |
| To Ditto for Waſhing the Surplus | 50 |
| To Edward Lively Sexton at the Lower Church the Same | 570 |
| To Lucy Gills towards her Maintainanc | 624 |
| To John Miller towards his Mantainanc | 300 |
| To Ann Glaſbrook for keeping Samuell Pauley | 738 |
| To Capᵗ William Hockaday for four Communions | 400 |
| To Ditto his Account given the Veſtry | 1000 |
| To Robert Taylor toward his Maintainanc | 600 |
| To Tho: Maples for keeping Anderſon Odals Child | 500 |
| To Auguſtine Shelbourn for keeping Sarah Taylor | 300 |
| To Capᵗ Doran for Sallevating Eliz filbates | 350 |
| To Mʳˢ Mary Kenney for keeping Eliz forgiſon | 400 |
| To Mʳ John Richardson for the Quitrents of the Gleibe | 44 |
| To the Churchwardens for the uſe of James filbates | 300 |
| To William Farthing for keeping Tho: Linſey two years | 1224 |

| | |
|---|---:|
| To Coll Baſsett by Orde of Charles Rawſon for keeping Honour Moore | 520 |
| To tobacco Levied to be Sold for the Uſe of the pariſh | 5000 |
| To Major Dandridge for two Copies of the Liſt | 36 |
| To Mʳ Matt Kemp | 18 |
| To Julius K Burbidge the Ballanc of his Accᵗ | 197 |
| | 33659 |
| To Sallary @ 6 pʳ Cᵗ on D° | 2020 |
| | 35679 |
| To a Dipositum in the Collectors hands | 147 |
| | 35826 |

Turn over

[54]

Turn Over

it is Ordered by this preſent Veſtry that John Maning bee diſcharged from paying Pariſh Levies

it is Ordered by this present Veſtry that William Fox be discharged from paying Parish Levies

it is Ordered by this preſent Veſtry that Auguſtin Shelbourn for keeping Sarah Taylor this Insuing year five hundred of tobb and Caſque

it is Ordered by this preſent Veſtry that the Church Wardens Take Care of William Tanner for the Insuing yeare and allow him what they think in their diſcretion is Neſecary for his Subsistance and bring their Account to the Veſtry and it Shall be alowed

it is Ordered by this preſent Veſtry that Ballard Dormar be alowed for this Insuing yeare Six hundred pounds of tobb and Caſque for Keeping and Maintaining David Dormar for the yeare Insuing it is Ordered by this preſent veſtry that Capᵗ John Doran adminesſter Such Cure as he Can poſsible to David Dormar for the Insuing yeare and that he bring his Account to the Next veſtry when the Levie is Laid and he Shall be paid

it is Ordered by this preſent Veſtry that the Widow Fiſhers Sons be diſcharged from paying Pariſh Levie this Insuing yeare

it is Ordered by this preſent Veſtry that Capᵗ John Doran and Mʳ William Mackain proportion the Pariſh Levie

Mʳ Georg Woodward this Veſtry hath Relinquiſhed his place of a Veſtry man and he is hereby diſmiſt from the Said Ofice

Capᵗ Edwin Dangerfeild is hereby Apointed a Veſtry man in the Roome of the Said Woodward for the future and Sworn Accordingly

Capᵗ John Doran and Mʳ Leonard Henley were Choſen Churchwardens and was Sworn Accordingly

it is Ordered that Samuell Curle have two hundred pounds of tobb alowed him out of his Rent the Next yeare for Reparations done on the Gleibe

Purſuant to an Order of Veſtry wee the Subſcribers have proportionᵈ the pariſh Levie and find it to be forty two pounds of tobb ℔ʳ poll and a depoſitum of one hundred and forty Seven pounds of tobb in the Collectors hands to be by him Accounted for at the Laying of the next pariſh Levie October yᵉ 20 1739

       John Doran
       William Mackain

[55]

it is Ordered by this preſent Veſtry yᵗ the pariſh Levie for this preſent yeare be forty & two pounds of tobb ℔ʳ polle & that Mʳ John Allen Sub-ſherif of this County is apointed to Collect and Receive the Said Summ of forty two pounds of tobb Every Indeviduall Tithable perſon within this pariſh & in Caſe of refuſiall of payment of any part thereof to Levie the Same by diſtreſs according to Law the Said Allen firſt Entring into Bond with good & Sufitient Security to the Veſtry of this pariſh for the payment of the Said Severall Sums of tobacco to the Severall reſpective pariſh Creditors to whome it is due According as they are Mentioned and Expreſt in the pariſh Charge and it is alſo ordered that the Clerk of the Veſtry take Bond as aforeſaid before he deliver a Copie of the of the pariſh Charg and of this Order of Veſtry to the Collector

                    C Thacker Miniſter
                    John Doran C Warden

            Teſt Frañ Cook Clerk Veſtry

[56]
At a Veſtry held for Bliſland Pariſh at the uper Church the 29ᵗʰ day of September 1740

                preſent
      the Reverend Mʳ Thacker Miniſter

| Coll William Baſsett | Capᵗ John Doran ⎫ warden |
| Capᵗ Edwin Dangerfield | Mʳ Leonard Henley ⎬ Church |
| Capᵗ William Hockaday | Mʳ Lanclot Woodward |
| | Mʳ John Richarson |

    This Veſtry proceeds to Lay the Pariſh Levie

| | |
|---|---:|
| To the Reverᵈ Chichley Thacker Miniſter his years Salery | 16000 |
| To Caſque to Dº. | 00640 |
| To Francis Cook Clerk at the uper Church | 02080 |
| to Tho Pettus Clerk at the Lower Church | 1248 |
| to Richard Warren Sexton at the Uper Church | 570 |
| to Ed: Liveley Sexton at the Lower Church | 607 |
| to the Maintainance of Lucy Gills | 624 |
| to John Miller toward his Maintainance | 300 |
| to Charles Rawſon for keeping Honour Moore | 570 |
| to Mʳ Henley for four Communions | 400 |
| to Mʳ Dandridg for two Copies of the Liſts of Tithes | 36 |

| | |
|---|---:|
| to Auguſtin Shelbourn for keeping Sarah Taylor | 300 |
| to Ann Glaſbrook for keeing Sam¹¹ Pauley | 400 |
| to Wᵐ Farthing for keeping Tho: Linſey | 600 |
| to Tho: Taylor for keeping Eliz: Hurts 3 Children | 400 |
| to Major Richardſon for his trouble with David Dormar | 300 |
| to Ballard Dormar for keeping his Son David | 624 |
| to Ann Evans for Maintainance of her Daughter Eliz. | 400 |
| to James Foreſter for one Levie overchared Laſt yeare | 42 |
| to Mʳ John Dandridg his Accᵗ alowed | 125 |
| to the Clerk of James Citty | 18 |
| to Julious Burbidge for Tho Smith | 162 |
| to Mʳ John Allen his Account for delinquents | 691 |
| | 27037 |
| To 6 ℔ Cᵗ to D° | 1627 |
| | 28764 |
| Cʳ By 826 at 35 ℔ polle | 28910 |
| To a depoſitum in The Collectors hands | 146 |

John Power John Allen & Richmond Terill Gent are Choſen Veſtrymen in the Roome of Wᵐ Mackain Georg Clough Deceaſt & Wᵐ Morris Gent Removed out of the County who Took the Oaths apointed by the Goverment and Subſcribed the Teſt Accordingly

[57]
Ordered that Charles Whitehead be discharged from paying Pariſh Levie for the year 1740

Ordered that Stephen Manning be discharged from paying pariſh Levie for the Enſuing yeare

Ordered that John Doran & Leonard Henley Genᵗ be Continued C Wardens

Ordered that Wᵐ Hockaday Leonard & John Allen Genᵗ Settle the Account between Coll William Baſsett & the pariſh

Ordered that the pariſh Levie for this preſent yeare be *28744 thirty five pounds of tobb ℔ʳ ℔olle & that Capᵗ John Doran and Mʳ Leonard Henley Churchwardens for this Pariſh are apointed to Collect and receive the Saide Summ of thirty five pounds of Tobb from Every Indeviduall Tithable perſon within this pariſh and in Caſe of refuſall of payment of any part thereof to Levie the Same by diſtreſs according to Law the Said Wardens firſt Entering into Bond with good & Suficent Security to the Veſtry of this pariſh for the payment of the Said Severall Sums of Tobb to the Severall Reſpective Pariſh Creditors to whome it is due According as they are Mentioned and Expreſt in the pariſh Charg and it is alſo Ordered that the Clerk of the Veſtry take Bond as aforeſaid before he deliver a Copie of the pariſh Charg and of this Order of Veſtry to the Collectors

      C. Thacker Miniſter
      John Doran Church Warden
      Leonard Henley Church Ward

[58]
At a Veſtry held for Bliſland Pariſh at the Lower Church the 15 day of October 1741

   Preſent yᵉ Reverᵈ Mʳ Thacker Miniſtʳ
Coll William Baſsett Capᵗ John Doran ⎫ Church
Capᵗ Edwin Dangerfield Mʳ Leonard Henley ⎬ Wardns
Capᵗ William Hocaday Mʳ Lanclot Woodward⎭
Mʳ John Richardſon Mʳ Richard Richᵈſon
Mʳ Richmon Terrell Mʳ Jeremiah Stanup

  This Veſtry proceds to Lay yᵉ Pariſh Levie
To the Reverend Mʳ Thacker his years Sallery 16000
to Caſque to Dᵒ 00640
to Francis Cook Clerk of yᵉ Uper Church his Sallery 02080
to Tho Pettus Clerk at yᵉ Lower Church his Sallery 01248
to Richᵈ Warren Sexton & waſhing yᵉ Surplus 00570

*These five figures erased in original, but still legible.—C. G. C.

| | |
|---|---|
| to Edward Liveley to Dº | 00570 |
| to the Maintainanc of Lucy Gills | 00624 |
| towards the Maintainanc of John Miller | 00300 |
| to Mʳ Henley for four Comunions | 00400 |
| to Mʳ John Dandridg for two Copies of the Liſtˢ | 00036 |
| to Mʳ Benj Waller for one Copie | 00018 |
| to Richᵈ Gaddey for Burying Eliz Evans | 00150 |
| to Auguſtin Shelbourn for Keeping Sarah Taylor 6 moneths & burying | 00520 |
| to James Shelbourn for keeping his Brother till this time | 00800 |
| to Ballard Dormar for keeping his Son David till now | 00624 |
| to Mʳˢ Thoˢ Oakley for keeping Honour Moore | 00700 |
| to Mʳˢ Mary Holdcraft for Makeing the harbour | 00035 |
| to Edward Linſey for burying Eliz Hurt | 00100 |
| to Mʳ William Rountree Junʳ his Accᵗ | 00160 |
| to Sarah Haukins for keeping Eliz Baker Six moneths | 00300 |
| to Charity Bracket for keeping John Son of Randal Wᵐˢ for the time paſt it being Six Moneths | 00300 |
| to Capᵗ John Doran for keeping keen foulks & Caſque | 02080 |
| to Capᵗ Doran for Francis Day & Caſque | 00832 |
| Towards paying Coll Baſsettˢ Accᵗ | 03000 |
| to Capᵗ Doran for Prudence Fiſher | 00400 |
| to Mʳ John Allen for Delinquents & Quitrents | 00271 |
| | 32758 |
| To 6 ℔ Cᵗ for Sallery on 32758 | 01965 |
| By Mʳ Leonard Henley for Supernumary tithes | 00234 |
| By Capᵗ Wᵐ Hockaday Francis Brookers Levie | 00034 |
| | 34902 |
| By 831 Tiths at 42 ℔ pole | 35171 |
| To Depoſited in the Collectors hands to be Accounted for Next yeare | 448 |

[59]

It is Ordred by this preſent Veſtry that the Churchwardens do agree with Workmen to Cover yᵉ Dary on the Gleibe with Shingles & to Cover yᵉ Quarter with Clapboards & to build a Shed at yᵉ End of the Barn & Cover it with Shingles

it is agreed with Capᵗ Jnº Doran to keep Keen Foulks yᵉ Enſuing yeare for one Thouſand ˡˡ of Tobᶜᵒ & Caſk

agreed with Capᵗ Jnº Doran to find Francis Day in Medicins the Enſuing yeare without any farther Reward

Ordered yᵗ Francis Cook have 200 ˡˡ of Tobacco for keeping Henry yᵉ Enſuing yeare

Ordered yᵗ Mʳ William Slaterˢ Bond to Pauley be Comenᵈ to yᵉ Clerk of yᵉ pariſh

Ordered yᵗ Francis Day be diſchargᵈ from paying pariſh Levie yᵉ Ensuing yeare

Capᵗ Edwin Dangerfeild & Mʳ Lanclot Woodward are Choſen Churchwardens in the roome of Capᵗ Doran & Mʳ Henley & Sworn accordingly

Ordered yᵗ Richard Bull be dischargᵈ from paying pariſh Levie

It is Ordered by this preſent Veſtry yᵗ the pariſh Levie for this preſent yeare be forty & two pounds of Tobcco ℔ʳ pole & that Capᵗ Edwin Dangerfeild and Mʳ Lanclot Woodward Churchwardens for this pariſh do Collect the Said Summ of forty two pounds of Tobacco from Every Indeviduall Tithable perſon within this pariſh & upon refuſall of payment to Levie the Same by diſtreſs according to Law yᵉ Said wardens firſt Entering into Bond with good & Sufficient Security to the preſent Veſtry of this pariſh for the Uſe of the pariſh for the payment of the Said Sums of tobacco to the Severall reſpective parish Creditors to whome it is due by Inſpectors Notes by the Laſt day of May Next and it is alſo Ordered that the Clerk of the Veſtry take Bond as aforeſaid before he deliver a Copie of the parifh Charg & of this Order of Veftry to the Said Collectors

     Chichely Thacker Min'
     Edwin Daingerfield ⎱ Churchwardens
     Lanclot Woodward ⎰

[60]
At a Vestry held for Blisland Parish at the upper Church. the 15th Day of October Anno ᵈ 1742

      Prefent
    The Rever ᵈ C. Thacker Min'
  Maj'. Edwin Daingerfield ⎱ Church wardens
  M'. Lançelott Woodward ⎰
William Bafett Esq'   M' John Richardson
Cap' John Doran.    M' Leonard Henley
Cap' William Hockaday  M' Richmond Terrel

  This Veftry Proceds to lay the Parish Levy
             B. Parish D'.
To the Rever'd C. Thacker Minister his years Sallery  16000
To Cask to D°.            640
To M'. Francis Cook, Clerk of the Church & Vestry
  Including Cask          2080
To M'. Tho'. Pettus Clerk of the Lower Church In-
  cluding D°            1248
To Richard Warren Sexton at the upper Church &
  washing the Surplus         570
To Edward Lively Sexton at the Lower Church &
  washing the D°           570
To the Maintainance of Lucy Gills     624
To the Maintainance of John Miller     300
To the Maintainance of Tho'. Lindfey two years 1248
To the Maintainance of David Dormer    624
To M'. Francis Cook for keeping Henry bear  200
To Maj'. Edwin Daingerfield for four Communions 400
To Peter Ball for keeping Hon'. Moore    500

| | |
|---|---:|
| To Elenor Pitman | 300 |
| To M`r`. Tho`s`. Taylor for keeping Hurts three Children two years Past, & Randal Williams's Dec`d`. two months & a halfe, includeing Cask | 624 |
| To Francis Day | 300 |
| To M`r`. John Woodward Jun`r` & Charity Bracket for keeping John Williams Son of Randal Williams Dec`d`. | 600 |
| To M`r` Richard Allen on Levy overcharg'd | 42 |
| To James Shelbourn, for keeping Tho`s`. Shelbourn five months And Burying him 500`l`, & Cask 20`l` | 520 |
| To Sarah Hawkins, for keeping Eliz`th` Barker | 430 |
| To M`r`. Lancelott Woodward, for keeping Eliz`th` Barker | 460 |
| To D`o`. for Stephen Jones, & James Philbates Delinquents | 84 |
| To Maj`r`. John Dandridge for two Copies of the list of Titheables | 36 |
| To M`r`. Benjamine Waller for one D`o` | 18 |
| To M`r` John Allen the Ballance of his Acco`t`. | 657 |
| | 29075 |

Brought

[61]

| | |
|---|---:|
| Brought over | 29075 |
| To William Baſsett Esq`r`. to Discharge his acco`t`. Fifteen Pounds, Six Shillings & Eight Pence halfe penny | 2534 |
| To Maj`r`. Edwin Daingerfield, to the Ballance of his acco`t`. Four Pounds ten shillillings | 720 |
| To M`r`. Richmond Terrel the Ballance of his Acco`t`. Three Pound four shillings | 512 |
| To M`r`. Richard Gaddey the Ballance of his acc`t`. One Pound five shillings | 200 |

| | |
|---|---|
| To M‘. Benj‘. Allen the Ballance of his acco‘. Three Pound | 480 |
| To M‘. Lancelot Woodward the Ballance of his Acco‘. Seven shillings & ten Pence | 63 |
| To Cap‘. John Doran for keeping Keen Foulks last year One Thousand Pounds of Tob<sup>co</sup> & Cask | 1040 |
| To Cap‘. John Doran for Cutting of Keen Foulks's leg Eleven Hundred & Cask | 1144 |
| To Keen Foulks's Board from this time till this time twelvemonth | 1200 |
| | 36968 |
| To 6 ℙ Cent for Sallery on 36968 | 2242 |
| | 39210 |
| To Depositium in the Collectors hands to be acco<sup>td</sup>. for next year | 120 |
| | 39330 |
| Credit By 828 Tithes at 47½ ℙ Poll | 39330 |

Maj". Edwin Daingerfield & M‘. Lancelott Woodward are Continued Church Wardens

Order'd by this Prefent Vestry that Stephen Maning be Difcharg'<sup>d</sup> From Paying his Parish Levy

Order'd by this Prefent Veftry that Fancis Day be Discharg'd From Paying his Parish Levy

Order'd by this Prefent Veftry that the Churchwardens bind out John Williams Son of Randal Williams Dec<sup>d</sup>

Order'd by this Prefent Veftry that Samuel Curle be Difcharg'd From Paying his Parish Levy

Order'd by this Prefent Veftry that Tho'. Lyon Sen'. be Difcharg'd From Paying his Parish Levy

Turn over

[62]
Turn'd over

This Prefent Veftry Mr Francis Cook Declin'd being Clerk of The Church & Veftry, Dudley Williams was Chosen in his room Haveing Taken the Oaths accordingly

Richard Warren haveing Declin'd Serving as Sexton of the Uper Church, David Gray is Chosen in his room

Order'd by this Present Vestry that the Parish Levy for this Prefent year Be forty Seven Pounds & a halfe of Tob⁕ ℔ Poll & that Majr. Edwin Daingerfield & Mr. Lancelott Woodward Churchwardens for this Parish Do Collect the Sᵈ Sum of Forty Seven & a halfe pounds of Tob⁕. from Every indevidual Titheable Person within this Parish, and upon Refufal of Payment, to Levy the Same by distrefs according to Law The Sᵈ. Wardens first Entring into Bond with good & Sufficient Security To the Prefent Veftry of this Parish, for the use of the Parish, for the Payment of the Sᵈ. Sums of Tob⁕. to the Several refpective Parish Creditors to whom it is due, by Inspectors notes by the last day of May Next, and it is also order'd that the Clark of the Vestry take Bond As aforesᵈ, before he deliver a Copy of the Parish Charge and of The order of Veftry to the Sᵈ. Collectors

    Sign'd By
        Chicheley Thacker Minisr.
        Edwin Daingerfield ⎱
        Lancelott Woodward ⎰ Churchwardens

  Copy Test Dudley Williams Clark of the Vestry

[63]
At a Vestry held for Blisland Parish, at the upper Church The 17th Day of December 1742

            Prefent

Mr. Chicheley Thacker Minisr. William Bafsett Esq Capt John Doran; Majrr Edwin Daingerfield & Mr Lancelott

Woodward Churchwardens; Cap⁺ William Hockaday, Mʳ Jeremiah Stanup, Mʳ Jnº Richᵈſon, Mʳ Leonard Henley, Mʳ Richmond Terrell

Capᵗ. John Power being formerly Chosen a Veſtryman Was Sworn, by Wᵐ Baſsett Esq

Doctor Thoˢ Arnott Choſen a Vestryman in the room of Majʳ. Richard Richardson, order'd That he be Sworn accordingly

And Mʳ. Jnº. Ruſsel Junʳ. is Choſen a Vestryman in the Room of Mʳ. Jnº. Allen, who is remov'd out of the Parish And County; & Mʳ. Jnº. Ruſsel Junʳ. was Sworn Accordingly by Capᵗ. William Hockaday

Order'd by this preſent Vestry That Capᵗ William Hockaday, Capᵗ. John Power Mʳ John Richardson & Mʳ Leonard Henley, that they lay of a Yard at the Lower Church and Agree with workmen to brick it in

Order'd by this preſent Veſtry that Sarah Hawkins have Five Hundred Pounds of Tobº for Keeping John Hill, From this time till the laying the next Parish Levy

    Sign'd By  Chicheley Thacker Minʳ.
                  Edwin Daingerfield  ⎫ Church
                  Lancelott Woodward ⎭ Wardens

Copy Test. Dudley Williams Clk Vestry

[64]
At a Vestry held for Blesland Parish at the lower Church the 18th. day of october. 1743

                    ℔resent

The Rever'd Mʳ Thacker; Majʳ. Edwin Daingerfield & Mʳ. Lancelott Woodward, Churchwardens, Wᵐ Baſsett Esqʳ. Capᵗ. John Doran; Capᵗ. William Hockaday; Mʳ. Jeremiah Stanup; Mʳ. Leonard Henley; Mʳ. John Richardson; Mʳ. Richmond Terrel; Capᵗ. John Power

84   VESTRY BOOK OF BLISLAND PARISH

  This Vestry proceeds to lay y<sup>e</sup>. parish Levy
Blisland Parish               Dr.

| | |
|---|---:|
| To the Rever'd M<sup>r</sup>. Thacker, his years Sallery | 16000 |
| To Cask to Ditto | 640 |
| To M<sup>r</sup>. Tho<sup>s</sup>. Pettus Clark of the lower Church includeing Cask | 1040 |
| To Dudley Williams Clark of the upper Church includeing Cask | 1560 |
| To David Gray Sexton of the upper Church & washing the Surp<sup>s</sup>. | 570 |
| To Edward Lively Sexton of the lower Church & washing the Surp<sup>s</sup>. | 570 |
| To the maintainance of Lucy Gills | 624 |
| To the maintenance of John Miller | 300 |
| To the maintenance of Tho<sup>s</sup>. Lindsey | 624 |
| To the maintenance of David Dormer | 624 |
| To Joseph Lindsey | 300 |
| To Elenor Pitman | 300 |
| To M<sup>r</sup>. William Parks, for advertiseing workmen for the Ch. wall | 56 |
| To Maj<sup>r</sup>. John Dandridge, for two copies of the list of Titheables | 36 |
| To M<sup>r</sup>. Benj<sup>a</sup>. Waller for one copy of the list of Titheables | 18 |
| To Sarah Hawkins for keeping Eliz<sup>th</sup>. Barker | 700 |
| To M<sup>r</sup>. Richmond Terrel for Keeping Richard Bull | 500 |
| To Cap<sup>t</sup>. John Doran for Cureing Anne Gibson | 1040 |
| To Rich<sup>d</sup>. Farthing for keeping Jn<sup>o</sup>. Williams Son of Randal Williams Dec<sup>d</sup> till the last day of Nov<sup>r</sup>. | 600 |
| To M<sup>r</sup>. John Woodward Jun<sup>r</sup>. for keeping the Same child | 100 |
| To M<sup>r</sup>. Fra's Cook, for Henry Nears | 300 |
| To M<sup>r</sup>. Lancelott Woodward for one delinq<sup>t</sup>. Tythe | 47½ |
| To Maj<sup>r</sup>. Edwin Daingerfield for four Communions | 400 |

| | |
|---|---|
| To M\*. John Allen | 219 |
| To Coll°. Wᵐ Baſsett, for cloathing Keen Foulks & Hon\*. More | 300 |
| To Majʳ Edwin Daingerfield for makeing Bricks, & makeing A Brick wall round the Church | 16000 |
| | 43468½ |

Debt

[65]

| | |
|---|---|
| Debt brought over | 43468½ |
| Credit By Mʳ. Lancᵗᵗ. Woodward for Samˡ Curll's rent in the year 1742 | 235 |
| | 43233½ |
| To 6 P. Cent for Sallery on 43233½ᶫᵇ Tob° | 2594 |
| | 45827 |
| Credit By 858 Tythes at 53½ ℔ poll | 45903 |
| To a Depositium in the collectors hands to be Paid to the Parish next year | 76 |

Capᵗ. John Doran sherriff is appointed collector, giveing Bond and Security as usual

Capᵗ. John Power, & Mʳ Richmond Terrel are chosen Ch wardens in the room of Majʳ. Edwin Daingerfield & Mʳ. Lancelott Woodward, & Sworn accordingly

Order'd by this present Vestry, that Samˡˡ. Curll, be discharg'd from paying his rent on the glebe two year, & build a Tob°. house on it four & twenty foot long & sixteen foot wide, & do it workman-like, & also that he be discharg'd from paying his quitrents two year

Order'd that the register-books that did belong to Wilmington Parish, be carried to, the Rev. Mʳ. Thackers

Order'd that the Ch. wardens, Majʳ. Edwin Daingerfield, Capᵗ. William Hockaday, Mʳ. Lancᵗᵗ. Woodward, Mʳ.

Leonard Henley. & M[r]. John Richardson or any three of them, go with the Surveyor of James City County, & run the line between Blisland Parish and St peters Parish. according to the act of aſsembly

'Tis agreed by this present Vestry that Maj[r]. Edwin Daingerfield have the Sixteen thousand pounds of Tob[o]. that is levied for the Church wall at twelve Shillings & Six pence ℔ hundred, & that The Collector pay it to him by July Court next

    Sign'd By Chicheley Thacker Min[r]
       John Power   } Ch wardens
       Richmond Terrel
   Copia Test. Dudley Williams Cler Vestry
               Order'd

[66]

Order'd by this present Vestry that the Parish levy for this p'ſent year be fifty three & a halfe pounds of Tob[o]. p[r]. poll. & that John Doran Gent. do collect the Said Sum of fifty three & a halfe pounds of Tob[o]. from every Individual titheable person within this Parish and upon refusal of payment to levy the Same by distreſs accord[g]. to Law, the S[d]. John Doran Gent. first entring into Bond with good & Sufficient Security, to the present Vestry of this Parish, for the use of the Parish, for the payment of the S[d]. Sums of Tob[o]. to the Several respective Parish Creditors to whom it is due, by Inspectors notes by the last day of May next, and it is also order'd that the Clark of the Vestry take Bond as afores'd before he deliver a copy of the Parish charge and of the order of Vestry to the Said collector

     Test Dudley Williams Clk. Vestry

[67]

At a vestry held for Blisland Parish at the uper Church the 15th Day of October 1744,

Present,

The Rev. M'. Thacker Cap'. John Power & M' Richmond Terrill Churchwardens, Maj' Edwin Daingerfield, Cap'. William Hockaday, M'. Jeremiah Stanhope, M'. Tho'. Arnott, M'. Lancelott Woodward, M'. Leonard Henley, M'. John Richardson, & M'. John Ruſsel Jun'

This vestry proceeds to lay the Parish Levy

| Blisland Parish | D'. |
|---|---:|
| To the Rev'd M'. Thacker his years Sallery | 16000 |
| To Cask to Ditto | 640 |
| To Tho'. Pettus Clerk of the lower Church 1000 & Cask 40 | 1040 |
| To Dudley Williams Clerk of the uper Church & vestry 1500 & Cask 60 | 1560 |
| To David Gray Sexton at the upper Church 500 & washing the Surplice 70 | 570 |
| To Edward Lively Sexton at the lower Church 500 & washing the Surplice 70 | 570 |
| To the maintainance of Lucy Gills | 624 |
| To the maintainance of John Miller | 300 |
| To the maintainance of Tho'. Lindsey | 624 |
| To the maintainance of David Dormer | 624 |
| To Joseph Lindsey | 500 |
| To Eleanor Pitman | 300 |
| To Maj'. John Dandridge for two copies of the list of Titheables | 36 |
| To M'. Benj'. Waller for one D°. | 18 |
| To the maintainance of Hon'. Moore, to be paid M'". Thornton | 800 |
| To the maintainance of Hon'. Moore 3 months, to be paid Charles Rawson | 200 |
| To Sarah Hawkins for keeping Elizabeth Barker | 700 |
| To Sarah Hawkins for keeping John Hill till this time | 700 |

| | |
|---|---|
| To M$^r$. Richmond Terril for keeping Richard Bull last year | 600 |
| To Francis Day | 1000 |
| To Cap$^t$. John Power four Commun$^s$. | 400 |
| To Cap$^t$. John Power for his cash acco$^t$. £ 6‖9$^s$‖11$^d$ at 9$^s$ ℔ Cent | 1446 |
| To Sarah Tirey | 1000 |
| To M$^r$. Richmond Terrel for 2½ Barrels of corn at 8$^s$ ℔ Barrel | 227 |
| To Keen Foulks | 1000 |
| To Tho$^s$. Oakley | 275 |
| To Tho$^s$. Oakley for cash | 7 |
| To David Pryour for keeping Tho$^s$. Holdcroft's child | 624 |
| To Julius K. Burbidge for Delinq$^{ts}$ | 695 |
| To pay the Surveyor for running the Parish line | 450 |
| | 33530 |
| To 6 p Cent on 33530$^{lt}$ Tob$^o$ for Collecting | 2011 |
| | 35541 |
| D$^o$. C$^r$. By 892 Tythes at 40 ℔ poll | 35680 |
| A Depositium in the Collectors hands of | 139 |

Turn over

Cap$^t$.

[68]

Cap$^t$. William Hockaday Sherriff is appointed Collector for this present year, giving Bond and Security as usual;

Order'd that the Churchwardens agree with Some person to build a Smoak houſe for The Rev. M$^r$. Thacker 12 foot square

M$^r$. Thruston James is appointed a Vestryman in the room of of W$^m$. Baſsett Gen$^t$, Dec'd

M$^r$. David Williams was this day Sworn a Vestryman in the room of John Doran Gen$^t$. Dec'd;

Doctor Tho⁸. Arnott was this day Sworn a Vestryman in the room of Richard Richardson Gen$^t$. Dec'd;

Cap$^t$. John Power, & M$^r$. Richmond Terril are continued Churchwardens for the enſuing year

    Sign'd By C. Thacker Minister
        John Power   ⎫
        Richmond Terril ⎭ Ch Wardens
Copia Test Dudley Williams Cler. Vestry

Tis order'd by this present Vestry that the Parish levy for this present year be forty pounds of Tob°. p. poll & that William Hockaday Gent. do collect the Said Sum of forty pounds of Tob° from every individual Titheable person within this Parish, and upon refusal of payment to levy the Same by distreſs according to Law the Said William Hockaday Gent. first entring into Bond with good and Sufficient Security to the present Vestry of this Parish for the use of the Parish for the paym$^t$. of the Said Sums of Tob°. to the Several respective Parish creditors to whom it is due by Inspectors notes by the last day of May next; and it is also order'd that the Clerk of the Vestry take Bond as aforesaid before he deliver a Copy of the Parish Charge and order of Vestry to the Said Collector

  Test Dudley Williams Clerk of the Vestry

At a Vestry held for Blisland Parish at the upper Church the 23$^d$. day of Sept$^r$. 1745.

Present; the Rev. M$^r$. Thacker; Cap$^t$. John Power, and M$^r$. Richmond Terril, Church Wardens; Maj$^r$. Edwin Daingerfield, Cap$^t$. William Hockaday, M$^r$. Lancelott Woodward. M$^r$. John Richardson, M$^r$. Leonard Henley, M$^r$ John Ruſsel, and M$^r$. Thruston James

M$^r$. Thruston James being chosen a Vestryman the last Vestry, was this day Sworn accordingly

Cap*ᵗ*. Rob*ᵗ*. Pennington is chosen a Vestryman in the room of M*ʳ*. Jer. Stanhope Dec'd

M*ʳ*. Julius K. Burbidge is chosen a Vestryman in the room of M*ʳ*. David Williams Dec'd

'Tis order'd by this present Vestry that the Churchwardens give publick notice (by advertizeing in the Gazetts) that the upper Church in Blisland Parish is to be repair'd as followeth, (Viz.) to be new cover'd with Cypres Shingles & a new floor laid, whitewash'd & painted inside and out, the Church yard wall repair'd, & new gates made

'Tis order'd that the Churchwardens give notice for the workmen to meet the Gent. of the Vestry, the Second Tuesday in Nov*ʳ*. next at the upper Church to agree about repairing the Church

    Sign'd By  C. Thacker Min*ʳ*.

      John Power   } Ch warden
      Richm*ᵈ*. Terrel

Test Dudley Williams Clerk o' the Vestry

At

[69]

At a Vestry held for Blisland Parish at the lower Church the 8th Day of October 1745

Present the Rev. M*ʳ*. Thacker, Cap*ᵗ*. John Power and M*ʳ*. Richmond Terrell Church wardens, Cap*ᵗ*. William Hockaday, Cap*ᵗ*. Robert Pennington, M*ʳ*. Leonard Henley, M*ʳ*. John Richardson, M*ʳ*. Julius King Burbidge and M*ʳ* Thruston James

  This Vestry proceeds to lay the Parish levy

| Blisland Parish | D*ʳ*. |
|---|---|
| To the Rev. M*ʳ*. Thacker his years Sallery 16000 To Cask to D° 640 | 16640 |
| To M*ʳ*. Tho*ˢ*. Pettus Clerk of the lower Church 1000 To Cask to D° 40 | 1040 |

| | |
|---|---:|
| To Dudley Williams Clerk of the upper Church and Vestry 1500 To Cask to D°. 60 | 1560 |
| To David Gray Sexton at the upper Church 500 To Cask to D°. 20 | 520 |
| To Edward Lively Sexton at the lower Church 500 To D°. to D°. 20 To washing Surp'. 50 | 570 |
| To the maintainance of Lucy Gills | 624 |
| To the Ditto of Tho'. Lindsey | 624 |
| To D°. David Dormer | 200 |
| To D°. Joseph Lindsey | 800 |
| To D°. Eleanor Pitman | 300 |
| To D°. David Gray | 150 |
| To D°. Keen Foulks | 500 |
| To D°. Fran'. Day | 1000 |
| To D°. William Fox | 800 |
| To M'. Richard Allen for washing and mending the Surplice | 74 |
| To Maj'. John Dandridge for two Copies of the list of Tithes | 36 |
| To M'. Benj'. Waller for one D°. | 18 |
| To M'. John Merrideth for services done at the glebe | 480 |
| To Cap'. John Power for four Communions | 400 |
| To Keziah Charlton for keeping Elizabeth Barker and her child | 850 |
| To M'. Richmond Terrel for keeping Richard Bull | 600 |
| To D°. his acco'. £ 3‖9' Tob° at 1½ ℔'. pound | 552 |
| To D°. his acco'. for quitrents of the Glebe land two years | 192 |
| To Ballard Dormer for one Tythe overcharg'd | 40 |
| To M'. John Allen | 60 |
| To D°. for James Holdcroft Son of Tho'. Holdcroft | 1000 |
| To David Pryor | 624 |
| To repairing the Church | 13000 |
| | 43354 |

| | |
|---|---:|
| Dº. Cr. By Capt. William Hockaday Parish Collector | 1059 |
| | 42295 |
| Dº. Dr. To 6 ₱ Cent for Collecting 42295ˡˡ Tob | 2537 |
| | 44832 |
| Dº. Cr. By 876 Tythes at 51½ ₱r. poll | 45113 |
| To a Depositium in the Collectors hands | 281 |

Capt

[70]

Capt. William Hockaday and Mr. Thruston James are chosen Church Wardens (in the room of Capt. John Power and Mr. Richmond Terrell) and was Sworn accordingly

Capt. William Hockaday Sherriff and Churchwarden is appointed Collector for the enſueing year giveing Bond and Security as uſual

Order'd by this present Vestry that Susa. Wallis be discharg'd from paying her Parish levy

Order'd that the Rev. Mr. Thacker Send for a Set of Plate for the lower Church

Order'd that the Churchwardens receive five pounds Current money of Capt. Robert Pennington which was given to the poor of the Parish by Capt. William Kenney Dec'd

Agreed with Mr. John Allen that he take James Holdcroft Son of Thoˢ. Holdcroft immediately from David Pryors and keep him clear of any Charge of the Parish in Consideration of which he is to have a thousand pounds of Tobº. the ensuing year

Order'd that Capt. John Power Capt. Robert Pennington and Mr. Julius K. Burbidge meet and proportion the Parish Levy

Order'd that Moll a Negro Woman belonging to Mary Crutchfield be discharg'd from paying her Parish levy

Cap$^t$. Robert Pennington and M$^r$. Julius King Burbidge being chosen Vestrymen last Vestry were this day Sworn accordingly

Order'd that the lower Church be painted inside and out, when the upper Church is painted

   Sign'd By  C Thacker Min$^r$
        William Hockaday Ch warden
        Thruston James Ch warden
 Copy Test  Dudley Williams Clerk o' th' Vestry

'Tis order'd by this present Vestry that the Parish levy for this present year be fifty one and a halfe pounds of Tob°. p. poll and that William Hockaday Gent Sherriff of New Kent County do collect the Said Sum of fifty one pounds and a halfe of Tob°. from every individual Titheable person within this Parish and upon refusal of payment to levy the Same by distreſs according to law the Said W$^m$. Hockaday first entring into Bond with good and Sufficient Security to the present Vestry of this Parish for the use of the Parish for the payment of the Said Sums of Tob°. to the Several respective Parish Creditors to whom it is due by Inspectors notes by the last day of May next, and it is also order'd that the Clerk of the Vestry take Bond as aforesaid before he deliver a Copy of the Parish charge and order of Vestry to the Said Collector

    Test  Dudley Williams Clerk o' the Vestry

                      At

[71]

At a Vestry held for Blisland Parish at the upper Church the 18$^{th}$. day of April 1746

Present, The Rev. M$^r$. Thacker, Cap$^t$ William Hockaday and M$^r$. Thruston James Church Wardens Maj$^r$. Edwin Daingerfield, Cap$^t$. John Power, M$^r$. Lancelott Woodward, M$^r$. Leonard Henley, M$^r$. John Richardson, M$^r$. Richmond

Terrel, Mr. Julius K. Burbidge and Mr. John Ruſsel Junior

Agreed by the Said Vestry that an addition be made to the upper Church in the said Parish as followeth (viz) Thirty three feet long from outside to outside, and twenty three feet wide from outside to outside, and two sash windows on each side the S$^d$. Addition, and a folding door at the end the addition made of brick, (and the Ile laid with brick,) and cover'd with Cypres Shingles, and plaister'd and whitewash'd

Order'd that the Church Wardens give public notice (by advertiseing in the Gazetts) for workmen to meet the Gentlemen of the Vestry the Second Tuesday in May next at the upper Church of the Said Parish to agree about undertakeing the Said Addition

Order'd that the Church Wardens sell the Tob°. which is levied for repairing the Church at publick auction

Mr. Richard Allen is chosen a Vestryman in the room of Mr. Thomas Arnott, and was Sworn accordingly by Majr. Edwin Daingerfield

Order'd that Robert Manning be discharg'd from paying his Parish levy

Order'd that Nicholas Valentine be discharg'd from paying his Parish Levy

Order'd that Isabella Gray be Sexton of the upper Church till laying the next Parish levy

   Sign'd By C Thacker Minr
       William Hockaday ⎫
       Thruston James ⎬ Ch. Wardens
Copy Test Dudley Williams C Vestry

At a Vestry held for Blisland Parish at the upper Church the 9$^{th}$. day of Sepr 1746

Present The Rev: Mr. Thacker, Capt. William Hockaday, and Mr. Thruston James Churchwardens; Capt. Robt.

Pennington, M$^r$. Leonard Henley, M$^r$. John Richardson, M$^r$. Richmond Terrel, & M$^r$. Richard Allen

'Tis order'd that the Church Wardens Sell the Tob°. that is levied for repairing the Church at publick Auction at next New Kent Court and if they cannot get nine Shill$^r$. and Six pence ℔. Cent. for it, it is further order'd that they receive the Tob°. for the uſe of the Parish, and have it repriz'd

    Sign'd By C. Thacker Min$^r$
        William Hockaday Ch Warden
        Thruston James Ch Warden
 Copy Test Dudley Williams Clerk o' th' Vestry
                At

[72]

At a Vestry held for Blisland Parish at the upper Church the 8th day of October 1746

       Present
  The Rev. M$^r$. Thacker Minister
  Cap$^t$ William Hockaday ⎫
  M$^r$ Thruston James   ⎬ Church Wardens
Maj$^r$. Edwin Daingerfield  M$^r$. John Richardson
Cap$^t$. John Power     M$^r$. Richard Allen, and
M$^r$. Lancelott Woodward  M$^r$ Richmond Terrel

This Vestry proceeds to lay the Parish levy
Blisland Parish                D$^r$.
To the Rev. M$^r$. Thacker his Years Sallery 16000$^{ll}$ $^{Tobo}$
 To Cask to D° 640$^{ll}$         16640
To M$^r$. Tho$^s$. Pettus Clerk o' the lower Church 1000
 To Cask to D°. 40          1040
To Dudley Williams Clerk o' the upper Church, & Vestry 1500. To Cask to D°. 60      1560
To Iſabella Gray Sexton of the upper Church 500
 To Cask to D°. 20 To washing Surp$^s$. 50  570
To Edward Lively Sexton of the lower D°. 500 To
 Cask to D°. 20 To washing Surp$^s$. 50   570

| | |
|---|---|
| To the maintainance of Lucy Gills | 624 |
| To Widow Lindsey for Tho⁸. Lindsey | 624 |
| To David Dormer | 250 |
| To Anne Lindsey | 300 |
| To Elenor Pitman | 300 |
| To Keen Foulks | 500 |
| To Francis Day | 1000 |
| To William Fox | 800 |
| To Majʳ. John Dandridge for the list of Tithes | 36 |
| To Mʳ. Ben: Waller for D° | 18 |
| To Capᵗ. William Hockaday for four Communions | 400 |
| To Ditto paid Keziah Charlton, for keeping Elizᵃ. Barker | 850 |
| To Mʳ. Richmond Terrel for keeping Richard Bull | 600 |
| To Capᵗ. William Hockaday for Quitrents of the Glebe land | 144 |
| To Mʳ. John Allen for keeping James Holdcroft Son of Thoˢ. Holdcroft Decd | 1000 |
| To Benjamine Tirey for keeping two of Sarah Tirey's Children | 936 |
| To Majʳ. Edwin Daingerfield for Margarett Gray | 1000 |
| | 29762 |
| Ditto Cʳ. By Capᵗ William Hockaday | 281 |
| | 29481 |
| D°. Dʳ. To 6 ℔ Cent for Collecting 29481¹¹ Tob°. | 1768 |
| | 31249 |
| D°. Cʳ. By 907 Tithes at 34½ ℔ poll | 31291½ |
| A Depositum in the Collector's hands to be accounted for at laying yᵉ. next levy | 42½ |

Capᵗ

[73]

Cap$^t$. William Hockaday and M$^r$. Thruston James are Continued Church Wardens

M$^r$. Gill Armistead D. Sher. is appointed Collector the enſuing Year giving Bond as uſual

M$^r$. Julius K. Burbidge Resign'd being a Vestryman, and M$^r$. William Hogg is Elected in his Stead.

Order'd that the Church Wardens agree with workmen to build a corn houſe on the Glebe

Iſsabella Gray Resign'd being Sexton, John Taylor is Choſen in her Stead

Order'd that M$^r$. Julius K. Burbidges letter of Resignation be recorded in the Vestry book—Which is as follows (Viz)

To The Vestry of Blisland Parish

Gentlemen

I am not inclined to serve as a Vestry Man any longer, therefore deſire you'l Elect one in my Stead, which I wish may be M$^r$. Ratcliffe

I am

Your hble Serv$^t$.

October. 8. 1746              Julius K. Burbidge

Tis order'd by this present Vestry that the Parish levy for this present Year be thirty four and a halfe pounds of Tob$^o$. ℔ poll and that M$^r$. Gill Armistead D Sher. do Collect the S$^d$. Sum of thirty four & a halfe pounds of Tob$^o$. from every individual Titheable person within this Parish, and upon refusal of payment to levy the Same by distreſs according to law the S$^d$. Gill Armistead first entring into Bond with good and Sufficient Security to the present Vestry of this Parish for the uſe of the Parish for the payment of the S$^d$ Sums of Tob$^o$. to the Several Respective Parish Creditors to whom it is due, by Inspectors notes by the last day of May next, and it is also order'd that the Clerk of the Vestry take Bond as aforesaid before he deliver a Copy of the Parish charge and order of Vestry to the S$^d$. Collector

        Sign'd By C Thacker Minister
        William Hockaday } Ch. Wardens
        Thruston James

Copy Test
        Dudley Williams Clerk o' the Vestry

                                                  At

[74]

At A Vestry held for Blisland Parish, at the Lower Church the 14$^{th}$. day of October 1747

                Present

The Rev. M$^r$. Thacker         M$^r$. Leonard Henley
Cap$^t$. William Hockaday )Church   M$^r$. John Richardson
M$^r$ Thruston James    (Wardens   M$^r$. Richmond Terrel
Cap$^t$. Robert Pennington       M$^r$. Richard Allen, and
        M$^r$. William Hogg Gent$^n$.

This Present Vestry proceeds to lay the Parish Levy, Which is as followeth.

| | |
|---|---:|
| Blisland Parish | D$^r$. |
| To the Rev. M$^r$. Thacker, his Years Sallery, 16000$^{lb}$ Tob$^o$. To Cask to D$^o$. 640 | Tob$^o$ lb 16640 |
| To Dudley Williams Clerk of the upper Church & vestry 1500, To Cask to D$^o$. 60 | 1560 |
| To M$^r$. William Slater for Serving as Clerk of the lower Church | 520 |
| To John Taylor Sexton of the upper Church 500. To Cask to D$^o$. 20, To washing the Surplice 50 | 570 |
| To Ditto for Cleaning the Church Yard | 200 |
| To Edward Lively Sexton of the lower Church 500, To Cask to D$^o$. 20, To Washing the Surp$^e$ 50 | 570 |
| To Ditto for mending the Surplice | 50 |
| To Tho$^s$. Oakley for Lucy Gills 800 To Cask to D$^o$. 32 | 832 |

| | |
|---|---|
| To the Maintainance of Tho˚. Linsey | 500 |
| To Anne Linsey | 300 |
| To Elenor Pitman | 500 |
| To Francis Day | 800 |
| To William Fox | 800 |
| To Majʳ. John Dandridge for the List of Tithes 40, other Charges 77 | 117 |
| To Mʳ. Ben: Waller for the list of Tithes | 18 |
| To Capᵗ. William Hockaday for four Communions | 400 |
| To Ditto for Eliz˚. Barker | 140 |
| To Nicholas Valentine for Eliz˚ Barker 637½ To Cask to D˚. 25 | 663 |
| To Mʳ. Richmond Terrel for Richard Bull | 200 |
| To Benjˢ, Tirey for keeping Sarah Tirey's to Children 1,000 To Cask to D˚. 40 | 1040 |
| To Majʳ. Edwin Daingerfield for Margᵗᵗ. Gray | 1000 |
| To Tho˚. Hight for the Support of William Hight | 1000 |
| To Samuel Curll for Grace Hix | 375 |
| To Macoy Williamson for D˚. | 125 |
| To Mʳˢ, Mary Thornton, for her trouble with Mary Reece | 250 |
| To Mʳ. Gill Armistead his Accoᵗ | 421 |
| To John Merrideth his Accoᵗ ( £8‖11‖6½ Tob˚ at 12/6 ⅌ Cᵗ) for building a Cornhouse on the Glebe | 1372 |
| To Prudence Bates | 300 |
| To Martha Pickett | 800 |
| To The Rev. Mʳ. Thacker one Tithe overcharg'd last Year | 34½ |
| To Mʳ Richmond Terrel one Tithe overcharg'd in the Year 1745 | 51½ |
| | 32149 |
| D˚. Cʳ. By Tob˚ in Mʳ. Gill Armistead's hands last Year | 42½ |
| | 32107½ |

| | |
|---|---:|
| D°. D'. To 6 ℔ Ct for Collecting 32107½ℓᵇ Tob° | 1926 |
| | 34033½ |
| D°. C'. By 940 Tithes at 36ˡᵇ ℔ poll | 33840 |
| D°. D'. To the Collector | 193½ |
| | M'. |

[75]

M'. Gill Armistead D She'. is appointed Collector for the Ensuing Year, giving Bond & Security as Uſual

Capᵗ. Robert Pennington, and M' Richard Allen are Chosen Church Wardens in the room of Capᵗ. William Hockaday, & M'. Thruston James, and were Sworn accordingly

Griſsle Henderson is appointed Sexton, in the room of John Taylor

Sign'd By  C Thacker Min'.

Robert Pennington ⎫<br>Richard Allen     ⎬ Ch Wardens<br> 

Copy Test Dudley Williams Clerk O' the Vestry

Memorandum

That at A Vestry held for Blisland Parish at the upper Church the 8ᵗʰ. Day of October 1746. M'. William Hogg was Chosen a Vestryman, in the room of M'. Julius K. Burbidge, and was accordingly Sworn, at the upper Church the 8th Day of September, 1747. by M'. Thruston James.

Test Dudley Williams Clerk O' the Vestry

Tis order'd by this present Vestry that the Parish levy for this present year be thirty Six pounds of Tob°. ℔ poll and that M'. Gill Armistead D. She'. do Collect the Said Sum of thirty Six pounds of Tob°. from every individual Titheable person within this Parish, and upon refusal of payment to levy the Same by

distreſs according to Law the S$^d$. Gill Armist$^d$. first entring into Bond with good & Sufficient Security to the present Vestry of this Parish, for the use of the Parish for the paym$^t$. of the S$^d$. Sums of Tob$^o$. to the Several respective Parish Creditors to whom it is due, by Inspectors notes by the last day of May next; and it is also order'd that the Clerk of the Vestry take Bond as aforesaid, before he deliver a Copy of the Parish Charge & order of Vestry to the Said Collector
   Test
      Dudley Williams Clerk of the Vestry

                At

[76]
At A Vestry held for Blisland Parish, at the upper Church the 14$^{th}$. Day of October 1748.

       Present
| | |
|---|---|
| The Rev. M$^r$. Thacker | M$^r$. John Richardſon |
| M$^r$. Richard Allen, Churchwarden | M$^r$. Lancelott Woodward |
| Cap$^t$. William Hockaday | M$^r$. Richmond Terrel |
| Cap$^t$. John Power | M$^r$. Thruston James |
| M$^r$. Leonard Henley | M$^r$. John Ruſsel & |

      M$^r$ William Hogg

This Vestry proceeds to lay the Parish Levy
Blisland Parish                D$^r$.
To the Rev. M$^r$ Thacker, his Years Sallery 16000$^{lb\ Tob^o}$. lb Tob$^o$
 To Cask to d$^o$. 640           16640
To M$^r$ William Slater Clark of the lower Church 1000 &
 Cask to d$^o$. 40            1040
To D$^o$. for one Month not alow'd in last years Acco$^t$.  83
To Dudley Williams Clark of the upper Church & Vestry
 1500. & Cask            1560
To John Gaddey Sexton of the upper Church 500. & Cask
 20                520

| | |
|---|---:|
| To Edward Lively Sexton of the lower Church 500 & Cask. & washing Surp⁸. | 570 |
| To the Maintainance of Lucy Gills 800. & Cask 32 | 832 |
| To the Maintainance of Thomas Lindsey | 500 |
| To the Maintainance of Anne Lindsey | 500 |
| To the Maintainance of Elenor Pitman | 600 |
| To the Maintainance of Francis Day | 800 |
| To the Maintainance of William Fox | 800 |
| To Majʳ. John Dandridge for the list of Tithes | 32 |
| To Mʳ. Benjᵃ. Waller for Dᵒ. | 18 |
| To Mʳˢ. Ann Pennington, for four Communions | 400 |
| To Prudence Fisher, for Elizᵃ. Barker | 700 |
| To Ditto for John Hill | 300 |
| To Ditto for Cloathing John Hill 19ˢ. Tobᵒ. at 12/6 | 152 |
| To Benjamine Tyree, for Keeping Sarah Tyree's two Children | 1040 |
| To the Maintainance of Margarett Gray | 1000 |
| To Gristle Henderson, for Grace Hix | 800 |
| To Mʳ. Gill Armistead his Accᵗ. | 697 |
| To James Jones, for Prudence Bates | 300 |
| To Martha Pickett | 800 |
| To Majʳ. John Dandridge | 27 |
| To Mʳ. Samuel Woodward for Rite Roberts | 500 |
| To Dᵒ. for Richard Creed Curll | 200 |
| To Mʳˢ. Ann Pennington for 1 Tithe overcharg'd last year | 36 |
| To Mʳ. Richmond Terrel for Corn for Jane Henry 20/ Tobᵒ. at 12/ | 166 |
| To Mʳ. John Chandler for Corn for Mary Laffoon 10/ Tobᵒ. at 12/ | 83 |
| To Mʳ. Richard Allen his Accᵗ | 295 |
| To Joſiah Maples | 500 |
| To Mʳ. Jeremiah Taylor 1 Tithe overcharg'd in 1746 | 35 |
| | 32526 |

| | |
|---|---|
| To 6 ⅌. Cent for Collecting 32526ˡᵇ Tobᵒ. | 1951 |
| | 34477 |
| Dᵒ. Cʳ. By 942 Tithes at 36½ ⅌. poll | 34383 |
| The Collector Dʳ. to the Parish | 94 |

Capᵗ.

[77]

Capᵗ. William Hockaday and Mʳ. Richard Allen are Chosen Churchwardens for the enſuing Year, & accordingly Sworn

Mʳ. Francis Ratcliffe, and Mʳ. Isaac Goddin, were choſen Veſtrymen, in the Stead of Majʳ. Edwin Daingerfield, and Capᵗ. Robert Pennington dec'd, and Mʳ. Isaac Goddin was accordingly Sworn.

Order'd that the Church wardens receive the money that was given by Capᵗ. William Kenney to this Parish for a piece of Plate, for the Church

Mʳ. John Richardson Sher. is appointed Collector for the enſuing Year, on his giving Bond & Security as Uſual

'Tis order'd by this preſent Veſtry that the Parish Levy for this preſent Year be Thirty Six & a half pounds of Tobacco ⅌ poll, and that John Richardson Gent. Sheriff of New Kent County do Collect the Said Sum of Thirty Six pounds and a half pounds of Tobacco from every Individual Titheable perſon within this Parish and upon refusal of payment to levy the Same by distreſs according to Law the Said Richardſon first entring into Bond with good and Sufficient Security to the preſent Veſtry of this Parish for the use of the Parish for the payment of the Said Sums of Tobᵒ. to the Sev'ral Parish Creditors to whom it is due by Inſpectors Notes by the last day of May Next. And it is also order'd that the Clark of the Vestry take Bond as aforesaid before he deliver a Copy of the Parish Charge and Order of Vestry to the Said Collector

    Sign'd By C. Thacker Min'.
         William Hockaday ⎱ Church Wardens
         Richard Allen ⎰

Copy Test

    Dudley Williams, Clark of the Vestry

               At

[78]

At a Vestry held for Blisland Parish at the lower Church the 10ᵗʰ. day of October 1749

     Present

Cap'. William Hockaday ⎱ Church  M'. Richmond Terrel
M'. Richard Allen  ⎰ Wardens M'. Thruston. James
Cap'. John Power       M'. John Ruſsel
M'. Leonard Henley      M'. Iſaac Goddin

  And M'. Francis Ratcliffe who was This
   day Sworn, before the Vestry Set.

This Vestry ℔roceeds to lay the Parish-levy
Blisland Parish            Dʳ

                ᵗᵇ Tobᵒ.

To The Rev. M'. Thacker his Sallery 16000. To Cask to
 Ditto 640            16640
To M'. William Slater Clark of the lower Church 1000.
 To Cask to D°. 40         1040
To Dudley Williams Clark of the upper Church & Vestry
 1500. To Cask to D°. 60      1560
To Edward Lively Sexton of the lower Church 500. &
 Cask 20. And washing y°. Surp'. 100  620

| | |
|---|---:|
| To John Gaddey Sexton of the upper Church 500. & Cask 20. And washing yᵉ. Surpˢ. 100 | 620 |
| To the Maintainance of Lucy Gills 800. & Cask 32 | 832 |
| To the Maintainance of Thomas Linsey | 500 |
| To the Maintainance of Anne Linsey | 500 |
| To the Maintainance of Elenor Pitman | 600 |
| To Francis Day | 800 |
| To William Fox | 800 |
| To Majʳ. John Dandridge for two Copies of the list of Tithes | 36 |
| To Mʳ. Ben: Waller for one Dº. | 18 |
| To Capᵗ. William Hockaday for four Communions | 400 |
| To William Fisher, for keeping Elizᵗ. Barker 2000 And Cask 80 | 2080 |
| To Capᵗ. William Hockaday, for the use of John Taylor's family | 600 |
| To Burnal Jones, for his trouble with Grace Hix | 300 |
| To James Jones, the Balˢ. of his Accoᵗ. for his trouble with Prudence Bates | 228 |
| To Martha Picket | 800 |
| To Mʳ. Samuel Woodward, for his trouble with Rite Roberts | 400 |
| To Josiah Maples | 200 |
| To Capᵗ. William Hockaday, for the use of Richard Gilmett | 700 |
| To James Wade, for keeping Hannah Bowles | 400 |
| To James Wade, for his trouble with Rite Roberts | 100 |
| To Capᵗ. William Hockaday the Balˢ. of his Accoᵗ, £15‖6‖3½. Tobº. at 12/6 | 2450 |
| To Mʳˢ Sarah Timberlake, for keeping Sarah Tyrees two Children ten Months | 866 |
| To Mʳ. Thruston James, the Balˢ. of his Accoᵗ. £1‖16‖6 Tobº. at 12/6 | 292 |

To M`r`. Richard Allen his Acco`t`, £1||13||8 Tob°. at 12/6    269
To M`rs`. Hannah Daingerfield her Acco`t`, £—||18`s`||—`d`
　Tob°, at 12/6    144
To M`r`. Richmond Terrel for two Barrels of Corn
　£1. Tob`s`. at 12/6    160

34955

At
[79]

At a Vestry held for Blisland Parish, at the upper Church, the 31`st`. day of October 1749.

### Present

| Cap`t`. W`m` Hockaday ⎫ Church | M`r`. John Richardson |
| M`r`. Richard Allen ⎰ wardens | M`r`. Thruston James |
| Cap`t`. John Power | M`r`. Isaac Goddin & |

M`r`. Francis Ratcliffe

This Vestry Proceeds to Conclude laying the Parish Levy. And to Receive the Procefsioners Returns

　Blisland Parish    D`r`.
                                                  lb Tobacco
To Debt brought over from the other Side, dated Octo-
　ber the 10`th`. 1749.    34955
To M`r`. Gill Armistead his Acco`t`. for Delinquents    779
To M`r`. Gill Armistead his Acco`t`. Cash £5||2||4 Tob°
　at 12/6    818½
To M`rs`. Hannah Daingerfield for 20 Bushels of lyme
　for the Glebe 10/ Tob°. at 12/6    80
To M`r`. William Hogg for a Barrel of Corn for Rich`d`.
　Gilmett 10/ Tob°. at D°    80

| | |
|---|---:|
| To James Wade for burying Hannah Bowles, & a further allowance for her Maint<sup>c</sup>. | 400 |
| To Edward Valentine for building a Henhouſe on the Glebe £4\|\| Tob°. at 12/6 | 640 |
| To Nicholas Valentine Senior | 400 |

| | lb Tob°. |
|---|---:|
| | 38152½ |
| To 6 ₩ Cent for Collecting 38152½ | 2289 |
| | 40441½ |
| Ditto C<sup>r</sup>. By Bal<sup>a</sup>. in M<sup>r</sup>. Gill Armistead's hands last year | 94 |

| | lb Tob°. |
|---|---:|
| | 40347½ |
| By 955 Tithes at 42½ ₩ Poll | 40587½ |

Deposited in the Collector's hands, till laying the next Parish Levy    240

Order'd by this Present Vestry, that Cap<sup>t</sup>. W<sup>m</sup> Hockaday, Cap<sup>t</sup>. John Power, and M<sup>r</sup> Iſaac Goddin (or any two of them) Agree with a Workman to build a fram'd Veſtryhouſe, on the Land of M<sup>r</sup> Iſaac Goddin, twelve by Sixteen, with a brick Chimney, & underpinn'd with brick; floor'd with Plank, & Shingl'd; & Ciel'd below Joiſt; & lath'd, & plaister'd. And that they get a lawful Deed of the S<sup>d</sup>. Iſaac Goddin for half an Acre of land to Set the Said houſe on, before they agree with a Workman, to build the S<sup>d</sup>. houſe for the uſe of this Parish. To be Compleated before the laying the Next Parish Levy. And the charge thereof to be levied at the laying the next Parish Levy

M<sup>r</sup>. John Richardson Sheriff is appointed Collector the Enſuing Year, giving Bond and Security as uſual

M<sup>r</sup>. Iſaac Goddin, and M<sup>r</sup>. Francis Ratcliffe are Choſen Church Wardens in the Stead of Cap<sup>t</sup>. William Hockaday, & M<sup>r</sup>. Richard Allen, and Accordingly Sworn

Order'd that the Clark of the Vestry Record the Sev'ral Returns of the Proceſsioners.

Sign'd By Iſaac Goddin } Church Wardens
Francis Ratcliffe

Copy Test

Dudley Williams Clark o' the Vestry

'Tis

[80]

'Tis order'd by this present Vestry, that the Parish Levy for this present Year be forty two and a half pounds of Tob°. ⅌. Poll. And that John Richardson Gent. Sheriff of New Kent County do Collect the S$^d$. Sum of forty two and a half pounds of Tob°. from every Individual Titheable Perſon within this Parish; and on refusal of Payment to levy the Same by distreſs according to Law. The S$^d$. John Richardson first entring into Bond with good & Sufficient Security to the Present Vestry of this Parish, for the use of the Parish, for the Payment of the S$^d$. Sums of Tob°., to the Sev'ral respective Parish Creditors, to whom it is due by Inspectors Notes by the last day of May next. And it is also Order'd that the Clark of the Vestry take Bond as aforesaid, before he deliver a Copy of the Parish Charge and Order of Vestry to the Said Collector

Teſt   Dudley Williams Clark o' the Vestry

At a Vestry held for Blisland Parish at the upper Church the 18$^{th}$ day of May 1750.

Preſent

The Rev. M$^r$. Thacker              M$^r$. Richmond Terrel
M$^r$. Francis Ratcliffe Church Warden   M$^r$. Richard Allen
Cap$^t$. William Hockaday            M$^r$. Thruston James
M$^r$. John Richardson                       and
M$^r$. Leonard Henley                M$^r$. William Hogg

The Petition of M<sup>r</sup>. George Baker praying that his Negro Girl (who thro. the infirmity of nature is render'd incapable of doing any Service) be exempted Paying her Parish Levy, which Said Petition is granted by the Vestry.

William Garland (on his Petition to be discharg'd from paying his Parish Levy) is discharg'd from paying his Parish Levy

M<sup>r</sup>. John Shermer is Choſen a Vestryman in the room of M<sup>r</sup>. Lancelot Woodward deceas'd

              Sign'd By C. Thacker Min<sup>r</sup>.
                    Francis Ratcliffe Ch. Warden
  Copy Test    Dudley Williams Clark o' the Vestry

[81]

At a Vestry held for Blisland Parish at the upper Church the 9<sup>th</sup>. day of October 1750.

### Present

The Rev. M<sup>r</sup>. Thacker        Cap<sup>t</sup>. Thruston James
M<sup>r</sup>. Francis Ratcliffe ⎫ Church   M<sup>r</sup>. Leonard Henley
M<sup>r</sup>. Iſaac Goddin   ⎭ Wardens  M<sup>r</sup>. Richmond Terrel
Maj<sup>r</sup>. John Power             M<sup>r</sup>. Richard Allen, &
Cap<sup>t</sup>. William Hockaday      M<sup>r</sup>. William Hogg
Cap<sup>t</sup>. John Richardson

This Vestry Proceeds to lay the Parish Levy: (Viz<sup>t</sup>.)

| Blisland Parish | D<sup>r</sup> |
|---|---|
| | lb Tob<sup>o</sup>. |
| To the Rev. M<sup>r</sup>. Thacker's Sallery 16000. To Cask to Ditto at 4 ℔ C<sup>t</sup>. 640 | 16640 |
| To M<sup>r</sup>. William Slater Clark of the lower Church 1000. To Cask to D<sup>o</sup>. 40 | 1040 |
| To Dudley Williams Clark of the upper Church & Vestry 1500. To Cask to D<sup>o</sup>. 60 | 1560 |

| | |
|---|---|
| To John Gaddey Sexton of the upper Church 500. & Cask 20. & washing the Surplice 100 | 620 |
| To Edward Lively Sexton of the lower Church 500. & Cask 20 & washing the Surplice 100 | 620 |
| To the Maintainance of Lucy Gills 600 & Cask 24 | 624 |
| To the Maint˚. of Tho˚. Linsey | 375 |
| To the Maint˚. of Ann Linsey | 400 |
| To the Maint˚. of Elenor Pitman | 500 |
| To the Maint˚. of Francis Day | 600 |
| To the Maint˚. of William Fox | 600 |
| To Majr. John Dandridge Clark of N. Kent Court for two Copies of th' list o' Tithes | 36 |
| To Ditto his Accot agt. the Parish on Accot of Frances Henry | 100 |
| To Mr. Iſaac Goddin, for four Communions | 400 |
| To Mr. Benjn. Waller Clark of James City County Court for a Copy of the list o' Tithes | 18 |
| To Sarah Fisher, for keeping Eliza. Barker | 2000 |
| To Prudence Fisher, for keeping John Hill | 875 |
| To Mr. Samuel Woodward, for keeping Richard Creed Curll, 2 Months & 6 Days | 440 |
| To Capt. Wm. Hockaday for the uſe of John Taylor's family | 450 |
| To Martha Pickett | 600 |
| To Joſiah Maples | 400 |
| To Richard Gilman | 525 |
| To Mrs. Sarah Timberlake, for keeping Sarah Tyree's two Children | 500 |
| To Nicholas Valentine Senr | 300 |
| To John Lyon Constable, for moving Tho˚. Lucas's Child to Mr. John Tyler's in James City Parish | 40 |
| To John Wall | 300 |
| To Mr. Frans. Ratcliffe, his Acco t. £3‖2s.‖5d. levied in Tob˚. at 15/ ℔ 100 | 416 |

| | |
|---|---|
| To M$^r$. Iſaac Goddin, his Acco$^t$. £6‖7‖6 D°—D°. at 15/ ℔ 100 | 850 |
| To M$^r$. W$^m$. Slater, for making a Coffin for Margarett Gray 10/ Levied in Tob°. at 15/ ℔ 100 | 66 |
| To M$^r$. Richmond Terrel his Acco$^t$. £3‖18‖3½ levied in Tob°. at 15/ ℔ 100 | 521 |
| To M$^r$. William Armistead his Acco$^t$. for Delinquents | 214 |
| To Cap$^t$. W$^m$. Hockaday, for a Lawyer's fee Employ'd ag$^{st}$. Fra$^s$. Henry 15/ | 100 |
| To M$^{rs}$. Daingerfield, for two Levies overcharg'd last Year 42½ Each | 85 |
| To Matthew Cole, for one Tithe overcharg'd in the year 1748 | 36½ |
| To Benj$^a$. Haselwood, for building a Quarter on the Glebe £10: Levied in Tob° at 15/ | 1333 |
| | 34184½ |
| Ditto C$^r$. By Bal$^e$. in M$^r$. William Armistead's hands last Year | 240 |
| | 33944½ |
| D°. D$^r$. To 6 ℔ C$^t$. for Collecting 33,944½$^{lb\ Tob°}$. | 2036 |
| | 35980½ |
| D°. C$^r$. By 944 Tithes at 38$^{lb}$ Tob°. ℔. Poll | 35872 |
| Balance Due to the Collector | 108½ |

M$^r$

[82]

M$^r$. William Armistead is appointed Collector the Enſuing Year, giving Bond & Security as Uſual

M$^r$. Francis Ratcliffe, & M$^r$. Iſaac Goddin, are Continued Church Wardens.

The Order of Vestry which was made for building a Vestry-houſe last Year, is Continued.

Sign'd By  C Thacker Min<sup>r</sup><br>
Fra<sup>s</sup>. Ratcliffe. C. W.<br>
Iſaac Goddin C. W.<br>
Test   Dudley Williams, Clark o' the Vestry

'Tis Order'd by this present Vestry, that the Parish Levy for this present year be Thirty Eight Pounds of Tob°. ℔ Poll; And that M<sup>r</sup>. W<sup>m</sup>. Armistead Deputy Sheriff in New Kent County do Collect the S<sup>d</sup>. Sum of Thirty Eight Pounds of Tob°. from ev'ry Individual Titheable Perſon within this Parish; And on refuſal of Payment to levy the Same by distreſs according to Law. The S<sup>d</sup>. W<sup>m</sup>. Armistead first Ent'ring into Bond with good and Sufficient Security to Preſent Vestry of this Parish, for the uſe of the Parish, for the Payment of the S<sup>d</sup>. Sums of Tob°. to the Sev'ral reſpective Parish Creditors to Whom it is due, by Inſpectors Notes, by the last day of May next. And it is also Order'd, that the Clark of the Vestry take Bond as aforesaid, before he deliver a Copy of the Parish Charge & Order of Vestry to the Said Collector

Test   Dudley Williams. Clark o' the Vestry

At a Vestry held for Blisland Parish, at the lower Church, March the 6<sup>th</sup>. 1750.

Present

| | |
|---|---|
| The Rev. M<sup>r</sup>. Thacker | Cap<sup>t</sup>. John Richardson |
| M<sup>r</sup>. Isaac Goddin, Ch. Warden | M<sup>r</sup>. Leonard Henley |
| Maj<sup>r</sup>. John Power | M<sup>r</sup>. Richard Allen |
| Cap<sup>t</sup>. William Hockaday | Cap<sup>t</sup>. Thruston James, and |

M<sup>r</sup>. William Hogg.

M<sup>r</sup>. Gill Armistead is Chosen a Vestryman, in the room of M<sup>r</sup>. Francis Ratcliffe deceas'd

Mr. William Hogg is Chosen Church Warden, in the room of Mr. Francis Ratcliffe deceas'd, and was Accordingly Sworn

'Tis Order'd by this Prefent Vestry, that the Parish Collector keep the Tob°. in his hands, which was levied for Benjª. Haselwood, for building a Quarter on the Glebe, till he has Compleated the Same

Sign'd By   C. Thacker Minr
Ifaac Goddin, Ch. Warden
William Hogg Ch. Warden

Test  Dudley Williams Clark of the Vestry

At

[83]

At a Vestry held for Blisland Parish at the lower Church, the 16th. Day of October 1751.

Prefent

| | |
|---|---|
| The Rev. Mr. Thacker | Capt. John Richardson |
| Mr. Isaac Goddin ⎫ Ch. | Mr. Leonard Henley |
| Mr. William Hogg ⎭ Wardens | Mr. Richmond Terrel |
| Majr. John Power | Capt. Thruston James |
| Capt. William Hockaday | Mr. Richard Allen |

Mr John Rufsel

Mr. John Shermer ⎫
Mr. Gill Armistead ⎭ Were both Sworn this day

Blisland Parish   Dr

| | lb Tobo |
|---|---|
| To the Rev. Mr. Thacker his Sallery 16000lb. To Cask at 4 ℔ Ct. 640. To 4 ℔ Ct. on 16000 for Shrinkage 640 | 17280 |
| To Mr. John Burnett Clark of the upper Church 1000 & 4 ℔ Ct. for Cask 40 | 1040 |
| To Dudley Williams Clark of the lower Church & Vestry 1500, & 4 ℔ Ct. for Cask 60 | 1560 |

| | |
|---|---|
| To John Gaddey Sexton of the upper Church 500 & 4 ℔ C$^t$. on D$^o$. 20. To D$^o$. for washing the Surplice 100 | 620 |
| To Edward lively Sexton of the lower Church 500 & 4 ℔ C$^t$. on D$^o$. 20. To D$^o$. for washing the Surplice 100 | 620 |
| To the Maintainance of Lucy Gills | 600 |
| To the Maintainance of Thomas Linsey | 400 |
| To Elenor Pitman | 600 |
| To Francis Day | 600 |
| To M$^r$. Ben. Waller, for the List of Tithes | 18 |
| To M$^r$. Isaac Goddin for four Communions | 400 |
| To M$^r$. Benj$^a$. Tyree for keeping two of Sarah Tyrees Children two Months in the Year 1749 | 163 |
| To M$^r$. Isaac Goddin, for Eliz$^a$. Barker 1500 & Cask to D$^o$. 60 | 1560 |
| To William Hawkins for keeping John Hill one Month | 100 |
| To Cap$^t$. William Hockaday, for Stephen Jones's keeping Ruth Brooks | 600 |
| To Sarah Fisher, for Cloathing for Eliz$^a$. Barker in the Year 1749 | 250 |
| To James Charles, for keeping Richard Creed Curll | 500 |
| To Cap$^t$. William Hockaday, for John Taylor's family | 800 |
| To Martha Pickett | 800 |
| To Richard Gilman | 800 |
| To Nicholas Valentine Sen$^r$. | 600 |
| To Mary Farthing, for the Maintainance of her Child | 300 |
| To Benj$^a$. Haselwood for keeping his Father one Month | 83 |
| To M$^r$. Richmond Terrel, for keeping Howard Burdett one Month which he was not paid for | 100 |
| To M$^{rs}$. Mary Baker, for one Tithe Overcharg'd in 1749 | 42½ |
| To M$^{rs}$. Daingerfield, for work at the Glebe & Lyme 12/ Levied in Tob$^o$. at 15/ ℔ 100 | 80 |

| | |
|---|---:|
| To William Fisher, for keeping Howard Burdett One Month & a halfe | 105 |
| To D°. his Acco' for burying D°. 7/10½ levied in Tob°. at 15/ ℔ 100 | 52 |
| To M'. William Hogg his Acco'. £9‖9‖8 Levied in Tob°. at 15/ ℔ 100 | 1263 |
| To M'. Isaac Goddin his Acco', 7‖1‖1½ Levi'd in Tob°. at 15/ ℔ 100 | 940 |
| To M'. Lewis Delony his Acco' £19‖2‖5 Levied in Tob°. at 15/ ℔ 100. to be in the hands of Cap'. W". Hockaday. Cap'. John Richardson, & M'. Gill Armistead till M'. Delony renders a Satisfactory Acco'. to them ag". the Parish | 2549 |
| To M'". Hanah Crittenden, her Acco'. for W". Jeffers £2‖8 levied in Tob°. at 15/ ℔ 100 | 320 |
| To M'. William Armistead, the Bal'. of his Acco'. | 270½ |
| | 36016 |
| D°. C'. By Dudley Williams, for Rent of the Glebe 35/ levied in Tob°. at 15/ ℔ 100 | 233 |
| | 35783 |
| D°. D'. To 6 ℔ Cent for Collecting 35783<sup>lb Tob°.</sup> | 2146 |
| | 37929 |
| Deposited in the Collector's hands, to be by him Paid to the Parish at laying the next levy | 431 |
| | 38360 |
| D°. C'. By 959 Tithes at 40<sup>lb</sup> Tob°. ℔. Tithe | 38360 |

M'. William Armistead, is appointed Collector the Ensuing Year, on giving Bond & Security as uſual.

M' John Shermer is appointed Church Warden (with M'.

W^m. Hogg) In the Stead of M^r. Isaac Goddin, & was accordingly Sworn

    Sign'd By  C. Thacker Min^r
          William Hogg ⎫ Church Wardens
          John Shermer ⎭

    Test: Dudley Williams Clark o' the Vestry

'Tis

[84]

'Tis Order'd by this Present Vestry that the Parish Levy for this present Year be Forty Pounds of Tob°. p. poll And that M^r. W^m. Armistead Deputy Sheriff in New Kent County do Collect the S^d. Sum of Forty pounds of Tob°. from ev'ry Individual Titheable Perſon within this Parish, and on refusal of payment to levy the Same by distreſs According to Law. The S^d. W^m. Armistead first Ent'ring into Bond with good & Sufficient Security to the present Vestry of this Parish, for the uſe of the Parish for the payment of the S^d. Sums of Tob°. to the Sev'ral respective Parish Creditors to whom it is due, by Inspectors Notes by the last day of May next. And it is also Order'd that the Clark of the Vestry take Bond as aforesaid, before he deliver a Copy of the Parish Charge and Order of Vestry to the Said Collector.

    Test  Dudley Williams Clark o' the Vestry

At

[85]

At a Vestry held for Blisland Parish at the upper Church October the 3^d. 1752.

        Present

The Rev. M^r. Thacker    M^r. Leonard Henley
M^r. John Shermer ⎫ Church  M^r. Richmond Terrell
M^r. William Hogg ⎭ Wardens M^r. Richard Allen
Cap^t. William Hockaday   M^r. Isaac Goddin &
Cap^t. John Richardson    M^r. Gill Armistead

This Vestry Proceeds to lay the Parish Levy
Blisland Parish                                                   D$^r$.

| | lb Tob°. |
|---|---:|
| To the Rev. M$^r$. Thacker his Sallary 16000$^{lb}$ & 4 ⍩ C$^t$. on d°. 640 & 4 ⍩ C$^t$. on d°. for Shrinkage 640 | 17280 |
| To M$^r$. John Burnett Clark of the upper Church 1000 & Cask on d°. 40 | 1040 |
| To Dudley Williams Clark of the lower Church & Vestry 1500 & Cask on d°. 60 | 1560 |
| To John Gaddey Sexton of the upper Church 500 & Cask on d°. 20. & Washing the Surplice 100 | 620 |
| To Edward Lively Sexton of the lower Church 500 & Cask on d°. 20 & Washing the Surplice 100 | 620 |
| To the Maint$^n$. of Lucy Gills | 750 |
| To Ann Linsey | 600 |
| To Thomas Linsey | 400 |
| To Cap$^t$. William Hockaday for finding Ann Linsey last Year | 600 |
| To M$^r$. John Shermer for finding Elenor Pitman last Year | 600 |
| To Ditto for Ditto this Year | 600 |
| To M$^r$. Ben: Waller for a Copy of the List of Tithes | 18 |
| To Maj$^r$. John Dandridge for two Copies of the list of Tithes last year & two d°. this year | 72 |
| To M$^r$. John Shermer for four Commun$^s$. | 400 |
| To D°. his Acco$^t$. for his Orders ⍩ Keziah Charlton £10 levied in Tob°. at 13/ ⍩ 100 | 1538 |
| To D°. paid Doctor Ken. Mackenzie's Acco$^t$. for John Swiney £1∥12∥6 ⎫ £. s. d. To D°. paid D°. his Acco$^t$. for ⎬ 3∥2∥6 in Tob° at 13/ Suf$^a$. Thomas 1∥10∥ ⎭ | 480 |
| To Stephen Jones for keeping Ruth Brooks one Month | 60 |
| To Cap$^t$. William Hockaday for John Taylor's family | 800 |
| To Martha Piggett | 800 |
| To Richard Gilman in the Churchwarden's hands | 800 |
| To Nicholas Valentine Sen$^r$. | 600 |

| | |
|---|---:|
| To M$^r$. William Hogg's Acco$^t$. £3\|8$^s$·\|—$^d$· ¾ levied in Tob°. at 13/ ℔ 100 | 523 |
| To Cap$^t$. William Hockaday's Acco$^{ts}$. deliver'd to the Vestry £6\|—$^s$·\|11¼$^d$· Tob°. at 13/ | 930 |
| To M$^r$. John Burnett's Acco$^t$. £3\|17\| in Tob°. at 13/ | 592 |
| To Doctor William Harwood's three Acco$^{ts}$. deliver'd to the Vestry £3\|16$^s$·\|9$^d$· Tob°. at 13/ | 590 |
| To Tho$^s$. Ratcliff's Acco$^t$. for Corn for Ann Brown £—\|10$^s$·\|—$^d$·\| in Tob°. at 13/ | 76 |
| To Tho$^s$. Oakley for his trouble & Charge with Ruth Brooks dec'd £1\|17\|— Tob°. at 13/ | 284 |
| To M$^r$. William Armistead for delinquents | 140 |
| To John Gaddey for keeping James Brown Son of James Brown dec'd last year | 500 |
| To the Support of John Gilman in the Church Warden's hands | 400 |
| To the Rev. M$^r$. Thacker for building a Dairy, & lathing the Quarter on the Glebe | 500 |
| | 34773 |

Blisland Parish C$^r$

| | |
|---|---:|
| By M$^r$. William Armistead deposited in his hands last year 431 $^{lb}$ | |
| By D° for Tob° levied for Elenor Pitman last year 600 } 1031 | 1031 |
| D°. D$^r$. | 33742 |
| To 6. ℔. Cent for Collecting 33742$^{lb}$ Tob°. | 2024 |
| | 35766 |
| Deposited in the Collector's hands, to be by him paid to the Parish at laying next Levy | 159 |

| | |
|---|---:|
| D°. C$^r$. By 958 Tithes at 37½ ℔. Poll | 35925 |

M$^r$. Gill Armistead, M$^r$ William Armistead, & Dudley Williams, are appointed to meet & proportion the Parish Levy on or before the last day of October.

John Sheriff on his Pettition is discharg'd from paying his Parish Levy.

The Church Wardens are appointed to Send for a Sett of Plate for the Parish, & to Receive Cap$^t$. William Kenney's Legacy in Part of Payment for the Same.

M$^r$.

[86]

M$^r$. Gill Armistead is Chofen Church Warden (in the Stead of M$^r$. William Hogg) With M$^r$. John Shermer & this day Sworn Accordingly.

M$^r$. William Armistead is appointed Collector the Enfuing Year on giving Bond & Security as Ufual.

Sign'd By   C. Thacker. Min$^r$.
John Shermer ⎫
G$^l$. Armistead ⎬ Church Wardens

Test.
Dudley Williams. Clerk o' the Vestry.

Pursuant to an Order o' Vestry of Blisland Parish, We the Subfcriber have met and Proportioned the Parish Levie for the Enfuing year & find it to be Thirty Seven and a half Pounds of Tobacco ℔ Poll. January 6th 1753/

William Armistead
G$^l$. Armistead
Dudley Williams

'Tis Order'd by this Present Vestry that the Parish Levy for this present Year be Thirty Seven & one half Pounds of Tobacco ℔. Poll. and that M$^r$. William Armistead D. Sheriff in New Kent County do Collect the S$^d$. Sum of Thirty Seven &

one half Pounds of Tob°. from ev'ry Individual Titheable Perſon within this Parish, And on refusal of Payment to Levy the Same by distreſs According to Law. The S⁴. William Armistead first Entr'ing into Bond with good & Sufficient Security to the Present Vestry of this Parish for the uſe of the Parish, for the Payment of the S⁴. Sums of Tob°. to the Sev'ral respective Parish Creditors to whom it is due, by Inspectors notes by the last day of May next. And it is also Order'd that the Clark of the Vestry take Bond as aforesaid before he deliver a Copy of the Parish Charge and Order of Vestry to the Said Collector.

Test    Dudley Williams Clark o' the Vestry

At

[87]

At a Vestry held for Blisland Parish at the lower Church October the 9ᵗʰ. 1753.

### Present

The Rev. Mʳ. Thacker               Majʳ. John Power
Mʳ. John Shermer ⎫ Church          Majʳ. John Richardson
Mʳ. Gill Armistead ⎭ Wardens       Capᵗ. Thruston James &
Majʳ. William Hockaday             Mʳ. William Hogg

This Vestry proceeds to lay the Parish Levy

Blisland Parish    Dʳ.

| | lb Tob°. |
|---|---|
| To the Rev. Mʳ. Thacker's Sallary 16000ˡᵇ Tob. & 4 p. Cᵗ. for Cask 640ˡᵇ & 4 ⅌ Cᵗ. for Shrinkage 640ˡᵇ. | 17280 |
| To Mʳ. John Burnett Clark of the upper Church 1000. & 4 ⅌. Cᵗ. for Cask 40 | 1040 |
| To Dudley Williams Clark of the lower Church & Vestry 1500. & 4 ⅌ Cᵗ. for Cask 60 | 1560 |
| To John Gaddey dec'd Sexton of the upper Church 500 & Cask 20. & for washing the Surplice 100 | 620 |
| To Edward Lively Sexton of the lower Church 500 & Cask 20. & for washing the Surplice 100 | 620 |

| | |
|---|---|
| To John Ball, for the Maintainance of Lucy Gills | 600 |
| To Ann Linsey | 600 |
| To Thomas Linsey | 400 |
| To Thomas Jones for keeping Eliz$^a$. Williams | 600 |
| To Elenor Pitman | 600 |
| To M$^r$. Ben: Waller for a Copy of the List of Tithes | 18 |
| To Coll$^o$. John Dandridge for two Copies of the List of Tithes | 36 |
| To M$^r$. John Shermer for four Communions | 400 |
| To M$^{rs}$. Ann Pennington for paying Keziah Charlton, the Ch. Warden's order for 1500$^{lb}$ Tob$^o$. For Elizabeth Barker | 1500 |
| To M$^{rs}$. Ann Pennington for paying the Ch. Wardens order to Mary Row for 20/ in Tob$^o$. @ 13/ | 153 |
| To Maj$^r$. William Hockaday for John Taylor's family | 800 |
| To Martha Piggett | 800 |
| To Maj$^r$. William Hockaday for Richard Gilman | 800 |
| To Nicholas Valentine Sen$^r$ | 600 |
| To John Yates his Acco$^t$. for keeping & burying John Gilman 1$^£$‖11$^S.$‖6$^{d.}$ in Tob$^o$. @ 13/ | 242 |
| To Eliz$^a$. Feer for her trouble with Mary Richardson in her Sickneſs £2‖10$^S.$: in Tob @ 13/ | 384 |
| To Rebecca White for keeping George Smith's Child Six months | 500 |
| Present M$^r$. Leonard Henley. To M$^r$. Gill Armistead's Acco$^t$ 3$^£$‖5$^S.$‖9½$^{d.}$ in Tob$^o$. at 13/ | 505½ |
| To Maj$^r$. William Hockaday for digging a grave & finding a Coffin for Mary Richardson | 100 |
| To Burnal Ruſsell for keeping John Swiney Eleven Months in 1752 | 400 |
| To M$^r$. John Shermer, for paying Thomas Albriton 15/ for Carrying Diana Sutton To Hanover, in Tob$^o$. at 13/ | 115 |
| To Honor Grace for her trouble with John Gaddey dec'd 7/6 in Tob$^o$. at 13/ | 58 |

| | lb Tob°. |
|---|---|
| To Majr. William Hockaday, for 6lb Sugar & ½ Bushel of Wheat for Wm. Garland 5/9 in Tob @ 13/ | 44 |
| To Majr. John Richardson, for paying John Sheriff's Levy in 1752. From which he was discharg'd by the Vestry in 1752 | 37½ |
| Carried over to the other Side | 31413 |

To

[88]

| Blisland Parish Dr. | lb Tob°. |
|---|---|
| To Debt brought over from the other Side | 31413 |
| To Doctor William Harwood's Acco‘. for attendance on John Gaddey's family and finding them means £3‖4‖6 in Tob°. @ 13/ ℔ 100 | 496 |
| To William Pitblado for keeping Lucy, the Daughter of Joseph Haselwood dec'd | 400 |
| To Richard Linsey for keeping Richard, the Son of Joseph Haselwood dec'd | 250 |
| To Sarah Gaddey for keeping James Brown, Son of James Brown dec'd | 500 |
| To Francis Day | 600 |
| To the Rev. Mr. Thacker for a glaſs to mend the Glebe Windows 5/ Tob°. @ 13 | 38 |
| To the Support of Reb*. Wall | 300 |
| To Mr. William Armistead the Bal*. of his Acco‘. | 37½ |
| To James Charles for Richard Creed Curle in 1752 | 100 |
| To the Church Wardens for work done at the Glebe by Mrs. Daingerfield's Workmen £4‖15S.‖3d. levied in Tob° @ 13/ | 732 |
| To the Church Wardens, to pay Mr. William Brown for Repairing the Church | 5600 |
| To Mr. William Hogg for 350 feet of 1½ Inch plank for a threshing floor for the Glebe And for Carting the Same £1‖15‖6 in Tob°. @ 13/ | 273 |
| Towards an Addition to the upper Church | 10000 |

| | |
|---|---|
| To Mary Farthing for the Support of her Child | 400 |
| To Grifsell Sanders for keeping John Gilman two Months | 150 |

51289½

Blisland Parish Cr. By Mr William Hogg 5s.‖8½d. in Tobo. @ 13/     44

51245½

Do. Dr. To 6 ℔. Cent. for Collecting 51245½lb Tobo.    3074

54319½

Deposited in the Collector's hands    457½

Do. Cr. By 961 Tithes at 57lb Tobo. ℔. Poll    54777

Order'd that the 2549lb Tobo. which was Levied for Mr. Lewis Delony be Sold by the Church Wardens (with the 10000lb Tobo. which was levied for an Addition to the upper Church) Purfuant to an Order of Vestry dated April 18th. 1746

Majr. John Richardson is appointed Church Warden, (with Mr. Gill Armistead) in the Stead of Mr. John Shermer and was Sworn accordingly

Edward Newman is Appointed Sexton at the upper Church, in the Stead of John Gaddey deceas'd

Mr. William Armistead is appointed Collector the Enfuing year, on giving Bond & Security as Ufual.

Memorandum. that the Balr. due to the Parish last year, was not accounted for this year.

         Sign'd By    C. Thacker Minr.
                     John Richardson Ch. Warden
                     Gl. Armistead Ch. Warden
     Test.   Dudleyy Williams Clark o' the Vestry

                                       'Tis

[89]

'Tis order'd by this Present Vestry that the Parish Levy for this present year be Fifty Seven pounds of Tob. ℔. Poll, and that W$^m$. Armistead D. Sheriff of New Kent County do Collect the S$^d$. Sum of Fifty Seven pounds of Tob. from ev'ry Individual Titheable Perſon in this Parish, and on refusal of Payment to Levy the Same by distreſs according to Law. The S$^d$. W$^m$. Armistead first ent'ring into Bond with good & Sufficient Security to the present Vestry of this Parish, for the uſe of the Parish, for the Payment of the S$^d$. Sums of Tob. to the Sev'ral respective Parish Creditors to whom it is due by Inspectors notes by the last day of May next. And it is also Order'd that the Clark of the Vestry take Bond as aforesaid before he deliver a Copy of the Parish Charge and order of Vestry to the S$^d$. Collector.

Test. Dudley Williams. Clark o' the Vestry

At a Vestry held Blisland Parish at the upper Church June the 22$^d$. 1754.

Present

The Rev. M$^r$. Thacker  
Maj$^r$. John Richardson ⎫ Ch.  
Cap$^t$. Gill Armistead ⎬ wardens  
Maj$^r$. William Hockaday  

Maj$^r$. John Power  
M$^r$. Richmond Terrel  
M$^r$. Richard Allen. and  
M$^r$. William Hogg  

Order'd that the Church Wardens of this Parish do Sell the Glebe Land in James City County, Purſuant to an Act of Aſsembly made in 1753. And that they give twelve months credit from the day of Sale for the Payment of the money. The purchaser giving Bond and Security for the payment of the money to the Church Wardens & their Succeſsors.

Order'd, that the Church Wardens do Sell the 5600¹ᵇ. Tob°. which was Levied in the Church Wardens hands for M͏ʳ. William Brown, for Repairing the Lower Church.
Sign'd by   C. Thacker Min͏ʳ.
John Richardson } Church Wardens.
Gill Armistead
Test. Dudley Williams. Clark o' the Vestry

At

[90]
At a Vestry held for Blisland Parish at the upper Church October 17ᵗʰ. 1754.

Present

The Rev. M͏ʳ. Thacker.
Maj͏ʳ. John Richardson } Church Wardens
Cap͏ᵗ. Gill Armistead
Maj͏ʳ. William Hockaday.   M͏ʳ. Richard Allen,
Maj͏ʳ. John Power.   M͏ʳ. John Shermer,
M͏ʳ. Leonard Henley,   Cap͏ᵗ. Thruston James, And,
M͏ʳ. William Hogg

This Vestry Proceeds to lay the Parish Levy

| | Blisland Parish | D͏ʳ. |
|---|---|---:|
| | | lb Tob°. |
| To the Rev. M͏ʳ. Thacker's Sallary 16000ˡᵇ ᵀᵒᵇ°. & 4 ℔ C͏ᵗ. for Cask 640ˡᵇ. & 4 ℔ C͏ᵗ. for Shrinkage 640ˡᵇ | | 17280 |
| To John Burnett Clark of the upper Church 1000ˡᵇ, & 4 ℔ Cent for Cask 40ˡᵇ | | 1040 |
| To Dudley Williams Clark of the Lower Church & Vestry 1500ˡᵇ, & 4 ℔. C͏ᵗ. for Cask 60ˡᵇ | | 1560 |
| To Edward Newman Sexton at the upper Church 500ˡᵇ & Cask 20. For washing Surplice 100ˡᵇ | | 620 |
| To Edward Lively Sexton at the Lower Church 500ˡᵇ & Cask 20. For washing the Surplice 100ˡᵇ | | 620 |

| | |
|---|---:|
| To the Support of Lucy Gills | 600 |
| To the Support of Ann Linsey | 600 |
| To the Support of Thomas Linsey | 300 |
| To Thomas Jones, for keeping Eliz*. Williams | 700 |
| To Elenor Pitman | 600 |
| To M*r*. Ben: Waller, for a Copy of the List of Tithes | 18 |
| To Col. John Dandridge for two Copies of d°. | 36 |
| To the Support of Martha Piggett | 600 |
| To Nicholas Valentine Sen*r*. | 600 |
| To Francis Day | 600 |
| To Richard Linsey, for keeping Richard Haselwood Son of Joseph Haselwood dec'd | 600 |
| To Maj*r*. John Richardson, for four Communions for the Lower Church | 500 |
| To Cap*t*. Gill Armistead for four Commun*s*. for the upper Church last year & four this year | 1000 |
| To David Dormer, For keeping Eliz*. Barker | 1560 |
| To Maj*r*. William Hockaday, For John Taylor's family | 800 |
| To         d°.         for Richard Gilman | 800 |
| To Reb*. White, For keeping George Smith's Child | 800 |
| To Sarah Gaddey, For keeping James Brown, Son of James Brown dec'd | 500 |
| To Mary Farthing, For the Support of her Child | 400 |
| To the Support of Ifsabella Gray | 200 |
| To the Church Wardens, for Isaac Tyree | 700 |
| To M*r*. John Shermer, To Satisfy David Johnson, for Curing Diana Sutton of a Cancer 10*ₛ*‖15* Tob°. at 10*. | 2150 |
| To the Bal*. of Cap*t*. William Macon's Acco*t*. for Plank for the Glebe 7/ in Tob°. at 10/ | 70 |
| To Doctor William Harwood's Acco*t* £ 1‖9*.‖3*d*. Levied in Tob°. at 10/ ℔ 100 | 295 |
| To John Jones Patroler, for his Levy Paid last year | 57 |

| | |
|---|---:|
| To Charles Hankin d°. for d°. 57¹ᵇ. To Richᵈ. Gaddey d°. for d°. 57¹ᵇ | 114 |
| To Richard Martin d°. for d°. 57¹ᵇ. To Landey Linsey d°. for d°. 57¹ᵇ | 114 |
| Towards an Addition to the upper Church | 10000 |
| | 46434 |
| D°. Cʳ. By Mʳ. Willᵐ. Armistead for Depositum in his hands last year | 457 |
| | 45977 |
| D°. Dʳ. To 6 ℈. Cent for Collecting 45977ˡᵇ Tobo. | 2758 |
| | 48735 |
| Deposited in the Collector's hands | 72 |
| D°. Cʳ. By 986 Tithes at 49½¹ᵇ ℈. Poll is | 48807 |

Mʳ

[91]

Mʳ. Richard Allen is Chosen Church Warden in the Stead of Capᵗ. Gill Armistead, and was Accordingly Sworn.

On the Motion of Edward Lively to be discharg'd from his Parish Levy, he is accordingly discharg'd.

Order'd that the 93½¹ᵇ Tob°. in the hands of the Sheriff of James City County taken by Execution of the Estate of Susᵃ. Thomas, be return'd to the Said Susᵃ. Thomas.

Order'd that Mary Sheriff be discharg'd from Paying her Parish Levy.

Order'd that Mʳ. William Armistead give Mʳ. Richard Allen Cʳ. Out of the Depoſitum in his hands for two Tithes (vizᵗ) Aca and Oda, On Account of their blindneſs

Mʳ. William Armistead is appointed Collector the Enſuing year, On giving Bond & Security as Uſual

Order'd that Mʳ William Armistead give Edward Lively Cʳ. for his Levy this present Levy.

  Sign'd By  C. Thacker Minʳ.
     John Richardson ⎫
     Richard Allen   ⎬ Church Wardens.

 Test. Dudley Williams Clark of the Vestry.

'Tis Order'd by this Present Vestry, that the Parish Levy for this Present Year, be Forty Nine and a half Pounds of Tobº. ℔. Poll, and that Mʳ William Armistead D. Sher. in New Kent County do Collect and receive the Said Sum of Forty nine & a half Pounds of Tobº. from Every Individual Titheable Person within this Parish. And on refusal of Payment to Levy the Same by diſtreſs according to Law. The Said William Armistead first Entring into Bond, With good & Sufficient Security to the Present Vestry of this Parish, for the uſe of the Parish, for the Payment of the Said Sums of Tobº. to the Several Respective Parish Creditors to whom it is due, by Inspectors Notes by the last day of May next. And it is also Order'd that the Clark of the Vestry take Bond as aforesaid, before he deliver a Copy of the Parish Charge And Order of Vestry to the Said Collector.

  Test.

   Dudley Williams Clark o' th' Vestry

              At

[92]

At a Vestry held for Blisland Parish, at the upper Church the Second day of Sepʳ. 1755.

Present, The Rev. Mʳ. Thacker, Majʳ. John Richardson, & Mʳ. Richard Allen Ch. Wardens. Majʳ. William Hockaday, Mʳ. Richmond Terrel, Capᵗ. Gill Armistead, Mʳ. William Hogg, and Mʳ. Isaac Goddin.

Order'd that Maj$^r$. John Richardson & M$^r$. Richard Allen, Gent. Church Wardens, Immediately Agree with Workmen to Undertake the Addition to the upper Church Pursuant to an Order of Vestry, dated July 29$^{th}$. 1755.
 Sign'd By   C. Thacker Min$^r$.
      John Richardson  ⎫
      Rich$^d$ Allen     ⎬ Church Wardens.
 Test. Dudley Williams Clark O' the Vestry

      Articles of Agreement.
 A Brick Addition to the upper Church in Blisland Parish, to be made twenty four feet in Length added to the Old Building, of the Same width as the Old, to have four Pews of Each Side. Two Sash Windows in Each Side: and two in the End: Each Window to have Eighteen Panes of glaſs ten by twelve. The Pulpit to be moved to the North Side of the Church, and to be fixed According to the Rev. M$^r$. Thacker's direction. The Floors and Pews above the Pulpit to be taken up, and Set down, in good Order with thoſe below: The Windows Old and New, with the Doors & Eaves of the Said Church to be well Prim'd & Painted white with white lead, Inside & Out. THE COMMUNION to be Moved, and decently fitted with New Rails and Banisters. The Addition to be a Compaſs Ceiling, Cover'd with Plank and good Cypreſs Shingles, to be lath'd and Plaister'd, and the whole Church Whitewash'd. The Wall of the Yard to be lengthen'd and Carried Eight feet Clear of the S$^d$ Addition. Two new gates made of good Season'd White Oak. The Whole to be Compleated (Workmen like) by October 1756. The Present Church Wardens to Inspect all the Bricks and Timber to be uſed about the Said Building: The Foundation to be laid as low as the Graves (where they Interfere) of the Church Yard.
 The above I agree to do (or Cause to be done) by October in the Year 1756. for the Sum of One Hundred and

Twenty Nine Pounds. IN PURSUANCE of which I have Paſsed a Bond dated Sep'. the 2ᵈ. 1755. And rec'd of Maj'. John Richardson & M'. Richard Allen Bond for the Sum abovemention'd. Witneſs our hands

        Sam¹. Du Val
 Sep'. the 2ᵈ. 1755  Christo'. Ford Juʳ.
Test.
 Dud. Williams.  John Richᵈson ⎫
 Samˡˡ. Ashley   Richᵈ. Allen  ⎬Ch. ward⁸.

            At

[193]

At a Vestry held for Blisland Parish, at the Lower Church Octoʳ. 15. 1755.

      Present

    The Rev. M'. Thacker,

 Maj'. John Richardson, ⎫
  & M'. Richard Allen  ⎬Ch. Wardens
Maj'. William Hockaday, Cap'. Gill Armistead,
M'. Leonard Henley   M'. John Shermer,
Cap'. Thruston James,    And
        M'. Isaac Goddin

This Vestry Proceeds to lay the Parish Levy

| Blisland Parish | Dʳ. |
|---|---|
| | lb Tob°. |
| To the Rev. M'. Thacker's Sallary 16000ˡᵇ ᵀᵒᵇᵒ· & 4 ₱ Cᵗ. for Cask 640ˡᵇ. & 4 ₱ Cᵗ. for Shrinkage 640ˡᵇ | 17280 |
| To M'. John Burnett Clark of the upper Church 1000ˡᵇ & 4 ₱ Cᵗ. for Cask 40 | 1040 |
| To Dudley Williams Clark of the Lower Church & Vestry 1500ˡᵇ & 4 ₱ Cᵗ. for Cask 60 | 1560 |

| | |
|---|---|
| To Edw<sup>d</sup>. Lively Sexton of the Lower Church 500<sup>lb</sup> & Cask 20, & for washing the Surplice 100<sup>lb</sup> | 620 |
| To Edw<sup>d</sup>. Newman Sexton of the upper Church 500<sup>lb</sup> & Cask 20, & for washing the Surplice 100<sup>lb</sup> | 620 |
| To the Maint<sup>e</sup>. of Lucy Gills 600.—To the Maint<sup>e</sup>. of Ann Linsey 600 | 1200 |
| To the Maint<sup>e</sup>. of Tho<sup>s</sup>. Linsey | 300 |
| To M<sup>r</sup>. Benj<sup>a</sup>. Tyree, for keeping Eliz<sup>a</sup>. Williams three Months | 175 |
| To M<sup>r</sup>. Jeremiah Woodward, for keeping Eliz<sup>a</sup>. Williams nine Months | 525 |
| To Elenor Pitman | 600 |
| To M<sup>r</sup>. Ben: Waller, for a Copy of the List of Tithes | 18 |
| To Coll. John Dandridge, for two Copies of d°. | 36 |
| To Nicholas Valentine Sen<sup>r</sup>. 500.— To Fra<sup>s</sup>. Day 500 | 1000 |
| To Richard Linsey, for keeping Richard Haselwood, Son of Joseph Haselwood dec'd | 700 |
| To M<sup>r</sup>. Richard Allen, for four Commun<sup>s</sup>. for the upper Church | 400 |
| To Maj<sup>r</sup>. John Richardson, for four d°. for the lower d°. | 400 |
| To M<sup>rs</sup> Ann Pennington her Acco<sup>t</sup> £5‖0<sup>s</sup>.‖11½<sup>d</sup>. to be paid by the Church Wardens | |
| To William Fisher's Acco<sup>t</sup>. for burying Eliz<sup>a</sup>. Barker 7.<sup>s</sup>. 6.<sup>d</sup>. To be paid by d°. | |
| To Edw<sup>d</sup>. James, for making a Coffin for John Eacho 5/. To be paid by d°. | |
| To M<sup>r</sup>. Jos. Watkins, for 2 Quarts of Rum, for John Eacho's funeral 2.<sup>s</sup>. 6.<sup>d</sup>. to be paid by d°. | |
| To Maj<sup>r</sup>. John Richardson, for a Barrel of Corn, for Widow Eacho. 10/. To be paid by d°. | |
| To Sarah Pitblado, for keeping Richard Gilman | 400 |
| To Maj<sup>r</sup>. William Hockaday, for John Taylor's family | 666 |
| To Reb<sup>a</sup>. White, for keeping George Smith's Child | 666 |

| | |
|---|---:|
| To Sarah Gaddey, for keeping James Brown, Son of Jam⁸. Brown dec'd | 416 |
| To Mary Farthing, for her Child | 333 |
| To Ifsabella Gray | 166 |
| To Mʳ. Isaac Goddin, ℔ Ch. Wardˢ. Order, for Simon Frazier being Sick at his house 15 days £3 Levied in Tobᵒ. at 15/℔ 100 | 400 |
| To Jam⁸. Jones, for taking care of Mary Samson in her late Sickneſs | 100 |
| | 29621 |
| To 6 ℔. Cent for Collecting 29621ˡᵇ Tobo | 1777 |
| | 31398 |
| Deposited in the Collector's hands | 284 |
| Dᵒ. Cʳ. By 1022 Tithes at 31ˡᵇ. ℔ Poll | 31682 |

order'd

[94]

Order'd that the Church Wardens Repair to the Glebe, and See what Repairs are wanting thereon, and agree with workmen, to build and make Such Repairs as they Shall think neceſsary: And for the Church Wardens to bring their Accoᵗ. for the Same, at the laying the next Parish Levy.

Order'd that the Church Wardens Enquire, whether Ann Leavor have any right to freedom dues; and if She has, that they pay her the Same, Purſuant to an agreement this Vestry made with Mʳ. Roger Williams April 24, 1725. And bring their Accoᵗ. to the laying the next Parish Levy.

Majʳ. John Power is Chosen Church Warden, in the Stead of Majʳ. John Richardson (with Mʳ. Richard Allen) and Order'd that he be Sworn Accordingly.

M$^r$. William Armistead is Appointed Collector, on giving Bond and Security as uſual.
        Sign'd by   C. Thacker Min$^r$.
                  Rich$^d$ Allen Church Warden
   Test.  Dudley Williams Clark O' the Vestry.

'Tis Order'd By this present Vestry, that the Parish Levy for this present year, be Thirty one pounds of Tob°. ℔ Poll, and that M$^r$. William Armistead D. She. in New Kent County, do Collect the S$^d$. Thirty one Pounds of Tob°. from every Individual Titheable person in this Parish, And on refusal of payment to Levy the Same by distreſs according to Law. The S$^d$. William Armistead first Entring into Bond with good and Sufficient Security to the present Vestry of this Parish, for the use of the Parish, for the Payment of the S$^d$. Sums of Tob°. to the Sev'ral respective Parish Creditors to whom it is due, by Inspectors notes by the last day of may next. And it is also Order'd that the Clark of the Vestry take Bond as aforesaid, before he deliver a Copy of the Parish Charge and Order of Vestry to the Said Collector
    Test
          Dudley Williams Clark o' th' Vestry

                                             At
[95]
At a Vestry held for Blisland Parish at the Upper Church October the 12$^{th}$. 1756.

                     Present

The Rev. M$^r$. Thacker         M$^r$. Richmond Terrel
Maj$^r$. John Power  ⎫            M$^r$. William Hogg
M$^r$. Richard Allen  ⎬ Ch. Wardens  Cap$^t$. Thruston James
Maj$^r$. William Hockaday      Cap$^t$. Gill Armistead
Maj$^r$. John Richardson        M$^r$. John Shermer.

This Vestry Proceeds to Lay the Parish Levy
Blisland Parish                              Dr.

| | |
|---|---:|
| To the Rev. Mr. Thacker, his Salary 16000lb. & 4 ℔ Ct. for Cask, & 4 ℔ Ct. for Shrinkage | 17280 |
| To Dudley Williams, Clark of the Upper Church 1500lb, & 4 ℔ Ct. for Cask 60 | 1560 |
| To Mr. John Burn' Estate for Serving as Clr. from Ocr. 15, 1755. till June 25. 1756 | 693 |
| To Mr. William Slater, for Officiating as Clr. lowr. Ch. from June 25. 1755. till Ocr. 12. 1756. | 347 |
| To Edward Newman Sexton at the upper Ch. 500. & 4 ℔ Ct. 20. for washing the Surpl'. 100 | 620 |
| To Edward Lively d°. at the lower d°. 500 & d°. 20 for d°. 100 | 620 |
| To Daniel Steward, for keeping Lucy Gills 11 Months | 600 |
| To John Ball for keeping        d°.      1 d°. | 50 |
| To the Maintainance of Tho'. Linsey | 300 |
| To Benj'. Tyree, for keeping Eliz'. Williams | 700 |
| To Elenor Pitman | 600 |
| To Mr. Ben: Waller, for the List of Tithes | 18 |
| To Mr. William Clayton, for two Copies of d°. | 36 |
| To Nicholas Valentine, for a Levy Overcharg'd in 1754 | 49½ |
| Present, Mr. Isaac Goddin.— To Nicho'. Valentine | 600 |
| To Richard Linsey, For keeping Richard Haselwd. Orphan of Jos. Haselwd. dec'd | 700 |
| To Mr. Richard Allen, Ch. W'rd'n For four Commun'. for the Upper Church | 400 |
| To Majr. John Power       d°.     For d°.     d°. for the Lower d°. | 400 |
| To John Jeffers, for keeping Richard Gilm. 5 Months at 900lb. ℔ Ann. | 375 |
| To D°. for his trouble with    d°    in his Sickness | 100 |
| To Reb'. White, for keeping Geo. Smith's Child | 666 |

| | |
|---|---|
| To Thoˢ. Smith, for Jamˢ. Brown, Son of Jamˢ. Brown dec'd. He is to keep him Three Years at the rate of 300ᵇ, ℔ Annum: And then to keep him for the future, Clear from being any Charge to the Parish | 300 |
| To Mary Farthing, for the Support of her Child | 333 |
| To Iſabella Gray | 166 |
| To William Wood, for keeping Sarah Taylor 3 Months | 200 |
| To Prudence Fisher, For her trouble with Rebˢ. Williams | 200 |
| To James Jones for his trouble with Mary Samson from Ocʳ. 15. 1755 till Febʳ. 17. 1756. at £8. ℔ Annum £2‖13‖4 Levied in Tobᵒ. at 15/ ℔ 100 | 355 |
| To James Jones, for his trouble and Charge in, burying Mary Samson | 100 |
| Dʳ. Carᵈ. Over | 28368½ |

To
[96]                Blisland Parish Dʳ

| | lb. Tobᵒ. |
|---|---|
| To Debt broᵗ. over, from the Other Side | 28368½ |
| To Majʳ. William Hockaday, his Accoᵗ. £2‖—‖11. Levied in Tobᵒ. at 15/ | 272½ |
| To Fraˢ. Day | 500 |
| To Doctʳ. William Harwood his Accᵗ. for Sundry perſons £13‖18. Levied in Tobᵒ. at 15/ ℔ 100 | 1853 |
| To Mary Charlton, For the Support of her Son William | 500 |
| To Majʳ. John Power his Accᵗ. 15/ Levied in Tobᵒ. at 15/ ℔ 100 | 100 |
| To the Ch. Wardens, For William Bennett, for repairs done at the Glebe | 4000 |

| | |
|---|---|
| To D°. To pay Mʳ. Samˡ Duval his Balᵗ. for an Addition to the Upper Church | 4000 |
| | 39594 |
| To 6 ⨊. Cent. for Collecting 39594ˡᵇ Tobo. | 2375 |
| | 41969 |
| Deposited in the Collector's hands | 59 |
| | 42028 |
| Blisland Parish Cʳ. | |
| By 1064 Tithes at 39½ ⨊. Poll | 42028 |

Order'd that Mʳ. William Armistead, pay Capᵗ. Gill Armistead 284ˡᵇ Tob°. Which was deposited in his hands at the laying the last Parish Levy.

Capᵗ. Gill Armistead Sheʳ. is Appointed Collector the Ensuing Year, on giving Bond and Security at Uſual

Order'd that the Church Wardens demand and Receive Capᵗ. William Kenney's Legacy to this Parish, for a Piece of Plate.

Majʳ. John Power, and Mʳ. Richard Allen, are Continued Church Wardens the Enſuing Year

Mem°. That Capᵗ. Gill Armistead lodg'd his Accoᵗ, with the Clark o' th' Vestry.

Order'd that the Collector Pay the 284ˡᵇ Tob°. which was deposited in the Collector's hands last year, and the 59ˡᵇ. Tob°. deposited in his his hands this year, to Dunkerton Henry

     Sign'd by C. Thacker Minʳ.
          John Power  ⎱
          Richᵈ. Allen  ⎰ Ch. wardens
 Test.

    Dudley Williams. Clark O' th' Vestry

                 'Tis

[97]
'Tis Order'd by this present Vestry that the Parish Levy for this present Year, be Thirty Nine & one half Pounds of Tob°. P. poll: And that Cap$^t$. Gill Armistead Sheriff of New Kent County do Collect the Said Thirty Nine and a half Pounds of Tob°. from Every Individual Titheable Person in this Parish; And on refusal of Payment, to Levy the Same by distreſs according to Law. The S$^d$. Gill Armistead first Entring into Bond, with good and Sufficient Security, to the present Vestry of this Parish for the use of the Parish, for the Payment of the S$^d$. Sums of Tob°. to the Several Respective Parish Creditors to whom it is due by the last day of May next. And it is also Order'd that the Clark of the Vestry take Bond as aforesaid, before he deliver a Copy of the Parish Charge, & Order of Vestry, to the S$^d$. Collector.

 Test.
    Dudley Williams. Clark o' th' Vestry

[98]
At a Vestry held for Blisland Parish at the upper Church October the 6$^{th}$. 1757.

     Present
    The Rev. M$^r$. Thacker

Maj$^r$. John Power, &   } Churchwardens
M$^r$. Richard Allen    }

M$^r$. Richmond Terrel,   M$^r$. John Shermer, &
Cap$^t$. Thruston James   Col Burwell Baſsett; who was
Cap$^t$. Gill Armistead    this day Choſe, and Sworn
M$^r$. William Hogg,

 This Vestry proceeds to lay the Parish Levy

| Blisland Parish | | D$^r$. |
|---|---|---|
| To the Rev. M$^r$. Thacker, his Salary | 16000$^{lb\ Tob°.}$ | lb Tob°. |
| To 4 ℔ C$^t$ for Cask on 16000$^{lb}$ | 640 | 17280 |
| To 4 ℔ C$^t$. for Shrinkage on 16000$^{lb}$ | 640 | |

| | |
|---|---:|
| To Dudley Williams, Clark of the upper Church & Vestry 1500ᵇ. To 4 ℔ Cᵗ. on dº. 640 | 1560 |
| To Mʳ. William Slater, Clark of the lower Church 1000ᵇ. To 4 ℔ Cᵗ. on dº. 40 | 1040 |
| To Edward Newman, Sexton at the upper Church 500, & Cask 20. for washing the Surpˢ. 100 | 620 |
| To Edward Lively, Sexton at the lower Church 500ᵇ & Cask 20. for washing the Surplice 100 | 620 |
| To John Yates, for keeping Lucy Gills | 650 |
| To Ann Linsey | 450 |
| To Dº. Omitted last Year. To Majʳ. William Hockaday's Estate | 600 |
| To the maintenance of Thomas Linsey | 300 |
| To Stephen Jones, for keeping Elenor Pitman | 600 |
| To Benjamin Tyree, for keeping Elizˢ. Williams | 700 |
| To Nicholas Valentine Senʳ. | 600 |
| To Mary Farthing, for the Support of her Child | 300 |
| To Francis Day | 800 |
| To Thomas Smith, for keeping James Brown, Son of James Brown dec'd | 300 |
| To Mʳ. Ben: Waller for a Copy of the List of Tithes | 18 |
| To Mʳ. William Clayton, for two Copies of the List of Tithes | 36 |
| To Richard Linsey, for keeping Richard Haselwood, Orphan of Joseph Haselwood dec'd | 700 |
| To Majʳ. John Power, for four Communions, for the lower Church | 400 |
| To Mʳ. Richard Allen for four dº. for the upper Church | 400 |
| To Rebˢ. White, for keeping George Smith's Child | 666 |
| To Mʳˢ. Martha Gooch, for keeping Sarah Taylor | 400 |
| To Elizˢ. Linsey, for keeping Ann Linsey | 173 |
| To Joel Willis, for keeping Joseph Willis Eight weeks | 300 |

NEW KENT COUNTY, VIRGINIA, 1721-1786    139

| | |
|---|---|
| To M$^r$. William Armistead, his Acc$^t$. for Bricks for the Glebe 23/ in Tob$^o$. @ 15/ | 153 |
| To M$^{rs}$. Hannah Daingerfield, her Acc$^t$. her Acc$^t$ of £ 18\|\|12\|\|11 reduced to £ 15\|\|14\|\|10½. Levied in Tob$^o$. @ 15/ ℔ C$^t$. | 2098 |
| To Cap$^t$. Gill Armistead, to pay Sam$^l$. Woodward, for Shingles for the Glebe | 800 |
| To Matthew Cole, for keeping two Children of John Eacho dec'd, from January the 21$^{st}$. last, till now, @ 1200$^{lb}$ & Cask ℔ Ann | 884 |
| Carried forward — | 33448 |

[99] Brought

| | |
|---|---|
| Brought forward | 33448 |
| To Prudence Fisher, for keeping Lydda Paul from Nov$^r$. 29$^{th}$. 1756 till now, And for Curing Rebekah Williams's knee | 800 |
| To William Bennett, a Levy Overcharg'd last Year | 39½ |
| To Cap$^t$. Gill Armistead, his Acc$^t$. for Delinquents | 815 |
| To M$^r$. John Shermer, For Carrying Diana Sutton to David Johnson's in Hanover 15/ Levied in Tob$^o$. @ 15/ ℔ C$^t$. | 100 |
| To Edward Lively | 400 |
| To Cap$^t$. Gill Armistead, the Bal$^e$. of his Acc$^t$. 28/ Levied in Tob$^o$. @ 15/ | 186 |
| To Isabella Gray | 200 |
| To Mary Charlton, for her Son William | 500 |
| To John Yates, for keeping Daniel Steward's Child | 500 |
| To Col. Burwel Ba∫sett, for work done at the Glebe, valued by M$^r$. Sam$^l$. Duval at £ 24\|\|10. Levied in Tob$^o$. @ 15 ℔ C$^t$. | 3266 |
| To the Collector, for the Ball$^e$. due to William Bennett, for Repairs done at the Glebe | 2200 |

|  |  |
|---|---|
| To Ann Brown, for Freedom dues (in Compliance with an Agreement this Vestry made with Mʳ. Roger Williams the 24ᵗʰ. day of April 1725) £ 3‖10 Levied in Tobº. @ 15/ ℔ Cᵗ. | 466 |
|  | 42920½ |
| To 6 ℔. Cent for Collecting 42920ˡᵇ Tobº. | 2575 |
|  | 45495½ |
| Deposited in the Collector's hands | 405 |
|  | 45900 |
| Blisland Parish Cʳ. |  |
| By 1080 Tithes @ 42½ ℔ Poll | 45900 |

Col. Burwel Baſsett was this day Chosen a Vestryman, in the room of Majʳ. William Hockaday dec'd, and Accordingly Sworn.

Col. Burwel Baſsett, and Capᵗ. Thruston James, are Chosen Churchwardens, in the Stead of Majʳ. John Power, & Mʳ. Richard Allen; and Accordingly Sworn.

Capᵗ. Gill Armistead Sher. is Appointed Collector the Enſuing Year, on giving Bond and Security as Usual.

    Sign'd By  C. Thacker Minʳ

        Burwell Baſsett } Ch. wardens
        Thruston James

Test.

    Dudley Williams. Clark o' the Vestry

[100. This page of the MS. is blank.—C. G. C.]

[101].

At a Vestry held for Blisland Parish at the lower Church October the 16ᵗʰ. 1758.

Present

The Rev. Mʳ. Thacker,
Col. Burwell Baſsett & } ch. wardⁿˢ.
Majʳ. Thruston James

Mʳ. Leonard Henley,     Col. Gill Armistead,
Col. John Richardson,     Mʳ. John Shermer,
Majʳ. John Power,     Mʳ. Richard Allen and
Mʳ. Richmond Terrel,     Mʳ. William Hogg.

This Vestry proceeds to lay the Parish Levy

| Blisland Parish | | Dʳ. |
|---|---|---|
| To the Rev. Mʳ. Thacker, his Salary 16000$^{lb\ Tob^o.}$ | } lb Tobᵒ. | |
| To 4 ℔ Cᵗ. on dᵒ. for Cask 640 | } 17280 | |
| To 4 ℔ᵗ. on dᵒ. for Shrinkage 640 | | |
| To Dudley Williams Clark of the upper Church & Vestry 1500$^{lb}$. To 4 ℔ Cᵗ. on dᵒ. 60$^{lb}$. | | 1560 |
| To William Slater Clark of the lower Church 1000$^{lb}$. To 4 ℔ Cᵗ. on dᵒ. for Cask 40 | | 1040 |
| To Edward Newman Sexton at the upper Church 500. To 4 ℔ Cᵗ. on dᵒ. 20 For washing the Surplice 100. | | 620 |
| To Edward Lively Sexton at the lower Church 500. To 4 ℔ Cᵗ. on dᵒ. 20, for washing the Surplice 100. | | 620 |
| To Dunkerton Henry, for keeping Lucy Gills | | 650 |
| To Ann Linsey | | 450 |
| To Thomas Linsey | | 300 |
| To James Glasebrook, for keeping Elizᵃ. Williams | | 700 |
| To Nicholas Valentine Senʳ. Refer'd to the Church-wardens | | — |
| To Francis Day | | 500 |
| To Thomas Smith, for keeping James Brown, Orphan of James Brown, dec'd | | 300 |
| To Mʳ. Ben: Waller, for a Copy of the List of Tithes | | 18 |

| | |
|---|---|
| To M<sup>r</sup>. William Clayton, for two Copies of the Lest of Tithes | 36 |
| To Maj<sup>r</sup>. Thruston James, for Four Commun<sup>s</sup>. at the lower Church | 400 |
| To Mary Farthing, for the Support of her Son Edward | 300 |
| To Reb<sup>a</sup>. White, for keeping George Smith's Child | 600 |
| To Sarah Laffoon, for her trouble with Sarah Taylor in her Sickneſs & burying her | 100 |
| To Matthew Cole, for keeping two Children of John Eccho dec'd at 1200 & Cask ℔ Ann | 1248 |
| To William Fisher, the Bal<sup>e</sup>. of his Acco<sup>t</sup>. for his trouble with Lydday Paul, and burying her | 55 |
| To Edward Lively, Exclusive of his Salary | 350 |
| To Isabella Gray, refer'd to the Ch. wardens | —— |
| To John Yates, for keeping Dan<sup>l</sup>. Steward's Child | 400 |
| To    D<sup>o</sup>.    for keeping William Fletcher | 1440 |
| Debt Carried forward | 28967 |

[102]

| | lb Tob<sup>o</sup>. |
|---|---|
| Debt bro<sup>t</sup>. forward | *28967* |
| To M<sup>r</sup>. John Timberlake, his Acc<sup>t</sup>. for Setting up Benches and horseblocks &c at the supper Church £4∥4∥4. Levied in Tob<sup>o</sup>. @ 2<sup>d</sup>. | 508 |
| To Elenor Banks, for keeping William Curle, Son of Jeremiah Curle four Months, & finding him Shoes and Stockings 25/ Levied in Tob<sup>o</sup>. @ 2<sup>d</sup>. | 150 |
| To Col. Burwel Baſsett, the Bal<sup>e</sup>. of his Acc<sup>t</sup>. 24/2 levied in Tob<sup>o</sup>. @ 2<sup>d</sup>. | 145 |
| To Maj<sup>r</sup>. Thruston James, paid Doctor Carter his acc<sup>t</sup> ag<sup>t</sup>. Prud<sup>e</sup>. Fisher 19/ Levied in Tob<sup>o</sup>. @ 2<sup>d</sup> | 114 |

| | |
|---|---:|
| To Richard Creed Curle, for keeping Reb⁸. Curle, daughter of Jeremiah Curle 25/ Levied in Tob°. @ 2ᵈ | 150 |
| To George Crump Patroler, Overcharg'd a Levy last year | 42½ |
| To Adam Byrd    d°.    d°.    d°. | 42½ |
| To Ben. Ratcliffe    d°.    d°.    d°. | 42½ |
| To William Vadin, for one Levy Overpaid last Year | 42½ |
| To Majʳ. Thruston James, for a Barˡ. of Corn for Sarah Fox 8/ in Tob°. @ 2ᵈ | 48 |
| To Col. Gill Armistead, the Balˢ. of his Accoᵗ. | 568½ |
| To James Jones, for keeping David Dormer three months | 100 |
| To John Ashwel, for keeping two of James Goodin's Children Eight Months £5. Levied in Tob°. @ 2ᵈ | 600 |
| | 31520 |
| To 6 ℔ Cᵗ. for Collecting 31520ˡᵇ ᵀᵒᵇᵒ. | 1891 |
| | 33411 |
| Deposited in the Collector's hands | 189 |
| | 33600 |

Blisland Parish Cʳ

By 1050 Tithes at 32 ℔ Poll    33600

Capᵗ. William Armistead is Chosen a Vestryman in the Stead of Mʳ. John Ruſsel dec'd.

Jemima Curle is appointed Sexton of the upper Church, in the room of Edward Newman.

Mʳ. Richmond Allen D. She. is appointed Collector for the Ensuing Year, on giving Bond & Security as usual.

Col. Burwel Bafsett, & Majʳ. Thruston James, are Continued Churchwardens for the Ensuing year.

Order'd that the Collector pay Stephen Jones 100ˡᵇ Tobᵒ. for keeping Elenor Pitman Out of the depositum in his hands.

Sign'd by Chicheley Thacker Minʳ.
Burwell Bafsett  
Thruston James   Ch. Wardens

Test.
Dudley Williams, Clark o' the Vestry.

[103]

At a Vestry held for Blisland Parish at the upper Church the 9ᵗʰ. day of Octoʳ. 1759.

Present

The Rev. Mʳ. Thacker

Col. Burwel Bafsett, & } Ch. Wardˢ.
Majʳ. Thruston James }

Col. John Richardson        Mʳ. Richard Allen, &
Mʳ. Leonard Henley          Col. Gill Armistead.
Majʳ. John Power

This Vestry proceeds to lay the Parish Levy

Blisland Parish Dʳ.

lb Tobᵒ.

| | |
|---|---:|
| To the Rev. Mʳ. Thacker's Salary 16000ˡᵇ Tobᵒ. To 4 ℔ Cᵗ. on dᵒ. for Cask 640ˡᵇ. To 4 ℔ Cᵗ. for Shrinkage 640ˡᵇ | 17280 |
| To Dudley Williams, Clark of the upper Church & Vestry 1500ˡᵇ. To 4 ℔ Cᵗ. on dᵒ. for Cask 60 | 1560 |
| To William Slater, Clark of the lower Church 1000. To 4 ℔ Cᵗ. on dᵒ. for Cask 40 | 1040 |
| To Jemima Curle, Sextonefs at the upper Ch. 500 & Cask 20. & for washing the Surplice 100 | 620 |
| To Edward Lively, Sexton at the lower Ch. 500 & Cask 20. & for washing the Surplice 100 | 620 |

| | |
|---|---|
| To Ann Linsey | 600 |
| To Thomas Linsey | 300 |
| To John Richardson, for keeping Eliz⁎. Williams | 700 |
| To Nicholas Valentine Sen. | 600 |
| To Francis Day | 500 |
| To Mʳ. Ben: Waller, for a Copy of the List of Tithes | 18 |
| To Mʳ. William Clayton, for two Cop⁎. dº. | 36 |
| To Majʳ. Thruston James, for four Commun⁎. for the lower Church | 400 |
| To Mary Farthing, for the Support of her Son Edward | 300 |
| To Rebⁿ. White, for keeping George Smith's Child | 600 |
| To John Linsey, for keeping Iſabella Gray | 150 |
| To Elenor Banks, for keeping William, the Son of Jeremiah Curle | 500 |
| To Richard Creed Curle, for keeping Rebⁿ. a daughter of Jerem. Curle, from Octoʳ. till March | 250 |
| To John Yates, for keeping Lucy Gills two months at the rate of 650 ℔ Ann  108 | |
| To Dº. for keeping John, Son of Danˡ. Steward last year  400 | 508 |
| To Richard Grout, for keeping William Bruce, from last March till this time | 200 |
| | 26782 |
| To 6 ℔ Cᵗ. for Collecting 26782ˡᵇ ᵀᵒᵇᵒ. | 1606 |
| | 28388 |
| Deposited in the Collector's hands | 311½ |
| | 28699½ |
| Blisland Parish Cʳ. By 1083 Tithes at 26½ ℔ poll | 28699½ |

1759 Octo$^r$. 9$^{th}$.
Blisland Parish                                      D$^r$.
                    For Sundry Cash Acco$^{ts}$.
Viz$^t$. To Henry Dormer, his Acc$^t$. for burying
John Bates, finding &c.                    £ 1‖ 8‖ 6
    To Maj$^r$ Thruston James for 7 Bar$^s$. Corn
@ 10/ £3‖10                                    3‖10‖—
    To D$^o$. for paid Jam$^s$. Hockad. for Sund$^s$.
for W$^m$ Garland 11/10                        —‖11‖10
    To D$^o$. his Acc$^t$. for Ha∫socks for the
lower Church                                   —‖ 9‖ 8½

Carried forward to the Other Side              £ 6‖—‖—½
  [104]
    Blisland Parish              D$^r$.
    To the amount of Cash Acco$^{ts}$ bro$^t$. for-
ward from the Other Side                       £ 6‖—‖—½
    To Martha Pigget, for keeping Mary Rowe
5 Months @ 5/ ℔ month                          1‖ 5‖—
    To Kirby Washer, for keeping two of
John Eacho's Children                          3‖—‖—
    To Col. Gill Armistead, his Acco$^t$       2‖ 3‖ 4½
    To M$^r$. Thomas Cowles, his Acco$^t$. for
blocks & benches at the lower Church           3‖ 5‖—
    To Maj$^r$. John Power, for paid Doct$^r$. Har-
vey his Acco$^t$. 11/6                         —‖11‖ 6
    To Col John Richardson for a Bar$^l$. Corn,
for Widow Eacho @ 10/                          —‖10‖—
    To William Fisher, for keeping John, Or-
phan of John Eacho dec'd two months            12‖ 6

                            £ 17‖ 7‖ 5

    The above Acco$^{ts}$ amounting to £17‖7‖5 is Order'd
to be paid by M$^r$. Richard Allen, Out of the Bal$^e$. that is
due from him to the Parish.

Maj$^r$. John Power & Cap$^t$. William Armistead, are Chosen Church Wardens in the Stead of Col. Burwel Baſsett & Maj$^r$. Thruston James.

Order'd that the Church Wardens Enquire into what repairs are wanting at the Glebe, and Agree with Workmen to do the Same.

Order'd that the Church Wardens agree with Workmen to Make Such Repairs to the Upper Church as they Shall See neceſsary.

M$^r$. Richmond Allen D. Sher. is appointed Collector the Enſuing Year, on giving Bond & Security as uſual.

Order'd that the Church Ward$^s$. agree with Workmen to build a house for the poor of this Parish on the Old Glebe.

    Sign'd by C. Thacker Min$^r$.
       John Power Ch. Warden

Test
  Dudley Williams, Clark O'the Vestry.

              At

[105]

At a Vestry held for Blisland Parish, at the lower Church, the 10$^{th}$. day of Nov$^r$. 1760.

    Present

    Maj$^r$. John Power, and  ⎫
    Cap$^t$. William Armistead ⎬ Ch. ward$^s$.
Col. John Richardson,     Col. Gill Armistead
Maj$^r$. Thruston James,       And
Col. Burwel Baſsett       M$^r$. Richard Allen

 This Vestry proceeds to lay the Parish Levy
    Blisland Parish        D$^r$.
              lb Tob$^o$.

To the Rev. M$^r$. Thacker his Salary 16000$^{lb}$ Tob$^o$.
 To 4 ℔ C$^t$. on d$^o$. for Cask 640$^{lb}$. & 4 ℔ C$^t$.
  for Shrinkage 640$^{lb}$        17280

| | |
|---|---:|
| To Dudley Williams, Clark of the upper Church & vestry 1500ᶫᵇ. To 4 ℔ Cᵗ. on dº. for Cask 60ᶫᵇ. | 1560 |
| To Richardson Henley, Clark of the lower Church 1000ᶫᵇ. To 4 ℔ Cᵗ. on dº. for Cask 40ᶫᵇ | 1040 |
| To Jemima Curle, Sextoneſs at the upper Church 500ᶫᵇ & Cask 20. & for washing the Surplice 100ᶫᵇ. | 620 |
| To Edward Lively, Sexton at the lower Church 500ᶫᵇ. & Cask 20ᶫᵇ. & for washing the Surplice 100 | 620 |
| To Ann Linsey | 600 |
| To Thomas Linsey | 300 |
| To Mʳˢ. Elizᵃ. Burnett, for keeping Elizᵃ. Williams | 700 |
| To Francis Day | 500 |
| To Mary Farthing, for the Support of her Son Edward | 300 |
| To Mʳ. Benjᵃ. Waller, for a Copy of the List of Tithes | 18 |
| To Mʳ. William Clayton, for a Copy of the List of Tithes | 18 |
| To Majʳ. John Power, for four Communions, for the lower Church | 400 |
| To Capᵗ. William Armistead, for four Communions for the upper Church | 400 |
| To Eleanor Banks, for keeping William, the Son of Jeremiah Curle | 600 |
| To Edward Lively, Exclusive of his Salary as Sexton | 400 |
| To Rebᵃ. White, for keeping George Smith's Child | 600 |
| To John Linsey, for keeping Iſsabella Gray | 250 |
| To Richard C. Curle | 400 |
| To James Jones, for keeping David Dormer Eight Months at 1500ᶫᵇ ℔ Annum | 1000 |
| To Elizᵃ. Wall, for her Care & trouble with Wᵐ. Garland's Children from the time of his death | 200 |

| | |
|---|---|
| To Marg⁺. Manning, for keeping two of Sackvile M'hone's Children last Year | 800 |
| To Sarah Fox, for keeping two of Joseph Foxes Children last Year | 400 |
| To Charles Hankin, for boarding Mary Row, finding Shoes &c. | 550 |
| To Matthew Cole, for keeping Benj⁴. Eacho | 500 |
| To Joel Willis, for keeping Tho˙. Twin's Child Eighteen Months | 600 |
| To John Ashwel, for keeping James Goodin's Child two Years | 800 |
| To M⁴. Richmond Allen, Collector, Bal⁴. of his Acc⁴⁸. in 1759 & 1760 | 264½ |
| | 31720½ |
| To Tob°. for the Ch. Wardens to pay the Several Cash Acco⁴⁸. hereafter mention'd &c. | 7000 |
| | 38720½ |
| To 6 ⅌ C⁴. for Collecting 38720ˡᵇ ᵀᵒᵇᵒ. | 2323 |
| | 41043½ |
| To Deposited in the Collector's hands, to be paid the Church Wardens | 797 |
| Blisland Parish C⁴. By 1046 Tithes at 40 ⅌ poll | 41840 |

Cash acco⁴⁸. carried over

[106]

1760 Nov⁴. 10ᵗʰ.

Blisland Parish, To Sundry Cash Acco⁴⁸.    D⁴.
    Viz⁴.

| | |
|---|---|
| To Jemima Curle, for mending the Surplice, Communion Cloth, Pulpit Cloth & Cushion | £—‖10‖— |

| | |
|---|---|
| To Doctor William Harvey, his Acco‘. for Elizᵃ. Kitson's board & finding her medicines to be paid Col. Gill Armistead | 3‖18‖— |
| To Col. Gill Armistead Exõr of Mʳ. John Ruſsel dec'd, his Accoᵗ | 3‖12‖— |
| To Col. Gill Armistead & Cᵒ. Accoᵗ. | 3‖11‖—¾ |
| To Col. Gill Armistead, his Accoᵗ | —‖8‖— |
| To Walter Rawleigh, his Accoᵗ. for Materials for the upper Church £1‖13‖—½ | |
| To Dᵒ. his Accoᵗ. for work done to the upper Church 8‖10‖— | 10‖ 3‖—½ |
| To James Tyree, his Accoᵗ. for boarding Walter Rawleigh & his 'prentices 71 days while at work on the upper Church £2‖10‖— | |
| To James Tyree, his Accoᵗ. for Wheat, & Lyme & bricks for the upper Church —‖ 7‖— | 2‖17‖— |
| To William Farthing, his Accoᵗ. for Bricklayer's work &c. at the upper Church | —‖18‖— |
| To Edward Valentine, for a Barˡ. of Corn, for Richard Creed Curle | —‖12‖ 6 |
| To Col. Burwel Baſsett, his Accoᵗ. for Plank &c for the upper Church | 3‖ 3‖ 1¾ |
| To James Wade, his Accoᵗ. for five Barˢ. Corn for Edwᵈ. Lively, & 3 Barˢ. for Betty Jones, in all Eight Barˢ. at 11/ ⅌ Barˡ. | 4‖ 8‖— |
| To Edward James, his Accoᵗ. for Sundries for John Eacho | —‖ 9‖— |
| To William Mutlow, for keeping Mary Row two months at 5/ ⅌ month | —‖10‖— |

To Maj$^r$. John Power, for paid M$^r$. William Brown, for Six Bushels of Corn, for Widow Charlton   —‖12‖—

The amount of the Sundry Cash Acco$^{ts}$. to be paid by the Ch. Wardens    £ 35‖11‖ 9

M$^r$. William Smith D. Sher, is appointed Collector, on giving Bond & Security.

Maj$^r$. John Power & Cap$^t$. William Armistead are Continued Church Wardens.

Order'd the Church Wardens have Such repairs made on the Glebe as they Shall See neceſsary.

Betty, a Negrowoman belonging to M$^r$. Julius K. Burbidge is Exempted from paying her Parish Levy, on Account of her blindneſs.

John Taylor, Son of John Taylor dec'd, is Exempted from paying his Parish Levy, on Account of his Infirmity.

    Sign'd by    John Power      } Ch. wardens.
                   William Armistead

Test.
     Dudley Williams, Clark O'the Vestry.

At

[107]

At a Vestry held for Blisland Parish at the upper Church the 19$^{th}$. day of October 1761.

Present

The Rev: M$^r$. Thacker Min$^r$.
Maj$^r$. William Armistead, Ch. warden,

| | |
|---|---|
| Col. John Richardson | Col Burwel Baſsett |
| M$^r$. Richmond Terrel, | Maj$^r$. Thruston James |
| M$^r$. Richard Allen | and |
| Col. Gill Armistead | M$^r$. John Shermer. |

This Vestry proceeds to lay the Parish Levy

Blisland Parish     D$^r$.

    lb. Tob$^o$.

| | |
|---|---:|
| To the Rev. M$^r$. Thacker his salary 16000$^{lb}$ Tob$^o$. To 4 ℔ C$^t$. on d$^o$. for Cask 640$^{lb}$. & 4 ℔ C$^t$. for Shrinkage 640$^{lb}$ | 17280 |
| To Dudley Williams Clark of the upper Church & Vestry 1500$^{lb}$ To 4 ℔ C$^t$. on d$^o$. for Cask 60 | 1560 |
| To Richardson Henly Clark of the lower Church 1000. To 4 ℔ C$^t$. on d$^o$. for Cask 40 | 1040 |
| To Jemima Curle Sexton$^*$. of the upper Church 500 & Cask 20 for washing the Surplice 100 | 620 |
| To Edward Lively Sexton of the lower Church the same | 620 |
| To Ann Linsey | 600 |
| To Thomas Linsey | 300 |
| To Elizabeth Burnett for keeping Elizabeth Williams | 700 |
| To Mary Farthing for the support of her son Edward | 300 |
| To M$^r$. Benjamin Waller for a Copy of the list of Tithes | 18 |
| To M$^r$. William Clayton, a Copy of     d$^o$. | 18 |
| To Maj$^r$. John Power for four Communions for the lower Church | 400 |
| To Maj$^r$. William Armistead for four Communions for the upper Church | 400 |
| To the Church Wardens for William the son of Jeremiah Curle | 600 |
| To Rebekah White for keeping George Smiths Child | 600 |
| To Richard Creed Curle towards his Maint$^*$ | 400 |
| To Richard* Tharp for keeping David Dormer | 1500 |

*Note! This name may be "Sharp"; it is hard to decipher.—C. G. C.

| | |
|---|---|
| To David Allen for keeping William Charlton | 1200 |
| To Matthew Cole for keeping Benjˢ. Eacho | 600 |
| To William Hart for keeping Thomas Duco | 600 |
| To dᵒ. for keeping the widow Rowe | 600 |
| To William Geddy for keeping Clift Duco | 600 |
| To Mary Jones towards his maintᵉ | 400 |
| To Burnal Ruſsell for keeping two of William Garlands Children | 900 |
| To Sarah Fox for keeping two of Joseph Foxes Children | 500 |
| To Joel Willis for keeping Thomas Twin's Child | 400 |
| To Elizˢ. Farthing, for keeping Elizˢ. Dunkerton Seven Months | 400 |
| | 33156 |
| Cʳ. By Mʳ. William Smith, the Balˢ. of his Accoᵗ. | 792 |
| | 32364 |
| Dʳ. To 6 ℔ Cent for Collecting 32364ˡᵇ ᵀᵒᵇᵒ. | 1941 |
| | 34305 |
| Blisland Parish Cʳ By 1069 Tithes at 32ˡᵇ. Tobᵒ. ℔ poll | 34208 |
| Due to the Collector | 97 |

1761 Octʳ. 19ᵗʰ.

Dʳ. Blisland Parish. To Sundry Cash Accoᵗˢ. Vizᵗ.

| | | | |
|---|---|---|---|
| To William Jones, for keeping Lucy Tyree, Orphan of Roger Tyree dec'd | £ 5 | — | — |
| To Capᵗ. William Richardson, for Expences in burying Thomas Dugar | — | 15 | — |
| To William Geddy, for Clothing Clift Dugar | 1 | — | 3 |
| To Frances Foulkes, for mending the Surplice, finding linen & Thread | — | 8 | 6 |
| To Col. Gill Armistead & Cᵒ. balˢ. of Accoᵗ. | 6 | 8 | 5½ |

| | |
|---|---|
| To Col. Gill Armistead, balʳ. of his Accᵗ | —‖ 4‖ 2 |
| To John Yates, for keeping Wᵐ. Fletcher three months from laying the Levy in 1759 | 3‖—‖— |
| | £ 16‖16‖ 4½ |

[108]

Order'd that Majʳ. William Armistead pay the several Cash Accoᵗˢ. levied by the Parish, together with other Cash Accoᵗˢ. which are unsettled, Out of the Balʳ. of Cash in his hands.

Mʳ. William Smith D. Sher. is Appointed Collector the Ensuing Year, on giving Bond and Security as Usual.

Capᵗ. William Richardson, Capᵗ. William Macon, and Capᵗ. Edward Power are chosen Vestrymen in the stead of Mʳ. Leonard Henley dec'd, Mʳ. Isaac Goddin dec'd and Mʳ. William Hogg dec'd.

Mʳ. John Shermer and Col. Gill Armistead are Chosen Churchwardens in the Room of Majʳ. John Power and Majʳ. William Armistead.

Order'd that the Church Wardens agree with workmen to build a workhouse, for the poor of this Parish, on the old Glebe, pursuant to and Order of Vestry 1759, of Such dimentions as they Shall think neceſsary.

Order'd that the Church Wardens Send to Great Britain for Table linen for the Communion Table.

Order'd that the Church Wardens demand and receive of the Representatives of Capᵗ. William Kenney dec'd the Legacy given by the Sᵈ. Kenney for a piece of plate for this Parish, pursuant to a former Order of Vestry.

Sign'd by   C. Thacker Minʳ.

John Shermer  } Churchwardens
G. Armistead  }

Test
     Dudley Williams, Clark O' the Vestry

At

[109]
At a Vestry held for Blisland Parish, at the upper Church, the 12th. day of November 1762.

### Present

The Rev. Mr. Thacker Minr.  
Mr. John Shermer Ch. Warden,  
Col. John Richardson,  
Majr. John Power,  
Majr. Thruston James,  

Mr. Richard Allen,  
Capt. William Macon,  
And  
Capt. Edward Power.  

This Vestry proceeds to lay the Parish Levy.

Blisland Parish Dr.

lb Tobo.

| | |
|---|---:|
| To the Rev. Mr. Thacker, his Salary 16000lb Tobo. To 4 ℔ Ct. on do. for Cask 640lb. & 4 ℔ Ct. for shrinkage 640lb | 17280 |
| To Dudley Williams, Clark of the upper Church & Vestry 1500lb. To 4 ℔ Ct. on do. for Cask 60lb. | 1560 |
| To Richardson Henley, Clark of the lower Church 1000lb. To 4 ℔ Ct. on do. for Cask 40lb. | 1040 |
| To Jemima Curle, Sextoness of the upper Church 500lb & Cask 20lb & for washing the Surplice 100lb | 620 |
| To Edward Lively, Sexton of the lower Church 500lb & Cask 20lb. & for washing the Surplice 100lb | 620 |
| To Thomas Linsey 300lb. To Ann Linsey 600lb | 900 |
| To Mrs. Eliza, Burnett, for keeping Eliza, Williams | 700 |
| To Mary Farthing, for the Support of her Son Edward | 300 |
| To Mr. Benjn. Waller, for a Copy of the List of Tithes | 18 |
| To Capt. William Clayton, for two Copies of the List of Tithes | 36 |

| | |
|---|---:|
| To Col. Gill Armistead's Estate, for four Communions, for the upper Church | 400 |
| To Mr. John Shermer, for four Communions for the lower Church | 400 |
| To Reb{a}. White, for keeping George Smith's Child | 600 |
| Present Majr. William Armistead | |
| To Richard Creed Curle, a further allowance towards his Maintainance | 400 |
| To Majr. Thruston James, for keeping David Dormer | 1500 |
| To David Allen, for keeping William Charlton | 1000 |
| To William Hart, for keeping widow Rowe | 800 |
| To Thomas Smith, for keeping Cliff Dugar | 500 |
| To Mary Jones | 600 |
| To Burnal Ruſsel, for keeping two of William Garland's Children | 900 |
| To Sarah Fox, for keeping two of Joseph Foxes children | 600 |
| To Joel Willis, for keeping Thomas Twin's child 500$^{lb}$, and 100$^{lb}$ Omitted last year 100$^{lb}$ | 600 |
| To David Haselwood, for keeping Eliza. Dunkerton | 800 |
| To Majr. William Armistead, for Margt. Mannings keeping two of Sackvile M'hone's Children two Year, to be paid her | 1600 |
| To John Yates, for keeping John, the Son of Daniel Steward dec'd | 350 |
| To Matt{w}. Cole, for Lydda Gadberry's keeping John Goodin from January the 8$^{th}$. 1761, till October 29$^{th}$. 1762 | 800 |
| Debt Carried Over | 34924 |

[110]

| | |
|---|---:|
| 1762 Novr. 12$^{th}$. Blisland Parish    Dr. | lb Tob{o}. |
| To Debt brought over from the Other Side | 34924 |

| | |
|---|---|
| To Majr. William Armistead, for Mary Jeffers' keeping three of the Children of John Jeffers dec'd from April the 12th. 1762 till Novr. 12th. 1762 | 600 |
| To Edward Lively, Exclusive of his Salary as Sexton | 400 |
| To Mr. William Smith Collector, the Balt. of his Accot. | 193 |
| To Majr. William Armistead, to pay Several Cash Accots. | 3500 |
| | 39617 |
| To 6 ℔ Ct. for Collecting 39617lb Tobo. | 2377 |
| | 41994 |
| Blisland Parish      Cr By 1088 Tithes at 38½lb Tobo. ℔ poll | 41888 |
| Due to the Collector | 106 |

Order'd that Majr. William Armistead, Mr. William Smith & Dudley Williams, meet as Soon as Conveniently they can, and proportion the Parish Levy.

Mr. William Smith D Sher. is appointed Collector the Ensuing Year, on giving Bond & Security as Usual.

William Hart is Chosen Sexton of the lower Church, in the Stead of Edward Lively, who resign'd that Office.

Mr. William Daingerfield is Chosen a Vestryman in the Stead of Col. Gill Armistead dec'd.

Capt. William Macon, and Capt. Edward Power, are Chosen Church Wardens, in the Stead of Col. Gill Armistead dec'd, & Mr. John Shermer, who resign'd that Office.

                 Sign'd by     C. Thacker Minr.
                           John Shermer Ch. wardn.

Test
         Dudley Williams, Clark O' the Vestry

Pursuant to an Order of Vestry dated Nov. 12th. 1762, We the Subscribers have met, and proportion'd the Parish Levy, & find it to be Thirty Eight & a half pounds of Tobº. ℔ poll, & One hundred & Six pounds of Tobº. due to the Collector from the Parish, as above. Witneſs Our hands January the 28th. 1763.

      William Armistead
      Wm. Smith
      Dud. Williams
           At

[111]
At a Vestry held for Blisland Parish, at the upper Church, the 25th. day of April 1763.

      Present
   Capt. William Macon, Ch. warden.
  (who was this day Sworn into that Office)

Mr. Richmond Terrel,  Mr. John Shermer,
Majr. John Power,  Majr. William Armistead,
Majr. Thruston James,  Col. Burwel Baſsett, and
Mr. Richard Allen,  Mr. William Daingerfield.

Order'd that Dudley Williams, Clark of the Vestry, take the Register Books of this Parish into his care, And that the Clarks of Each Church give notice, that the Births & deaths in this Parish, are to be Registered by the Sd. Williams.

Order'd that Richard Creed Curle, be discharged from paying his Parish Levy on Account of his Infirmity.

Order'd that Majr. William Armistead pay Mr. John Timberlake Fifteen Shillings, for making and fixing a Dialpost, for the upper Church.

    Sign'd by  William Macon, Ch. warden.
 Test
    Dudley Williams, Clark O'the Vestry.

At a Vestry held for Blisland Parish, at the upper Church, the 13$^{th}$. day of June 1763.

Present

Cap$^t$. William Macon } Ch. wardens
Cap$^t$. Edward Power }

M$^r$. Richmond Terrel,    M$^r$. John Shermer,
Maj$^r$. John Power,       Col. Burwel Ba∫sett,
Maj$^r$. Thruston James,   Maj$^r$. William Armistead, and
M$^r$. Richard Allen,      Cap$^t$. William Richardson.

The Rev. M$^r$. Price Davies, having offered to Serve this Parish as Minister; the S$^d$. Vestry do agree to Accept of him as the Minister of this Parish: And the S$^d$. Vestry do agree to allow him at the laying the next Parish Levy, according to Act of A∫sembly, for the discharge of his Ministerial Function, from the 22$^d$. day of May last, till laying the Levy; and also to allow the S$^d$. M$^r$. Davies for his Board the S$^d$. time, in Consideration of his not being in po∫se∫sion of the Glebe.

M$^r$. James Hockaday is Chosen a Vestryman, in the Stead of Col. John Richardson dec'd.

Sign'd by  Price Davies Minister
           William Macon  } Church Wardens
           Edward Power   }

Test
     Dudley Williams, Clark O' the Vestry

At

[112]

At a Vestry held for Blisland Parish at Chiswel's Ordinary, the 21$^{st}$. day of November 1763.

Present

Cap$^t$. Edward Power, Ch. warden

Maj$^r$. John Power           Cap$^t$. William Richardson,
Maj$^r$. Thruston James,              and
M$^r$. Richard Allen          M$^r$. James Hockaday
Maj$^r$. William Armistead

This Vestry proceeds to lay the Parish Levy.

Blisland Parish                                             D$^r$.

| | lb Tob$^o$. |
|---|---|
| To the Rev. M$^r$. Thacker's Estate, late Minister of this Parish, Salary from laying the Levy in 1762 till the 19$^{th}$ of March 1763 at 16000$^{lb}$ ⅌ Ann. 6749$^{lb\ Tob^o}$. To 4 ⅌ C$^t$. on d$^o$. for Cask 271$^{lb}$, & 4 ⅌ C$^t$. for Shrinkage 271$^{lb}$ | 7291 |
| To the Rev. M$^r$. Price Davies, present Minister of this Parish, his Salary, from the 22$^d$. day of May last till October the 22$^d$. 1763, at 1600$^{lb}$ Tob$^o$. ⅌ Ann. 6665$^{lb}$, To 4 ⅌ C$^t$. on d$^o$. for Cask 266$^{lb}$, and 4 ⅌ C$^t$. for Shrinkage 266$^{lb}$. | 7197 |
| To Dudley Williams, Clark of the upper Church & Vestry, 1500$^{lb}$, & 4 ⅌ C$^t$. for Cask 60 | 1560 |
| To Richardson Henley, Clark of the lower Church, 1000$^{lb}$. & 4. ⅌ C$^t$. for Cask 40 | 1040 |
| To Jemima Curle, Sextoneſs of the upper Church, 500$^{lb}$ & Cask 20$^{lb}$. To d$^o$. for washing the Surplice 100$^{lb}$ | 620 |
| To William Hart, Sexton of the lower Church 500$^{lb}$ & Cask 20$^{lb}$, & for wash$^g$. Surplice 100$^{lb}$. | 620 |
| To Thomas Linsey | 300 |
| To M$^{rs}$. Eliz$^a$. Burnett, for keeping Eliz$^a$. Williams | 700 |
| To Mary Farthing, for the Support of her Son Edward | 300 |
| To M$^r$. Ben: Waller, for a Copy of the List of Tithes | 18 |
| To Cap$^t$. William Clayton, for two Copies of the List of Tithes | 36 |
| To Jeremiah Martin, for keeping Ann Linsey | 1065 |
| To William Hart, for keeping Mary Rowe 950$^{lb}$, and for keeping William Garland's two Children till this time 1000$^{lb}$ | 2050 |

Present Col. Burwel Baſsett & Mr. William Daingerfield
To Matthew Cole, for keeping widow Gadberry's
 Child & John Goodin 1200

Dr. Carried forward 23997
1763
[113]
1763. Nov 21st.
 Blisland Parish Dr.
 lb Tobo.
To Debt brought forward 23997
To Sarah Fox for keeping Joseph Foxes two Children 750
To David Allen, for keeping William Charlton till
 June 6th. 1763 533
To Robert Buchan, in Majr. William Armistead's
 hands, for keeping Betty Kitson, till 1763,
 & burying her 600
To Capt. William Macon, for keeping Cliff Dugar 500
To Do. for two Communions for the upper Church 250
To William Geddy, for keeping Thomas Dugar,
 who is to be bound to the Sd. Geddy, & Geddy
 to Clear him from further Charge to the
 Parish 600
To Richard Creed Curle, a further allowance towards his Maintainance 400
To Majr. Thruston James, for keeping David Dormer 1500
To Mary Jones, in Majr. William Armistead's hands 800
To Joel Willis, for keeping Thomas Twins Child 500
To David Haselwood, for keeping Eliza. Dunkerton 1000
To Margt. Manning, for keeping two of Sackvile
 M'hone's Children 800
To Edward Lively 800

To Ann Taylor, (in Maj'. William Armistead's hands) for the Support of her Son John Taylor  600
To Mr. William Smith, D. Sher. & Collector, his Acco't  595
To Cap't. Edward Power, for two Communions, for the lower Church  250

34475
To 6 ℔ Ct. for Collecting 34475ᵇ Tob°.  2068

36543

Blisland Parish  Cr
lb Tob°.
By 1100 Tithes at 34ᵇ. Tob°. ℔ pole  37400
The Debt as above, is  36543

Deposited in the Collector's hands  857 Tob°. to be paid to the Church wardens towards repairs on the Glebe

N. B. The Cash Accoˢ. & Orders Carried over to the other Side

1763.
[114]
1763. November the 21ˢᵗ.
Blisland Parish  Dr

To Sundry Cash Accoˢ, to be paid by Majr William Armistead Out of the Balˢ. of Tob° in his hands

Vizt. To Mr Richard Allen, for boarding the Rev. Mr Price Davies Minister of this Parish from June 21ˢᵗ. last till laying the levy, for the deficiency of the Glebe's not being in his poſseſsion, at the rate of £ 25 ℔ Annum
£ S. d.
10‖ 8‖ 4

| | | | |
|---|---|---|---|
| To David Allen's Acc$^t$. for burying William Charlton | 1 | 5 | 6 |
| To William Mutlow, his Acc$^t$. for Corn to Sundry persons | 3 | 6 | — |
| To M$^r$. John Timberlake, for Corn for Mary Jeffers, ℔ Cap$^t$. William Macon's Order | 1 | — | — |

£ 15‖19‖10

M$^r$. William Smith D. Sher. is appointed Collector, on giving Bond & Security as usual.

M$^r$. Richard Allen is Chosen Church Warden, in the Stead of Cap$^t$. William Macon, with Cap$^t$. Edward Power.

William Swiney is discharg'd from paying his Parish Levy, on Account of his being lame in his Arm

  Sign'd by

    Edward Power  Church Wardens.
    Richard Allen

Test

  Dudley Williams, Clark O' the Vestry.

              At

[115]

At a Vestry held for Blisland Parish at the upper Church the 12$^{th}$. day of October 1764.

     Present

  The Rev. M$^r$. Price Davies Min$^r$.
  M$^r$. Richard Allen  } Church Wardens
  Cap$^t$. Edward Power

Col. Burwel Baſsett   Maj$^r$. William Armistead
Maj$^r$. Thruston James  Cap$^t$. William Richardson
M$^r$. John Shermer     And
        M$^r$. James Hockaday

This Vestry proceeds to lay the Parish Levy, and to Examine the Returns of Proceſsioners.

| | |
|---|---|
| Blisland Parish | Deb$^r$. |

To the Rev. M$^r$. Price Davies Min$^r$. his Salary 16000$^{lb}$.
To 4 ℔ C$^t$. on d$^o$. for Cask 640$^{lb}$. & 4 ℔ Ct. for lb Tob$^o$.
Shrinkage 640$^{lb}$. — 17280

To Dudley Williams, Clark of the upper Church & Vestry 1500$^{lb}$. To 4 ℔ C$^t$. on d$^o$. for Cask 60 — 1560

To Richardson Henley, Clark of the lower Church 1000$^{lb}$.
To 4 ℔ C$^t$. on d$^o$. for Cask 40 — 1040

To Jemima Curle, Sextone∫s of the upper Church (in the hands of M$^r$. Richard Allen Church Warden) 500$^{lb}$. & Cask 20$^{lb}$. & for washing the Surplice 100$^{lb}$ — 620

To William Hart Sexton of the lower Church 500$^{lb}$ & Cask 20, & for washing the Surplice 100$^{lb}$ — 620

To Thomas Linsey — 300
To M$^{rs}$. Eliz$^a$. Burnett, for keeping Eliz$^a$. Williams — 800
To Mary Farthing, for the Support of her Son Edward — 300
To M$^r$. Ben. Waller, for a Copy of the List of Tithes — 18
To Cap$^t$. William Clayton, for two Copies of the List of Tithes — 36
To Mary Farthing, for keeping Ann Linsey — 1065
To William Hart, for keeping two of the Children of William Garland dec'd — 1200
To William Hart, for Clearing the lower Church Yard — 50
To Matthew Cole, for keeping the wid$^o$. Gadberry's Child & John Goodin — 1200
To Sarah Fox, for keeping Joseph Foxes two Children — 800
To M$^r$. Richard Allen, Church Warden, for four Commun$^s$. for the upper Church — 500
To Cap$^t$. Edward Power, Church Warden, for four Commun$^s$. for the lower Church — 500
To Benj$^a$. Allen, for keeping Mary Row — 950
Present M$^r$. William Daingerfield
To Maj$^r$. Thruston James, for keeping David Dormer — 1500

| | |
|---|---|
| To Maj$^r$. William Armistead, for Mary Jones | 1000 |
| To Joel Willis, for keeping Tho$^s$. Twin's Child | 500 |
| To David Haselwood, for keeping Eliz$^a$. Dunkerton | 1000 |
| To Marg$^t$. Manning's Est$^a$. for keeping two of Sackv$^o$. M'hone's Children | 1000 |
| To Edward Lively | 1000 |
| To Ann Taylor, for the Support of her son John Taylor | 700 |
| Debt Carried Over | 35539 |

Blisland

[116]

| Blisland Parish | Deb$^r$. |
|---|---|
| 1764 October 12$^{th}$. | lb Tob$^o$. |
| To Debt bro$^t$. Over | 35539 |
| To John Wall, for keping two Children of John Jeffers dec'd | 900 |
| To d$^o$. for d$^o$. Short paid last Year | 43 |
| To the Bal$^a$. of M$^r$. William Smith's Acco$^t$. | 306 |
| To James Tyree, for keeping John, Son of Dan$^l$. Steward dec'd from 1762 till this time | 800 |
| To Tob$^o$. in Maj$^r$. William Armistead's hands, to pay Sundry Cash Acc$^{ts}$. | 3000 |
| | 40588 |
| To 6 ⅌ C$^t$. for Collecting 40588$^{lb}$ Tob$^o$. | 2435 |
| | 43023 |
| Deposited in the Collector's hands | 135 |
| | 43158 |

| Blisland Parish | Cred$^r$. |
|---|---|
| By 1121 Tithes @ 38½ ⅌ poll | 43158 |

M$^r$. William Smith D. Sher. is appointed Collector the Ensuing Year, on giving Bond & Security as usual.

Mr. William Daingerfield & Capt. William Richardson, are Chosen Church-Wardens, in the Stead of Mr. Richard Allen, & Capt. Edward Power.

On the Pettition of Mr. John Timberlake, to have an Old Negro man Jack, to be discharg'd from paying his Parish Levy, he is accordingly discharg'd on account of his being unable to do any Service.

The Returns of the Several Procefsioners in this Parish, were this day Examin'd by the Vestry, and Order'd to be Recorded in the Vestrybook of this Parish, for that purpose.

    Sign'd by Price Davies Rector
     William Daingerfield ⎱ Ch. Wardens
     William Richardson ⎰
  Test
     Dudley Williams, Clark O' the Vestry.

             At

[117]

At a Vestry held for Blisland Parish at the lower Church October the 21st. 1765.

     Present
   Col. William Daingerfield ⎱ Ch. wardens
   Capt. William Richardson ⎰

Majr. Thruston James      Mr. John Shermer
Mr. Richard Allen         and
Majr. William Armistead     Mr. James Hockaday

This Vestry proceeds to lay the Parish Levy, & Examine the Entry of the Procefsioners Returns.

  Blisland Parish          Debr.
To the Rev. Mr. Price Davies Minr. his Salary 16000lb.
  To 4 ℔ Ct. on do. for Cask 640lb, & 4 ℔ Ct.   lb Tobo.
  for Shrinkage 640lb           17280
To Dudley Williams, Clark of the upper Church & Ves-
  try 1500lb. To 4 ℔ Ct. on do. for Cask 60    1560

| | |
|---|---:|
| To Richardson Henley, Clark of the lower Church 1000ᵇ. To 4 ℔ Cᵗ. on dº. for Cask 40 | 1040 |
| To John Yates, Sexton at the upper Church 500 & Cask 20, & for washing the Surplice 100 | 620 |
| To William Hart Sexton at the lower Church 500 & Cask 20, & for washing the Surplice 100 | 620 |
| To Mʳ. Ben. Waller, for a Copy of the List of Tithes | 18 |
| To Capᵗ. William Clayton, for two Copies of the List of Tithes | 36 |
| To Martha Bush, for keeping Thoˢ. Linsey | 300 |
| To Mary Farthing, for keeping Ann Linsey 1065ᵇ and for her Son Edward 300ᵇ | 1365 |
| To Mʳˢ. Elizᵃ. Burnett, for keeping Elizᵃ. Williams | 800 |
| To Col. William Daingerfield, for four Communˢ. for the upper Church | 500 |
| To Capᵗ. William Richardson, for four dº. for the lower Church | 500 |
| To William Hart, for keeping two Children of William Garland dec'd | 1200 |
| To Sarah Fox, for keeping two Children of Jos. Fox dec'd | 800 |
| To Ben. Allen, for keeping Mary Row | 950 |
| To Richard Linsey, for keeping a Child of Wᵐ. Gadberry dec'd & a Child of Jamˢ. Goodin dec'd | 1200 |
| To Majʳ. Thruston James, for keeping David Dormer till July 5ᵗʰ. last past | 1120 |
| To Col. Wm Daingerfield, for Mary Jones, to be divided between Stephen Jones and Jemima Curle according to Each persons Expence | 1000 |
| To David Haslewood, for keeping Elizᵃ Dunkerton from Octoʳ. 12ᵗʰ. till Nov. 24ᵗʰ. & burying her | 250 |
| To Sarah Manning, for keeping two Children of Sackvˡ. M'hone dec'd | 1000 |
| To Elizᵃ. Lively | 500 |
| To Ann Taylor, for the Support of her Son John | 600 |

|  |  |
|---|---|
| To John Wall, for keeping three Children of John Jeffers dec'd | 1000 |
| To William Smith Collector, the Bal<sup>e</sup>. of his Acco<sup>t</sup> | 522 |
| To 2000 in Maj<sup>r</sup>. William Armistead's hands, towards paying the Cash Acco<sup>ts</sup>. And repairs for the upper Church | 2000 |
|  | 36781 |
| To 6 ⅌ C<sup>t</sup>. for Collecting 36781<sup>lb</sup> Tob<sup>o</sup>. | 2206 |
|  | 38987 |

Blisland Parish              Cred<sup>r</sup>.

| By 1096 Tithes at 35½<sup>lb</sup> Tob<sup>o</sup>. ⅌ poll | 38908 |
|---|---|
| Due to the Collector | 79 |

N. B. The Sundry Cash Acco<sup>ts</sup>. allow'd by this Vestry, are Over on the Other side

                                                                         Blisland

[118]

Blisland Parish                  Deb<sup>r</sup>.

1765 October 21<sup>st</sup>.

To Sundry Cash Acco<sup>ts</sup>, to be paid with the Bal<sup>e</sup>. in Maj<sup>r</sup>. William Armistead's hands Viz<sup>t</sup>.

|  | £ | s | d |
|---|---|---|---|
| To the Bal<sup>e</sup>. of Col. William Daingerfield's Acco<sup>t</sup> | 4 | 9 | — |
| To William Jones for keping Lucy Tyree | 5 | — | — |
| To Charles Hankin's Acco<sup>t</sup> for 5 Bar<sup>s</sup>. Corn at 10/ | 2 | 10 | — |
| To Tho<sup>s</sup>. Hatton's Acco<sup>t</sup> for a Coffin for David Dormer | — | 15 | — |
| To Dud. Williams & James Hockaday's Acco<sup>t</sup>. for Sund<sup>s</sup>. for Lucy Tyree | 1 | — | 8 |
| To William Geddy's Acco<sup>t</sup>. for work done to the lower Church | 3 | 2 | 6 |
|  | £16 | 17 | 2 |

Col. William Daingerfield and Cap‘. William Richardson are Continued Church Wardens for the Ensuing Year.

Order'd that Maj'. William Armistead Settle and pay Ben. Allen his Acco‘. for his Expences in Burying Mary Row, Out of the Cash in his hands.

Order'd that Col. William Daingerfield & Maj'. William Armistead, meet and proportion the Parish Levy, & return it to the Clark of the Vestry to Enter Accordingly.

M'. Wm Smith D. Sher. is appointed Collector the Ensuing Year, on giving Bond & Security as usual.

This day, the Entry of the Returns of the Proce∫sioners in 1764 in the Vestrybook, were Examined by the Vestry, from the Several Copies return'd; And are found to be Enter'd Agreable to the Said Copies.

Toney, a Negro man, belonging to M". Reb‘. Hockaday, is discharged from paying his Parish Levy, on Account of his Age and Infirmity.

    Sign'd by   Wm Daingerfield } Ch. Wardens.
                   Wm Richardson

   Test
       Dudley Williams, Clark O' the Vestry.

Pursuant to an Order of Vestry dated October 21". 1765 We the Subscribers have met, and proportioned the Parish Levy, and find it to be $35\frac{1}{2}^{lb}$ of Tob°. ℔ poll, and a Bal‘. of $79^{lb}$ Tob°. due to the Collector. Given under Our hands this $24^{th}$. day of March 1766

           William Daingerfield
           William Armistead

   Test
       Dudley Williams, Clark O' the Vestry

At

[119]
At a Vestry held for Blisland Parish at the upper Church October 20th. 1766.

Present

The Rev. Mr. Price Davies Minr.
Capt. William Richardson Ch. Warden,
Col. Burwell Baſsett,     Mr. Richard Allen,
Mr. Richmond Terrell,     Mr. John Shermer
Majr. Thruston James,     and
Majr. William Armistead,     Capt. Edward Power.

This Vestry proceeds to lay the Parish Levy

| Blisland Parish | Debr. |
|---|---|
| To the Rev. Mr. Price Davies Minr. his Salary 16000lb lb Tobo. Tobo., To 4 ℔ Ct. on do. for Cask & 4 ℔ Ct. for Shrinkage 1280lb | 17280 |
| To Dudley Williams, Clark of the upper Church & Vestry, 1500lb. To 4 ℔ Ct. on do. for Cask 60 | 1560 |
| To Richardson Henley, Clark of the lower Church 1000lb. To 4 ℔ Ct. on do. for Cask 40 | 1040 |
| To John Yates, Sexton at the upper Church 500 & Cask 20 & for washing the Surplice 100 | 620 |
| To William Hart, Sexton at the lower Church 500 & Cask 20 & for washing the Surplice 100 | 620 |
| To Col. William Daingerfield, for four Communions, for the upper Church | 500 |
| To Capt. William Richardson, for four do. for the lower do. | 500 |
| To Mr. Ben. Waller, for a Copy of the List of Tithes | 18 |
| To Capt. William Clayton, for two Copies of do. | 36 |
| To Martha Bush, for keeping Thos. Linsey | 300 |
| To William Banks, for keeping Ann Linsey till Sepr. 12th. 1766 @ 1200 ℔ Annum | 1100 |
| To John Piggett, for keeping two Children of William Garland dec'd | 1200 |

| | |
|---|---|
| To Sarah Fox for keeping a Son of Joseph Fox, dec'd | 400 |
| To Richard Linsey, for keeping a Child of Wm Gadberry dec'd & a Child of James Goodin dec'd | 1400 |
| To Sarah Manning, for keeping two Children of Sackvile M'hone dec'd | 800 |
| To Eliz*. Lively. 500 To Ann Taylor, for the Support of her Son John Taylor 600 | 1100 |
| To John. Wall, for keeping a Child of John Jeffers dec'd | 550 |
| To Dickson Haslewood, for keeping a Child of d°. dec'd | 400 |
| To Mary Farthing, for the Support of her Son Edward Farthing | 500 |
| To Elisha Bennett, for keeping Sarah Valentine Seven Months | 700 |
| To Mary Hogg, for keeping d° Three Months | 300 |
| To Joel Willis, for keeping Tho*. Twin's Child last year 300. & for d°. this year 200 | 500 |
| To M$^r$. Wm Smith Collector, the Bal$^a$. of his Acco$^t$. Including 79 due to him last year | 647 |
| To Tob°. in Maj$^r$. William Armistead's hands to pay the Several Cash Acco$^{ts}$. & repairing up$^r$. Ch. | 3000 |
| | 35071 |
| To 6 ℔ C$^t$. for Collecting 35071$^{lb}$ Tob°. | 2104 |
| | 37175 |
| Deposited in the Collector's hands | 277½ |
| | 37452½ |
| Blisland Parish Cred$^r$. | |
| By 1055 Tithes @ 35½ ℔ poll | 37452½ |

Cash Acco$^t$. for this Vestry Carried Over

Blisland

[120]

| Blisland Parish To Sundry Cash Acco<sup>ts</sup>. 1766 October 20<sup>th</sup>. | Deb<sup>r</sup>. |

To John Lewis & C°. for Sund<sup>s</sup>. ⅌ James Taylor as
⅌ Acco<sup>t</sup>   £ 2‖ 6‖11
To Reb<sup>a</sup>. Lilly for keeping Lucy Tyree   5‖—‖—
To Mary Ashcraft, for one Bar<sup>l</sup>. Corn   —‖15‖—
To Eliz<sup>a</sup>. Lively for two Bar<sup>s</sup>. Corn   1‖10‖—
To Daniel Slater, for Sund<sup>s</sup>. for William Jeffers as
⅌ Acco<sup>t</sup>.   1‖ 9‖ 6
To M<sup>r</sup>. Tho<sup>s</sup>. Cowles, for Setting up benches at the
lower Ch.   1‖10‖—
To William Banks, for Expences in burying Ann
Linsey   —‖15‖—
To Ben. Tyree, for keeping Priscilla Day's Child
3½ months   1‖15‖—

            15‖ 1‖ 5

M<sup>r</sup>. Will. Smith D. Sheriff, is appointed Collector the Ensuing Year, on giving Bond & Security as Usual.

M<sup>r</sup>. Richmond Allen is chosen a Vestryman, in the Stead of Cap<sup>t</sup>. William Macon dec<sup>d</sup>. And M<sup>r</sup>. Richardson Henley, is Chosen a Vestryman, in the Stead of Cap<sup>t</sup>. John Power, who is removed out of this Parish.

M<sup>r</sup>. James Hockaday & M<sup>r</sup>. Richmond Allen, a Chosen Church Wardens in the Stead of Col. William Daingerfield & Cap<sup>t</sup>. William Richardson.

     Sign'd by Price Davies Rector
          William Richardson Ch. Warden.

  Test

     Dudley Williams, Clark O' the Vestry

              At

[121]
At a Vestry held for Blisland Parish at the lower Church the 1ˢᵗ. day of October 1767.

Present

Mʳ. James Hockaday, ⎫ Ch.  Majʳ. William Armistead,
Capᵗ. Richmond Allen, ⎭ wardˢ.  Mʳ. John Shermer,
Majʳ. Thruston James,  Capᵗ. William Richardson,
Col. Burwell Baſsett,  Col. William Daingerfield, and
Mʳ. Richard Allen,  Mʳ. Richardson Henley.

This Vestry proceeds to lay the Parish Levy, and Appoint Proceſsioners.

| Blisland Parish | Debʳ. |
|---|---|
| To the Rev. Mʳ. Price Davies Minʳ. his Salary 16000ˡᵇ lb Tobᵒ. Tobᵒ., & 4 ℔ Cᵗ. on dᵒ. for Cask, & 4 ℔ Cᵗ. for Shrinkage 1280ˡᵇ | 17280 |
| To Dudley Williams, Clark of the upper Church & Vestry 1500ˡᵇ & 4 ℔ Cᵗ. on dᵒ. for Cask 60 | 1560 |
| To Mʳ. Richardson Henley, Clark of the lower Church 1000ˡᵇ, & 4 ℔ Cᵗ. for Cask 40 | 1040 |
| To John Yates, Sexton at the upʳ. Church 500ˡᵇ & Cask 20, & for washing the Surplice 100ˡᵇ | 620 |
| To Elizˢ. Hart, Sextoneſs at the lower Church 500ˡᵇ & Cask 20, & for washing the Surplice 100ˡᵇ | 620 |
| To Capᵗ. Richmond Allen, for four Communˢ. for the upʳ. Church | 500 |
| To Mʳ. James Hockaday, for four Communˢ. for the lower Church | 500 |
| To Mʳ Ben. Waller, for a Copy of the List of Tithes | 18 |
| To Capᵗ. William Clayton, for two Copies of the List of Tithes | 36 |
| To Martha Bush, for keeping Thoˢ. Linsey | 240 |
| To Mary Farthing, for the Support of her Son Edward | 400 |

| | |
|---|---:|
| To Tho⁸. Smith, for keeping Sarah Valentine from Octo'. 27ᵗʰ. last at 1000 ℔ Annum | 926 |
| To Ann Taylor, for the Support of her Son John Taylor | 480 |
| To M'. Lancelott Woodward, for keeping Eliz⁸. Williams two months & twelve days from laying the Levy in 1765 & for Burying her | 200 |
| To William Hart's Estate, for keeping James Garland, Orphan of William Garland dec⁴. And John Goodin, Orphan of James Goodin dec⁴. from Nov'. 17ᵗʰ. last @ 1200 ℔ Ann | 1050 |
| To John Wall, for keeping an Orphan of John Jeffers dec⁴. | 550 |
| To Sarah Fox, for keeping an Orphan of Joseph Fox dec⁴. | 400 |
| To Sarah Manning, for keeping two Children of Sackvile Mahone dec⁴. | 400 |
| To Eliz⁸. Lively | 400 |
| To M'. William Smith Collector, his Acco'. | 568 |
| To 3000ᴸᵇ Tob°. in Maj'. William Armistead's hands, to pay Sundry Cash Acco'ˢ. | 3000 |
| | 30788 |
| D°. C'. By Depositum in the Collector's hands last year, not taken from his Acco'. | 277½ |
| | 30510½ |
| D°. D'. To 6 ℔ C'. for Collecting 30510½ᴸᵇ Tob° | 1830 |
| | 32340½ |
| D°. Cred'. By 1042 Tithes @ 31 ℔ poll | 32302 |
| Due to the Collector | 38½ |

Blisland

[122]

| | | |
|---|---|---|
| Blisland Parish    To Sundry Cash Acco$^{ts}$. | | Deb$^r$ |
| 1767, Octo$^r$. 1$^{st}$. | | £  S.  d. |
| To John Piggett, for keeping William Garland, Orphan of Will$^m$. Garland dec$^d$. | | —‖12‖ 6 |
| To Rebecca Lilly, for keeping Lucy Tyree | | 5‖—‖— |
| To William Jones, for keeping a Child of Susannah Sanders from Feb$^y$. 1$^{st}$. last @ £5. ℔ Ann | | 3‖ 8‖ 8 |
| To William Manning, for keeping a Child of Priscilla Days | | 4‖—‖— |
| To M$^r$. James Hockaday, for 6 Bushels of Corn for Patience Linsey | | —‖15‖— |
| To D$^o$. for paid M$^{rs}$. Pasteur, for making a Surplice, & finding thr$^d$. & butt$^s$. | | 1‖ 7‖— |
| To Marg$^t$. Haselwood, for a Bar$^l$. of Corn for Patience Linsey | | —‖12‖ 6 |
| To Maj$^r$. John Prentis, for 12 Yards of hol$^d$. @ 7/6 for a Surplice | | 4‖10‖— |
| To M$^r$. John Lewis, his Acco$^t$. | | 4‖ 8‖10 |
| To Cap$^t$. Richmond Allen Churchwarden, his Acco$^t$ | | 4‖12‖ 3 |
| To Doct$^r$. William Harvey, of his Acco$^t$ of £4‖15 | | 2‖10‖— |
| To William Jones, for keeping Susannah Sanders' Child the Year 1765 | | 5‖—‖— |
| To Col. William Daingerfield's Acco$^t$. | | 1‖10‖ 3 |
| To Rebecca Lilly, her Acco$^t$. for Sund$^s$. for Lucy Tyree two Years | | 2‖ 9‖ 2 |
| To William Jones, his Acco$^t$. for Sund$^s$. for d$^o$. the Year 1763 Omitted | | 1‖ 6‖— |
| To John Ball, for making a Coffin for Jemima Curles Child | | —‖ 7‖ 6 |
| | | 42‖ 9‖ 8 |

M$^r$. James Hockaday, & Cap$^t$. Richmond Allen, are Continued Ch. Wardens.

Mr. William Smith D. Sheriff is appointed Collector the Ensuing Year, on giving Bond and Security as Usual.

Order'd that the Church Wardens Endeavour to purchase that part of land of David Chandler, which lies between the Glebe and the Swamp, to be Annexed to the Glebe.

James Hockaday } Ch. Wardens
Richmond Allen }

Test  Dudley Williams, Clark O' the Vestry

[124]

At a Vestry held for Blisland Parish, at the upper Church, the 10th. day of October 1768.

### Present

The Rev. Mr. Price Davies Minr.  Mr. Richard Allen,
Mr. James Hockaday } Ch.   Mr. John Shermer,
Capt. Richmond Allen } Wards.  Col. Burwel Bassett,
Mr. Richmond Terrel,   Majr. William Armistead, &
Majr. Thruston James,   Capt. Richardson Henley

This Vestry proceeds to lay the Parish Levy.

| Blisland Parish | Debr. |
|---|---|
| To the Rev. Mr. Price Davies Minr. his Salary 16000lb, lb Tobo. & 4 ℔ Ct. on do. for Cask, & 4 ℔ Ct. for Shrinkage 1280 | 17280 |
| To Dudley Williams, Clark of the upper Church & Vestry 1500lb, & 4 ℔ Ct. for Cask 60 | 1560 |
| To Capt. Richardson Henley, Clark of the lower Church 1000lb, & 4 ℔ Ct. for Cask 40 | 1040 |
| To John Yates, Sexton at the upr. Church 500 & Cask 20, & for washing the Surplice 100 | 620 |
| To John Piggott, Sexton at the lower Church 500 & Cask 20, & for washing the Surplice 100 | 620 |
| To Capt. Richmond Allen, for four Communions, for the upper Church | 500 |

| | |
|---|---:|
| To M$^r$. James Hockaday, for four Communions, for the lower Church | 500 |
| To M$^r$. Ben. Waller, for a Copy of the List of Tithes | 18 |
| To Maj$^r$. William Clayton, for two Copies of the List of Tithes | 36 |
| To Mary Farthing, for the Support of her Son Edward | 400 |
| To James Valentine, for keeping his Mother from Dec$^r$. 22$^d$ last till laying the Levy at 1000 ℔ ⅌ Ann | 800 |
| To Ann Taylor, for the Support of her Son John Taylor | 500 |
| To Tho$^s$. Smith, for keeping Sarah Valentine 26 days from laying the levy last year | 74 |
| To Moses Swiney, for keping Jam$^s$. Garland, Orphan of William Garland dec$^d$. and John Goodin, Orphan of Jam$^s$. Goodin dec$^d$ | 1000 |
| To John Wall, for keeping Richard Jeffers, Orphan of John Jeffers dec$^d$, from Octo$^r$. 1$^{st}$. till March 1$^{st}$. @ 550 ⅌ Ann | 229 |
| To Daniel Slater, for keeping Richard Jeffers, Orphan of John Jeffers dec$^d$. from March 1$^{st}$, till Oct$^r$. 10$^{th}$ at 550 ⅌ Ann | 325 |
| To Sarah Manning, for keeping two Children of Sackv$^l$. M'hone dec$^d$ | 400 |
| To Elizabeth Lively | 400 |
| To Sarah Ramsey, for keeping Matthew Curle, from Octo$^r$. 1$^{st}$. 1767 till Mar. 4$^{th}$. 1768 | 150 |
| To John Manning, for keeping a Child of Susanna Sanders's 18 Months, & funeral Charges | 500 |
| To M$^r$. William Smith Collector, his Acco$^t$ | 554½ |
| To 6000$^{lb}$, in Maj$^r$. William Armistead's hands, to pay Sundry Cash Acco$^{ts}$. | 6000 |
| Debt Carried forward | 33506½ |

[124]

| | |
|---|---|
| Blisland Parish | Deb<sup>r</sup>. |
| 1768. Octo<sup>r</sup>. 10<sup>th</sup>, | lb Tob<sup>o</sup> |
| To Debt bro<sup>t</sup>. forward | 33506½ |
| To 6 ℔ C<sup>t</sup>. for Collecting 33506½<sup>lb</sup> Tob<sup>o</sup>. | 2010 |
| | 35516½ |
| Deposited in the Collector's hands | 255½ |
| | 35772 |
| Blisland Parish | Cred<sup>r</sup>. |
| By 1084 Tithes at 33<sup>lb</sup> Tob<sup>o</sup>. ℔ poll | 35772 |

Blisland Parish, To Sundry Cash Acco<sup>ts</sup>.    Deb<sup>r</sup>.
    Viz<sup>t</sup>.

| | |
|---|---|
| To M<sup>r</sup>. John Lewis & C<sup>o</sup>. Acco<sup>t</sup> | £ 3‖13‖ 7 |
| To William Jones, for keping Lucy Tyree, & a Child of Susan<sup>h</sup>. Sand<sup>s</sup> | 8‖—‖— |
| To M<sup>r</sup>. James Hockaday, for two Bar<sup>s</sup>. Corn for Patience Linsey | 1‖—‖— |
| To Cap<sup>t</sup>. Richmond Allen, his Acco<sup>t</sup>. Including Doct<sup>r</sup>. William Harvey's Acc<sup>t</sup>. of 35/ | 4‖ 1‖ 7 |
| To David Chandler, his Acco<sup>t</sup>. for Rent of his house, & going to Mill for Tho<sup>s</sup>. M'gary | —‖10‖ 5 |
| To M<sup>r</sup>. John Ball, for a Coffin, for Tho<sup>s</sup>. M'gary's Child | —‖ 7‖ 6 |
| To the Rev. M<sup>r</sup>. Price Davies, for a Tract of Land bo<sup>t</sup>. of David Chandler, Annexed to the Glebe | 25‖—‖— |
| | 42‖13‖ 1 |
| Blisland Parish      Cred<sup>r</sup>. | |
| By M<sup>r</sup>. James Hockaday, a Fine Rec<sup>d</sup>. of Sarah Manning | 2‖10‖— |
| Bal<sup>s</sup>. of Cash Acco<sup>ts</sup>. due from the Parish | £40‖ 3‖ 1 |

This day M*r*. Richmond Terrel resign'd the Office of a Vestryman of this Parish.

M*r*. Bartholomew Dandridge, is this day Chosen a Vestryman, in the room of M*r*. Richmond Terrel.

Maj*r*. William Armistead, & Cap*t*. Richardson Henley, are Chosen Church Wardens in the Stead of M*r*. James Hockaday, & Cap*t*. Richmond Allen, & Accordingly Sworn.

Bartlet Williams D. Sheriff is appointed Collector of the Parish Levy the Ensuing Year, on giving Bond & Security as Usual.

Eight of the Procefsioners returns were this day Examin'd by the Vestry, & Ordered to be Recorded.

   Sign'd by
    Price Davies Rector,
    William Armistead, } Church Wardens
    Richardson Henley, }

 Test
    Dudley Williams, Clark O' the Vestry

[125]

At a Vestry held for Blisland Parish, at the lower Church, the 23*d*. day of October 1769.

### Present

Maj*r*. William Armistead, } Ch. M*r*. John Shermer,
Cap*t*. Richardson Henley, } wardens Cap*t*. William Richardson
Maj*r*. Thruston James,    and
M*r*. Richard Allen,    Cap*t*. Richmond Allen.
Col. Burwell Bafsett.

This Vestry proceeds to lay the Parish Levy.

Blisland Parish         Deb*r*.

To the Rev. M*r*. Price Davies Min*r*. his Salary } lb Tob*o*.
 16000$^{lb}$ $^{Tobo}$., & 4 ℈ C*t*. on d*o*. for Cask 640$^{lb}$, and }
 4 ℈ C*t*. on d*o*. for Shrinkage 640$^{lb}$    } 17280

| | |
|---|---:|
| To Dudley Williams, Clark of the upper Church & Vestry 1500¹ᵇ, & 4 ℔ Cᵗ. on dº. for Cask 60¹ᵇ | 1560 |
| To Capᵗ. Richardson Henley, Clark of the lower Church, 1000 & 4 ℔ Cᵗ. on dº. for Cask 40 | 1040 |
| To John Yates, Sexton at the upper Church 500¹ᵇ & Cask 20¹ᵇ, & for washing the Surplice 100¹ᵇ | 620 |
| To John Piggot, Sexton at the lower Church 500 & Cask, 20, & for washing the Surplice 100¹ᵇ | 620 |
| To Majʳ. William Armistead, Ch. warden, for four Communˢ. for the upper Church | 500 |
| To Capᵗ. Richardson Henley, Ch. warden, for four Communˢ. for the lower Church | 500 |
| To Mʳ. Ben. Waller, for a Copy of the List of Tithes | 18 |
| To Majʳ. William Clayton, for two Copies of the List of Tithes | 36 |
| To Majʳ. William Armistead, for the Support of Sarah Valentine | 1000 |
| To Mʳ. William Smith, late Collector, his Accoᵗ. Short Cast last year 100 | 100 |
| To Moses Swiney, for keeping James Garland, Orphan of William Garland decᵈ. and John Goodin, Orphan of James Goodin decᵈ. | 700 |
| To Daniel Slater, for keeping Richard Jeffers, Orphan of John Jeffers decᵈ. | 500 |
| To Martha Bush, for keeping Thomas Linsey | 500 |
| Cʳ. | 24974 |
| By Bartlet Williams Collector | 523½ |
| Dʳ. | 24450½ |
| To 6 ℔ Cent. for Collecting 24450¹ᵇ Tobº | 1467 |
| | 25917 |

C$^r$.

| | | |
|---|---|---|
| By 1132 Tithes @ 23$^{lb}$ Tob°. ℔ Tithe | 26036$^{lb}$ $^{Tob°.}$ | |
| Deposited in the Collector's hands | 119 | |
| | 26036 | |

Blisland Parish     To Sundry Cash Acco$^{ts}$.    Deb$^r$.

| | |
|---|---:|
| To Ann Taylor, for the Support of her Son John Taylor | £ 4‖ 3‖ 4 |
| To Pearson Piggot, for finding Plank & Making a Coffin for Thomas M'gary | —‖15‖— |
| To Stephen Jones, in part of his Acco$^t$. of £2‖7‖6 for moving Tho$^s$. M.gary &c. | 1‖—‖— |
| To M$^r$. John Lewis, his Acco$^t$ | —‖14‖— |
| To Cap$^t$. William Richardson, his Acco$^t$. for Corn, for Mary Banks, & Tho$^s$. M'gary | 2‖ 5‖10 |
| To William Jones, for keeping Lucy Tyree £5. and for keeping Susan$^a$. Sanders's Child £5. | 10‖—‖— |
| To M$^r$. John Shermer, for his Acco$^t$. for 68½$^{lb}$ Bacon @ 6$^d$ | 1‖14‖ 3 |
| To Eliz$^a$. Harman, for keeping Mary M'Cormick, from March 5$^{th}$, till Octo$^r$. 23$^d$ | 3‖10‖— |
| To John Manning, his Acco$^t$. for 156$^{lb}$ beef, for John Harris & Eliz$^a$. Cumbo | 1‖ 7‖— |
| To Eliz$^a$. Deaton, for keeping Priscilla Day's Child | 3‖ 5‖— |
| To Cap$^t$. Richardson Henley, to pay George Flack for teaching Mary Banks's Children, when the year is Expired | 1‖—‖— |
| Carried Over | £29‖14‖ 5 |

[126]

1769 October 23$^d$ Blisland Parish    Deb$^r$.

| | |
|---|---:|
| To the amount of the Cash Acco$^{ts}$. bro$^t$. Over | £29‖14‖ 5 |
| To 6 ℔ Cent for Collecting £29‖14‖5 | 1‖15‖ 7 |
| | 31‖10‖— |

D°. C⁽. By 1132 Tithes @ 6¾ᵈ ℔ Tithe £31‖16‖9
Deposited in the Collector's hands                6‖ 9

                                                £31‖16‖ 9

Majʳ. William Armistead, and Capᵗ. Richardson Henley, are Continued Church Wardens.

Richard Linsey is Chosen Sexton of the lower Church, in the Stead of John Piggott, who resign'd.

Majʳ. William Armistead this day made return of his transactions as Treasurer of the Parish, from the Year 1760 to this day; and the Balˢ. due to the Parish is £9‖6

Bartlet Williams D. Sheriff is appointed Collector the Ensuing Year, on giving Bond and Security.

Sign'd by

William Armistead ⎫ Ch. wardˢ.
Richardson Henley ⎭

Test

Dudley Williams, Clark O' the Vestry.

[127]

At a Vestry held for Blisland Parish, at the upper Church, the 23ᵈ. day of October 1770

Present

The Rev. Mʳ. Price Davies Minʳ.

Majʳ. William Armistead ⎫ Ch. Wardens,
Capᵗ. Richardson Henley ⎭

Col. Burwel Baſsett,          Capᵗ. William Richardson,
Mʳ. Richard Allen,            Mʳ. James Hockaday,
Mʳ. John Shermer,                       and
                              Mʳ. Bartholomew Dandridge.

This Vestry proceeds to lay the Parish Levy.

Blisland Parish                                  Debʳ.

To the Rev. Mʳ. Price Davies Minʳ. his Salary 16000ˡᵇ ⎫
  Tob°.., To 4 ℔ Cᵗ. on d°. for Cask 640ˡᵇ and 4 ℔ ½lb Tob°. ⎬
  Cᵗ. on d°. for Shrinkage 640                  ⎭ 17280

NEW KENT COUNTY, VIRGINIA, 1721-1786

| | |
|---|---:|
| To 6 ℔ Cent. for Collecting 17280$^{lb}$ Tob°. | 1036 |
| | 18316 |
| Deposited in the Collector's hands, to be accounted for next year | 98 |
| | 18414 |

| Blisland Parish | Cred$^r$. |
|---|---:|
| | lb Tob°. |
| By 1116 Tithes at 16½$^{lb}$ Tob°. ℔ poll | 18414 |

Blisland Parish   To Cash Deb$^r$.

| | £ | S. | d. |
|---|---:|---:|---:|
| To Dudley Williams, Clark of the upper Church & Vestry | 15 | — | — |
| To Cap$^t$. Richardson Henley, Clark of the lower Church | 10 | — | — |
| To John Yates, Sexton at the upper Church, & for washing the Surplice | 5 | — | — |
| To Richard Linsey, Sexton at the lower Church, & for washing the Surplice | 5 | — | — |
| To Maj$^r$. William Armistead Ch. warden, for four Commun$^s$. for the upper Church | 5 | — | — |
| To Cap$^t$. Richardson Henley, Ch. warden, for four Commun$^s$. for the lower Church | 5 | — | — |
| To M$^r$. Ben. Waller, for a Copy of the List of Tithes | — | 3 | — |
| To Maj$^r$. William Clayton, for two Copies of the List of Tithes | — | 6 | — |
| To the Church Wardens, for Sarah Valentine | 8 | 6 | 8 |
| To Jeremiah Martin, for keeping James Garland, & Richard Jeffers | 7 | 1 | 8 |
| To Cap$^t$. William Richardson, for 5 Bar$^s$. Corn at 15/. for Mary Banks | 3 | 15 | — |

# VESTRY BOOK OF BLISLAND PARISH

| | |
|---|---|
| To Sarah Laffoon, for keeping Mary M'Cormick | 5‖—‖— |
| To Jeremiah Martin his Acco<sup>t</sup>. for Sund<sup>s</sup>. for Mary Banks | —‖ 8‖— |
| To William Jones, for keeping Lucy Tyree | 5‖—‖— |
| To Martha Bush, for keeping Tho<sup>s</sup>. Linsey | 5‖—‖— |
| To Moses Sweny, for keeping John Goodin, & Susanna Sanders's Child | 5‖—‖— |
| To Cap<sup>t</sup>. Richardson Henley, for 30<sup>lb</sup> bacon at 7<sup>d</sup>. for Keziah Allen, & Eliz<sup>a</sup>. Cumbo | —‖17‖ 6 |
| To Charles Hankin, for 10 Bar<sup>s</sup>. Corn at 12/6. for Eliz<sup>a</sup>. Lively | 6‖ 5‖— |
| To the Church Wardens, to Settle and to pay Doct<sup>r</sup>. William Pasteur's Acco<sup>t</sup>. for Thomas M'gary and Keziah Allen | 12‖12‖ 6 |
| Debt Carried Over | £104‖15‖ 4 |

[128]

### 1770 October 23<sup>d</sup>. Blisland Parish Deb<sup>r</sup>.

| | |
|---|---|
| To debt bro<sup>t</sup>. Over from the Other Side | £104‖15‖ 4 |
| To Ann Taylor, for the Support of her Son John Taylor | 4‖ 3‖ 4 |
| To Mary Jones, for keeping Keziah Allen 19 days in her sickneſs at 20/ ⅌ month | —‖13‖ 7 |
| To John Thomas Constable one Levy paid William Smith wrong listed in 1767 31<sup>lb</sup> Tob<sup>o</sup>. | —‖ 5‖ 2 |
| To Bartlet Williams Collector, bal<sup>s</sup>. of his Acco<sup>t</sup>. | 7‖ 5‖10¼ |
| To the Church Wardens, for repairs to be made on the Glebe | 10‖—‖— |
| | 127‖ 3‖ 3¼ |
| To 6 ⅌ Cent. for Collecting £127‖3‖3¼ | 7‖12‖ 7 |
| | 134‖15‖10¼ |

Deposited in the Collector's hands            1||1¾

                                     £134||17||—

| Blisland Parish | Cred$^r$. |
|---|---|
| By 1116 Tithes at 2$^s$· 5$^d$· ℔ Poll | £134||17||— |

Col. Burwel Baſsett, and Maj$^r$. William Armistead, are appointed to meet and proportion the Parish Levy according to the List of Tithes.

M$^r$. John Townes is Chosen a Vestryman in the Stead of Col. William Daingerfield, who is removed out of the Parish.

M$^r$. Barth$^w$. Dandridge, & M$^r$. John Townes are Chosen Church-Wardens for the Ensuing year, and M$^r$. Barth$^w$. Dandridge Sworn accordingly

At the request of Maj$^r$. William Armistead, it is agreed he shall Settle the bal$^s$. of his Acco$^t$. with the Church Wardens, and pay them the bal$^s$. if any remaining in his hands.

Bartlet Williams D. Sheriff is appointed Collector of the Parish levies the Ensuing Year, on giving Bond & Security.
                     Signed by
                               Price Davies Rector
                               B. Dandridge Ch. Warden
       Test   Dud. Williams Clark O' the Vestry.

Pursuant to an Order of Vestry dated October 23$^d$. 1770, We the Subscribers have met and Proportion'd the Parish Levy, and find it to be Sixteen & a half pounds of Tob°. ℔ poll, and two Shillings & five pence Cash ℔ Poll, leaving a depositum of Ninety Eight pounds of Tob°. and one Shilling and one penny three farthings Cash. Witneſs Our hands this 27$^{th}$. of Feb$^y$. 1771.
                               Burwel Baſsett.
                               William Armistead.
           Test   Dud. Williams, Clark O' the Vestry.

[129]

At a Vestry held for Blisland Parish, at the lower Church, the 29th. day of October 1771.

### Present

M$^r$. Bartholomew Dandridge, Church Warden.

| | |
|---|---|
| Maj$^r$. Thruston James. | Cap$^t$. William Richardson, |
| M$^r$. John Shermer, | Cap$^t$. Edward Power, |
| M$^r$. Richard Allen, | Cap$^t$. Richmond Allen, and |
| Cap$^t$. Richardson Henley | |

This Vestry proceeds to lay the Parish Levy, and to Appoint Proceſsioners.

| | |
|---|---:|
| Blisland Parish | Deb$^r$. |
| To the Rev. M$^r$. Price Davies, Rector, his Salary 16000$^{lb}$ Tob$^o$. To 4 ⅌ Cent. on 16000$^{lb}$ Tob$^o$. for Cask 640$^{lb}$ & 4 ⅌ Cent on d$^o$. for Shrinkage 640$^{lb}$ | lb Tob$^o$. 17280 |
| To Bartlet Williams Collector, his Acco$^t$. for Insolvents | 247½ |
| | 17527½ |
| C$^r$. By bal$^e$. deposited in the Collector's hands last year | 98 |
| | 17429½ |
| D$^r$. To 6 ⅌ Cent for Collecting 17429½$^{lb}$ Tob$^o$. | 1045½ |
| Whole Tob$^o$. debt | 18475 |
| C$^r$. By 1150 Tithes at 16$^{lb}$ Tob$^o$. ⅌ Poll | 18400 |
| Due from the Parish to the Collector | 75 |

| | |
|---|---:|
| Blisland Parish | Deb$^r$. |
| To Dudley Williams Clark of the upper Church & Vestry | £ 15‖—‖— |
| To Cap$^t$. Richardson Henley, Clark of the lower Church | 10‖—‖— |

| | |
|---|---|
| To Richard Linsey, Sexton at the lower Church | 5‖—‖— |
| To John Yates, Sexton at the upper Church | 5‖—‖— |
| To Mr. John Townes, Ch. Warden, for four Communions for the Upper Church, and four do. for the lower Church | 10‖—‖— |
| To Mr. Ben. Waller, for a Copy of the List of Tithes | —‖ 3‖— |
| To Col. William Clayton, for a Copy of the List of Tithes | —‖ 6‖— |
| To Jeremiah Martin, for keeping Thomas Linsey | 7‖—‖— |
| To do. for keeping James Garland | 3‖—‖— |
| To William Jones, for keeping Lucy Tyree | 5‖—‖— |
| To Moses Sweny, for keeping Richmond Jeffers £2 and for keeping Susannah Sanders's Child £5 | 7‖—‖— |
| To Thomas Smith, for keeping John Goodin | 1‖15‖— |

Debt Carried Over October 29th, 1771 £ 69‖ 4‖

[130]

1771 October the 29th. Blisland Parish Debr

| | |
|---|---|
| To debt bro' Over from the Other Side | £ 69‖ 4‖— |
| To Mr. John Lewis, for Clothing for John Goodin | —‖15‖— |
| To Mary Jones, for keeping Sarah Valentine | 8‖—‖— |
| To David Williams, for three barrels of Corn, for John Taylor and two barrels of Corn, for Patience Linsey at 12/6 | 3‖ 2‖ 6 |
| To Mr. John Shermer, for Six and a half barrels of Corn, for Stephen Jones, and Rebekah Williams, at 12/6 | 4‖ 1‖ 3 |
| To Peter Rue, for four & a half barrels of Corn at 15/ ℔ barrel for Stephen Jones | 3‖ 7‖ 6 |
| To Mr Richard Allen, for two barrels of Corn, for Jemima Curle | 1‖ 5‖— |

| | |
|---|---|
| To M'. John Timberlake, his Acco'. for Pork & Corn, for d°. | 3‖ 7‖ 9 |
| To M'. Ben. Moore, for 4 Gall°. Molaſses at 2/6 for Patience Linsey, and 2ᵇ Sugar at 8ᵈ. for Stephen Jones | —‖11‖ 4 |
| To William Jennings, for keeping Elizᵃ. Williamson's Child from Febʸ. 23ᵈ. last, at £5 ℔ Annum | 3‖ 6‖ 8 |
| To Prudence Odal, for keeping Mary M'Cormick | 5‖—‖— |
| To M'. Bartholomew Dandridge, for Corn & Other things for Mildred Jennings's Children & Elizᵃ. Cumbo, the Acco'. to be Settled at next Vestry | 5‖—‖— |
| To Bartlet Williams Collector, his Cash Acco'. for Insolvents | 1‖16‖ 3 |
| | £108‖17‖ 3 |
| To 6 ℔ Cent for Collecting £108‖17‖3 | 6‖10‖ 7½ |
| The whole Cash debt | £115‖ 7‖10½ |
| Blisland Parish Credʳ. | |
| By 1150 Tithes, at 2/ | 115‖—‖— |
| Due to the Collector | —‖ 7‖10½ |
| | £115‖ 7‖10½ |

M'. Bartholomew Dandridge, & M'. John Townes, are Continued Church Wardens the Ensuing year.

M'. Bartholomew Dandridge, & M'. John Townes, Churchwardens, are Chosen Collectors of the Parish Levies, on giving Bond & Security as Usual.

     Sign'd by

        B Dandridge Church Warden

  Test

     Dudley Williams, Clark o' the Vestry

NEW KENT COUNTY, VIRGINIA, 1721-1786    189

[131]
At a Vestry held for Blisland Parish, at the upper Church, the 19th. day of October 1772.

### Present
The Rev. Mr. Price Davies Minr.

Mr. Bartholomew Dandridge } Churchwardens.
Mr. John Townes

Col. Burwell Baſsett,          Mr. John Shermer,
Majr. Thruston James,          Capt. William Richardson,
Majr. William Armistead,       Capt. Richmond Allen,
Mr. Richard Allen,             Mr. James Hockaday, and
          Capt. Richardson Henley.

This Vestry proceeds to lay the Parish Levy, and receive the Proceſsioners returns.

| Blisland Parish | Debr. |
|---|---|
| To the Rev. Mr. Price Davies Minr. his Salary 16000lb lb Tobo. Tobo. To 4 ℔ Ct. on 16000lb Tobo. for Cask 640lb, & 4 ℔ Ct. on do. for Shrinkage 640lb | 17280 |
| To Bartlet Williams Collector, Due to him ... last year | 75 |
| To do balt. of his Acco.t of Tobo. | 192 |
|  | 17547 |
| Cr. By Bartlet Williams Collector 1 Levy recd. of John Churn for 1770     16½ By St. Peter's Parish, for Lawrence Egmon's Levies     325 | 341½ |
|  | 17205½ |
| Dr. To 6 ℔ Cent. for Collecting 17205½lb Tobo. | 1032 |
|  | 18237½ |
| Deposited in the Collector's hands | 50½ |
|  | 18288 |
| Cr. By 1143 Tithes, at 16lb Tobo. ℔ Poll | 18288 |

1772 October 19th. Blisland Parish   Debr.
To Dudley Williams, Clark of the Upper Church
    & Vestry      £ 15||—||—
To Capt. Richardson Henley, Clark of the lower
    Church      10||—||—
To John Yates, Sexton at the upper Church    5||—||—
To Richard Linsey, Sexton at the lower Church    5||—||—
To Mr. John Townes Churchwarden, for four
    Communions for the Upper Church £5.
    And for four do. for the lower Church £5.    10||—||—
To Mr. Ben. Waller, for a Copy of the List of
    Tithes      —|| 2|| 3
To Col. William Clayton, for two Copies of the
    List of Tithes      —|| 4|| 6
To Jeremiah Martin, for keeping Thos. Linsey    8||—||—
To Eliza. Sanders, for keeping Susannah Sanders'
    Child      5||—||—
To Mr. Richard Allen Junr. for Clothes for John
    Goodin      4||—|| 2½
To Elisha Bennett, for 77lb. beef, for Jemima
    Curle      —||12||10
To Cornelius Jones, for half a barl. of Corn, for
    Stephen Jones      —|| 6|| 8

    Debt Carried forward      £ 63|| 6|| 5½

[132]

1772 Octor. 19th.  Blisland Parish   Debr.
To debt brot. forward      £ 63|| 6|| 5½
To Mr. John Slater's Accot. for 2½ bars. Corn
    for Jemima Curle, and 3 Bars. do. for
    Ann Taylor @ 15/      4|| 2|| 6
To Mr. John Townes, for paid Mr. James Under-
    wood, for 17lb. windo. lead @ 6d      —|| 8|| 6

To Sarah Ramsey, of her Acco‘. of £2||3||9 for
  keeping & burying Lucy Tyree                1|| 3|| 9
To Mʳ. Thoˢ. Cowles, his Accoᵗ. for horseblocks
  & benches, at the lower Church              5||—||—
To Mʳ. William Tyree, his Accoᵗ for dº. & dº.
  at the upper Church                         4||13|| 4
To Capᵗ. William Richardson, for a barˡ. of
  meal for Margᵗ. Haslewood                   —||16||—
To Isaac Fox's Accoᵗ. for his Sister Sarah, her⎫
  board 9 weeks in her Sickneſs, Coffin, ⎬
  and funeral Charges                   ⎭    4||10||—
To Thoˢ. Rawson, for Accomodating the Glazier
  7 days, when glazing the Church windows    —||16|| 3
To John Bradenham, for a barˡ. Corn, for
  Patience Linsey                             —||15||—
To Benjⁿ. Moore's Accoᵗ. for Molaſses &c.     —||13|| 1
To Mʳ. John Townes, for 2 barˢ. Corn for
  Jemima Curle                                1||10||—
To Doctʳ. Andrew Anderson's Accoᵗ. for Salley
  Fox                                         6||11|| 6
To Mʳ. John Townes, for a Napkin              —|| 2|| 6
To Joel Willis, for 17 Yards of Virginia Cloth,
  for Mary M'Comick @ 2/                      1||14||—
To Mʳ. John Townes, his Accoᵗ. for work on the⎫
  upper Church & Glebe, and for materials⎬   10||12|| 9½
To Mʳ. John Lewis Merchᵗ. the balˢ. of his⎫
  Accoᵗ. from 1765 till this time         ⎬   2|| 7|| 2
To Mʳ. David Lewis & Cº. Accoᵗ. for 6 Ells⎫
  Oznbˢ. and 1½ Yard of plains for Jemima⎬
  Curle                                    ⎭  —||10|| 6
To William Jennings, for keeping Elizᵗ. Wil-
  liamson her child, a year                   5||—||—
To Mʳ. Bartholʷ. Dandridge Ch. warden, the
  balˢ. of his Accoᵗ.                         4||13||10½

| | |
|---|---|
| To Turner Cumbo, for keeping Eliz⁎. Cumbo | 3∥—∥— |
| To Mʳ. William Hankin, for 5 barˢ. Corn for Stephen Jones, at 15/ | 3∥15∥— |
| To Mʳ. Daniel Taylor, for the Rent of his house, for Patience Linsey | 1∥ 5∥— |
| To Mʳ. William Hankin, for 6 barˢ. Corn, for Mary Banks @ 15/ | 4∥10∥— |
| | 131∥17∥ 2½ |
| To 6 ℔ Cent. for Collecting £131∥17∥2½ | 7∥18∥ 2¾ |
| | 139∥15∥ 5¼ |
| Deposited in the Collector's hands, to be accounted for at laying the next Parish Levy | 5∥ 9∥ 8¼ |
| | £145∥ 5∥ 1½ |
| Credʳ. By 1143 Tithes at 2/6½ | £145∥ 5∥ 1½ |

[133]

1772 October 19ᵗʰ.

Burnal Ruſsell is discharged from paying his Parish Levy for the future.

Order'd that the Clark of the Vestry Record the Returns of the Several Proceſsioners, in Order to have them examin'd.

Vizᵗ. The Return of Stephen Willis and John Ames.
The Return of John Harman and Julius Vadin.
The Return of Edward Warren and Geo. Clough.
The Return of David Williams and William Tyree.
The Return of James Allen and John Richardson.
The Return of Walter Rawleigh and Andʷ. Banks.
The Return of Richard Gaddey and John Hankin.
The Return of William Hankin and Thoˢ. Hatton.
The Return of William Geddy and William Spraggins.
The Return of Philemon Woodward and Randolph Woodward.

Col. Burwell Baſsett, and Majʳ. Thruston James, are Chosen Churchwardens for the Ensuing year.

Majʳ. Thruston James Churchwarden, and Mʳ. William Armistead Junʳ. are Chosen Collectors of the Parish Levies the ensuing year, on giving Bond and Security as Usual.

   Sign'd by

      P. Davies Rector
      Burˡ. Baſsett } Churchwardens
      Thruston James }

Test

    Dudley Williams, Clark O' the Vestry.

[134]

At a Vestry held for Blisland Parish at the lower Church, the 29ᵗʰ, day of November 1773.

      Present

  The Rev. Mʳ. Price Davies, Rector,
  Col. Burwell Baſsett, } Church wardens.
  Majʳ. Thruston James, }

Majʳ. William Armistead,    Mʳ. James Hockaday,
Capᵗ. William Richardson,    Capᵗ. Richmond Allen, and
    Capᵗ. Richardson Henley

  This Vestry proceeds to lay the Parish Levy.
   Blisland Parish      Debʳ.

To the Rev. Mʳ. Price
 Davies Minʳ his Salary
 16000ˡᵇ Tobᵒ.
To 4 ℔ Cent. on dᵒ. for } 17280ˡᵇ Tobᵒ· at 12/6 £108||—||—
 Cask 640 and 4 ℔ Cent.
 for Shrinkage 640

To Dudley Williams, Clark of the upper Church
 and Vestry             15||—||—
To Capᵗ. Richardson Henley, Clark of the lower
 Church              10||—||—

| | |
|---|---|
| To John Yates, Sexton at the upper Church | 5\|\|—\|\|— |
| To Richard Linsey, Sexton at the lower Church | 5\|\|—\|\|— |
| To Col. Burwell Baſsett, Ch. warden, for four Communions, for the upper Church | 5\|\|—\|\|— |
| To Majʳ. Thruston James, Ch. warden, for four Communions for the lower Church | 5\|\|—\|\|— |
| To Ben. Waller Esqʳ. for a Copy of the List of Tithes | —\|\| 3\|\|— |
| To Col. William Clayton, for a Copy of the List of Tithes | —\|\| 6\|\|— |
| To Mʳ. George Bridges, for keeping Thoˢ. Linsey | 8\|\|—\|\|— |
| To the Churchwardens, for Susannah Sanders' Child | 5\|\|—\|\|— |
| To Majʳ. Thruston James Ch. warden, for Clothing for John Gooding, and Kirby Washer's Children, ℔ Mʳ. John Lewis's Accoᵗ. | 2\|\|17\|\|— |
| To Mʳ. William Norvell, his Accoᵗ. for 3 barˢ. Corn for John Buffin in 1770, at 12/6, and 9 barˢ Corn this year for Stephen Jones, at 15/ | 8\|\|11\|\|— |
| To Mʳ William Brown, for 7 barˢ. Corn, for Mary Banks at 15/ | 5\|\| 5\|\|— |
| To Mʳ. William Hankin, for 5 barˢ. Corn, for Stephen Jones, at 13/3, Omitted last year | 3\|\| 6\|\| 3 |
| To Mary Banks, for keeping a Child of Margᵗ. Haslewood's 9½ Months | 4\|\|—\|\|— |
| To Elizˢ. Austin, for keeping two of Jeſse Hall's Children from Febʸ. 27ᵗʰ. last | 8\|\|—\|\|— |
| To Majʳ. Thruston James, to pay Eleanor Allen, for the Rent of a Plantation, for Stephen Jones | 3\|\|10\|\|— |
| To Mʳˢ. Rebˢ. Hockaday, for ½ barˡ. Corn for Patience Linsey | —\|\| 6\|\| 3 |

| | |
|---|---|
| To M$^r$. William Tyree, for keeping and maintaining Richard Curle, Orphan of Richard Curle dec$^d$. he is to keep him from being any Charge to the Parish for the future | 8‖—‖— |
| To Doctor Andrew Anderson's Acco$^t$. for Mary Yates, and Richmond Jeffers | 1‖14‖— |
| To James Odal's Acco$^t$. for keeping Mary M'Comick about five weeks, and for her funeral charges | 2‖10‖— |
| To John Ball Sen$^r$. for a Coffin for Elisha Frazier | —‖15‖— |
| To M$^r$. Barth$^w$. Dandridge's Acco$^t$. | 5‖ 9‖ 3 |
| To Turner Cumbo, for keeping his Mother | 3‖10‖— |
| To Benj$^a$. Wall, for keeping his brother John's Son Tho$^s$. from Jan$^y$. 2$^d$. last | 1‖10‖— |
| To William Jennings, for keeping Eliz$^a$. Williamson's Child from October 1772 and a Child of Mildred Jennings's | 7‖10‖— |
| Carried forward | £233‖ 2‖ 9 |

[135]
1773 Nov$^r$. 29$^{th}$. Blisland Parish Deb$^r$.

| | |
|---|---|
| To debt bro$^t$. forward | £233‖ 2‖ 9 |
| To Eliz$^a$. Deaton, bal$^a$. of her prov'd Acco$^t$ for boarding and keeping James Day the year 1768 | 4‖—‖— |
| To Col. Burwell Baſsett Church warden, his Acco$^t$. | 4‖14‖ 3¾ |
| To William Jones, for a Coffin, for Lucy Tyree | —‖15‖— |
| To Rachel Wall, for 9 yards of Virginia Cloth & p$^r$. of Shoes and Stockings, for a Child of John Wall dec$^d$. | 1‖ 1‖ 9 |
| To M$^r$. David Lewis and C$^o$. Acco$^t$. | 4‖14‖ 5½ |

| | |
|---|---|
| To David Williams's Acco⁺. of £7‖17‖6 for work done on the Glebe | 6‖—‖— |
| To Bartlet Williams, balⁿ. of his Accᵗ. for Insolvⁿ. last year | 1‖11‖ 5½ |
| To Mʳ. W. Smith's Accᵗ. agᵗ. Benjⁿ. Haslewood decᵈ. for the years 1764. 1765. 1766, 1767 and 1768 .... 769ˡᵇ Tobᵒ. at 2ᵈ | 6‖ 8‖ 2 |
| To Mʳ. John Brown, Collector for Majʳ. Thruston James. balⁿ. of his Tobᵒ. Accᵗ. for Insolvⁿ 38½ˡᵇ Tobᵒ. | —‖ 4‖ 9¾ |
| To Mʳ. Benjⁿ. Moore, for 2 Gallⁿ. Molaſses, for Stephen Jones | —‖ 5‖ 6 |
| To Col. Burwell Baſsett Ch. warden, to pay for repairs done on the Glebe | 10‖—‖— |
| To the Church wardens, towards an Addition to the lower Church | 75‖—‖— |
| To the Church wardens, towards Erecting a workhouse | 25‖—‖— |
| | £372‖18‖ 2½ |

Credʳ.

| | | |
|---|---|---|
| By Mʳ. John Brown, Collector for Majʳ. Thruston James | £2‖ 4‖ 8 | |
| By Mʳ. William Armistead Collector | 2‖14‖10 | 4‖19‖ 6 |
| | | 367‖18‖ 8½ |

Debʳ.

| | |
|---|---|
| To 6 ℈ Cent. for Collecting £367‖18‖8½ | 22‖ 1‖ 6¼ |
| | £390‖—‖ 2¾ |

Credʳ.

| | |
|---|---|
| By 1133 Tithes at 6ˢ 9½ᵈ (or 68ˡᵇ Tobᵒ. at the Option of the payer) | 384‖14‖11½ |
| Due to the Collector | 5‖ 5‖ 3¼ |

| | | |
|---|---|---|
| Or | Blisland Parish | Deb$^r$. |

lb Tob°.

To the above £384||14||11½ to purchase Tob°. at
10/ ℔ C$^t$.  76949½
Deposited in the Collector's hands  94½

77044

Cred$^r$.

lb. Tob°.

By 1133 Tithes at 68$^{lb}$. Tob°. (or 6$^s$.||9½$^d$. Cash, at the Option of the payer)  77044

Col. Burwell Baſsett, and Maj$^r$. Thruston James, are Continued Church wardens, for the ensuing year.

M$^r$. William Armistead D Sheriff in New Kent, is appointed Collector of the Parish Levies the ensuing year, on giving Bond and Security as Usual.

Order'd that the Church wardens Advertise an Addition and repairs to the lower Church in this Parish.

Order'd that the Churchwardens Rent, or build a workhouse, for the poor of this Parish, at the Expence thereof; and that they also purchase neceſsaries for the poor.

M$^r$. Armistead Ruſsell, and M$^r$. William Hankin, are Chosen Vestrymen, in the room of M$^r$. Richard Allen dec'$^d$, and M$^r$. John Townes, who is removed out of the Parish.

Burnal Ruſsell, is Chosen Sexton, at the lower Church, in the room of Richard Linsey, who resign'd that Office

Sign'd by   P. Davies Rector
            Bur$^l$. Baſsett   } Church wardens.
            Thruston James

Test

Dudley Williams, Clark O' the Vestry.

[136]

At a Vestry held for Blisland Parish, at the upper Church, the 31$^{st}$. day of October 1774

## Present

The Rev. Mʳ. Price Davies, Rector
Col. Burwell Baſsett, } Church wardens,
Majʳ. Thruston James,
Majʳ. William Armistead   Capᵗ. Richmond Allen, and
Capᵗ. William Richardson   Mʳ. William Hankin.
Mʳ. James Hockaday

This Vestry proceeds to lay the Parish Levy
Blisland Parish        Debʳ.
                                                    lb Tobº.

| | |
|---|---:|
| To the Rev. Mʳ. Price Davies, Rector, his Salary 16000ᶫᵇ Tobº., To 4 ℔ Cent. on dº. for Cask 640ᶫᵇ. and 4 ℔ Cent. on dº. for Shrinkage 640ᶫᵇ | 17280 |
| To 6 ℔ Cent. for Collecting 17280ᶫᵇ Tobº. | 1036 |
| | 18316 |
| Dº. Credʳ. By 1071 Tithes at 17ᶫᵇ Tobº. ℔ Poll | 18207 |
| Due to the Collector | 109 |

1774 October 31ˢᵗ.   Blisland Parish     Debʳ.

| | |
|---|---|
| To Dudley Williams, Clark of the upper Church, and Vestry | £ 15‖—‖— |
| To Capᵗ. Richardson Henley, Clark of the lower Church | 10‖—‖— |
| To John Yates, Sexton at the upper Church | 5‖—‖— |
| To Burnal Ruſsell, Sexton at the lower Church | 5‖—‖— |
| To Col. Burwell Baſsett, Churchwarden, for four Communions, for the upper Church | 5‖—‖— |
| To Majʳ. Thruston James, Churchwarden, for four Communions, for the lower Church | 5‖—‖— |

| | | |
|---|---|---|
| To M$^r$. Ben. Waller, for a Copy of the List of Tithes 20$^{lb}$. Tob$^o$. at 1½$^d$ | —‖ 2‖ 6 | |
| To Col. William Clayton, for two Copies of the List of Tithes 40$^{lb}$. Tob$^o$. at 1½$^d$ | —‖ 5‖— | |
| To M$^r$. George Bridges, for maintaining Thomas Linsey | 8‖—‖— | |
| To M$^r$. William Brown, for 19½ Bushels of Corn for the Widow Banks, and 5 Bushels of Corn, for William Swiney at 12/6 ℔ barrel | 3‖ 1‖ 3 | |
| To M$^r$. Benjamin Moor, for 2 Gallons of Molaſses, for Stephen Jones | —‖ 5‖ 6 | |
| To the Churchwardens, for Susannah Sanders' Child | 3‖—‖— | |
| To Joel Willis and wife, for Carrying Eliz$^a$. Pond's Child to Col. Robert Carter's, in Westmoreland County, and for their trouble with Mary Thomson, in her Sickneſs | 3‖10‖— | |
| To Mildred Thomas, for the maintainance of Philemon Chandler's Son Philemon | 3‖—‖— | |
| To M$^r$. William Hankin, for 3½ Bar$^s$. Corn for Kirby Washer, at 12/6, and 1 Bar$^l$. of Corn For William Banks at 11/ | 2‖14‖ 9 | |
| To the Churchwardens, for the maintainance of two of Jeſse Hall's Children one year | 8‖—‖— | |
| To M$^{rs}$. Eleanor Allen, for the Rent of her Land to Stephen Jones | 3‖10‖— | |
| To M$^r$. Daniel Slater, for a Bar$^l$. of Corn, for Patience Linsey | —‖12‖ 6 | |
| To William Jennings, for maintaining a Child of Eliz$^a$. Williamson's, and a Child of Mildred Jennings's | 6‖—‖— | |

| | |
|---|---|
| To Rachel Wall, for maintaining a Child of John Wall dec^d | 3‖10‖— |
| To M^r. David Lewis's Acco^t. for Sundries | 1‖ 3‖ 1½ |
| To Julius Allen, for a Barrel of Corn, for Stephen Jones in 1772 | —‖15‖— |
| Debt Carried forward | £ 92‖ 9‖ 7½ |

[137]

1774 October 31^st. Blisland Parish Deb^r.

| | |
|---|---|
| To Debt brought forward | £ 92‖ 9‖ 7½ |
| To M^r. Charles Hankin, for a Barrel of Corn, for Rachel Wall | —‖12‖ 6 |
| To M^r. William Armistead Jun^r. D. Sheriff, and Collector, the bal^r. of his Acco^t | 8‖ 8‖ 9¼ |
| To Col. Burwell Baſsett, towards an addition to the lower Church | 94‖—‖— |
| | 195‖10‖10¾ |
| To 6 ℞ Cent. for Collecting £195‖10‖10¾ | 11‖14‖ 7¾ |
| | 207‖ 5‖ 6½ |
| Deposited in the Collector's hands | 4‖ 7 |
| | £207‖10‖ 1½ |
| Blisland Parish Cred^r. | |
| By 1071 Tithes at 3^s 10½^d ℞ Poll | £207‖10‖ 1½ |

Cap^t. William Richardson, and Cap^t. Richmond Allen are chosen Churchwardens, for the ensuing year, in the room of Col. Burwell Baſsett, and Maj^r. Thruston James, and Sworn accordingly.

Cap^t. William Richardson Church warden, is Chosen Collector of the Parish Levies the ensuing year, on giving Bond and Security as usual.

Sign'd by   Pryse Davies Rector
            W$^m$. Richardson    } Churchwardens
            Richmond Allen       }

Test
            Dudley Williams, Clark o' the Vestry

[138]

At a Vestry held for Blisland Parish, at the lower Church the 30$^{th}$. day of October 1775.

Present

The Rev. M$^r$. Pryse Davies, Rector
Cap$^t$. William Richardson,  } Churchwardens.
Cap$^t$. Richmond Allen,      }
Maj$^r$. Thruston James,      M$^r$. Bartholomew Dandridge,
Col. Burwell Ba∫sett,                      and
Maj$^r$. William Armistead    M$^r$. William Hankin.
M$^r$. James Hockaday,

This Vestry proceeds to lay the Parish Levy, and to appoint Proce∫sioners.

| Blisland Parish | Deb$^r$. |
|---|---|
| | lb Tob$^o$. |
| To the Rev. M$^r$. Pryse Davies Rector, his Salary 16000$^{lb}$ Tob$^o$. To 4 ℔ Cent. on d$^o$. for Cask 640$^{lb}$ | |
| To 4 ℔ Cent on d$^o$ for Shrinkage 640$^{lb}$ | 17280 |
| To 6 ℔ Cent on 17280$^{lb}$ Tob$^o$. for Collecting | 1036 |
| | 18316 |

| Blisland Parish | Cred$^r$. |
|---|---|
| By 1075 Tithes at 17$^{lb}$ Tob$^o$. ℔ Poll | 18275$^{lb}$ Tob$^o$. |
| Due to the Collector | 41 |
| | 18316 |

Blisland Parish                                Debr

| | |
|---|---|
| To Dudley Williams, Clark of the upper Church, and Vestry | £ 15\|—\|— |
| To Capt. Richardson Henley, Clark of the lower Church | 10\|—\|— |
| To John Yates, Sexton at the upper Church | 5\|—\|— |
| To Burnal Ruſsell's Estate, for Serving as Sexton at the lower Church | 5\|—\|— |
| To Capt. Richmond Allen, Ch. warden, for four Communions for each Church | 10\|—\|— |
| To Mr. Benjamin Waller, Clark of James City County Court, for a Copy of the List of Tithes | —\| 2\| 6 |
| To Mr. George Bridges, for the maintainance of Thomas Linsey | 8\|—\|— |
| To Elizabeth Sanders, for keeping and maintaining Susannah Sanders's child | 3\|—\|— |
| To Mr. John Hockaday, for a Coffin for, and burying Elizabeth Cumbo | 1\|—\|— |
| To Burnal Ruſsell's Estate, for the maintainance of two of Jeſse Hall's children | 8\|—\|— |
| To Mr. John Allen, for the Rent of Land, to Stephen Jones | 3\|10\|— |
| To Thomas Wilks for the maintainance of Thomas, and Joseph Smith, Orphans of Thomas Smith dec'd from the 4th. of April | 5\|—\|— |
| To Amelia Thomas, for maintaining and Schooling Philemon Chandler, Son of Philemon Chandler | 6\|—\|— |
| To John Valentine, for maintaining and Schooling William Smith, Son of Thomas Smith dec'd, from the 4th. of April at £6\|5 ℔ Annum | 3\|10\| 7 |

| | | |
|---|---|---|
| To Prudence Odal, for the maintainance of Mary Thomson | | 4‖—‖— |
| To M`r`. M`r`. John Brown, Collector, his Cash Acco`t`. for Insolvents return'd | £3‖16‖9½ | |
| To d°. his Tob°. Acco`t`. for Insolvents and 109`lb` due at laying the Levy Last year included, is 466`lb` Tob°. at 20/· | 4‖13‖2¼ | 8‖–9‖11¾ |

|  |  |
|---|---|
|  | £ 95‖13‖—¾ |
| To 6 ⅌ Cent. for Collecting £95‖13‖—¾ | 5‖14‖ 9¼ |
|  | £101‖ 7‖10 |
| Deposited in the Collector's hands | 10‖ 2¼ |
|  | £101‖18‖—¼ |

| Blisland Parish | Cred`r`. |
|---|---|
| By 1075 Tithes at 1` 10¾`d` ⅌ Poll | £101‖18‖—¼ |

M`r`. William Smith, is chosen a Vestryman, in the room of Cap`t`. Richardson Henley, who is removed out of the Parish; and M`r`. Silvanus Prince, is chosen a Vestryman, in the room of M`r`. John Shermer dec'd.

Cap`t`. William Richardson, and Cap`t`. Richmond Allen, are continued Churchwardens, for the ensuing year.

Dudley Williams is chosen Collector of the Parish Levies the ensuing year, on giving Bond and Security, as usual.

  Signed by
    Pryse Davies, Rector
    William Richardson ⎱ Church wardens.
    Richmond Allen ⎰
 Test
   Dudley Williams, Clark o' the Vestry.

[139]

At a Vestry held for Blisland Parish at the lower Church the 29th. day of July 1776.

Present the Rev. Pryse Davies, Rector, Capt. William Richardson, and Capt. Richmond Allen Church wardens, Major Thruston James, Col. Burwell Baſsett, Capt. James Hockaday, Capt. Edward Power, and Mr. William Hankin.

This Vestry proceeds to examine the Addition to the lower Church in this Parish, built by Mr. Daniel Lyon, which he agreed with this Vestry to do, and for the performance of which entered into Articles of agreement with Col. Burwell Baſsett, and Major Thruston James, the then Church wardens of this Parish the        day of 1774. The said Vestry agrees with Mr. William Moſs, Executor of the abovesaid Daniel Lyon deceas'd to receive the said Addition; and the said William Moſs agrees to and with the said Vestry, to repaint the inside of the Windowsashes, the Door, and Eaves of the said Addition, and to reshingle the the valleys of the Roof if neceſsary. And the said Vestry agrees that Col. Burwell Baſsett pay the said William Moſs the balance due to the said Daniel Lyon's Estate, for the said Addition.

    Signed by    Pryse Davies Rector

                 William Richardson } Church wardens
                 Richmond Allen

    Test

        Dudley Williams Clark of the Vestry.

At a Vestry held for Blisland Parish at the upper Church the 28th. day of April 1777.

NEW KENT COUNTY, VIRGINIA, 1721-1786    205

Present

The Rev. M.ʳ. Pryse Davies, Rector,
Capt. Richmond Allen, Church warden.
Maj.ʳ. Thruston James,   Capt. Edward Power,
Col. Burwell Baſsett,    M.ʳ. William Hankin
Capt. James Hockaday,    Capt. Silvanus Prince, and
M.ʳ. Armistead Ruſsell

The Vestry proceeds to lay the Parish Levy.
Blisland Parish                  Deb.ʳ.

To the Rev. M.ʳ. Pryse Davies,
  Rector, his Salary        16000ˡᵇ
  Tob°. for the year 1776
To 4 ℔ Cent. on 16000ˡᵇ Tob°. for
  Cask                       00640
To 4 ℔ Cent. on d°. for Shrinkage 00640
To his Salary from Octo.ʳ. 15.ᵗʰ. till
  Dec.ʳ. 31.ˢᵗ. at 17280ˡᵇ ℔ Ann  03645

                20925 Tob°.
  at 20/ ℔ 100ˡᵇ                          £209|| 5||—
To Dudley Williams, Clark of the upper
  Church and Vestry, till the last day of
  December 1776 at £15 ℔ Annum            17||10||—
To Capt Richardson Henley, Clark of the
  lower Church till the last day of Decem-
  ber 1776 at £10 ℔ Annum                  11||13|| 4
To John Yates, Sexton at the upper Church  5||—||—
To Rebecca Ruſsell, Sextoneſs at the lower
  Church                                   5||—||—
To   d°   for maintaining two of Jeſse
  Hall's Children                          8||—||—
To Capt. William Richardson, for 7 Com-
  munions, for the two Churches            8||15||—

| | |
|---|---|
| To M#. Benjamin Waller, for a Copy of the List of Tithes | —‖ 2‖ 6 |
| To Capt. Richmond Allen, for 4 Communions for the two Churches, since last October | 5‖—‖— |
| To M#. John Allen, for the Rent of his Plantation to Stephen Jones | 3‖10‖— |
| To M#. George Bridges, for maintaining Thomas Linsey | 8‖—‖— |
| Debt carried forward | £281‖15‖10 |

[140]

Blisland Parish           Deb#.
1777 April 28#.

| | |
|---|---|
| To Debt bro#. forward from the other side | £281‖15‖10 |
| To Elizabeth Feare, for maintaining Dorril Feare, Orphan of Hamner Feare, dec# | 4‖—‖— |
| To Capt. Richmond Allen, for M#. Mary Hogg's maintaining a Child of Thomas Smith dec#. till this time at £5 ℔ Annum | 7‖10‖— |
| To Thomas Wilks, for maintaining two of Tho#. Smith's Children till Octo#. last | 10‖—‖— |
| To Prudence Odell, for maintaining Mary Thomson from October 1775 till this time at £4 ℔ Annum | 6‖—‖— |
| To M#. William Tyree, for a Coffin for Isaac Fox, and a d°. for his Daughter | 1‖10‖— |
| To Turner Cumbo, for maintaining two of George Jennings's Children a year, at £5 each | 10‖—‖— |
| To the Estate of M#. Danel Lyon, dec#. for making a Sashwindow for the upper Church | 1‖10‖— |

| | |
|---|---|
| To the Estate of M⁽ʳ⁾. Daniel Lyon dec⁽ᵈ⁾. for a mistake in his calculation when he undertook the Addition to the lower Church in 1774 | 40‖—‖— |
| To M⁽ʳ⁾. John Lewis's Acco⁽ᵗ⁾ for Sundries in 1773 and 1774 | 2‖ 4‖ 5¼ |
| To Elizabeth Sanders, for maintaining Laney Jones Sanders, Child of Susannah Sanders dec⁽ᵈ⁾. 8 Months, and for his Funeral charges | 4‖19‖ 2 |
| To Maj⁽ʳ⁾. Thruston James, for 2 Bar⁽ˢ⁾. Corn, for Kirby Washer | 1‖ 5‖— |
| To M⁽ʳ⁾. John Brown, for half a Bar⁽ˡ⁾. Corn, for William Sweeny in 1774 | —‖ 6‖ 3 |
| To £11 of Thomas Rawson's Acco⁽ᵗ⁾ of £15, for boarding Richmond Jeffers, making his Clothes, and funeral charges | 11‖—‖— |
| To John Manning, for maintaining George Jennings's daughter Priscilla till this time | 6‖—‖— |
| | 388‖—‖ 8¼ |
| Cred⁽ʳ⁾. By bal⁽ˢ⁾. due from Dudley Williams Collector ℔ Acco⁽ᵗ⁾ | 8‖18‖ 4 |
| | 379‖ 2‖ 4¼ |
| Deb⁽ʳ⁾. To 6 ℔ Cent. for collecting £379‖2‖4½ | 22‖14‖11½ |
| | 401‖17‖ 3¾ |
| Deposited in the Collector's hands | 000‖14‖ 8¼ |
| | £402‖12‖— |
| Cred⁽ʳ⁾. By 1098 Tithes at 7⁽ˢ⁾‖4⁽ᵈ⁾ ℔ Poll | £402‖12‖— |

M⁽ʳ⁾. John Timberlake is chosen a Vestryman, in the room of M⁽ʳ⁾. William Smith, who is removed out of the Parish.

Capt. James Hockaday, and Mr. William Hankin are chosen Church wardens in the room of Capt. William Richardson, and Capt. Richmond Allen, and accordingly sworn.

Dudley Williams is chosen Collector of the Parish Levies, on giving Bond and Security.

Sign'd by     P. Davies, Rector

Jams. Hockaday   } Church wardens.
Wm Hankin

Test

Dudley Williams, Clark of the Vestry

[141]

At a Vestry held for Blisland Parish at the upper Church the 23d. day of Feby. 1779.

Present the Rev. Mr. Pryse Davies, Rector, Capt. James Hockaday, the hon. Bartholomew Dandridge Esq. Capt. Richmond Allen, Capt. Edward Power, Mr. George Bridges, Mr. John Timberlake, Mr. Andrew Banks, Mr. John Lewis, and Mr. John Goddin.

N. B. The above Vestry was chosen by the freeholders of Blisland Parish, pursuant to an Act of Aſsembly, which diſsolved the late Vestry of this Parish, agreeable to a pettition from the inhabitants of the Parish: in which Election Col. Burwell Baſsett, Capt. Silvanus Prince, and Mr. William Allen, were chosen Vestrymen also with the nine abovementioned, but did not attend Vestry this day.

This Vestry proceeds to lay the Parish Levy for the years 1777 and 1778.

Blisland Parish                      Debr.

To Doctr. Elisha Hall, of his Accot. of
    £30||17 for visits and medicines for
    Thomas Smith, Orphan of Thomas
    Smith decd. from Decr. 1777           £ 20||17||—

To Do. 5 ℔ Cent. on £20||17 two years       2|| 1|| 8

| | |
|---|---|
| To M\*. William Tyree, for a Coffin for the abovesaid Orphan Thomas Smith | 1‖—‖— |
| To Capt. James Hockaday, for 2½ Barrels of Corn, for Widow Merriman 30/ | 3‖15‖— |
| To John Valentine for maintaining and schooling William Smith, Orphan of Thomas Smith dec⁴ | 3‖—‖— |
| To Mary Green, for maintaining Elizabeth Hall and her child a year to Oct\*. 12ᵗʰ. 1778 | 50‖—‖— |
| To Thomas Wilks, for maintaining Thomas Smith, Orphan of Thomas Smith dec⁴. from Octo\*. 1776 till May 1778. including funeral charges | 35‖—‖— |
| To Dᵒ. for maintaining Joseph Smith, Orphan of Thomas Smith dec⁴. from Oct\*. 1776 till this 23ᵈ. of February 1778 | 25‖—‖— |
| To M\*. George Bridges, for maintaining Thomas Linsey a year to Octo\*. 1777 | 8‖—‖— |
| To M\*. William Fisher, for maintaining Thomas Linsey a year to Octo\*. 1778 | 10‖—‖— |
| To John Allen, for rent to Stephen Jones 1777 £3‖10<br>To Dᵒ. for rent to 1778 £4 and half a Barrel of Corn to dᵒ. 10/ | 8‖—‖— |
| To Jeremiah Wade, for rent to Widow Merriman 1777 £2. for dᵒ. to dᵒ. 1778 £3 | 5‖—‖— |
| To Prudence Odell, for maintaining Mary Thomson, from April 28ᵗʰ. 1777 till this time | 30‖—‖— |
| To the hon Barthʷ. Dandridge, for 100ˡᵇ Bacon for widow Merriman | 12‖10‖— |
| To John Brooker, for maintaining Elizabeth Hall and her child two months | 16‖12‖ 8 |

| | |
|---|---|
| To M`r`. John Timberlake, for maintaining Isaac Fox, Orphan of Isaac Fox dec`d`. from April 1`st` 1777 till Feb`y`. 6`th` 1778 | 6‖—‖— |
| To M`r`. John Cowles, for maintaining William Smith, Orphan of Thomas Smith dec`d`. from April 1777 till January 24`th` 1778 | 3‖15‖— |
| Carried forward | £240‖11‖ 4 |

[142]

1779 Feb`y`. 23`d`    Blisland Parish    Deb`r`

| | |
|---|---|
| To debt brought forward | £240‖11‖ 4 |
| To Lucy Yates, for maintaining Francis Oakley 14 Months | 12‖—‖— |
| To John Manning, for maintaining Priscilla, Orphan of George Jennings dec`d`. from April 1777 till this time | 15‖—‖— |
| To John Manning, for maintaining Thomas Merriman, Orphan of James Merriman dec`d`. from Octo`r`. last till this time | 5‖—‖— |
| To Rebecca Rufsell's Estate, for maintaining two of Jefse Hall's Children from Octo`r`. 1776 till Dec`r`. 1778 | 25‖—‖— |
| To Turner Cumbo, for maintaining one of George Jennings's Children the year 1777 | 5‖—‖— |
| To the Churchwardens, to pay M`r`. William Norvell his Acco`t`. of £18. and Cole Ashlock his Acco`t`. of £25, both for Philley Jones and her three Children, if the said Wardens do find that the said Philley Jones belongs to this Parish, and the Acco`ts`. are just | 43‖—‖— |

To the Churchwardens, for the use of the
    Parish, if found neceſsary                  150||—||—
To Dudley Williams, Clark of the Vestry         20||—||—

                                                515||11|| 4
Cred'. By Dudley Williams Collector, balᵉ.
    of his Accoᵗ.                                1|| 4|| 2

                                                514|| 7|| 2
Dʳ. To 6 ₰ Cent. for collecting £514||7||2      30||17|| 2

                                                545|| 4|| 4
    Deposited in the Collector's hands           3||18|| 8

                                                £549|| 3||—
Cred'. By 1046 Tithes at 10/6                    549|| 3||—

Ordered that the Churchwardens meet and proportion the Parish Levy as soon as they conveniently can.

Meſsʳˢ. John Timberlake, and John Lewis are chosen Churchwardens the present year.

Dudley Williams is chosen Collector of the Parish Levies, on giving Bond and Security as usual.

    Signed by    P. Davies, Rector

        John Timberlake } Church wardens.
        John Lewis

Pursuant to an Order of Vestry dated the 23ᵈ. day of February 1779, we the subscribers have proportioned the Parish Levy, and find it to be ten shillings and six pence ₰ Tithe, and a depositum of £3||18||8 deposited in the

Collector's hands, to be accounted for at the laying the next parish Levy.

March 18th. 1779 Signed by
>John Timberlake.
>John Lewis.

Test,
>Dudley Williams, Clark o' the Vestry.

[143]

At a Vestry held for Blisland Parish at the lower Church the 8th. day of November 1779

Present the Rev. Mr. Pryse Davies, Rector, Mr. John Timberlake Churchwarden, Capt. James Hockaday, Capt. Richmond Allen, Capt. Edward Power, Mr. George Bridges, Capt. William Allen, Mr. Andrew Banks, and Mr. John Goddin.

This Vestry proceeds to lay the Parish Levy

| Blisland Parish | Debr. |
|---|---|
| To William Tyree, for maintaining James Merriman 4 Months at £40 ⅌ Ann | £ 13\|\| 6\|\| 8 |
| To Edmund Taylor, for maintaining Isaac Fox, a year to February 6th. 1779 | 8\|\|—\|\|— |
| To Ditto for Ditto Ditto from Feby. 6th. till Novr. 8th. 1779 | 22\|\|10\|\|— |
| To William Fisher, for maintaining Thomas Linsey from Octor. 8th. 1778 till this 8th. of November 1779. at £40 ⅌ Annum | 43\|\| 6\|\| 8 |
| To John Ames, for maintaining Elizabeth Hall from the 23d. of Feby. last till this 8th. of Novr. at £100 ⅌ Annm. £70\|\|13\|\|8 deduct for half a barrel of Corn of the Ch. wards. 7\|\|10 | 63\|\| 3\|\| 8 |
| To Prudence Odell, for maintaining Mary Thomson from Feby. 23d. till this time | 85\|\|—\|\|— |

| | |
|---|---:|
| To John Manning, for maintaining a Child of George Jennings dec⁴. and a Child of James Merriman dec⁴. from Feb⁷. 23ᵈ last till this time | 70‖13‖ 8 |
| To Jeremiah Martin, for maintaining Dorril Feare 16 months in the years 1776 and 1777 | 8‖—‖— |
| To Ditto, the half of 31/6 for 3 Parish levies overcharged for 1777 and 1778, they being out of the Parish in 1777 | 15‖ 9 |
| To Daniel Slater the half of 21/ for 2 Parish levies in the same manner | 10‖ 6 |
| To Thomas Potter the half of 21/ for 2 Ditto Ditto | 10‖ 6 |
| To John Gadberry the half 21/ for 2 Ditto Ditto | 10‖ 6 |

Thus fär was levied November the 8ᵗʰ. 1779    £ 316‖ 7‖11

1780 February the 3ᵈ. the Vestry met again at the lower Church

Present The Rev Mʳ. Pryse Davies Rector, Meſsʳˢ. John Timberlake, and John Lewis, Church wardens, Capt. Richmond Allen, Mʳ. George Bridges, Capt. William Allen, Mʳ. Andrew Banks, Mʳ. John Goddin, and Mʳ. Edmund Hockaday, who was chosen a Vestryman the 8ᵗʰ. day of November 1779, in the room of Capt. Silvanus Prince, who refused to qualify as a Vestryman.

This Vestry proceeds to finish laying the Parish Levy which was begun the 8ᵗʰ. day of November last (as above) and to appoint Proceſsioners in the several districts in this Parish

The above £316‖7‖11 carried forward and charged.

[144]
    1780 February 3ᵈ Blisland Parish    Debʳ.

| | |
|---|---:|
| To debt levied Novʳ. 8ᵗʰ. 1779 brought forward | £ 316‖ 7‖11 |
| To Mʳ. John Lewis, Churchwarden, the balance of his Accoᵗ | 123‖10‖— |

Present Capt. James Hockaday.

| | |
|---|---:|
| To John Manning, for maintaining Thomas Merriman Orphan of James Merriman decᵈ. from the 8ᵗʰ. of Nov. last till the 15ᵗʰ. of January last | 10‖—‖— |
| To Lucy Yates, for maintaining Francis Oakley, from February the 23ᵈ. last, and putting him to School 4 Months | 50‖—‖— |
| To John Woodward, for maintaining Mary Austin from January the 10ᵗʰ. till this 3ᵈ. of February 1780 . . . 24 days | 10‖—‖-- |

Present Capt. Edward Power.

| | |
|---|---:|
| To John Ames, for keeping Elizabeth Hall, till the 28ᵗʰ. of this Inst. (Febʳ.) the balʳ. of £100 (£70‖13‖8 being levied Nov. 8ᵗʰ. last) | 29‖ 6‖ 4 |
| To Dudley Williams, Clerk of the Vestry | 100‖—‖--- |
| To the Churchwardens, for contingent charges | 350‖—‖— |
| | £ 989‖ 4‖ 3 |
| Cʳ. By Dudley Williams, Collector, balʳ. of his Accoᵗ. due the Parish | 98‖—‖10 |
| | 891‖ 3‖ 5 |
| Dʳ. To 6 ⅌ Cent. for collecting £891‖3‖5 | 53‖ 9‖ 4 |
| | 944‖12‖ 9 |
| Deposited in the Collector's hands, to be accounted for at laying the levy | 32‖15‖ 3 |
| | £ 977‖ 8‖— |
| Cʳ. By 1086 Tithes at 18/ | £ 977‖ 8‖— |

Mr. John Timberlake, and Mr. John Lewis, are continued Church wardens, the present year.

Ordered that the Church wardens settle with Mr. William Norvell, for the maintainance of Philarity Jones, and her children.

Mr. John Timberlake, Sheriff of New Kent County, is appointed Collector of the Parish levies this present year, on giving Bond and Security as usual.

   Sign'd by P. Davies Rector.
     John Timberlake } Churchwardens.
     John Lewis

Test
  Dudley Williams Clerk of the Vestry

[145]

At a Vestry held for Blisland Parish, at the lower Church the 20th. day of December 1780.

Present Mefs.rs John Timberlake, and John Lewis, Churchwardens, Capt. James Hockaday, Mr. George Bridges, Capt. William Allen, Capt. Andrew Banks, Capt. John Goddin, and Mr. Edmund Hockaday.

  This Vestry proceeds to lay the Parish Levy.
  Blisland Parish       Debr.

To William Fisher, for maintaining Thomas Linsey from March 1st. till this time, at £400 ⅌ Annum   £ 330||—||—

To William Ammons, for maintaining Elizabeth Hall, from Febr. 14th. 1780, till Febr. 14th. 1781   580||—||—

To Prudence Odell, for maintaining Mary Thomson a year, to Febr. 3d. 1781   300||—||—

To John Manning, for maintaining a Child of George Jennings decd. a year from Novr. 8th. 1779   300||—||—

| | |
|---|---|
| To Warwick Woodward, for maintaining a Child of James Meriman dec⁴ | 306‖—‖— |
| To Mʳ. John Lewis, Churchwarden, the balˢ. of his Accoᵗ | 189‖10‖— |
| To Mʳ. William Norvel's Accoᵗ. for Corn, for Philarity Jones, and her three children, in 1778, levied in the Churchwarden's hands, till the said Wardens were satisfied whether the said Philarity Jones belonged to this Parish, which not being determin'd in 1778, the Collector did not pay, and credited the Parish for in his Accoᵗ. £ 18. eight prices being allowed in consideration of depreciation of money in two years, and not being paid when required | 144‖—‖— |
| To Cole Ashlock's Accoᵗ. for Corn for the said Philarity Jones, and her three Children, levied at the same time, under the same circumstances, which the Collector did not pay, and Credited the Parish for £ 25. allowed as above | 200‖—‖— |
| To James Jones, for maintaining Richard Hall, a year to Febʳ. 14ᵗʰ. 1781 | 332‖—‖— |
| To William Jennings, for maintaining Ann, a Child of Susannah Curle | 200‖—‖— |
| To Mʳ. John Timberlake, Churchwarden, balˢ. of his Accoᵗ. | 170‖16‖ 8 |
| To Ditto his Accoᵗ. for Mary Austin | 250‖—‖— |
| To Joseph Hix, for maintaining Hardiman, a Child of Preston Hix dec⁴ | 150‖—‖— |
| To John Allen, for rent of his land to Stephen Jones £ 100, last year £ 30 | 130‖—‖— |

Capt. John Goddin, and Capt. Andrew Banks were chosen Churchwardens in the stead of Meſsʳˢ. John Timberlake, and John Lewis.

This Vestry is adjourned till Wednesday the 3ᵈ. of January next. But, as the militia of James City, and New Kent Counties were called on duty at that time, it prevented the Vestry's meeting till January 30ᵗʰ. the proceedings of which, being annexed to this, to conclude laying the Parish Levy, is carried over

Debt levied Decʳ. 20ᵗʰ. 1780 carried over to the other charges of January 30ᵗʰ. 1781    £ 3582‖ 6‖ 8

[146]

At a Vestry held for Blisland Parish, at Mʳ. Adam Birds, the 30ᵗʰ. day of January 1781.

Present Meſsʳˢ. John Timberlake, and John Lewis, Churchwardens, James Hockaday, George Bridges, William Allen, Andrew Banks, and John Goddin, Gent.

This Vestry proceeds to finish laying the Parish levy, which begun the 20ᵗʰ. day of December 1780.

| Blisland Parish | Debʳ. |
|---|---|
| To debt laid Decʳ. 20ᵗʰ. 1780, and brought over | £ 3582‖ 6‖ 8 |
| To Mʳ. John Timberlake, a further allowance for Mary Austin | 150‖—‖— |
| To Dudley Williams, Clark of the Vestry | 500‖—‖— |
| To the Churchwardens, for contingent charges | 600‖—‖— |
| | 4832‖ 6‖ 8 |
| To 6 ℔. Cent. for collecting £4832‖6‖8 | 289‖18‖ 9½ |
| | £ 5122‖ 5‖ 5½ |

| | |
|---|---|
| Cʳ. By 1020 Tithes at £5 | 5100‖ |

| | |
|---|---|
| Due to the Collector | 22‖ 5‖ 5½ |

Davy, a Negroman, belonging to Mʳ. John Timberlake, is exempted from paying his Parish levy, in consideration of his being unable to labour for many years past.

Dudley Williams, is appointed Collector of the Parish levies, on giving Bond and Security as usual.

    Signed by
      John Goddin  ⎱
      Andrew Banks ⎰ Churchwardens.
Test
    Dudley Williams, Clark of the Vestry.

Davy a Negroman belonging to Mʳ John Timberlake is exempted from paying any taxes the present year

[147]

At a Vestry held for Blisland Parish, at Mʳ. Adam Byrds thee 3ᵈ. day of November 1781.

Present Andrew Banks, and John Goddin, Gent. Churchwardens, James Hockaday, George Bridges, Edward Power, John Lewis, and William Allen, Gent.

This Vestry proceeds to lay the Parish Levy.

| Blisland Parish | Debʳ. |
|---|---|
| To Mʳ. George Bridges, for maintaining Thomas Linsey, from March 1ˢᵗ. till this time at £8 ℔ Ann. | 5‖ 8‖ 8 |
| To Ditto for a Coat for Ditto | —‖14‖— |
| To John Ames, for maintaining Elizabeth Hall from Febʳ. 14ᵗʰ. till this time at £5 ℔ Ann | 3‖12‖ 4 |

To Prudence Odell, for maintaining Mary
Thomson, from Feb$^r$. 3$^d$. till this time at
£6 ℔ Ann                                                    4‖ 9‖ 9

To John Manning, for maintaining a Child of
George Jennings dec$^d$                                      4‖—‖—

To Randolph Woodward, for maintaining
Thomas, an Orphan of James Merriman
dec$^d$. from Jan$^y$. 1$^{st}$ @ £3                         2‖10‖ 5½

To John Allen, for rent of his land, to Stephen
Jones                                                        5‖—‖—

To M$^r$. William Norvel, for 5 Bar$^s$. and 4 Bush$^s$.
Corn, for Stephen Jones, and Philarity
Jones @ 10/                                                  2‖18‖—

To Joseph Hix, for clothing for Preston Hixes
child                                                        —‖10‖—

To Julius Curle, for a Coffin, for Ann Manning               —‖10‖—

To William Jennings, for maintaining two
(Strange) Children from Sep$^r$. 1$^{st}$. till this
time at £4 ℔ Ann. each                                       1‖ 8‖—

To Sarah Bradley, for maintaining two (Ditto)
Ditto the same time, at the same rate                        1‖ 8‖—

To James Jones, for maintaining Richard
Hall, a Child of Eliz$^a$. Hall's from Feb.
14$^{th}$. till this time @ £4                               2‖18‖—

Carried to the Parish charge laid by the Vestry the 15$^{th}$. of Octo$^r$. 1782          £35‖ 7‖ 2½

1781 Nov. 3$^d$. Capt. John Goddin rendered an Acco$^t$. to the Vestry, of what money he received that was levied in the Church warden's hands, for contingent charges, the 30$^{th}$. day of January 1781

To wit

To paid Randolph Woodward                     £ 80‖—‖—

| To paid Nance Hitchcock, to buy Corn, for Mourning Hawkins | 120‖—‖— |

£ 200‖—‖—

| Cʳ. By Cash recᵈ. of Dudley Williams Collector | £ 200‖—‖— |

John Goddin, and Andrew Banks, Gent. are continued Church wardens, the ensuing year.

Order'd that the Church wardens, and Clark of the Vestry meet, as soon as the Lists of Tithes can be got, and proportion the Parish Levy: and that they proportion the said Parish Levy that hath been this day levied in Specie, in paper Currency, agreeable to the Value that the grand Jury at the succeeding general Court shall settle it at.

Dudley Williams is appointeed Collector of the Parish Levies the ensuing year, on giving Bond and Security as usual.

Sign'd by

John Goddin  
Andrew Banks } Church wardens.

N. B. The above charge of £35‖7‖2½ was not proportion'd, because the List of Tithes was not taken, as the interruption of the English Army, in this part of the State prevented it. And the said charge of £35‖7‖2½ is carried over, and added to the charge levied by the Vestry the 15ᵗʰ. day of October 1782. and proportion'd with it.

Test

Dudley Williams, Clark of the Vestry.

[148]

At a Vestry held for Blisland Parish, at the lower Church the 15ᵗʰ. day of October 1782.

Present John Goddin, and Andrew Banks, Gent. Church wardens, James Hockaday, George Bridges, John Timberlake, John Lewis, Edward Power, and Edmund Hockaday Gent.

The Vestry proceeds to lay the Parish Levy.

Blisland Parish                      Deb$^r$.

| | |
|---|---|
| To the amount of Acco$^t$. levied Nov. 3$^d$. 1781 being never proportion'd, collected nor paid, brought over from the other side | 35‖ 7‖ 2½ |
| To M$^r$. George Bridges, for maintaining Thomas Linsey from Nov. 3$^d$ 1781 till Jan$^y$. 1$^{st}$. 1782 | 2‖11‖ 4 |
| To William Fisher, for maintaining Thomas Linsey from January 1$^{st}$. till this time at £12 ℔ Ann | 9‖10‖— |
| To John Ames, for maintaining Eliz$^a$. Hall, from Nov. 3$^d$. 1781, till Feb. 14$^{th}$. 1782 | 4‖—‖— |
| To William Ammons, for maintaining Eliz$^a$. Hall, from Feb. 14$^{th}$. till this time at £15 ℔ Ann | 10‖—‖— |
| To Prudence Odell, for maintaining Mary Thomson, part of the year | 6‖10‖— |
| To John Manning, for maintaining a Child of George Jennings dec$^d$ | 4‖—‖— |
| To Randolph Woodward, for maintaining a Child of James Merriman dec$^d$ | 1‖10‖— |
| To M$^r$. William Norvel's Acco$^t$. of 88½ Bush$^s$. Corn @ 2/6 for Jones, and Philarity Jones | 11‖ 1‖ 3 |
| To James Jones, for maintaining Richard, a Child of Eliz$^a$. Hall, from Nov. 3$^d$. till this time | 4‖—‖— |
| To William Jennings, for two Strange Children, from Nov. 3$^d$. 1781 till Feb. 22$^d$ 1782 @ £14 ℔ Ann | 4‖ 5‖11 |

| | |
|---|---|
| To Sarah Bradley, for two Ditto...from Ditto, til.. Ditto, at...Ditto | 4‖ 5‖11 |
| To John Allen, for Rent of his Land to Stephen Jones | 5‖—‖— |
| To Nance Hitchcock, for maintaining Mourning Hawkins | 5‖—‖— |
| To Isham Christian, for four Barrels of Corn, for Nathan Hixes Children | 3‖—‖— |
| To Jamees Pride, for one Ditto...for..Ditto | —‖15‖— |
| To Capt. Andrew Banks, for one Ditto... for...Ditto | —‖15‖— |
| To... Ditto,... for half a Barl. Corn, for Philarity Jones | —‖ 7‖ 6 |
| To the Churchwardens, for contingent charges | 6‖—‖— |
| To Dudley Williams, two years Salary as Clark of the Vestry | 12‖10‖— |
| | 130‖ 9‖ 1½ |
| Cr. By Dudley Williams Collector, bal'. of his Acco't. £727‖14‖6½ paper money, reduced to Specie according to the Scale of Depreciation for May 1781 at 150 for 1 | 4‖17‖— |
| | 125‖12‖ 1½ |
| Dr. To 6 ₱ Cent. for collecting £125‖12‖1½ | 7‖10‖ 8½ |
| | 133‖ 2‖10 |
| Cr. By 964 Tithes at 2/9 | 132‖11‖— |
| Due to the Collector | 11‖10 |

Col. Edward Power, and Mr. Edmund Hockaday, are chosen Church wardens, in the room of Andrew Banks, and John Goddin, Gent.

The Sheriffs of James City and New Kent Counties, are chosen Collectors of the Parish levies the ensuing year, on giving Bond and Security as usual.

Sign'd by

    Edward Power  ⎱ Church wardens
    Edmund Hockaday ⎰

 Test
    Dudley Williams, Clark o' the Vestry

[149]

At a Vestry held for Blisland Parish at the House of M$^r$ Charles Harvey the 23$^d$. day of February 1784.

Present Edward Power, and Edmund Hockaday Gent. Churchwardens, James Hockaday, John Timberlake, Richmond Allen, Andrew Banks, William Allen, and John Goddin Gent.

  This Vestry proceeds to lay the Parish Levy
  Blisland Parish      Deb$^r$.

| | |
|---|---:|
| To Moses Sweny, for maintaining Thomas Linsey, last year | £ 8‖—‖-- |
| To William Fisher, for maintaining Thomas Linsey two Months and a half in 1782 | 2‖10‖— |
| To William Ammons, for maintaining Eliz$^a$. Hall, last year, and clothing her | 15‖—‖— |
| To Bennett Curle, for maintaining & clothing James Rawleigh, Orphan of Walter Rawleigh dec$^d$ | 6‖—‖— |
| To Mary Hix, for maintaining George Hix, Orphan of Nathan Hix dec$^d$ | 6‖—‖-- |
| To Eliz$^a$. Sanders, for her trouble with Sarah Glasebrook from Jan$^y$. 8$^{th}$. to Mar. 8$^{th}$. and funeral charges | 5‖—‖— |

224   VESTRY BOOK OF BLISLAND PARISH

| | |
|---|---|
| To Jemima Curle, for maintaining & clothing Cliffe Chandler, Orphan of David Chandler dec⁴ and putting him to School six Months | 12‖—‖— |
| To James Jones, for maintaining and clothing Richard Hall | 5‖—‖— |
| To M⁺ Edmund Hockaday, for half a Bar¹. Corn, for Sarah Glasebrook, when at Mʳˢ. Sanders's | —‖ 7‖ 6 |
| To James Odell, for expences in burying Mary Thomson | 2‖—‖— |
| To Warwick Woodward, for maintaining Sarah Hix, Orphan of Sarah Hix a year | 3‖—‖— |
| To Capt. Andrew Banks, for two years rent of his plantation to Isaac Green | 4‖—‖— |
| To the Estate of Docʳ. Andrew Anderson dec⁴ for his attendance on William Smith, when his Arm was fractur'd and for medicines | 5‖ 7‖ 6 |
| To James Wade, for four Barˢ. and a half of Corn, for Stephen Jones | 3‖ 7‖ 6 |
| Present the Hon'ble Bartholomew Dandridge Esqʳ. | |
| To Nance Hitchcock, for maintaining Mourning Hawkins a year | 6‖—‖— |
| To John Manning, for maintaining a Child of George Jennings dec⁴ | 4‖—‖— |
| To John Allen, for rent of his Land to Stephen Jones last year | 5‖—‖— |
| To David Williams, for maintaining four strange Children a Month in 1782 | 1‖—‖— |
| To Dudley Williams, Clark of the Vestry | 5‖—‖— |
| | 98‖12‖ 6 |

| | |
|---|---|
| To 6 ℔ Cent. for collecting £98‖12‖6 | 5‖18‖ 4 |
| | 104‖10‖10 |
| In the Collectors hands, to be accounted for in making up their Acco^ts. with the Vestry | 1‖—‖10 |
| | £ 105‖11‖ 8 |
| Cred^r. By 905 Tithes at 2/4 | £ 105‖11‖ 8 |

Col. Richmond Allen Sheriff, and Collector, render'd an Acco^t. of his part of the Parish Collection, by which there is £7‖13‖6 due to the Parish, which he is to pay to the Church Wardens.

The Parish Levy as above being 2/4 Cash, which every person is to pay for each Tithe in this Parish or 12^lb Tob^o. at the Option of the payer.

John Yates is exempted from paying his Parish Levy in future, on account of his age and inability.

M^r. David Lewis, and M^r. John James, are chosen Vestrymen in the room of M^r. George Bridges, who has resign'd, and M^r. John Lewis, who is removed out of the Parish.

N. B. The remaining part of this days proceedings is carried over.

[150]

1784 February 23^d.

This days proceedings continued from the other side.

Col. Edward Power, and M^r. Edmund Hockaday, are continued Church Wardens this present year.

Col. Richmond Allen, Sheriff of New Kent County, and Capt. William Allen D. Sheriff of James City County are appointed Collectors of the Parish Levies this present year, on giving Bond and security as usual.

    Sign'd by

        Edward Power } Church Wardens.
        Edmund Hockaday

Test

    Dudley Williams Cl'k o' the Vestry

*O! Lord most holy and merciful God, look down with a compassionate eye upon the feeble tenements of mortality: thou knowest the fraileties of human nature

[151]

At a Vestry held for Blisland Parish at the upper Church the 30$^{th}$. day of October 1784.

Present Edmund Hockaday Gent. Church Warden, James Hockaday, John Timberlake, Richmond Allen, John Goddin, David Lewis, and John James Gent.

This Vestry proceeds to lay the Parish Levy.

| Blisland Parish | Deb$^r$. |
|---|---|
| To Martha Breeding, for the maint$^t$. of Thomas Linsey from the last of Feb$^y$. till this time £8 ⏁ Ann | 5\|\| 6\|\| 8 |
| To John Ames, for the maint$^t$. of Eliz$^a$. Hall, from the last of Feb$^y$. till this time at £15 ⏁ Ann | 10\|\|—\|\|— |
| To Mary Banks, for the maint$^t$. of George Hix, Orphan of Nathan Hix dec$^d$. from the last of Feb$^y$. till this time at £4 ⏁ Ann | 2\|\|13\|\| 4 |
| To James Jones, for the maint$^t$. of Richard Hall, from the last of Feb$^y$. till this time at £5 ⏁ Ann | 3\|\| 6\|\| 8 |

*Note! The following three lines are in a different hand.—C. G. C.

To Mary Hix, for the maintª. Sarah Hix, Or-
phan of Nathan Hix decᵈ   8||—||—
To Capt. Andrew Banks, for the rent of his
plantation to Isaac Green   2||—||—
To John Shay, for the maintª. of John Walker,
Orphan of Charles Walker about 4 Months   1||10||—
Present Col. Edward Power, Church Warden.
To Mʳ. Edmund Hockaday, Church Warden,
the Balance of his Accoᵗ   —||18|| 3
To William Piggott, for a Coffin for Isaac
Green   1||—||—
To William Norvel, his Accoᵗ. for Corn, for
sundry Persons   7|| 3|| 6
To James Norvel Walker, for 2½ Bushels of
Corn, for Mary Perkins   —||12|| 6
To James Jennings, for the maintª. of Cath-
arine Harvey, from the 23ᵈ. of April till
this time, at 20/ a Month (deducting 1
Months pay)   5||—||—
To Rebecca Slater, for the hire of her Negro-
woman to Isaac Green   4||—||—
To Daniel Jones, for 2½ Bushels of Corn, for
Philarity Jones   —||12|| 6
To Ditto, for 1 Bushel d°. for Mary Perkins   —|| 5||—
To John Allen, for rent of his Land to Stephen
Jones   5||—||—
To Obadiah Wilks's Estate, for 2 Levies, by
Tithes wrong listed last year @ 2/4   —|| 4|| 8
To Nance Hitchcock, for maintª. of Mourn-
ing Hawkins, from the last of Febʳ. till
this time at £6 ℔ Ann   4||—||—
To John Manning, for maintª. of Priscilla,
Orphan of George Jennings from the last
of Febʳ. till this time, at £4 ℔ Ann   2||13|| 4

| | | |
|---|---|---|
| To Col. Edward Power, Collector for 1781, and 1782, the balance of his Acco$^t$. | —‖13‖— | |
| To Col. William Clayton, Cl. of New Kent Court, for a Copy of the List of Tithes 20$^{lb}$ Tob$^o$ | —‖ 2‖ 6 | |
| To Benjamin C. Waller, Cl. of James City Court, for a D$^o$. 20$^{lb}$. Tob$^o$. @ 1½$^d$ | —‖ 2‖ 6 | |
| To Dudley Williams, Cl. of the Vestry | 5‖—‖— | |
| To be paid, by the Collectors, to the Church Wardens, for the use of the Parish | 10‖18‖ 3 | |
| | 81‖ 2‖ 8 | |
| To 6 ℔ Cent. for collecting £81‖2‖8 | 4‖17‖ 4¼ | |
| | 86‖—‖—¼ | |
| Cred$^r$. By 860 Tithes at 2/ | 86‖—‖— | |

William Tinny, and James Ingram, are exempted from paying their Parish Levies, on account of their infirmit[ ]

David Lewis, and John James Gent. are chosen Church Wardens for the ensuing year, in the room of Edward Power, and Edmund Hockaday Gent.

The conclusion of this days proceedings is on the other side of this leaf.

[152]

1784 October 30$^{th}$.

The Sheriffs of James City, and New Kent Counties are appointed Collectors of the Parish Levies the ensuing year, on giving Bond and Security as usual.

    Sign'd by

      David Lewis  ⎱
      Jn$^o$. James   ⎰ Church Wardens.

 Test

    Dudley Williams, Clark of the Vestry

At a meeting of the former Vestry of Bliſland Parrish at the upper Church Novm. 8. 1785

Present M$^r$. David Lewis Jo$^n$. James Church Wardens, Cap$^t$. James Hockaday M$^r$. Jo$^n$. Timberlake, Cap$^t$. Jo$^n$. Goddin Collo Edw$^d$ power & M$^r$. Edm$^d$. Hockaday

This vestry proceeds To Choose a Clark, Jo$^n$. Boſswell Chose, C, of Vestry

This vestry proceeds to Lay the Arearages due from y$^e$ s$^d$. Vestry agreeable to an act of aſsembly paſ'd Oct$^r$. 18 1784

|  | Blisland Parish | D$^r$ | | |
|---|---|---|---|---|
|  |  | £ | S | D |
| To Martha Breeding for the ballc$^e$. of her acc$^t$. for maintain$^e$. Tho$^s$. Linsey from Oc$^t$. till Feb$^y$. 1785 | | 2 | 13 | 4 |
| To Mary Banks for ballc$^e$. due her for maintain$^e$. Ge$^o$. Hicks Orphan of Nathan Hicks from Octo$^r$. Till the Last of Feb$^y$. 1785 = £1∥6$^s$/8$^d$ To James Jennings for maint$^e$ Cathr$^n$ Harvey 2 m$^o$. £2 | | 3 | 6 | 8 |
| To Nance Hitchcock for Coffin for mourning Hawkings 15$^s$/ To Jo$^n$ manning for maintaining Priscilla Orphan of Geo. Ginnings from October till the Las of Feb$^y$. 1785 £1∥6$^s$∥8$^d$ | | 2 | 1 | 8 |
| To John Walker for y$^e$ Rent of his place for Stephen Jones in the year 1785 | | 5 | — | — |
| To Jo$^n$. Hankin for the rent of his place for Phillarity Jones £3∥10$^s$ To M$^{rs}$ Otey for for D$^o$. to: Mary Pirkins £3 To John Shea for maintain$^e$. John Walker | | 10 | 10 | — |
| To William Norvel for Corn &C To Jones & Perkins | | 3 | — | — |

To Ja⁸. Odel for maintaing Betty Hall one year £10   To Edwᵈ Farthing For maintainᵍ. Orphan of Nathan Hicks One year £6   To George Ballof Coffin For Suckey Curle £1   To John Boſwell as Clk of Vestry £1                                             18||—||—
To Collᵒ. Will Clayton for List Tyths 2ˢ/6ᵈ
To Ballcᵉ. in Collectors hands 9ˢ||1½ᵈ        —||11|| 7½

£ 45|| 3|| 3½
9|| 8|| 2¾

35||15|| 0¾
To 6⅌ʳ. Cᵗ. for Collecting £35||15ˢ||0¾ᵈ      02|| 2||11

£ 37||17||11¾

Cᵗ 1785
By the Ballcᵉ of James City Collectors accᵗ in   £   S   d
   the hands of John James                    1|| 2|| 4¼
By Dᵒ. in the hands of David Lewis            3||19|| 1½
By Dᵒ. in the hands of Newkent Collectors     4|| 6|| 9

                                    £ S d   £ 9|| 8|| 2¾
By 933 Tythes at 9¾ᵈ ⅌              37||17||3

The Sheriffs of N. Kent and James City County's are appointed Collectors of the Parrish Levy for the Enſuing year

                         David Lewis  }
                         Jnᵒ. James   } C W

        Test
                Jnᵒ. Boſwell C. O. V.

[153]
Pursuant to an Act of Aſsembly past at the City of Richmond the 17ᵗʰ of Novʳ. 1784 the Inhabetants of Blisland Parrish meet at Mʳ. Adams Byrds on Easter Munday being the 28ᵗʰ day of March 1785 and Elected the following Gent, To wit. as Vestrymen, Col. Burwell Baſsett The H'ble B Dandridge Capᵗ. James Hockaday Col. Richmond Allen Mʳ. Edmund Hockaday Col. Edward Power Capᵗ. John Hockaday Mʳ. David Lewis Mʳ. John James Capᵗ. John Goddin Capᵗ. Andrew Banks and Capᵗ. William Allen, we the Subscribers do agree to be conformable to the doctrine disciplin and worship of the Protestant Episcopal Church Incoperated by a law Specify'd as above

Burwell Baſsett  Burwell Baſsett Jr
James Hockaday  Stanup Richardson
Richmond Allen  George Baker
Edmund Hockaday
Edward Power,
John Hockaday.  David Lewis
John James

At a Vestry held for Blisland Parrish at the upper Church the 7ᵗʰ day of May 1785.
Present The Revᵈ Mʳ. Pryse Davies Rector Col. Burwell Baſsett Capᵗ. James Hockaday Col. Richmond Allen Mʳ. Edmund Hockaday Col. Edward Power Capᵗ. John Hockaday Mʳ. David Lewis and Mʳ. John James Gent
This Vestry Proceeds to Chose a Clark
Geo. Dillard is appointed Clark of the Vestry
Mʳ. David Lewis and Mʳ. John James Gent. is appointed Church wardens for the Ensuing year.
Col. Burwell Baſsett is appointed to represent the Parrish of Blisland in Convention with The Revᵈ. Mʳ. Pryse Davies to be held at Richmond the 18ᵗʰ day of this Instant

Mʳ. William Armistead Senʳ. is Chosen a Vestryman in the roome of The Hble B. Dandridge decᵈ
  Sighn'd by
        Pryse Davies Rector
        David Lewis  } Church Wardens
        John James   }
  Test
        Geo. Dillard Clark of the Vestry

[154]

At a vestry held for the Parrish of Blifsland at the Upper church October 11ᵗʰ. 1786

Present, The Reverⁿᵈ. Pryes Davies Mʳ David Lewis Church Warden, Collº. Burwell Bafsett, Mʳ. Edward Hockaday, John Hockaday, Burwell Bafsett Junier George Baker & Stanup Richardson Members

This Vestry proceeds to the chosing of a Clark, John Bofswell chosen clark of The Vestry & Clark of the upper church; John Yates Chosen Sexton of upper Church

Mʳ. David Lewis & Mʳ. Stanup Richardson are appointed Collectors of the Subscription for 1785

Mʳ. Burwell Bafsett Junʳ. and Mʳ. Stanup Richardson are appointed Church wardens in the room of Mʳ. David Lewis and Mʳ. John James

              { Pryes Davies Minister
  Sign'd by  { Burwell Bafsett  } Church Wardens
              { Stanup Richardson
  Test
      John Bofswell, C‖ O‖ Vestry

      *John Taylor      January

*John Augustine Taylor 1816

*William D Abbott, this day put his name upon this B[    ]

---

*These entries following the official record were inserted later.— C. G. C.

# APPENDIX

## CLERGYMEN

The following list contains the names of the ministers (incumbents of the parish and temporary supply preachers) who served Blisland Parish between 1721 and 1786. The numerals (in parentheses) preceding each clergyman's name indicate the number of the page in this volume on which the name first appears; the date (in parentheses) following the name indicates the year in which the clergyman is first mentioned in the Vestry Book.

| | |
|---|---|
| (1) | Taylor, Daniel (1721) |
| (39) | Mossom, ——— (1729) |
| (39) | Leneve, ——— (1729) |
| (40) | Thacker, Chicheley (1730) |
| (159) | Davies, Price (1763) |

### Notes

*Mossom,* ———. The Rev. Mr. Mossom referred to on page 39 was, doubtless, the Rev. David Mossom, minister of St. Peter's Parish, New Kent County, from 1727 until his death, in 1767.

*Leneve,* ———. The Rev. Mr. Leneve referred to on page 39 was, doubtless, the Rev. Wm. Le Neve (entered Cambridge University in 1707; ordained in 1722), who was minister of James City Parish, James City County, from 1722 to 1737. In 1723 and again in 1726 he served as chaplain of the General Assembly of the Colony.

Mr. Mossom and Mr. Le Neve were engaged as temporary supply preachers for the two churches in Blisland Parish. As, however, there is no record in the Vestry Book of any payment having been made them for services that they had rendered, it is entirely possible that the agreements made with them by the vestry of Blisland Parish never went into effect.

## CLERKS OF THE VESTRY

The following list contains the names of the clerks of the vestry of Blisland Parish between 1721 and 1786. The numerals (in parentheses) preceding each clerk's name indicate the number of the page in this volume on which the name first appears as that of the clerk; the date (in parentheses) following the name indicates the year in which the clerk began to officiate as such.

- (2)　　Holdcraft (Holdcroft), Henry (1721)
- (34)　　Cooke, Francis (1728)
- (82)　　Williams, Dudley (1742)
- (229)　Bosſwell (Boswell), John (1785)
- (231)　Dillard, Geo. (1785)
- (232)　Boſswell, John (1786)

## PHYSICIANS AND SURGEONS

The following list contains the names of the physicians and surgeons mentioned in this volume.

- (8)　　Burbidge, Robt. (1723)
- (13)　　Livingstone, Wm. (1724)
- (19)　　Brody, Jno. (1725)
- (21)　　Scott, Jno. (1725)
- (35)　　Jones, Philip (1728)
- (83)　　Arnott, Thos. (1742)

| | |
|---|---|
| (117) | Mackenzie, Ken. (1752) |
| (118) | Harwood, Wm. (1752) |
| (142) | Carter, ——— (1758) |
| (146, 150) | Harvey, Wm. (1759) |
| (184) | Pasteur, Wm. (1770) |
| (191) | Anderson, Andrew (1772) |
| (208) | Hall, Elisha (1779) |

### Notes

*Mackenzie, Ken.* In the years 1741 to 1749 a Dr. Alexander Mackenzie was practicing medicine in the neighboring parish of Petsworth, Gloucester County. (See *Vestry Book of Petsworth Parish, Gloucester County, Virginia, 1677-1793,* pages 262 to 279) Query: Were Dr. Ken. Mackenzie and Dr. Alexander Mackenzie brothers?

*Carter, ———.* In the year 1773 a Dr. William Carter was practicing medicine in the neighboring parish of Petsworth, Gloucester County (See *Vestry Book of Petsworth Parish, Gloucester County, Virginia, 1677-1793,* p. 349)

## ORDINARIES

The following list contains the names of the ordinaries (inns or taverns) mentioned in this volume.

| | |
|---|---|
| (26) | Furnea's Ordinary (1726) |
| (159) | Chiswel's Ordinary (1763) |

### Note

Chiswel's Ordinary was located about half-way between Williamsburg and the Pamunkey River on the main road running up the Peninsula. See Frontispiece Map.

# ERRATA

Page   2, line 21, "Richᵈ: *Halfield*" should probably be "Richᵈ: *Hatfield*."

Page  42, line 22, "Mʳ *Tha* Williams" should be "Mʳ *Tho.* Williams."

Page  69, line 7, *"Mᵉ* John Dandridg" should be *"Mʳ* John Dandridg."

Page 123, line 28, *"Dudleyy* Williams" should be *"Dudley* Williams."

Page 142, line 2, *"Lest* of Tithes" should be *"List* of Tithes."

Page 142, lines 22-23, *"supper* Church" should be *"upper* Church."

Page 152, line 33, asterisk should be after *"Tharp."*

Page 153, line 6, "To Mary Jones towards *his* maintᵉ" should be "To Mary Jones towards *her* maintᵉ."

Page 218, lines 14-15, To the entry, *"Davy a Negroman belonging to Mʳ John Timberlake is exempted from paying any taxes the present year,"* there should have been added the note: *"This entry appears to be in a different handwriting from that of the rest of the page."*

# INDEX

Abbott, William D., 232.
Aca, [a Negro (?)], 127.
Act of Assembly, authorizing feoffees of counties to purchase land and erect towns, xlviii; authorizing the sale of glebe land in James City Co., lv, 124; authorizing the sale of land in Blisland Parish, lv, lvi; Blisland Parish vestry dissolved by, 208; concerning persons allowed to tend tobacco, $10^2$, $11^2$; concerning the laying of arrearages, 229; establishing King and Queen County, xxiv, xxv; for dissolving Wilmington Parish, xxix, xxix (note), liii; for docking the entail of certain lands in James City County, lv; for improving the staple of tobacco, 9, $11^2$, $15^2$; law for the dissolving of Wilmington Parish, 15; passed in Richmond, Nov. 17, 1784, 231; regarding the salary of ministers, 159; relating to the church and particularly concerning the induction of ministers, li.
Act of Pardon, xlii.
Acts of Assembly, printed book of, xliii.
Adams, Ebenezer, liii.
Addison (?), Josi, xlvi.
Adkins, [ ]illiam, xliv.
Agreement, concerning f r e e d o m dues, 140; for binding out a bastard, 15, 16, 17; for binding out an apprentice, 44; for building an addition to the Lower Church, 204; for building an addition to the Upper Church, 129; with minister regarding tobacco casks in lieu of glebe, 1; with ministers to preach on alternate Sundays, 39.
Albriton, Thomas, 121.
Aldersey, Nicholas, churchwarden, 1, 2; justice of the peace, liii; successor to, appointed, 3, 42; vestryman, 4, 7, 12, 15, 33, 38.
Alexandria, x, lviii.
Alice, a Negro, 7.
Allen, Benj., 81, 164, 167, 169.
Allen, Daniel, 10, 25, 33.
Allen, Daniel, jr., 37, 66.
Allen, David, 153, 156, 161, 163.
Allen, Mrs. Eleanor, 194, 199.
Allen, James, processioner, 192.
Allen, John, 92, 96, 202, 206, 209, 216, 219, 222, 224, 227; deputy sheriff and collector of the levy, 73, 75; for delinquents and quitrents, 77, 80, 85, 91; successor to, appointed, 83; tobacco viewer and teller, 33, 37; vestryman, $75^2$.
Allen, Joseph, 63; churchwarden, $58^2$, 59; vestryman, 50, 52, 53, 54, 55, 56, 58.
Allen, Julius, 200.
Allen, Keziah, $184^3$.
Allen, Richard, 80, 91, 102, 106, 127, 146, 162, 187, 197; churchwarden, $100^2$, 101, 103, $104^2$, 106, 127, $128^2$, $129^2$, $130^3$, 131, 132, $133^2$, 134, $136^2$, 137, 138, $163^3$, $164^2$; successor to, appointed, 107, 140, 166; vestryman, 94, $95^2$, 98,

108, 109, 112, 113, 116, 124, 125, 141, 144, 147, 151, 155, 158, 159², 166, 170, 173, 176, 179, 182, 186, 189.

Allen, Richard, jr., 190.

Allen, Richmond, 178, 206²; churchwarden, 172, 173², 175², 176³, 200, 201², 202, 203, 204², 205; deputy sheriff and parish collector, 143², 147, 149, 225²; successor to, appointed, 179, 208; vestryman, 179, 186, 189, 193, 198, 208, 212, 213, 223, 226, 231⁴.

Allen, William, 208, 212, 213, 215, 217, 218, 223, 231; deputy sheriff of James City County, 225.

Allom, Anthony, petitioner, 41.

American Revolution, 1.

Ames, John, 192, 212, 214, 218, 221, 226.

Ammons, William, 215, 221, 223.

Ammunition, xliv.

Anderson, Andrew, 191, 195, 224, 235.

Anderson (Andersone), R o b e r t, xxii², xxiii, xlv, xlv (note)².

Andrewes, Giles, xlv.

Andrews, *Narratives of the Insurrections, 1675-1690* . . ., xxxiv (note), xxxv (note), xxxvi (note).

Appomattox River, xxvi, lx.

Apprentice, indenture for binding out, 44; surrendered by one person, bound to another, 44; to be taught weaving, 39; tobacco levied for binding out, 16, 17, 39, 41.

Apprentices, children of indigent parents to be bound out as, 16.

Archer, ———, clerk of James City County court, 27.

Armistead, Mrs. ———, 42.

Armistead, Gill, 99², 102, 106², 107, 115, 121, 126, 136, 139², 143, 146, 150³, 153, 154, 156, 157²; churchwarden, 119², 120, 123², 124, 125², 154²; deputy sheriff and collector, 97³, 100², 101, 136, 137², 140; member of committee to proportion the parish levy, 119²; successor to, appointed, 127; vestryman, 112, 113, 116, 128, 130, 133, 137, 141, 144, 147, 151.

Armistead, Gill, and Company, 150, 153.

Armistead (Arimstead), John, application of, for pew in Brick Church, 24; churchwarden, 8, 9, 11; declines to serve as churchwarden, 14; justice of the peace, 15; vestryman, 1, 4, 7, 15, 18, 23, 26, 30, 34.

Armistead, William, 111, 115, 118², 122, 127², 128, 136, 139, 148, 152, 154, 157, 161², 162², 165, 168², 169, 171, 174, 177, 180, 185, 196, 198; churchwarden, 147², 151³, 156, 179³, 180, 182², 183; deputy sheriff and parish collector, 111, 112, 115, 116, 119², 123, 124, 127, 128, 133², 197; member of committee to proportion the parish levy, 119, 157, 158, 169², 185²; successor to, appointed, 154; treasurer, 182; vestryman, 143, 158², 159², 163, 166, 170, 173, 176, 189, 193, 201, 232.

Armistead, William, jr., collector of parish levy, 193; deputy sheriff and collector of levy, 200.

Arnott, Thomas, physician, 234; vestryman, 83², 87, 89, 94.

Arrearages, due from vestry, 229.

Ashcraft, Mary, 172.
Ashley, Saml., 130.
Ashlock, Cole, 210, 216.
Ashwel, John, 143, 149.
Assumpsit in court, 21.
Attorney-general, 1.
Auctions, tobacco to be sold at public, 51, 94, 95.
August court, parish accounts to be settled the day after, 67.
Austin, Eliza., 194.
Austin, James, xlv, xlv (note), xlvi (note).
Austin, Mary, 214, 216, 217.
Austin. *See also* Oustin.
Awborne, Richard, xxxviii, xl.

Bacon, 181; for indigents, 184, 209.
Bacon, Nathaniel, xxxiii, xxxiv, xxxv, xxxvi, xxxix[6], xli.
Bacon, Nathaniel, sr., xxxv.
Bacon's Rebellion, xxii, xxxiv, xxxv, xxxvii[2], xlvii, xlix.
Baitch, Benjamin, 13.
Baker, Eliz., 77.
Baker, George, petitioner, 109; vestryman, 231, 232.
Baker, Mrs. Mary, 114.
Baker, Richd., 2.
Baker, Thomas, 2.
Ball, John, 121, 134, 175, 178.
Ball, John, sr., 195.
Ball, Peter, 52, 79.
Ballard, ———, 54.
Ballard, Tho., 12, 35.
Ballof, George, 230.
Bamshaw, Rich., lii.
Banks, Mrs. ———, 199.
Banks, Andrew, 222[2]; churchwarden, 217, 218[2], 220[2], 221; processioner, 192; rent for plantation, 224, 227; successor to, appointed, 222; vestryman, 208, 212, 213, 215, 217, 223, 231.
Banks, Eleanor (Elenor), 142, 145, 148.
Banks, Mary, 181[2], 183, 184, 192, 194[2], 226, 229.
Banks, William, 170, 172, 199.
Barker, Elizabeth, 27, 29[2], 31, 46, 77, 80[2], 84, 87, 91, 96, 99[2], 102, 105, 110, 114[2], 121, 126, 131.
Barker, Susanna, 13.
Barn, 78; to be repaired or rebuilt, 60, 61.
Barnatt, Gregory, xlvi, xlvi (note).
Barnehouse, ———, xi[2].
Barnett, John, xlvi, xlvi (note).
Barnett, Wm., xlvi (note).
Barnhouse, [ ]icholas, xliv (note).
Barrett, Christopher, 10, 11[2].
Bassett, ———, 42, 44[2], 53, 72, 77.
Bassett, Burwell, lvi[2], lvii[4], lviii, 139, 142, 150, 200; churchwarden, 140[2], 141, 144[3], 193[3], 194, 195, 196, 197[2], 198[2]; successor to, appointed, 147, 200; to proportion the parish levy, 185[2]; to represent Blisland Parish in convention, 231; vestryman, 137, 140, 147, 151, 158, 159, 161, 163, 170, 173, 176, 179, 182, 189, 201, 204, 205, 208, 231[3], 232.
Bassett, Burwell, jr., churchwarden, 232[2]; vestryman, 231, 232.
Bassett, William, 14; vestryman, 1, 4.
Bassett, William, 46, 50, 75, 80, 83, 85, 88; churchwarden, xxxiii, li, 41, 42, 44[2], 45[3], 46, 48[2], 49, 51, 66, 67[2], 68, 70[2]; churchwarden and collector of the levy, 70[2]; committee to meet at home of,

67; successor to, appointed, 50; to build dairy, 45; to repair glebe house, 42, 70; to sell tobacco levied for parish debts, 43, 48; to sell tobacco raised toward building a church, 51; vestryman, 41, 42, 51, 54, 55, 56, 61, $62^2$, 64, 74, 76, 79, 82, 83.

Bassett's Landing, xviii, xxxiii.

Bastard, fine for having, 21, 32; tobacco levied for binding out, 13, 15, $16^2$, 17, 20, 24.

Bates, John, 44, 146.

Bates, Prudence, 99, 102, 105.

Bates, Thomas, 57, 59, 63, 66, $69^2$.

Baughan, John, xlv, xlv (note).

Beackey, Wm., xl.

Bear, Henry, 79.

Bed, owner paid for use of and damage to feather, 22.

Beds, xxxviii.

Beef, for indigent persons, 181, 190.

Benches, 52; for Lower Church, 146, 172, 191; for Upper Church, 142, 191.

Bennet, Richard, $xi^2$, xiii, xiv.

Bennett, Elisha, 171, 190.

Bennett, William, 135, $139^2$.

Bequest, of money to buy a piece of plate, 103, 119, 136, 154; to the poor of the parish, 92.

Berkeley, William, xii, xiii, xiv, xxxiv, xxxv, xxxv (note), xxxvi, xxxvi (note), xxxvii.

Berry (Berrie), John, xxxvii, xl, xli, xlii.

Betty, a Negro, 151.

Beverley (Beverlye), Robert, $xxxviii^2$, xl.

Binding out, of apprentice, 44; of bastards, 13, 15, 16, 17, 20; of indigent children, 16; of orphan, 81.

Bird, Adam. *See* Byrd, Adam.

Births, to be registered, 33, 158.

Bishop of London, 40.

Blackwell, James, xliv, xliv (note).

Blair, James, letter from, 40.

Blindness, exemption from parish levy on account of, 127, 151.

Blisland Parish, v, $ix^6$, xi, xii, xii (note), xiii, xiv, xv, xv (note), xvi (note), xvii (note), xix, xxi, xxiii, xxxiv, xxxvi, xxxvii, xlviii, l, lii, liii (note), liv, lv, lvi, lviii, $lix^6$, lx, lxi, 234; accounts of, to be settled, 67; addition to Upper Church in, 129; allowance to minister of, in lieu of glebe, 1, 4, 7, 12, 18, 26, 30, 34, 38, 159, 162; area and population of, liii; bequest to, for a piece of plate, 103, 119, 136; church to be built in the lower part of, 53, 54; clerk of, 1, 4, 7, 12, 19, 26, 30, 34, 38; clerk of the church and vestry, 82; clerk of the register, 33; clerks of the vestry of, 234; divided into precincts, xvii, 9, 10; dividing line between St. Peter's Parish and $xx^2$, xxxiii, 54, 64, 86; division of, confirmed, xxxiv; earliest consecutive records of, ix, x; establishment of, x-xvi, xxvii; facsimile of grievances, lx; grievances of some of the inhabitants of, xxii, xlii, xliii, 1; indenture signed by churchwardens of, 44, 45; levy laid for, 1, 4, 7, 12, 18, 26, 30, 34, 38, 46, 49, 52, 56, 57, 59, 62, 65, 68, 71, 74, 76, 79, 84, 87, 90, 95, 98, 101,

104, 106, 109, 113, 117, 120, 125, 130, 134, 137, 141, 144, 147, 152, 155, 160, 163, 166, 170, 173, 176, 179, 182, 185, 186, 189, 193, 198, 201, 205, 208, 212, 213, 215, 217, 218, 221, 223, 226; list of ministers of, 233; location of, v, ix, x; manuscript vestry book of, ix, x; minister of, $1^2$, $4^2$, 6, 7, 9, 11, 14, 18, 23, 25, 26, $30^2$, 32, 33, $34^2$, 36-38, 40-42, 44, $45^2$, $46^2$, $48^2$, $49^2$, $51^2$, $52^2$, $54^2$, 55, $56^2$, 58, 59, $61^2$, $62^2$, $64^2$, $67^2$, $68^3$, 70, $71^2$, $74^3$, $76^2$, $79^2$, $82^2$, $83^2$, 84, 86, $87^2$, $89^2$, $90^3$, $93^2$, $94^2$, $95^3$, $98^3$, 100, $101^2$, $104^2$, 106, 108, $109^3$, $112^2$, $113^3$, $116^2$, 117, 119, $120^2$, 123, 124, $125^3$, $128^2$, 129, $130^2$, $133^2$, 134, 136, $137^2$, 140, $141^2$, $144^3$, $147^2$, 151, 152, 154, $155^2$, 157, $159^2$, 160, 162, 163, 164, $166^2$, $170^2$, 172, 173, $176^2$, $179^2$, $182^2$, 185, 186, $189^2$, $193^3$, 197, $198^2$; origin of the name of, x; overdue levies, 28; part of Wilmington Parish added to, 15; patents to land in, xi, xii, xv; petition concerning division of, xxxiii; petition for repealing warehouse at Taskanask, lv; petition of the inhabitants of that part of, which was formerly a part of Wilmington Parish, liii; plate ordered for, 119; represented in Richmond convention, 231; St. Peter's Parish cut off from, xxxii, xxxiii; supply preachers for churches in, 233; territorial extent of, xvi-xxxii; tobacco levied for debts of, to be sold, 43; tobacco viewers and tellers appointed for, 10, 25, 33, 34, 37;

treasurer, 182; Upper Church in, to be repaired, 90; vestry chosen by freeholders, 208, 231; vestry dissolved and new one chosen, 208; vestry held for, 1, 4, 6, 9, 11, 14, 18, 23, 25, 26, 30, 33, 34, 36, 37, 38, 41, 42, 45, 46, 48, 49, $51^2$, 54, 55, 56, 59, 61, 62, 64, 67, 68, 71, 74, 76, 79, 82, 83, 86, 89, 90, 93, 94, 95, 98, 100, 101, 104, 106, 108, 109, 112, 113, 116, 120, 124, 125, 128, 130, 133, 137, 140, 144, 147, 151, 155, 158, $159^2$, 163, 166, 170, 173, 176, 179, 182, 186, 189, 193, 197, 201, $204^2$, 208, 212, 213, 215, 217, 218, 220, 223, 226, 229, 231, 232; vestry of, authorized to sell certain land in, lv; vestry of, favor induction of minister, li, lii; workhouse for the poor of, 147, 154, 196, 197; workmen engaged to build new church in, 55.

*See also* Lower Church; Upper Church.

Blocks. *See* Horseblocks.

Blomefield, John, xlvii.

Bond, for daughter's fine, 3; given to relieve the parish of the care of a bastard, 13, 24; parish collectors to give, 4, 6, 9, 14, 22, 24, 28, 32, 36, 39, 41, 48, 50, 51, 53, 58, 61, 64, 67, 70, 73, 74, 76, 78, 82, 85, 86, 88, 89, 92, 93, $97^2$, 100, 101, 103, 107, 108, 111, 112, 116, 119, 120, 123, 124, 127, 128, $133^2$, 136, 137, 140, 143, 147, 151, 154, 157, 163, 165, 169, 172, 176, 179, 182, 185, 188, 193, 197, 201, 203, 208, 211, 215, 218, 220, 223, 226, 228; passed between churchwardens and contractors, 130; to be

given for the performance of an order, xxxviii; workmen required to give, 56.
Bostwicke (Bostick, Bostike), Charles, xlv, xlv (note)³, xlix², 1².
Boswell (Bosswell), Jon., clerk of Blisland Parish vestry, 229, 230², 232², 234².
Bowles, Hannah, 105, 107.
Box, 43.
Bracket, Charity, 60, 77, 80.
Bradenham, John, 191.
Bradley, Sarah, 219, 222.
Bray, Thomas, liii.
Breeding, Benja., 35.
Breeding, John, tobacco viewer and teller, 33, 37.
Breeding, Martha, 226, 229.
Brewin, Wm., 3.
Brick, chimney to be built of, 70, 107; church aisle of, 94; church to be built of, 53, 54; door made of, 94; used in repairing glebe house, 42.
Brick Church, lix; built on land owned by parishioner, 25; meeting of Blisland Parish vestry held at, 1, 4, 6, 9, 14, 18, 25, 34, 41, 45, 48, 49, 51; proposal for a pew in, 24; to be built in the lower part of the parish, 53, 54.
Brick-house, xxxv, xxxvi³, lvii; location of, lv (note); town to be established at, xlviii; warehouse established at, lv.
Brick wall, around church, 85; around churchyard, 83.
Bricklayer, 150.
Bricks, for the glebe, 139; for the Upper Church, 150; made by E. Daingerfield, 85.

Bridges, George, 194, 199, 202, 206, 209, 218, 221; successor to, appointed, 225; vestryman, 208, 212, 213, 215, 217, 218, 221.
Bright, John, xlvii.
Bristol, [England], 67.
Bristol Parish, xxvi.
Bristol stone, church aisle to be of, 55.
Brody, John, 19², 234.
Brooker, Francis, 77.
Brooker, John, 209.
Brooks, Ruth, 114, 117, 118.
Browing, John, petitioner, 41.
Brown, ———, 58.
Brown, Ann, 118, 140.
Brown, James, petitioner, 68.
Brown, James, jr., 118, 122, 126, 132, 135, 138, 141.
Brown, James, sr., 118, 122, 126, 132, 135, 138, 141.
Brown, John, 196², 203, 207.
Brown, William, xxx, 20², 53, 122, 125, 151, 194, 199.
Bruce, William, 145.
Brunskill, John, minister, lii, liii.
Bruton (Brewton) Parish, xii (note), xvi (note)², xvii.
Brydon, G. MacLaren, lxi.
Buchan, Robert, 161.
Buffin, John, 194.
Bull, Richard, 78, 84, 88, 91, 96, 99.
Burbidge, ———, lvii, 66.
Burbidge, Julius (Julias, Julious) King, 69, 72, 75, 88, 151; collector of parish levy, 60, 61, 63, 64, 67; member of the committee to proportion the parish levy, 92; resigns as vestryman, 97; successor to, appointed, 100; vestryman, 90², 93, 94.

INDEX  243

Burbidge, Robert, 8, 234.
Burdett, Howard, 114, 115².
Burgesses, for York County, xv.
Burgis, Roger, xlvi.
Burials, charges for, of indigent persons, 5², 16, 30, 35, 59, 66², 69, 77³, 80, 107, 115, 121², 131, 135, 142², 146, 153, 163, 167, 169, 172, 174, 191, 202, 224. *See also* Funerals.
Burke, Mary, 13.
Burnett, Mrs. Eliza., 148, 152, 155, 160, 164, 167.
Burnett (Burn˚), John, 118, 134; clerk of the Upper Church, 113, 117, 120, 125, 130; tobacco viewer and teller, 33, 37.
Burton, Edward, xlv.
Bush, Martha, 167, 170, 173, 180, 184.
Buttons, for surplice, 175.
Byrd (Bird), Adam, 143, 217, 218, 231.

*Calendar of State Papers . . .,* xxxiii, xxxv (note), xxxvi (note), xlix (note)².
Cambridge University, 233.
Cancer, woman cured of, 126.
Carolina, xxxiv.
Carpenter, 2, 44.
Carpenter, Peter, tobacco viewer and teller, 11, 15, 26.
Carter, ———, liv, 142, 235.
Carter, John, liv.
Carter, Robert, 199.
Carter (?), William, xlvi, 235.
Casement, made, 42; altered, 43.
Cask. *See* Tobacco casks.
Catlin, ———, xxxv.
Chamberlayne, Mrs. ———, lvii, lviii².

Chamberlayne, Mrs. Elizabeth (Littlepage), lviii.
Chamberlayne, Mrs. Richard, lviii.
Chamberlayne, Thomas, lv.
Chamberlayne, William, lviii².
Chamberlayne, Mrs. William, lviii.
Chandler, Cliffe, 224.
Chandler, David, 176, 178², 224.
Chandler, John, 102.
Chandler, Philemon, jr., 199, 202.
Chandler, Philemon, sr., 199, 202.
Chaplain, 233.
Chapman, George, xiv, xxii.
Charles, James, 57, 58, 114, 122.
Charles, Philip, 51.
Charles City County, xxix², xxxi.
Charles Parish, xvi (note).
Charles River, xiv.
Charles River County, xxvii.
Charlton, Mrs. ———, 151.
Charlton, Christopr., 38.
Charlton, Keziah, 91, 96, 117, 121.
Charlton, Mary, 135, 139.
Charlton, William, 29, 138, 139, 153, 156, 161, 163.
Chescake Parish. *See* Chiskiack Parish.
Chicheley, Henry, xlix.
Chickahominy River, xxvi², xxix³, xxx², xxxi, xxxii.
Children, of indigent parents to be bound out as apprentices, 16; strange, supported by the parish, 219², 221, 224.
Chimneys, to be built of brick, 42, 70, 107.
Chiskiack (Chescake, Chickyack, Kiskeake, Kiskiacke, Kiskyacke, Kiskyake) Parish, xii (note), xiii, xvii, xxvii.
Chiswel's Ordinary, 159, 235².
Christ Church, Alexandria, lviii.

Christ Church Parish, xxvi; vestry of, favors induction of minister, lii.

Christian, Isham, 222.

Christians, sermon to be printed and distributed for the comfort of, liv.

Christopher Barrett's Landing, 10, 11².

Church, act relating to, li; deed to, land, 57; glebe house to be built after cost of building, has been paid, 58; repaired, 12, 122; to be built in lower part of parish, 53, 54; to be built on land given by Mrs. Holdcroft, 54, 55; tobacco levied toward building, 47², 50, 51, 53; workmen engaged to build, 55; workmen required to finish, in accordance with agreement, 66, 67.

Church of England, v.

Church plate, money bequeathed to parish for a piece of, 103, 136, 154; of Wilmington Parish, 53, 58; to be purchased, lvi, 92, 103, 119, 136.

Church windows, glazed, 191.

Churchwardens, 1, 4, 6, 9, 11, 14, 18, 23, 25, 26, 30, 33, 34, 36, 37, 38, 41, 42, 44, 45³, 46, 48², 49, 51², 52, 54², 55, 56², 58, 59, 61², 62³, 64², 67², 68², 70, 71, 74², 76², 79², 82³, 83², 85, 86, 87, 89, 90², 93², 94², 95², 98², 100, 101, 104², 106, 108², 109², 112², 113², 116², 119, 120, 123, 124, 125², 128², 129³, 130², 133², 136, 137, 140, 141, 144², 147², 151², 154², 155, 157, 158, 159³, 163³, 166³, 169⁴, 170, 172, 173, 175, 176², 179², 182², 185, 186, 189, 193, 197, 198, 200, 201², 203, 204², 205, 208², 211², 212², 213, 215³, 217², 218², 220², 221, 223², 225-232; appointed and reappointed, 3, 8, 14, 23, 28, 41, 50, 53, 58, 60, 63, 66, 70, 73, 75, 78, 81, 85, 89, 92, 97, 100, 103, 107, 111, 113, 115, 119, 123, 127, 132, 136, 140, 144, 147, 151, 154, 157, 163, 166, 169, 172, 175, 179, 182, 185, 188, 193, 197, 200, 203, 211, 215, 217, 220, 222, 225, 228, 231, 232; appointed parish collectors, 70, 76, 78, 82, 188, 193, 200; articles of agreement signed by, 129; authorized to buy land adjoining glebe, 176; authorized to have work on Lower Church finished, 67; copy of act relating to the church and induction of ministers sent to, li; enquire into a girl's right to freedom dues, 132; indenture signed by, 45; levy for contingent charges, 214, 217, 219, 222; of St. Peter's Parish, 64; of Wilmington Parish, 20; sworn, 3, 8, 14, 28, 41, 50, 58, 60, 63, 66, 70, 73, 78, 85, 92, 100, 103, 107, 113, 116, 119, 123, 127, 132, 140, 179, 185; to advertise work on Lower Church, 197; to advertise work on Upper Church, 90, 94; to bind out indigent children, an apprentice and orphan, 16, 44, 81; to build or rent a workhouse, 147, 154, 196, 197; to demand and receive bequest to the parish, 103, 119, 136, 154; to demand Wilmington Parish church plate, 53; to have barn repaired or rebuilt, 60; to have corn house built on glebe, 97; to have glebe repaired, 132, 147, 151; to have smokehouse built, 88; to make addition and repairs to the Upper Church, 129, 147; to order communion table linen, 154; to proportion the parish levy, 211, 220; to receive money bequeathed to the poor, 92; to run dividing line between St. Peter's and Blisland parishes, 64; to sell glebe land in James City County, lv, 124; to sell tobacco levied for repairing the church, 94, 95, 123, 125; to sell tobacco levied to build a glebe house, 62.

Churchyard, brick wall around, 83, 85; cleaned, 66, 69, 98, 164; committee appointed to lay off, 83; sexton paid for cleaning, 98; wall repaired, 90; walls of, lengthened, 129.

Churn, John, 189.

Clapboards, 78.

Clarke, Mrs. Hannah, xiii$^2$, xiv.

Clarke, Richard, petitioner, xxxvii, xxxviii, xxxix, xl.

Clayborne, William, xxiv (note).

Clayton, William, 134, 138, 142, 145, 148, 152, 155, 160, 164, 167, 170, 173, 177, 180, 183, 187, 190, 194, 199, 228, 230.

Clergymen, list of, 233.

Clerk of Blisland Parish, 1, 4, 7, 12, 19, 26, 30, 34, 38, 78; of General Court, xxxiv; of James City Co., 35, 46, 75; of James City County court, 27, 30, 110, 202, 228; of New Kent County, xxxvi, xxxvi (note), liv, 110, 228; of the church and vestry, 79, 82; of the court, 19, 31; of the Lower Church, 59, 62, 65, 68, 71, 74, 76, 79, 84, 87, 90, 95, 98, 101, 104, 109, 138, 141, 144, 148, 152, 155, 160, 164, 167, 170, 173, 176, 180, 183, 186, 190, 193, 198, 202, 205; of the Lower Church and vestry, 113, 117, 120, 125, 130; of the parish and vestry, 38; of the Upper Church, 59, 62, 68, 71, 74, 76, 84, 91, 113, 117, 120, 125, 130, 134; of the Upper Church and vestry, 65, 87, 95, 98, 101, 104, 109, 138, 141, 144, 148, 152, 155, 160, 164, 166, 170, 173, 176, 180, 183, 186, 190, 193, 198, 202, 205, 232; of the vestry, 2, 6, 7, 9, 11, 12, 14, 18, 19, 23, 25, 26, 29, 30, 33, 34$^2$, 36, 37$^2$, 39$^2$, 41, 44, 45$^2$, 48$^2$, 49, 51$^2$, 52, 54-59, 62, 64, 67, 68, 74, 82, 83, 86, 89, 90, 93, 94, 95, 98, 104, 108, 109, 112, 113, 116$^2$, 119, 120, 123-125, 128$^2$, 129, 133$^2$, 136, 137, 140, 144, 147, 151, 154, 157, 158, 159, 163,˙166, 169$^2$, 172, 176, 179, 182, 185$^2$, 188, 193, 197, 201, 203, 204, 208, 212, 214, 215, 217, 218, 220, 223, 224, 226, 228-232; of the vestry, collector of parish levies, 208, 211, 218, 220; of the vestry, member of the committee to proportion the parish levy, 220; of the vestry, to record births and deaths, 33, 158; of the vestry, to record processioners returns, 108, 192; of Wilmington Parish, 20.

Clerks, fees of, 5$^2$, 27, 35; of the vestry, list of, 234.

Cliff, ———, 43.

Clinch, Robt., 21.

Closet, added to glebe house, 42.

Cloth, purple, 43.

Clothing, for an apprentice, 45; for indigent persons, 13, 17, 32, 85, 102, 114, 153, 187, 190, 194, 207, 218, 219, 223², 224².

Clough, George, churchwarden, 50, 51², 52, 53, 54², 55², 56³; processioner, 192; successor to, appointed, 58, 75; vestryman, lii, 42, 45, 46, 49, 61, 62, 64, 68, 71.

Clough, Richard, tobacco teller and viewer, 10; successor to, appointed, 25.

Cocker, John, petitioner, xl, xli.

Coffins, for indigent persons, 12, 13, 111, 121, 131, 168, 175, 178, 181, 191, 195², 202, 206, 209, 219, 227, 229, 230.

Cole, Matthew, 111, 139, 142, 149, 153, 156, 161, 164.

Cole's Mill Creek, xxx.

Collectors, of parish levies, 6, 9, 13, 14, 22, 23, 24, 28, 32, 36, 39, 40, 48, 50, 53, 58, 61, 70, 73, 76, 82, 86, 89, 93, 97, 100, 103, 108, 112, 113, 115, 116, 119², 123, 124, 127, 128, 133², 136², 137, 140, 143, 144, 147, 149, 151, 154, 157², 158, 162, 163, 165, 168, 169, 171, 172, 174, 176, 179, 180, 182, 184, 185, 188², 189², 193, 196, 197, 200, 201, 203, 207, 208, 211², 214, 215, 218, 220, 222, 223, 225², 226, 228, 230, 232; of subscriptions for 1785, 232; required to give bond, 4, 6, 9, 14, 22, 24, 28, 32, 36, 39, 41, 48, 50, 51, 53, 58, 61, 64, 67, 70, 73, 74, 76, 78, 82, 85, 86, 88, 89, 92, 93, 97², 100, 101, 103, 107, 108, 111, 112, 116, 119, 120, 123, 124, 127, 128, 133², 136, 137, 140, 143, 147, 151, 154, 157, 163, 165, 169, 172, 176, 179, 182, 185, 188, 193, 197, 201, 203, 208, 211, 215, 220, 226, 228.

Commissioners for the Affairs of Virginia, xxxvii, xxxix, xl, xli.

Common Prayer books, 43.

Commonwealth, Parliament of, xv.

Communion, to be moved and fitted with new rails and banisters, 129.

Communion cloth, mended, 149.

Communion table, linen for, ordered from Great Britain, 154.

Communions, 12, 31, 35², 38, 49, 52², 57, 59, 63, 65, 68, 71, 74, 77, 79, 84, 88, 91, 96, 99, 102, 105, 110, 114, 117, 121; for the Lower Church, 126, 131, 134, 138, 142, 145, 148, 152, 156, 162, 164, 167, 170, 173, 177, 180, 183, 187, 190, 194, 198, 202, 205, 206; for the Upper Church, 126, 131, 134, 138, 148, 152, 156, 161, 164, 167, 170, 173, 176, 180, 183, 187, 190, 194, 198, 202, 205, 206.

Compass altar, 56.

Compass ceiling, 55, 129.

Constable, 110, 184.

Contractors, engaged to b u i l d church, 55; required to give bond, 56, 130.

Conway, ———, liv.

Cook (Cooke), Francis, 78, 84; clerk of the church and vestry, 79; clerk of the parish, 1, 4, 7, 12, 19, 26, 30, 34; clerk of the parish and vestry, 38; clerk of the register, 33; clerk of the Upper Church, 59, 62, 65, 68, 71, 74, 76; clerk of the vestry, 34, 36, 37², 39², 40, 41, 45², 46, 48², 49, 51², 52, 54, 55, 56, 57, 58, 59, 62, 64, 67, 68, 74, 234; resigns as clerk of the church and vestry, 82.

Corbett (Corbat, Corbet, Corbit), Joane (Jone), 8², 19, 35⁴.
Corley, Rch., xlv.
Corn, 88, 146, 168; for indigent persons, 16, 17, 70, 102², 106, 118, 131, 143, 146, 150², 151, 163², 172², 175², 178, 181, 183, 184, 187³, 188², 190², 191², 192², 194⁴, 199², 200², 207², 209², 216, 219, 220, 221, 222⁴, 224², 227⁴, 229.
Cornhouse, on glebe land, 97, 99.
Coroners, of New Kent County, liii.
Cotton, for indigent person, 70.
Council, xxix, xxxiii, xxxv, xxxv (note), xxxvii; act relating to the church and induction of ministers read at a, li; report to the governor, xlviii.
Counties, dividing line between, xxi; feoffees of, to purchase land and erect towns, xlviii; sermon to be printed and distributed in, liv; parishes co-terminous with, in area, xxvi.
County courts, grievance concerning the selling of strong drink on court days, xliii.
Court days, grievance concerning the selling of strong drink on, xliii.
Court martial, trial by, xxxvi (note).
Cousins, ———, 27.
Cowles, John, 210.
Cowles, Thomas, 146, 172, 191.
Cox, William, xiv, 35; churchwarden, 3, 4, 5, 7, 8; vestryman, 1, 9, 12, 15, 23, 26, 29, 30, 33, 34, 36, 37, 38, 41, 42, 48, 49, 50.
Coxe, George, xxii, xxiii², xlvii, xlvii (note)².
Cox's (Coxe's) Mill Creek, 10², 11.

Crafford, David, xliv.²
Crafford (Crarford, Crofford, Croford) Jane, 46, 49, 50, 52², 54, 60², 63, 66.
Crawford (Crafford, Crarford, Croford), Moses, sexton, 20, 21, 26, 30, 34, 38.
Creeks, Cole's Mill, xxx; Cox's Mill, 10²; Diascun, xxxii; John's (Jack's), xix², xx², xxii, xxiv², xxviii, xxix; King's, xxxv; Poropotank, xvi, xviii, xxii², xxviii²; Pouncey's, xii; Queen's, xii (note), xvi, xvii (note), xxvii; Scimino, xii (note)², xiii², xiv, xvi², xvi (note)², xvii², xvii (note), xviii, xxvii, xxviii², xxxi, liv; Tank's xii; Townsend, xii (note)²; Ware, xiv⁵, xv, xvii², xxxi, liv, 10; Warrany, xiv²; Yorktown, xii (note).
Crittenden, Mrs. Hannah, 115.
Crook, Mary, 45, 46, 49, 52, 53.
Croome, Joell, lii.
Crump, George, patroler, 143.
Crutchfield, Mary, 92.
Crutchley, Henry, 21.
Culpeper, Thomas (Lord), governor, xlviii.
Cumbo, Eliza., 181, 184, 188, 192, 202.
Cumbo, Gideon, 7.
Cumbo, Turner, 192, 195, 206, 210.
Curle, Ann, 216.
Curle, Bennett, 223.
Curle (Curles), Jemima, 143, 144, 148, 149, 152, 155, 160, 164, 167, 175, 187, 190², 191², 224.
Curle, Jeremiah, 142, 143, 145², 148, 152.
Curle, Julius, 219.

Curle, Matthew, 177.
Curle, Reba., 143, 145.
Curle, Richard, jr., 195.
Curle, Richard, sr., 195.
Curle (Curll), Richard Creed, 102, 110, 114, 122, 143, 145, 148, 150, 152, 156, 158, 161.
Curle (Curl, Curll, Curls), Samuel, 29, 36, 38, 39, 47, 50, 52, 57, 60, 63, $66^2$, 69, 73, 81, $85^2$, 99.
Curle, Suckey, 230.
Curle, Susannah, 216.
Curle, William, 142, 145, 148, 152.
Curnute (Cornute, K e r n u t e), James, 35, 38, $39^2$, 41, $44^2$, 47.
Currency, paper, 220.
Cushion, mended, 149.
Custis, ———, $lvii^2$.
Custis, Daniel Parke, lviii.
Custis, Martha (Dandridge), lvi, lviii.
Cypress shingles, 90, 94, 129.

Daingerfield, Mrs. ———, 111, 114, 122.
Daingerfield (Daingerfeild, Dangerfield), Edwin, 80, 86, 94, 96, 99; bricks made by, 85; churchwarden, 78, $79^2$, 81, $82^2$, $83^2$, 84; collector of parish levy, 78, 82; member of committee to run dividing line, 85; successor to, appointed, 85, 103; vestryman, 73, 74, 76, 87, 89, 93, 95.
Daingerfield, Mrs. Hannah, $106^2$, 139.
Daingerfield, William, 167, 168, 175; churchwarden, $166^3$, 167, $169^2$, 170; parish levy proportioned by, $169^2$; successor to, appointed, 172, 185; vestryman, 157, 158, 161, 164, 173.

Dairy, on glebe land, 45, 78, 118.
Dandridge, ———, 63, 69, 72, 74.
Dandridge, Mrs. ———, lvii.
Dandridge, Anna Maria, lvi.
Dandridge, Bartholomew, lvii, 188, 195, 209; churchwarden, $185^2$, 186, $188^2$, 189, 191; collector of parish levy, 188; successor to, chosen, 232; vestryman, 179, 182, 201, 208, 224, 231.
Dandridge, John, 46, 49, 52, 57, 59, 65, 69, 75, 77, 80, 84, 87, 91, 96, 99, $102^2$, 105, 110, 117, 121, 126, 131.
Daniell, William, xlvi.
Darling, Frank (Franck), 21.
Darling, Joseph, 21.
Darling, Susanna, 21.
David Lewis and Co., 191.
Davies, Price (Pryse), clergyman, lviii, $159^3$, 160, 162, 163, 164, $166^2$, $170^2$, 172, 173, $176^2$, 178, $179^2$, $182^2$, 185, 186, $189^2$, $193^2$, 197, $198^2$, $201^3$, 203, $204^2$, $205^2$, $208^2$, 211, 212, 213, 215, $231^2$, $232^2$, 233.
Davis, ———, lvi, lvii.
Davis, [ ]effery, xliv.
Davis, Roland, xxxiv.
Davis, Thomas, lviii.
Davy, a Negro, $218^2$.
Dawes, John, xlv.
Day, Francis, 59, 77, $78^2$, 80, 81, 88, 91, 96, 99, 102, 105, 110, 114, 122, 126, 131, 135, 138, 141, 145, 148.
Day, James, 195.
Day, Priscilla, 172, 175, 181.
Deaths, to be registered, 33, 158.
Deaton, Eliza., 181, 195.
Deed, to church land, 57; to land to build vestryhouse on, 107.
Deeds of sale, 25.

"Delaware Town" and "West Point" in King William County, Va., xxiv (note).
Delinquents (tax delinquents), 2, 5², 7², 13, 19, 20, 21, 27², 28, 46, 49, 60, 75, 77, 80, 84, 88, 106, 111, 118, 139.
Deloney (Delony), Lewis, 55, 56², 66, 67, 115², 123.
Demetrius, Emanuel, 19, 22, 31, 32.
Desk, for new church, 56.
Dial (dyall) post, 65, 158.
The Diaries of George Washington, 1748-1799, lvi.
Diascun Creek, xxxii.
Diascun Swamp, xxx.
Dibdall, Jno., lii.
Dibdall, Mrs. Margrett, 13.
Dillard, Geo., clerk of Blisland Parish vestry, 231, 232, 234.
Diocesan Convention of 1785, lix.
Diocese of Southern Virginia, xvii, lix².
Diocese of Virginia, lix²; historiographer of, lxi.
Distress, when to be made for tobacco due for levy, 4, 6, 9, 14, 22, 24, 28, 32, 36, 38, 39, 41, 61, 70, 73, 76, 78, 82, 86, 89, 93, 97, 101, 103, 108, 112, 116, 120, 124, 128, 133, 137.
Dividing line, between St. Peter's and Blisland parishes, xxxiii, 54, 64, 86, 88.
Door, made of brick, 94.
Doran, John, 8, 12, 13, 16, 17, 18, 19², 20, 28, 31, 32, 35², 38, 46, 58, 63, 69, 71, 77, 78², 81², 84, 88; churchwarden, 14², 18, 19, 22, 23², 25, 26, 28, 60, 61², 62², 64², 73, 74², 75, 76²; delinquents returned by, 5, 7, 21, 27; deputy sheriff and collector of parish levy, 3, 6, 8², 9, 12, 13, 14, 23, 24; member of the committee to proportion the parish levy, 73; sheriff, 2; sheriff and collector of the parish levy, 85, 86; successor to, appointed, 66, 78; vestryman, 14, 30, 33, 34, 36, 37, 38, 41, 45, 46, 48, 49, 51, 52, 53, 54, 55, 56, 59, 67, 68, 71, 79, 82, 83.
Dormer (Dormar), Ballard, 57, 59, 69², 72, 75, 77, 91.
Dormer (Dormar), David, 72, 73, 75, 77, 79, 84, 87, 91, 96, 126, 143, 148, 152, 156, 161, 164, 167, 168.
Dormer, Henry, 146.
Dorrell, Edward, xlvi.
Dowde, William, 7.
Downs (Downes), Rice, 35, 38.
Drew, ———, xxxv.
Drink, grievance concerning the selling of strong, xliii.
Drummond, ———, xxxv, xxxvi, xxxvii².
Ducerie, John, jr. See Lucerie, John, jr.
Duco, Clift, 153.
Duco, Thomas, 153.
Dugar, Cliff (Clift), 153, 156, 161.
Dugar, Thomas, 153, 161.
Dunkerton, Eliza., 153, 156, 161, 165, 167.
Dunkerton, Henry, 141.
Dunketon, Thomas, xi², xv.
DuVal (Duval), Samuel, 130, 136, 139.

Eacho, Mrs. ———, 131, 146.
Eacho, Benja., 149, 153.
Eacho, John, 131², 139, 142, 146, 150.
Eacho, John, jr., 146.

Eacho, John, sr., 146.
Eaton, ———, 65.
Eaton, John, deputy sheriff of James City County, 2.
Edwards, W. P., clerk of General Court, xxxiv.
Egmon, Lawrence, 189.
*Eltham,* lvi, lvii², lviii, lix.
England, x²; Church of, v.
English army, 220.
English government, commissioners sent over by, xlii.
English merchant ship, xxxvi.
English servants, xxxviii³, xl².
English settlers, xxiii, xxiv.
Entail, act for docking, of certain lands in James City County, lv.
Evans, Ann, 37, 46, 52, 57, 59, 63, 75².
Evans, Eliz., 75, 77.
Evans, John, 7, 63.
Evans, Thomas, 7.
Estate, executor of, of D. Lyon, 204; payment to, of Dr. A. Anderson, 224; Wm. Hart, 174; D. Lyon, 207; M. Manning, 165; B. Russell, 202; R. Russell, 210; Rev. C. Thacker, 160; O. Wilks, 227; tobacco taken in execution of an, returned, 127.
Evidence. *See* Witness.
*Executive Journals of the Council of Colonial Virginia,* xvii (note), xlix (note), 1 (note).

Falconer, Wm., xlvii.
Farnham Parish, xxvi.
Farthing, Edward, 142, 145, 148, 152, 155, 160, 164, 167, 171, 173, 177, 230.
Farthing, Eliza., 153.
Farthing, Mary, 114, 123, 126, 132, 135, 138, 142, 145, 148, 152, 155, 160, 164², 167, 171, 173, 177.
Farthing, Rebecca, 8, 12.
Farthing, Richd., 84.
Farthing, William, 66, 71, 75, 150.
Feare, Dorril, 206, 213.
Feare (Feer), Elizabeth, 121, 206.
Feare, Hamner, 206.
Feather bed, owner paid for the use of and damage to, 22.
Feathers, 43.
Fees, 2², 5², 19, 27, 35, 111.
Feoffees, land to be purchased by, and laid out for towns, xlviii.
Field, ———, 19.
Field, Mary, 19.
Filbates. *See* Philbates.
Filbeach, William, 7.
Fine, bond for daughter's, 3; due by assumpsit in court, 21; for having a bastard, 21, 32; paid in current money, 32; paid in pork, xxxvii; received of S. Manning, 178.
Fisher, Mrs. ———, 73.
Fisher, Prudence, 66, 77, 102, 110, 135, 139, 142.
Fisher, Sarah, 110, 114.
Fisher, Thomas, 2.
Fisher, William, 2, 105, 115², 131, 142, 146, 209, 212, 215², 221, 223.
Fitzhugh, ———, liv.
Fitzpatrick, John C., lvi, lvii.
Flack, George, 181.
Fleming, John, xlv, xly (note).
Fletcher, William, 142, 154.
Folding door, made of brick, 94.
Font, for new church, 56.
*Force's Tracts,* xxxvi (note).
Ford, Christor., jr., 130.
Forester, James, 75.
Forgison, Eliz., 71.

## INDEX

Fornea, Stephen. *See* Furnea, Stephen.
Fort duties, xliii.
Foster, John, tobacco teller, 11, 15.
Foster, Joseph, liii.
Foulkes, Frances, 153.
Foulks, Keen, 77, 78, 81², 85, 88, 91, 96.
Fox, Isaac, 191, 206, 210², 212.
Fox, Joseph, 149, 153, 156, 161, 164, 167, 171, 174.
Fox, Salley, 191.
Fox, Sarah, 143, 149, 153, 156, 161, 164, 167, 171, 174, 191.
Fox, William, 72, 91, 96, 99, 102, 105, 110.
Fry, Joshua, lx.
Frazier, Elisha, 195.
Frazier, Simon, 132.
Freedom dues, 132, 140.
Freeholders, vestry chosen by, 208.
Fringe, silk, 43.
Funeral, rum for, 131.
Funerals, charges for, of indigent persons, 177, 191, 195, 207², 209, 223.
*See also* Burials.
Furnea (Fornea), Stephen, 36, 37, 55².
Furnea's Ordinary, 26, 235.

Gadberry, Mrs. ———, 161, 164.
Gadberry, John, 213.
Gadberry, Lydda, 156.
Gadberry, Wm., 167, 171.
Gaddey, John, 101, 105, 110, 114, 117, 118, 120, 121, 122, 123.
Gaddey, Richard, 21, 77, 80, 127, 192.
Gaddey, Sarah, 122, 126, 132.
Gaddy, ———, 27.
*See also* Geddy.

Gaddyes (i. e., Gaddy's house or ordinary), 19.
Gallery, in new church, 55; windows in, 66.
Garland, James, 174, 177, 180, 183, 187.
Garland, William, 109, 122, 146, 148, 153, 156, 160, 164, 167, 170, 174, 175², 177, 180.
Garnatis (?), William, xlvi.
Garrett, James, xlv.
Garrot, Tho., petitioner, 50.
Gates, hooks and hinges for glebe, 43; two new, to churchyard, 129.
Geddes, Joseph W., lxi.
Geddy, William, 153², 161, 168; processioner, 192.
*See also* Gaddy.
Geeves (?), Thomas, xlvi.
General Assembly, xix, xxiv, xxx, xlviii, liii, liv, lv; chaplain of, 233.
General Court, xxxiii, xxxiv, 220.
George II, King, 65.
Gibson, Anne, 84.
Gills (Gill, Gilles), Lucy (Lucey, Lycy), 5, 8, 12, 19, 27, 29, 30, 35, 38, 47, 49, 52, 57, 59, 63, 65, 68, 71, 74, 77, 79, 84, 87, 91, 96, 98, 102, 105, 110, 114, 117, 121, 126, 131, 134², 138, 141, 145.
Gilman, John, 118, 121, 123.
Gilman, Richard, 110, 114, 117, 121, 126, 131, 134.
Gilmett (Gillmett), Richard, 7, 19, 21, 105, 106.
Ginnings. *See* Jennings.
Gittins, Thomas, xlv.
Glasbrook, Ann, 69, 71, 75.
Glasebrook, James, 141.
Glasebrook, Sarah, 223, 224.

Glass, 42; sash, 56; to mend glebe windows, 122.
Glasse, Thomas, xlv.
Glazier, 191.
Glebe, 8; "a quarter built on," 111, 113, 118; allowance to minister in lieu of, 1, 4, 7, 12, 18, 26, 30, 34, 38, 159, 162; bricks for, 139; cornhouse on, 97, 99; dairy on, 78, 118; henhouse on, 107; land adjoining, purchased, 176, 178; lime for, 106, 114; Negro quarters built on, 44; plank for, 126; quitrent of, 12, 71, 91; rent of, 29, 39, 85, 115; repaired, 38, 73, 132, 135, 139, 147, 151, 162, 184, 191, 196; shingles for, 139; smokehouse built on, 50; threshing floor for, 122; tobacco casks allowed minister in lieu of, 1, 4, 7, 12, 18, 26, 30, 34, 38; windows repaired, 122.
Glebe gate, hooks and hinges for, 43.
Glebe house, repaired, 42; new, to be built, 58; tobacco levied to pay for, 62, 63, 66, 69.
Glebe land, house to be built on, 58; in James City County, lv, 27, 124; quitrents for, 5, 91, 96; quitrents for old, 27; workhouse to be built on old, 147, 154.
Glebe plantation, rent of, 22.
Gloucester County, v, xlix; Petsworth Parish, 235[3]; tobacco riots in, xlviii, xlix.
Goddin, Isaac, 114, 115, 132, 154; churchwarden, 107, 108, 109, 110, 111[2], 112[2], 113[2], 114; member of building committee, 107; petitioner, 48; successor to, appointed, 116; vestryman, 103, 104, 106, 116, 128, 130, 134.
Goddin, John, churchwarden, 217, 218[2], 219, 220[2], 221; successor to, appointed, 222; vestryman, 208, 212, 213, 215, 217, 223, 226, 231.
Gooch, Henry, xxxv, xxxvi, xxxvii.
Gooch, Mrs. Martha, 138.
Gooch, William, letter from, 40, 65; letter from recorded, 66.
Goodin, James, 143, 149, 167, 171, 174, 177, 180.
Goodin (Gooding), John, 156, 161, 164, 174, 177, 180, 184, 187[2], 190, 194.
Goodin (Goodings), Martha, 17, 18, 19, 22.
Grace, Honor, 121.
Grand Assembly, xv[2].
Grand jury, to determine ratio of paper currency to specie, 220.
Grantham, ———, xxxvi.
Gray, Arthur P., lxi.
Gray, David, 91; sexton at Upper Church, 82, 84, 87, 91.
Gray, Edward, xliv.
Gray, Isabella (Issabella), 126, 132, 135, 139, 142, 145, 148; sextoness, 94, 95, 97.
Gray, Margarett, 96, 99, 102, 111.
Gray, William, lviii.
Great Britain, table linen ordered from, 154.
Green, Isaac, 224, 227[3].
Green, Mary, 209.
*Green Spring,* Gov. Berkeley's residence, xxxv, xxxvii.
Greene, Henry, xlvii, xlvii (note)[2].
Grey, Anne, condemned for murder, 1.
Grievance, of three planters of New Kent County, xl.

INDEX 253

Grievances, of some of the inhabitants of Blisland Parish, xxii; of the inhabitants of Blisland Parish, xliii, 1.
Grigsby, Hugh Blair, x².
Grout, Richard, 145.
Groves, ———, xxxv.
Gulick, Holland, 43.

Halfield, Richd., 2.
Hall, Betty, 230.
Hall, Elisha, 208, 235.
Hall, Elizabeth, 209², 212, 214, 215, 218, 219, 221³, 223, 226.
Hall, Jesse, 194, 199, 202, 205, 210.
Hall, John, 59.
Hall, Richard, 216, 219, 221, 224, 226.
Hall, T h o m a s, xxxvi, xxxvi (note).
Hall, Wilmer L., lxi.
Hampton Parish, xii, xii (note), xiii, xvi, xvi (note)⁵, xvii², xvii (note), xxvii⁶, xxviii.
Hankin, Charles, 127, 149, 168, 184, 200.
Hankin, John, 229; processioner, 192. *See also* Hankins, John.
Hankin, William, 192², 194, 199; churchwarden, 208²; processioner, 192; vestryman, 197, 198, 201, 204, 205.
Hankins, John, tobacco viewer and teller, 33, 37; unable to serve as tobacco teller, 37. *See also* Hankin, John.
Hanover, 121, 139.
Hanover County, xxvi, xxviii, xxxiv², xxxvi.
Harbour, 66, 77.
Harman, Eliza., 181.
Harman, Francis, 2, 21.

Harman, John, processioner, 192.
H a r m a n, [ ]obert, xliv, xliv (note).
Harman, William, tobacco viewer and teller, 15², 26, 34, 37.
Harris, John, 181.
Harris, Malcolm H., xxiii (note).
Harrison, Edward, xlvi.
Harry, a Negro, 48.
Hart, Eliza., sextoness, 173.
Hart, William, 44, 153², 156, 160, 164², 167, 174; sexton,. 157, 160, 164, 167, 170.
Hartwell, Wm., xxxviii, xl.
Harvey, Catharine, 227, 229.
Harvey, Charles, 223.
Harvey, William, 146, 150, 175, 178, 235.
Harwood, William, 118, 122, 126, 135, 235.
Haselwood (Haslewood), Benja., 111, 113, 114, 196.
Haselwood (Haslewood), David, 156, 161, 165, 167.
Haselwood, Joseph, 122², 126, 131, 134, 138.
Haselwood, Lucy, 122.
Haselwood (Haslewood), Margt., 175, 191, 194.
Haselwood, Richard, 66, 122, 126, 131, 134, 138.
*See also* Haslewood, Hazelwood.
Hasewell, Frances, 13.
Hasewell (Haswell), Mary, 13, 15, 16, 21, 24.
Haslewood, Dickson, 171.
*See also* Haselwood, Hazelwood.
Hassocks, for the Lower Church, 146.
Hatfeild, Sarah, 70.
Hatfeild, William, 66.

Hatfield, Richard, jr., petitioner, 22.
Hatfield, Richard, sr., 22.
Hatton, Thos., 168; processioner, 192.
Haward, Luke, xlv.
Hawkins, Joseph, 27.
Hawkins (Hawkings), Mourning, 220, 222, 224, 227, 229.
Hawkins (Haukins), Sarah, xliv, 69, 77, 80, 83, 84, 87².
Hawkins, William, 114.
Hazelwood, Mrs. ————, 13.
See also Haselwood, Haslewood.
Henderson, Grissle (Gristle), 100, 102.
Henderson, Thomas, 31, 35.
Henhouse, built on the glebe, 107.
Hening, *Statutes at Large* . . . , xiv (note), xv (note), xvi (note), xvii (note), xix (note), xxi (note), xxiv (note), xxvi (note), xxvii (note), xxix (note), xxxii (note), xxxvi (note), liii (note), lv (note), lviii (note.)
Henley, ————, 66, 78.
Henley, Leonard (Len), 20, 64, 77, 154; churchwarden, 73, 74², 75, 76², 77; churchwarden and collector of the levy, 76; member of committee to run dividing line, 86; vestryman, 64², 67², 71, 76, 79, 83³, 87, 89, 90, 93, 95, 98, 101, 104, 108, 109, 112, 113, 116, 121, 125, 130, 141, 144.
Henley, Richardson, 181, 184; churchwarden, 179³, 180, 182³, 183; clerk of the Lower Church, 148, 152, 155, 160, 164, 167, 170, 173, 176, 180, 183, 186, 190, 193, 198, 202, 205; successor to, appointed, 203; vestryman, 172, 173, 176, 186, 189, 193.
Henry [i. e., Henry Bear, see p. 79], 78.
Henry, Bryan, 3, 5³, 7, 8, 12², 19², 27², 29.
Henry, Mrs. Bryan, complainant, 29.
See also Henry, Dorothy.
Henry, Dorothy (Doll), 30³, 35, 38, 47, 49, 52, 57, 59, 63.
See also Henry, Mrs. Bryan.
Henry, Dunkerton, 136.
Henry, Edward, 2, 21, 31.
Henry, Frances, 110, 111.
Henry, Jane, 102.
Hickman, Richard, clerk of James City County court, 30, 35.
Hickory Neck Church, lxi.
Hicks. See Hix.
High sheriff. See Sheriff.
Hight, Thos., 99.
Hight, William, 99.
Hill, ————, lvii.
Hill, [ ]n, xliv, xliv (note).
Hill, John, xliv (note), 69, 83, 87, 102², 110, 114.
Hillsford, Charles. See Millsford, Charles.
Hinges, for glebe gates, 43.
Hitchcock, Nance, 220, 222, 224, 227, 229.
Hix (Hicks), George, 223, 226, 229.
Hix, Grace, 99, 102, 105.
Hix, Hardiman, 216.
Hix, Joseph, 216, 219.
Hix, Mary, 223, 227.
Hix, Nathan, 222, 223, 226, 227, 229, 230.
Hix, Preston, 216, 219 .
Hix, Sarah, 224², 227.

# INDEX 255

Hockaday, ———, 57, 60², 64.
Hockaday, Edmund (Edward), 224; churchwarden, 222, 223², 225, 226², 227; successor to, appointed, 228; vestryman, 213, 215, 221, 229, 231³, 232.
Hockaday, James, 146, 168, 175, 178², 209; churchwarden, 172, 173², 175, 176², 177, 208³; successor to, appointed, 179; vestryman, 159², 163, 166, 182, 189, 193, 198, 201, 204, 205, 212, 214, 215, 217, 218, 221, 223, 226, 231³.
Hockaday, John, lii, 2, 202; vestryman, 1, 12, 231³.
Hockaday, Mrs. Reba., 169, 194.
Hockaday (Hoccaday), William, xiv², xv³, 63, 75, 77, 96, 105³, 110, 111, 114², 115, 117², 118, 121³, 122, 126², 131, 135, 138; churchwarden, 58², 59², 60, 61², 63, 70², 71², 92, 93², 94², 95², 96, 97, 98², 99, 103, 104², 106; churchwarden and collector of parish levy, 70; member of committee to build vestryhouse, 107; member of committee to run dividing line, 85; successor to, appointed, 63, 100, 107, 140; sheriff and collector of parish levy, 88, 89, 92, 93; vestryman, 56, 58, 62, 64, 67, 68, 74, 76, 79, 83³, 87, 89, 90, 101, 108, 109, 112, 113, 116, 120, 124, 125, 128, 130, 133.
Hockaday family, xv (note).
Hogg, John, tobacco viewer and teller, 34, 37.
Hogg, Mary, 171.
Hogg, Mrs. Mary, 206.
Hogg, William, 106, 115, 118, 122, 123, 154; churchwarden, 113³, 116³; successor to, appointed, 119;
vestryman, 97, 98, 100, 101, 108, 109, 112, 120, 124, 125, 128, 133, 137, 141.
Holdcraft, Mrs. Mary, 77.
Holdcroft, Mrs. ———, gives land on which to build church, 54, 55.
Holdcroft (Holdcraft), Henry, 5², 31, 32; churchwarden, 8, 9, 11, 12, 14², 18, 19, 21, 22, 23², 24², 26, 27²; clerk of the vestry, 2, 4, 6, 7, 9, 11, 12, 14², 18, 19, 23, 25, 26², 29, 30, 33, 34, 234; collector of delinquent levies, 28; resigns as clerk of vestry, 34; successor to, appointed, 28; vestryman, 1, 4, 7, 30, 33.
Holdcroft, James, 91, 92, 96.
Holdcroft, Thomas, 88, 91, 92, 96.
Holdcroft's mill, xvii, 10.
Holland, Jno., 21.
Hollands for surplice, 175.
Holt, David, 2.
Hooks, for glebe gates, 43.
Hope, Jon., xiv.
Hopkins, Hannah, 27.
Horseblocks, 35², 52, 66; for the Lower Church, 146, 191; for the Upper Church, 31, 142, 191.
Horsl, Richard, xlvi, xlvi (note).
Horsley, Rowland (Rouland), xlvi, xlvi (note).
Hughes, Rees, xliv.
Hughes, Robert, xlv².
Hurt, ———, 80.
Hurt, Eliz., 60, 63, 66, 69, 75, 77.

Indenture, for binding out an apprentice, 44.
Indian reservation, in Pamunkey Neck, xxiv.

Indians, g r i e v a n c e concerning, xliii; war against, xxxiv.
Indigent persons, appropriations for the support of, 5, 8, 12, 13, 19, 20, 27, 29, 31, 35, 38, 46, 47, 49, 52, 57, 59, 60, 63, 65, 66, 69, 71, 72, 75, 77, 78, 79, 80, 81, 84, 85, 87, 88, 91, 92, 96, 99, 102, 105, 106, 107, 110, 114, 115, 117, 118, 121, 122, 126, 127 131, 132, 134, 135, 138, 139, 141, 142, 143, 145, 146, 147, 149-153, 155-157, 160-165, 167, 168, 170-175, 177, 178, 180, 181, 183, 184, 187, 188, 190-192, 194, 195, 196, 199, 200, 202, 203, 205-207, 209, 210, 212-224, 226, 227, 229, 230; bacon for, 184, 209; beef for, 181, 190; burial charges for, $5^2$, 16, 30, 35, 59, $66^2$, 69, $77^3$, 80, 107, 115, $121^2$, 131, 135, $142^2$, 146, 153, 163, 167, 172, 174, 191, 202, 204; children of, bound out as apprentices, $16^2$; clothing for, 13, 17, 32, 85, 102, 153, 194, 207, 219, $223^2$, 224; coffins for, 12, 13, 111, 121, 131, 168, 175, 178, 181, 191, $195^2$, 202, 206, 209, 219, 227, 229, 230; corn for, 16, 17, 70, $102^2$, 106, 118, 131, 143, 146, $150^2$, 151, $163^2$, $172^2$, $175^2$, 178, 181, 183, 184, $187^4$, $188^2$, $190^2$, $191^2$, $192^2$, $194^4$, $199^5$, $200^2$, 207, 209, 216, 219, 220, 221, $222^4$, $224^2$, $227^4$, 229; cotton for, 70; funeral charges for, 177, 191, 195, $207^2$, 209, 223; house and land rent paid for, 178, 192, 194, 199, 202, 206, $209^3$, 216, 219, 222, $224^2$, $227^2$, $229^3$; meal for, 191; meat for, 27; medicine for, 13, 19, 46, 78, 150, 208, 224; molasses for, 188, 191, 196, 199; money bequeathed to, 92; petticoat for, 70; pork for, 188; sent to Ireland, 67; shoes for, 142, 149, 195; stockings for, 142, 195; sugar for, 122, 188; sundries for, 146, 150, 168, $172^2$, $175^2$, 184, 200, 207; tobacco levied to pay for the curing of certain, 17, 19, 29, $31^2$, 35, 38, 46, $69^2$, 81, 84, 126; workhouse be built for, 147, 154, 197.
Induction, act concerning the, of ministers, li; response of certain parishes to the governor's letter concerning, lii.
Ingram, ———, $xxxv^2$, xxxvi, xxxix.
Ingram, James, 228.
Insolvents, 186, 188, $196^2$, $203^2$.
Inspectors notes, 48, 51, 53, 58, 61, 78, 82, 86, 89, 93, 97, 101, 103, 108, 112, 116, 120, 124, 128, 133.
Inventory, to be made of stolen goods, xxxviii.
Ireland, 67.

Jack, a Negro, 39, 166.
Jack's Creek. *See* John's Creek.
James, Edward, 131, 150.
James, John, 21, 22, 23, 230; churchwarden, $228^2$, 230, 231, 232; successor to, appointed, 232; vestryman, 225, 226, $231^3$.
James, Thruston, 105, 142, 143, 146, 156, 161, 164, 167, 194, $196^2$, 204, 207; churchwarden, 92, $93^2$, $94^2$, $95^2$, 97, $98^2$, $140^2$, 141, 142, $144^2$, 145, $193^3$, $194^2$, $197^2$, $198^2$; collector of the parish levy, 193, 196; successor to, appointed, 100, 147, 200; vestryman, 88, $89^2$, 90, 101, 104, 106, 108, 109, 112, 120, 125, 130, 133, 137, 147, 151, 155,

158, 159², 163, 166, 170, 173, 176, 179, 186, 189, 201, 204, 205.
James City, xix, xxxiii.
James City County, v, ix, xxix², xxxi², xxxii³, xxxiv², lv, lix², 5, 27, 57, 59, 63, 65, 75, 86; act for docking the entail of certain lands in, lv; clerk of, 35, 46; deputy sheriff of, 2, 225; dividing line between New Kent County and, lix; glebe land in, to be sold, lv, 124; list of titheables, 30, 35, 46, 57, 63, 65, 110, 202; militia of, 217; quitrents for glebe land in, 27; sheriff of, 127, 223, 228, 230; tobacco tellers appointed for that part of Blisland Parish lying in, 34.
James City County court, clerk of, 27, 30, 110, 202, 228.
James City Parish, xxix, xxx³, xxxi, 110, 233.
James River, xxvi², xxxiv, xxxv².
Jamestown, xxxiv², xxxv³, xxxv (note), xxxix, xlviii.
Jammeson, ———, 27.
See also, Jemmyson.
Jefery, a Negro, 37.
Jeffers, John, 134, 157, 165, 168, 171², 174, 177², 180.
Jeffers, Mary, 157, 163.
Jeffers, Richard, 177², 180, 183.
Jeffers, Richmond, 187, 195, 207.
Jeffers, William, 115, 172.
Jefferson, Peter, lx.
Jeffreys, Herbert, xxxvii, xxxix, xl, xli, xlii.
Jemmey, a Negro, 64.
Jemmyson, Elizabeth, fined, 32.
See also Jammeson.
Jenkins, Leoline, xlviii, xlix.
Jennett, John, 31.

Jennings (Ginnings), George, 206, 207, 210², 213, 215, 219, 221, 224, 227, 229.
Jennings, James, 227, 229.
Jennings, Mildred, 188, 195, 199.
Jennings, Peter, 20.
Jennings (Ginnings), Priscilla, 207, 210, 227, 229.
Jennings, William, 188, 191, 195, 199, 216, 219, 221.
Jesus, sermon refuting objections to the divinity and dignity of, liv.
John Lewis & Co., 172, 178.
John's Creek, xix², xx², xxii, xxiv², xxviii, xxix.
Johnson, David, 126, 139.
Johnson, Edward, xlv.
Jones, ———, 221, 229.
Jones, Betty, 150.
Jones, Burnal, 105.
Jones, Cornelius, 51, 190.
Jones, Daniel, 227.
Jones, Mrs. Elizabeth, 16.
Jones, Emanuel, minister, lii.
Jones, Evan (Evans, Even), 16², 35, 49, 57, 66.
Jones, Mrs. Evan, 16.
Jones, James, 102, 105, 132, 135², 143, 148, 216, 219, 221, 224, 226.
Jones, John, 126.
Jones, Mary, 35, 153, 156, 161, 165, 167, 184, 187.
Jones, Philarity, 215, 216³, 219, 221, 222, 227, 229.
Jones, Philip, 35, 234.
Jones, Philley, 210².
Jones, Richard, 13, 52.
Jones, Stephen, 51, 80, 114, 117, 138, 144, 167, 181, 187², 188, 190, 192, 194³, 196, 199², 200, 202, 206, 209², 216, 219², 222, 224², 227, 229.
Jones, Thomas, 121, 126.

Jones, William, 13, 21, 153, 168, 175², 178, 181, 184, 187, 195.
*Journals of the House of Burgesses of Virginia, 1659/60-1693,* xix (note), xxiv (note), xxv (note), xxix (note), liii (note), liv (note), lvi (note).
*Journals of the House of Burgesses of Virginia, 1727-1734, 1736-1740,* liv.
Justice, of the county, 15; of the peace, xlix, liii, 65.
Justices, one of his majesty's, 50.

Keeling, ————, 21.
Keeling, George, lii; vestryman, 1, 7, 9, 12, 18, 23, 25, 26, 30, 33, 36, 38, 41.
Keen, John, appointed tobacco viewer and teller, 10; declines to serve as tobacco viewer and teller, 25.
Kemp, Matthew, 46, 49, 52, 57, 59, 63, 65, 69, 72.
Kenney, Mrs. Mary, 71.
Kenney, William, liii², 5, 38, 42, 43, 92; bequest to parish to purchase a piece of plate, 103, 119, 136, 154; churchwarden, 1, 2, 3², 36, 37, 38, 41; magistrate, 1, 3; sheriff and collector of parish levy, 36, 39; vestryman, 9, 12, 18, 23, 26, 30, 33, 34, 42, 46, 48, 51, 52, 54, 55, 56, 59.
Kernute. *See* Curnute.
King and Queen County, v, xxiv, xxvii, xxviii, xxxiv², xxxvi.
King George II, 65.
King William County, xx, xxv, xxviii, xxxiv², xxxvi, 15.
King's Creek, xxxv.

Kitchen, brick chimney added to, 70; new roof on, 42.
Kitson, Betty, 161.
Kitson, Eliza., 150.
Knit, an apprentice taught to, 39.

Lace, purple silk, 43.
Laffoon (Lafoon, Lafoone), John, 20, 27, 35².
Laffoon, Mary, 102.
Laffoon, Sarah, 142, 184.
Land, adjoining glebe to be bought, 176; feoffees of counties to purchase, and erect towns, xlviii; patent to, in Pamunkey Neck, xlv (note); patent to, on the south side of the Mattaponi, xlv (note), xlvi (note); patents to, in Blisland Parish, xi, xii, xv; patents to, in York County, xi, xii, xiii, xiv; purchased, 178; vestry of Blisland Parish authorized to sell certain, lvi.
Landing, Capt. Bassett's, xviii.
Lands, act for docking the entail of certain, lv.
Lane, John, xlvii.
Langford, John, 2.
Langley, Mrs. Frances, 8.
Langly, ————, 27.
Laton, Reuben, 8.
Lawrence, ———— xxxv, xxxvi, xxxvii.
Lawsone, Nichols, xlv, xlv (note).
Lawsuits, parish vs. Cousins, Gaddy, Jammeson, Langly, Mackormack, 27; Mary Field, 19.
Lawyer, fee of, 111.
Lead, 42, 190.
Leather, 43.
Leaver (Lever), Anne, 16, 20, 132.
Leaver (Lever), Mary, 16, 20.

# INDEX 259

Legacy, to the parish, 119, 136, 154; to the poor of the parish, 92.
*Legislative Journals of the Council of Colonial Virginia,* . . ., lvi (note).
LeNeve (Leneve), Rev. Mr. ——, 39, 233$^4$.
Lenley's (Lendley) plantation, 10, 11.
Letter, concerning the induction of the minister of Blisland Parish, li; from James Blair, 40; from William Gooch, 40, 65; of Henry Chicheley, mentioned, xlix; of resignation, 97; of the secretary of Virginia, mentioned, xlviii.
Levy, fort duties, xliii; grievance concerning the imposition of 2 s. per hhd., xliv. *See also* Parish levy.
Lewis, Charles, liii.
Lewis, David, 200, 230; churchwarden, 228$^2$, 229, 230, 231, 232$^2$; collector of the subscription for 1785, 232; vestryman, 225, 226, 231$^4$.
Lewis, David, and Co., 191, 195.
Lewis, John, 175, 181, 187, 191, 194, 207; churchwarden, 211$^2$, 212, 213, 214, 215$^3$, 216, 217$^2$; vestryman, 208, 218, 221, 225.
Lewis, John, and Co., 172, 178.
Lewis, Robert, liii.
Library Board, v$^2$.
Lilly, Rebecca, 172, 175$^2$.
Lime, 106, 114, 150.
Lindley, Henry, 21.
Lindsey, Mrs. ————, 96.
Lindsey (Linsey), Anne (Ann), 96, 99, 102, 105, 110, 117$^2$, 121, 126, 131, 138$^2$, 141, 145, 148, 152, 155, 160, 164, 167, 170, 172.
Lindsey (Linsey), Joseph, 21, 47, 84, 87, 91.
Lindsey (Linsey), Thomas, 66, 71, 75, 79, 84, 87, 91, 96, 99, 102, 105, 110, 114, 117, 121, 126, 131, 134, 138, 141, 145, 148, 152, 155, 160, 164, 167, 170, 173, 180, 184, 187, 190, 194, 199, 202, 206, 209$^2$, 212, 215, 218, 221$^2$, 223$^2$, 226, 229.
Lindsey. *See also* Linsey.
Linen, for communion table, 154; for indigent person, 32; for mending surplice, 153.
Linsey, Edward, 35, 77.
Linsey, Eliza., 138.
Linsey, John, 145, 148.
Linsey, Landey, 127.
Linsey, Patience, 175$^2$, 178, 187, 188, 191, 192, 194, 199.
Linsey, Richard, 122, 126, 131, 134, 138, 167, 171; sexton, 182, 183, 187, 190, 194, 197.
Linsey. *See also* Lindsey.
*List of the Parishes, Tythables, Ministers, etc., in Virginia in July, 1702,* 1 (note).
*A List of Those That Have Been Executed for ye Late Rebellion in Virginia,* xxxvi (note).
Little, [ ] rancis, xliv.
Lively, Edward, 128, 150, 161, 165; petitioner, 127; sexton, 60, 63, 65, 68$^2$, 71, 74, 77, 79, 84, 87, 91, 95, 98, 102, 104, 110, 114, 117, 120, 125, 131, 134, 138, 139, 141, 142, 144, 148$^2$, 152, 155, 157.
Lively, Elizabeth, 167, 171, 172, 174, 177, 184.
Livingstone (Levingstone), William, 13, 15, 16, 21, 24, 27, 234.

Lockalere, Robt., 21.
London, Lord Bishop of, lii, 40; Public Record Office, xvii (note), xx, xxxi (note), xxxvii, xxxix (note), xl (note), xli (note), xliv (note), l (note), lii (note), liii, liv (note).
Longworthie, John, xliv.
Lord Bishop of London, lii.
Lossen, Nick., xlv.
Lovall, Charles, xlv².
Lowder, Robert, petitioner, xl, xli.
Lower Church, lix; addition to, 196, 197, 200, 204; benches for, 146, 172, 191; clerk of, 59, 62, 65, 68, 71, 74, 76, 79, 84, 87, 90, 95, 98, 101, 104, 109, 113, 117, 120, 125, 130, 134, 138, 141, 144, 148, 152, 155, 160, 164, 167, 170, 173, 176, 180, 183, 186, 190, 193, 198, 202, 205; communion plate and ornaments to be purchased for, lvi; communions for, 126, 131, 134, 138, 142, 145, 148, 152, 156, 164, 167, 170, 173, 177, 180, 183, 187, 190, 194, 198, 202; contractors required to finish, in accordance with agreement, 67; hassocks for, 146; horseblocks for, 146, 191; minister engaged for, 39; repaired, 168; set of plate for, 92; sexton at, 2, 12, 19, 21, 26, 34, 38, 43, 59, 63, 65, 68, 71, 74, 79, 84, 87, 91, 95, 98, 102, 104, 110, 114, 117, 120, 125, 131, 134, 138, 141, 144, 148, 152, 155, 157, 160, 164, 167, 170, 176, 181, 182, 183, 187, 190, 194, 197, 198, 202; sextoness at, 173, 205; to be painted, 93; tobacco levied for repairing, to be sold, 125; trees planted at, 69; vestry for Blisland Parish held at, 11, 23, 30, 38, 42, 46, 51, 54, 59, 64, 71, 76, 83, 98, 104, 112, 113, 120, 140, 147, 166, 173, 179, 186, 193, 201, 204, 212, 213, 215, 220; yard cleaned, 69, 164; yard to be laid off and bricked in, 83.
Lownell, Tho., xlv.
Lucas, Thos., 110.
Lucerie (?), John, jr., xliv, xliv (note).
Luck, John, 26, 34.
Lyon, Daniel, 204², 206, 207.
Lyon, John, constable, 110.
Lyon, Thos., 49.
Lyon, Thos., sr., 81.

M'Cormick (M'Comick), Mary, 181, 184, 188, 191, 195. *See also* Mackormack.
M'gary, Thomas, 178², 181³, 184.
Mackain, ———, 52, 57, 69.
McKain (Mackain, Mackaine, Makain), William, liv, 56, 58⁴, 63; churchwarden, 50, 51², 52, 53, 54², 55², 58; clerk of Wilmington Parish, 20; magistrate, 42, 60; member of the committee to proportion the levy, 73; petitioner, 64; vestryman, 41, 42, 45, 46, 59, 61, 62, 64, 67², 68, 71, 75.
Mackenzie, Alexander, 235².
Mackenzie, Ken., 117, 235³.
Mackormack, ———, 27.
*See also* M'Cormick.
Mackoy, John, xliv, xliv (note).
Macon, William, liii, 126, 161, 163; churchwarden, 157, 158², 159²; sheriff and collector of parish levy, 23, 53, 58; successor to, appointed, 163, 172; vestryman, 154, 155.

# INDEX

Magazine, fort duties levied toward building, xliii.
Magistrate, 1, 3, 8, 14², 28, 41², 42², 50, 60.
Mahone (M'hone), Sackvile, 149, 156, 161, 165, 167, 171, 174, 177.
Manning, Ann, 219.
Manning (Maning), John, 72, 177, 181, 207, 210², 213, 214, 215, 219, 221, 224, 227, 229.
Manning, Margt., 149, 156, 161, 165.
Manning, Robert, 94.
Manning, Sarah, 167, 171, 174, 177, 178.
Manning, Stephen, 75, 81.
Manning, William, 175.
Maple tree, xi.
Maples, Josiah, 102, 105, 110.
Maples, Richard, tailor, 44³.
Maples, Thomas, 64, 66, 69, 71.
Markland, John, 57.
Marks, ———, 35.
Marston Parish, xii (note), xvi², xvii, xvii (note)², xxvii, xxviii.
Martin, Jeremiah, 160, 183, 184, 187, 190, 213.
Martin, John, xxxvi (note).
Martin, Richard, 127.
Massie, Charles, liv.
Massie, Peter, xliv.
Massie, Thomas, liii.
Matchemeed Swamp, xi².
Mathews, Saml., xxxviii, xl.
Mattaponi River, xviii², xix², xx², xxi³, xxii³, xxii (note), xxiii, xxv², xxvi, xxviii, xxix, xxxv, xlvi (note).
Meade, *Old Churches, Ministers and Families of Virginia*, ix, ix (note), x (note), xxxii (note).
Meal, for indigent persons, 191.

Meat, for indigent person, 27.
Medicine, 235²; for indigent persons, 13, 19, 46, 78, 150, 208, 224.
Merchant ship, English, xxxvi.
Merideth, Rebeckah, 49.
Merrideth, John, 91, 99.
Merriman, Mrs. ———, 209³.
Merriman, James, 210, 212, 213, 214, 216, 219, 221.
Merriman, Thomas, 210, 214, 219.
Merritt, Edwd., 21.
Middlesex County, xxvi, lii; tobacco riots in, xlviii, xlix.
Mid[ ]lton, Martin, xlv.
Militia, fine assessed in pork for the use of, xxxvii; of James City Co. called out, 217; of New Kent Co. called out, 217.
Milkhouse, to be built, 45.
Miller, John, 49, 52, 57, 59, 63, 65, 68, 71, 74, 77, 79, 84, 87.
Millsford (?), Charles, xlv, xlv (note).
Mims, Thomas, xlvi.
Ministers, act concerning induction of, li; list of, 233.
Mohun, Warick, lii.
Molasses, for indigent persons, 188, 191, 196, 199.
Moll, a Negro, 92.
Money, bequeathed to parish to purchase a piece of plate, 103; bequeathed to the poor of the parish, 92; depreciation of, 216; fine paid in current, 32; levy payable in tobacco or, 225; paper, reduced to specie, 222; raised by selling tobacco, 48; to be raised to pay for glebe house, 62; work on glebe house paid for in current, 42.

Moore, Benjamin, 188, 191, 196, 199.
Moore, Honour, 67, 70, 72, 74, 77, 79, 85, 87².
Moore, James, xlvi.
Moore, John, 55, 56³, 67.
Mooreman, Thomas, xlv.
Morgan, Edward, xlvi.
Morris, Owen, 21.
Morris, William, churchwarden, 3, 4, 5, 6, 7, 41, 42, 44², 45, 46, 48, 49, 51; justice of the peace, liii; magistrate, 28, 42; sheriff and collector of parish levy, 53, 58; successor to, appointed, 8, 33, 50, 75; to sell tobacco belonging to the parish, 43; tobacco viewer and teller, 10; vestryman, 1, 9, 12, 18, 25, 26, 30, 33, 36, 37, 38, 41, 52, 54, 55, 56, 59, 61, 62, 64, 68, 71.
Moryson (Morison, Morrison), Francis, xxxvii, xxxix, xl², xli, xlii.
Moss (Mosse), William, xlvi, xlvi (note)², 204³.
Mossom, David, minister, liv, 39, 233³.
*Mt. Vernon,* lvi.
Mulatto, 16².
Murder, woman condemned for, 1.
Mutlow, William, 150, 163.

Nails, 12.
Nansemond County, xxxv.
Napkin, 191.
Narrows, xiv², xv.
Nears, Henry, 84.
Negroes, xxxviii², xl²; certain, levy free, 21, 37, 39, 48, 64, 92, 109, 151, 166, 169, 218; quarters for, on glebe, 44.

Netherland, John, xxx.
New Kent County, v, ix, xii (note), xiii, xiv, xvi, xvi (note), xvii, xvii (note), xviii⁴, xxv, xxvi², xxviii², xxix, xxx², xxxi², xxxii⁴, xxxiii, xxxiv³, xxxv, xxxv (note), xxxvi³, xxxvi (note), xxxvii², xliii, xlv (note), xlvii, xlviii², xlix², l, li, lii, lv², lvi³, lvii, lviii², lix², lxi, 233; area and population of, liii; boundary line of, xiii, xiv; clerk of, liv; collectors, 230; coroners of, liii; county lieutenant of, liv; deputy sheriff of, 112, 116, 119, 124, 128, 133, 197; dividing line between New Kent north side and south side, xxi; dividing line between James City County and, lix; established, xxvii; justices of the peace of, xlix, liii; militia of, called on duty, 217; parishes in, xxi, xxii; petitions of inhabitants of xxxvii, xl, xli, xlii; sheriff of, liii, 93, 103, 108, 137, 215, 223, 225, 228, 230; surveyor, liv; tobacco riots in, xlviii, xlix²; town to be established in, xlviii
New Kent County court, 48, 95; clerk of, xxxvi, 110, 228.
Newman, Edward, sexton, 123, 125, 131, 134, 138, 141, 143 .
New Pocoson (Poquoson) Parish, xvi (note), xvii.
Niccoll (?), James, xlv.
Nicholson, Francis, letter to, li.
Norfolk, x.
Norris, Nathaniel, 2, 5.
Northey, Edward, 1, li (note).
Norvell (Norvel), William, 194, 210, 215, 216, 219, 221, 227, 229.

Oakley, Francis, 210, 214.
Oakley, Thos., 88², 98, 118.
Oakley, Mrs. Thos., 77.
Oaths, action of vestry in reference to, 67; appointed for vestrymen, 61, 64, 75; governor's opinion regarding the taking of, 65; tobacco tellers required to take, 10², 11², 15².
Oda, [a Negro(?)], 127.
Odall (Odal), Anderson, 64, 66, 69, 70, 71.
Odall, Joyce, 70.
Odell (Odal, Odel), James, 195, 224, 230.
Odell (Odal), Prudence, 188, 203, 206, 209, 212, 215, 219, 221.
Oglesby, Charles, 21.
Oglesby, Mary, 12.
Old glebe. *See* Glebe land.
Old Rappahannock County, xxvi.
Orders, from Lord Bishop of London, 40.
Ordinaries, Chiswel's, 159, 235; Furnea's, 26, 235.
Ornaments, to be purchased for the Lower Church, lvi.
Otey, Mrs. ———, 229.
Otey, John, liii.
Oustin, Sam, xlvi (note). *See also* Austin.
Oznaburgs, 6 ells of, 191.

Page, Thomas, xlv.
Pamunkey Indians, xxxv.
Pamunkey Neck, xviii³, xix⁵, xix (note), xx⁶, xxii³, xxii (note), xxiii⁶, xxv⁴, xxviii², xxix, xxxiv, xlv, xlvi, xlvi (note); certain inhabitants of, restored to St. John's Parish, xxiv; English settlers in, xxiii, xxiv; Indian reservation in, xxiv; petition of the inhabitants of, xix; processioners in that part of, in St. Peter's Parish, xxiii, xlvii (note); settlement of, xxiii, xxiii (note).
Pamunkey River, xii, xvii, xviii⁶, xix, xx³, xxi⁵, xxii², xxiii, xxv, xxvi, xxviii², xxxii, xxxv², lv (note), lvi, lviii, 235.
Paper money, 220; reduced to specie, 222.
Parish, Jones, 52.
Parish, petition regarding the establishment of a, xix.
Parish levy, certain persons discharged from payment of, 21, 22³, 32, 37, 39, 41, 45, 47, 48, 50, 51², 64, 68, 72, 73, 75, 78, 81, 92, 94², 109, 119, 127², 151², 158, 163, 166, 169, 192, 218², 225, 228; charges for building vestry house to be laid at the laying of, 107; collectors of, 3, 6, 9, 13, 22, 23, 24, 28, 32, 36, 39, 41, 48, 50, 53, 58, 60, 61, 64, 70, 73, 76, 78, 82, 85, 86, 88, 89, 92, 93, 97², 100², 103², 107, 108, 111, 112, 115, 116, 119², 120, 123, 124, 127, 128, 133², 136, 137, 140, 143, 147, 151, 154, 157, 163, 165, 169, 172, 176, 179, 182, 185, 188, 193, 197, 201, 203, 208, 211, 215, 218, 220², 222, 223, 225², 226, 228, 230; collectors of, to give bond, 4, 6, 9, 14, 22, 23, 24, 28, 29, 32, 36, 39, 41, 48, 50, 53, 58, 61, 64, 67, 70, 73, 74, 76, 78, 82, 85, 86, 88, 89, 92, 93, 97², 100, 101, 103, 107, 108, 111, 112, 116, 119, 120, 123, 124, 127, 128, 133², 136, 137, 140, 143, 147, 151, 154,

157, 163, 165, 169, 172, 176, 179, 182, 185, 188, 193, 197, 201, 203, 208, 211, 215, 218, 220, 223, 226, 228; collectors to distrain for, 4, 6, 9, 14, 22, 24, 28, 32, 36, 39, 41, 61, 70, 73, 76, 78, 82, 86, 89, 93, 97, 101, 103, 108, 112, 116, 120, 124, 128, 133, 137; committee to proportion, 73, 92, 119, 157, 158, 169$^2$, 185, 211, 220; payable in cash or tobacco, 225; proportioned, 3, 6, 9, 13, 22, 28, 32, 36, 39, 40, 48, 50, 53, 58, 73, 76, 78, 82, 86, 87, 93, 97, 100, 103, 108, 112, 116, 119, 124, 128, 133, 137, 139; to collect overdue, 28.

Parish record books of colonial Virginia, x.

Parish register, births and deaths to be recorded in, 33.

Parish tobacco. *See* Tobacco.

Parish treasurer, report of, 182.

Parishes, early colonial, xii (note), xxvii, xxxii; counties co-terminous with, in area, xxvi; dividing line between, xxi; established during the period from 1643 to 1655, xxvi; in New Kent County, xxi, xxii, xxxii; in York County, xii (note), xvi (note), xvii; schedule of, in Virginia, xx.

Parks, William, 84.

Parliament of the Commonwealth, xv.

Pasteur, Mrs. ———, 175.

Pasteur, William, 184, 235.

Patents, to land in Blisland Parish, xi, xii, xv; to land in Pamunkey Neck, xlv (note); to land in York County, xi, xii, xiii, xiv; to land on the south side of the Mattaponi, xlv (note), xlvi (note).

Patroler, 126, 127$^2$, 143$^3$.

Paul, Lydda (Lydday), 139, 142.

Pauley, ———, 78.

Pauley, Samuel, 69, 71, 75.

Pease, [ ]sephe, xliv.

Pennington, ———, 70.

Pennington, Mrs. Ann, 102$^2$, 121$^2$, 131.

Pennington, Robert, 38, 103; churchwarden, 100$^2$; vestryman, 90$^2$, 92$^2$, 93, 95, 98.

Perkins, ———, 229.

Perkins (Pirkins), Mary, 227$^2$, 229.

Perrine, James, xliv.

Perry, *Historical Collections Relating to the American Colonial Church,* lii (note), liii (note).

Pethwood, John, 3, 8, 12$^2$.

Petitions, concerning parish levy, 21$^2$, 22$^2$, 32, 41, 47, 48$^2$, 50, 51$^2$, 64, 68, 109, 119, 166; for appointment as sexton, 21; for repealing the warehouse at Taskanask, lv; of inhabitants of Blisland Parish, xxxiii, 208; of Richard Clarke, xxxvii-xli; of Samuel Sutton, xxxvi (note); of some of the inhabitants of Blisland Parish, liii; of Stephen Tarleton, xli; of the inhabitants of Pamunkey Neck, xix; of three planters of New Kent County, xl.

Petsworth Parish, v, lii, 235$^3$.

Petticoat, for indigent person, 70.

Pettis, Jno., lii.

Pettus, Thomas, clerk of the

Lower Church, 59, 62, 65, 68, 71, 74, 76, 79, 84, 87, 90, 95.
Pew, offer for, in the Brick Church, 24.
Pews, for the Upper Church, 129; in the new church, 56.
Philbates (Filbates), Eliz., 69, 71.
Philbates (Filbates), James, 71, 80.
Phillips, George, xliv.
Phips, Sarah, 66.
Physic. See Medicine.
Physicians, list of, 234.
Pickett (Picket, Pigget, Piggett), Martha, 99, 102, 105, 110, 114, 117, 121, 126, 146.
Pigg, John, 65.
Piggett, Martha. See Pickett, Martha.
Piggot (Piggett, Piggott), John, 170, 175; sexton, 176, 180, 182.
Piggot, Pearson, 181.
Piggott, William, 227.
Pitblado, Sarah, 131.
Pitblado, William, 122.
Pitman, Elenor, 80, 84, 87, 91, 96, 99, 102, 105, 110, 114, 117$^2$, 118, 121, 126, 131, 134, 138, 144.
Plains, 191.
Plank, 12; for coffin, 181; for roofing, 56; for the glebe, 126; for threshing floor, 122; for Upper Church, 150.
Plant, Wm. (?), xlvii.
Plate. See Church plate.
Poll abatement, 50, 53, 58.
Pond, Eliza., 199.
Pond, Matt., 21.
Poor people. See Indigent persons.
Pork, fine assessed in, xxxvii; for indigent person, 188.

Poropotank Creek, xvi, xviii, xxii$^2$, xxviii$^2$.
Porter, Robert, petitioner, xl, xli.
Potter, Roger, xxxvii, xxxviii$^2$, xl.
Potter, Thomas, 213.
Pouncey, John, xi, xii, xiii.
Pouncey's Creek, xii.
Pouncie, Roger, xlvi, xlvi (note).
Power, Edward, churchwarden, 157, 159$^3$, 162, 163$^3$, 164, 222, 223$^2$, 225, 226, 227; collector, 228; successor to, appointed, 166, 228; vestryman, 154, 155, 170, 186, 204, 205, 208, 212, 214, 218, 221, 229, 231$^3$.
Power, John, 88$^2$, 91, 135, 138, 146, 148, 151, 152; churchwarden, 85, 86, 89$^3$, 90$^2$, 132, 133, 134, 136$^2$, 137, 147$^3$, 151$^2$; successor to, appointed, 92, 140, 154, 172; vestryman, 75, 83, 92, 93, 95, 101, 104, 106, 107, 109, 112, 113, 120, 124, 125, 141, 144, 155, 158, 159$^2$.
Powers, Henry, 56.
Preachers. See Ministers.
Precincts, parish divided into, xvii, 9, 10$^3$, 11, 15$^2$, 25, 37.
Prentis, John, 175.
*The Present State of Virginia*, liii.
Price, Edmund, xlvi.
Priddy, Robert, xiv.
Pride, James, 222.
Prinage, 43.
Prince, Silvanus, 203, 205, 208, 213.
Processioners, appointed, 173, 186, 201, 213; in Pamunkey Neck district, xxiii, xlvii (note); in St. Peter's Parish, xliv (note)$^4$, xlv (note)$^5$, xlvi$^5$, xlvii (note)$^5$, 1; list of, 192; re-

turns of, examined, 106, 163, 166, 179, 189; returns of, recorded, 108, 169, 179, 192.

Proclamation, xlii.

Protestant . Episcopal Church, parish record books belonging to, x; vestrymen subscribe to doctrine, discipline and worship of, 231.

*Protestant Episcopal Review and Church Register,* ix.

Pryor (Pryer, Pryour), David, 37, 63, 66, 88, 91, 92.

Pulpit, for the new church, 56; in the Upper Church, to be changed, 129.

Pulpit cloth, mended, 149.

Purple cloth, 43.

Purple silk lace, 43.

Purple silk tassels, 43.

Quarter, on the glebe for Negroes, 44, 78; tobacco levied for building, 111, 113; tobacco levied for lathing, 118.

Queen's Creek, xii (note), xvi, xvii, xxvii.

Quitrents, 77; of the glebe land, 5, 12, 71, 91, 96; of the glebe land in James City Co., 27; of the old glebe land, 27; Saml. Curl discharged from paying for two years, 85.

Ramsey, Sarah, 177, 191.

Rappahannock County, xxvi.

Rappahannock River, xxvi.

Ratcliffe, ———, 97.

Ratcliffe, Ben., 143.

Ratcliffe, Francis, 112, 113; churchwarden, 107, $108^2$, $109^2$, 110, 111, 112; vestryman, 103, 104, 106.

Rawleigh, James, 223.

Rawleigh, Walter, $150^2$, 192, 223.

Rawson, Charles, 70, 72, 74, 87.

Rawson, Thomas, 191, 207.

Recommendation, of minister by James Blair, 40; by William Gooch, 40.

Reece, Mary, 99.

Register books, of Blisland Parish, 33, 158; of Wilmington Parish, 85.

Register clerk, appointed, 33.

Rent, house and land, paid for indigent persons, 178, 192, 194, 199, 202, 206, $209^3$, 216, 219, 222, $224^2$, $227^2$, $229^3$; of the glebe, 22, 29, 39, 73, 85, 115; paid by Saml. Curl, 39, 57, 60, 63, 66, 69, 85.

Reynolds, John, 1.

Richardson, ———, $35^2$, 44, 46, 75.

Richardson, Benjamin, tobacco teller and viewer, 25, 33, 37.

Richardson, John, 46, 49, 65, 66, 69, 71, 115, 122, 126, $131^2$, 145, 146, 159; churchwarden, 63, $64^2$, 65, $67^2$, $68^2$, 123, 124, $125^2$, $128^2$, $129^2$, $130^2$; member of the committee to run dividing line, 86; processioner, 192; sheriff and collector of the parish levy, $103^2$, 107, 108; successor to appointed, 132; vestryman, $61^2$, 62, 74, 76, 79, $83^3$, 87, 89, 90, 93, $95^2$, 98, 101, 106, 108, 109, 112, 113, 116, 120, 133, 141, 144, 147, 151, 155.

Richardson, Mary, $121^2$.

Richardson, Richard, liii, 63, 89;

INDEX 267

churchwarden, 28, 30, 31, 33; magistrate, 8; sheriff and collector of the parish levy, 40, 48; successor to, appointed, 33, 83; tobacco viewer and teller, 10; vestryman, 4, 7, 9, 12, 15, 25, 26, 36, 38, 41, 42, 45, 46, 48, 51, 52, 54, 55, 56, 59, 61, 62, 64, 68, 74.

Richardson, Stanup, churchwarden, 232; collector of the subscription for 1785, 232; vestryman, 231, 232.

Richardson, William, 153, 181, 183, 191, 205; churchwarden, 166$^3$, 167, 169$^3$, 170$^2$, 172$^2$, 200, 201$^2$, 203, 204$^2$; successor to, appointed, 172, 208; vestryman, 154, 159$^2$, 163, 173, 179, 182, 186, 189, 193, 198.

Richmond, x, lv (note), lxi, 231.

Rivers, ridges between, dividing line between counties and parishes, xxi.

Robards, Evan, sexton, 19.

Roberts, Rite, 102, 105$^2$.

Robinson, Morgan P., lxi.

Rockahock, lvii.

Roe (?), John, xliv.

Rogers, John, xiii.

Roper, John, xxxiii, xlvii, xlvii (note)$^2$.

Rosse, Will., xlvii, xlvii (note)$^2$.

Rountree (Rowntree), John, 21; tobacco viewer and teller, 33, 37.·

Rountree, William, jr., 77.

Rowe, Mrs. ———, 153, 156.

Rowe (Row), Mary, 121, 146, 149, 150, 160, 164, 167, 169.

Rue, Peter, 187.

Rum, for funeral, 131.

Russell, ———, 66.

Russell, Armistead, vestryman, 197, 205.

Russell, Burnal, 121, 153, 156, 192; payments to the estate of, 202$^2$; sexton, 197, 198.

Russell (Russel), John, 143, 150; vestryman, 89, 101, 104, 113.

Russell (Russel), John, jr., vestryman, 83$^2$, 87, 94.

Russell, Rebecca, payment to the estate of, 210; sextoness, 205.

St. John's Parish, xix, xx$^2$, xxii (note), xxiv, xxv, xxix, xxxii.

St. Paul's Parish, xxvii.

St. Peter's Church, lviii$^2$, lix.

St. Peter's Parish, xviii$^2$, xix$^4$, xix (note), xx, xxi, xxii, xxviii, xxix, xxx$^4$, xxxi, xxxii$^4$, xliv (note)$^4$, xlv (note)$^5$, liii, liv, lvi, 189, 233; act concerning the inhabitants of Pamunkey Neck district of, xxiv; cut off from Blisland Parish, xxiii, xxxii; dividing line between Blisland Parish and, xx$^2$, xxxiii, 54, 64, 86; English settlers in, xxiv; established, xviii, xxiii; processioners in xlvi,$^5$ xlvii (note)$^5$, 1; vestry book of, xix (note), xx, xxxii, xxxiii, xlvi (note)$^5$, xlvii (note)$^5$; vestry of, opposed to induction of minister, lii; vestryman of, xlix, 1.

St. Stephen's Parish, xxi, xxii, xxiii.

Salivating, 13, 19, 46, 69, 71.

Salmon, Tho., 2, 5$^2$.

Samson, Mary, 132, 135$^2$.

Sanders, Mrs. ———, 224.

Sanders, Elizabeth, 190, 202, 207, 223.
Sanders, Grissell, 123.
Sanders, Laney Jones, 207.
Sanders, Susannah (Susanna), 175², 177, 178, 181, 184, 187, 190, 194, 199, 202, 207.
Sash glass, 56.
Sash windows, for the Upper Church, 129, 206.
Sawyer, Sarah, 45.
Sawyer, William, 45.
Schooling, payments for, of indigent children, 202², 209, 224.
Scimino Creek, xii (note)², xiii², xiv, xvi², xvi (note)², xvii², xvii (note), xviii, xxvii², xxviii², xxxi, liv.
Sclater, ———, 31, 35².
Sclater, John, 36, 38, 58; churchwarden, 28, 30; justice of the peace, liii; magistrate, 14², 41², 50²; sheriff and collector of parish levies, 28², 31, 32; vestryman, 4, 7, 9, 12, 15, 23, 26, 38, 41, 45, 46, 51, 52, 54, 55. *See also* Slater, John; Slaughter, John.
Scott, John, liii², 21², 27, 29², 31, 234.
Seats, Edmd. Walker paid for making, 66.
Sermon, to be printed and distributed, liv.
Servant, 13, 15, 21, 44.
Servants, English, xxxviii³, xl².
Sexton, 4, 5, 7², 46², 52², 57², 76; appointed, 43, 60, 82, 94, 97, 100, 123, 143, 157, 182, 197; at Lower Church, 2, 12, 19², 21, 26, 34, 38, 59, 63, 65, 68, 71, 74, 84, 87, 91, 95, 98, 102, 104, 110, 114, 117, 120, 125, 131, 134, 138, 141, 144, 148, 152, 155, 160, 164, 167, 170, 176, 180, 183, 187, 190, 194, 198, 202, 205; at Upper Church, 2, 12, 19, 26, 30, 34, 38, 46, 59, 63, 65, 68, 71, 74, 79, 84, 87, 91, 95 98, 101, 105, 110, 114, 117, 120, 125, 131, 134, 138, 141, 167, 170, 173, 176, 180, 183, 187, 190, 194, 198, 202, 205.
Sextoness, at Lower Church, 173, 205; at Upper Church, 94, 95, 97, 143, 144, 148, 152, 155, 160, 164.
Sharp, Andrew, xlvii.
Sharp (Tharp), Richard, 152.
Shea (Shay), John, 227, 229.
Shed, 78.
Shelbourn, Augustine, 71, 72, 75, 77.
Shelbourn, James, 77, 80.
Shelbourn, Mary, 21, 27², 31, 38.
Shelbourn, Thomas, 38, 80.
Shelbourn, Wm., 69.
Sheriff, John, 119, 122.
Sheriff, Mary, 127.
Sheriff, 4, 23, 27; collector of parish levy, 28, 32, 36, 39, 40, 48, 53, 58, 85, 88, 92, 93, 103, 107, 108, 136, 137, 140, 215, 223, 225², 228, 230; deputy, collector of parish levy, 3, 6, 9, 13, 22, 23, 50, 61, 73, 97, 100², 112, 116, 119, 124, 128, 133, 143, 147, 151, 154, 157, 163, 165, 169, 172, 176, 179, 182, 185, 197, 200; deputy, of James City County, 2, 225; deputy, of New Kent County, 112, 116, 119, 124, 128, 133, 197; of James City County, 127, 223, 225, 228, 230; of New Kent County, 93, 103, 108, 136,

# INDEX

137, 215, 223, 225, 228, 230; of York County, xlv (note), xlix².
Sheriffs, fees of, 19; grievance concerning, xliii.
Shermer, John, 117², 121², 126, 139, 156, 181, 187, 203; churchwarden, 115, 119, 120, 154², 155; successor to, appointed, 123, 157; vestryman, 109, 113, 125, 130, 133, 137, 141, 151, 158, 159, 163, 166, 170, 173, 176, 179, 182, 186, 189.
Sherwood, William, xxxv (note).
Shingles, 78², 139; cypress, 90, 94, 129.
Ship, trial by court martial on board of, xxxvi.
Ships, fort duties levied upon, xliii.
Shoemaker (Shomaker, Shoomaker), Francis, bond for daughter's fine, 3; petitioner, 32; sexton, 2, 5, 7, 12, 19, 43, 46, 49, 52, 57, 59; successor to, appointed, 60.
Shoes, for indigent persons, 142, 149, 195.
Shutters, wainscot, 56.
Sidwell, Richard, xlvi.
Silk fringe, 43.
Silk lace, 43.
Silk tassels, 43.
Skins, leather, 43.
Slater, Daniel, 172, 177, 180, 199, 213.
Slater, John, 190.
*See also* Sclater, John; Slaughter, John.
Slater, Rebecca, 227.
Slater, William, 78, 111; clerk of the Lower Church, 98, 101, 104, 109, 134, 138, 141, 144.

Slaughter, John vestryman, 1².
*See also* Sclater, John; Slater, John.
Smallpage (Smallepage), Sarah, 20, 27, 34, 35, 38, 46, 49.
Smith, Bryan, xxxviii⁴, xl², xli³.
Smith, George, xlvii, xlvii (note)², 121, 126, 131, 134, 138, 142, 145, 148, 152, 156.
Smith, James, xlvi.
Smith, Joseph, 202, 209.
Smith, Rebecca, 66.
Smith, Thomas, 75, 135, 138, 141, 156, 174, 177, 187, 202³, 206², 208², 209⁵, 210.
Smith, W., 196.
Smith, William, 153, 165, 168, 171, 174, 177, 180, 184; deputy sheriff and collector, 151, 154, 157, 162, 163, 165, 169, 172, 176; member of the committee to proportion the levy, 157, 158; successor to, appointed, 207; vestryman, 203.
Smith, William (orphan), 202, 209, 210, 224.
Smokehouse, to be built, 50, 88.
Snead, Henry, xlv.
Snell, Rutherford, lxi.
Southal, ———, lvii.
*Southern Churchman*, ix.
Southern Virginia, Diocese of, xvii.
Spanish brown, church doors and windows primed with, 56.
Speare, Robert, xlvii, xlvii (note)².
Specie, parish levy levied in, 220.
Specifications, for a church to be built in Blisland Parish, 53, 55²; for an addition to the

Upper Church, 94; for vestry house, 107.
Spencer, Nicholas, secretary of Virginia, xlviii.
Spraggins, William, processioner, 192.
Spraglinge, Andrew, xlv.
Stanup, John, lx.
Stanup (Stanhope), Jeremiah, 90; vestryman, 62$^2$, 64, 67, 68, 71, 76, 83$^2$, 87.
Steward, Daniel, 134, 139, 142, 145, 156, 165.
Steward, John, 145, 156, 165.
Stockings, for indigent persons, 142, 195.
Stone, church isle to be of Bristol, 55.
Storehouses, feoffees of counties to establish, xlviii.
Strange, Henry, xlvi.
Stratton Major Parish, v, xxi, xxii, xxii (note), xxiii, xxvii, xxviii, xxxii, xxxiv.
Strong drink, grievance concerning the selling of, xliii.
Stubs, Tho., xlvii.
Sub sheriff. *See* Sheriff, deputy.
Subscription for 1785, collectors of, 232.
Sugar, for indigent persons, 122, 188.
Supervisors, appointed, 56.
Surgeons, list of, 234.
Surplices, 43; laundered, 64, 68$^2$, 71, 76, 79$^2$, 84$^2$, 87$^2$, 91$^2$, 98$^2$, 102, 104, 105, 110$^2$, 114$^2$, 117$^2$, 120$^2$, 125$^2$, 131$^2$, 134$^2$, 138$^2$, 141$^2$, 144$^2$, 148$^2$, 152$^2$, 155$^2$, 160$^2$, 164$^2$, 167$^2$, 170$^2$, 173$^2$, 176$^2$, 180$^2$, 183$^2$; material for, 175$^2$; mended, 91, 98, 149, 153.

Surveyor, xxxiii, liv; of James City County, 86; paid for services, 88; to run dividing line, 64.
Sutton, Diana, 121, 126, 139.
Sutton, Samuel, xxxvi (note).
Swearing, fine for, 32.
Swiney, John, 117, 121.
Swiney (Sweny), Moses, 177, 180, 184, 187, 223.
Swiney (Sweeny), William, 163, 199, 207.
Syme, John, surveyor, liv.

Table, for the new church, 56.
Table linen, for communion table, 154.
Tailor, an apprentice to be taught the art of a, 44.
Tank's Creek, xii.
Tanner, William, 72.
Tarleton, Stephen, xli, xlix$^2$.
Taskanask, public warehouse at, liv, lv.
Tassels, silk, 43.
Taxes, grievance concerning, xliii.
Taylor, Ann, 162, 165, 167, 171, 174, 177, 181, 184, 190.
Taylor, Daniel, minister, li, lii, liv, 1$^2$, 2, 4$^2$, 5, 6, 7$^2$, 9, 11, 12, 14, 18$^2$, 21, 23, 25, 26$^2$, 27, 30$^2$, 32, 33, 34$^2$, 35, 36, 37, 38, 192, 233.
Taylor, Edmund, 212$^2$.
Taylor, Jeremiah, 102.
Taylor, John, 97, 98, 100, 105, 110, 114, 117, 121, 126, 131, 151$^2$, 162, 165, 167, 171, 174, 177, 181, 184, 187, 232.
Taylor, John Augustine, 232.
Taylor, Robert, 66, 69, 71.

# INDEX

Taylor, Sarah, 59, 63, 66, 69, 71, 72, 75, 77, 135, 138, 142.
Taylor, Tho., lii, 75, 80.
Terrell (Terrel, Terill, Terril), Richmond, xlvii, xlvii (note)[2], 80, 84, 88[2], 91[3], 96, 99[2], 102, 106, 111, 114; churchwarden, 85, 86, 87, 89[3], 90[2]; resigns as vestryman, 179; successor to, appointed, 92, 179; vestryman, 75, 76, 79, 83[2], 93, 94, 95[2], 98, 101, 104, 108, 109, 113, 116, 124, 128, 133, 137, 141, 151, 158, 159, 170, 176.
Thacker, Chicheley, minister, 40[2], 41, 42, 44, 45[2], 46[2], 48[2], 49[2], 50, 51[3], 52[2], 54[2], 55[2], 56[2], 57, 58, 59[2], 60, 61[2], 62[4], 64[2], 65, 67, 68[3], 70[2], 71[2], 74[3], 76[3], 79[3], 82[2], 83[2], 84, 85, 86, 87[2], 88, 89[2], 90[3], 92, 93[2], 94[2], 95[3], 98[3], 99, 100, 101[2], 104[2], 108, 109[3], 112[2], 113[3], 116[2], 117, 118, 119, 120[2], 122, 123, 124, 125[3], 128[2], 129[2], 130[2], 133[2], 134, 136, 137[2], 140, 141[2], 144[3], 147[2], 151, 152, 154, 155[2], 157, 233; salary paid to the estate of, 160; sermon by, to be printed and distributed, liv; thanked by burgesses for sermon, liv.
Tharp (Sharp), Richard, 152.
Thomas, Amelia, 202.
Thomas, John, 184.
Thomas, Mildred, 199.
Thomas, Susa., 117, 127[2].
Thompson, Roger, li.
Thomson, Mary, 199, 203, 206, 209, 212, 215, 219, 221, 224.
Thornton, ———, 5, 19, 38, 52.
Thornton, Mrs. ———, 87.
Thornton, John, liv, 2, 7, 12, 19, 27, 31, 35, 38, 42; churchwarden, 36, 38; successor to, appointed, 41; vestryman, 1, 4, 7, 9, 12, 18, 33, 34.
Thornton, John, 57; deputy sheriff and collector, 50.
Thornton, Mrs. Mary, 99.
Thread, for surplice, 153, 175.
Threshing floor, 122.
Tilsley, Thomas, xliv.
Timberlake, John, 142, 158, 163, 188, 210, 218[2]; churchwarden, 211[2], 212[2], 213, 215[3], 216; petitioner, 166; sheriff and collector of parish levy, 215; successor to, appointed, 217; vestryman, 207, 208, 221, 223, 226, 229.
Timberlake, Mrs. Sarah, 105, 110.
Tinny, William, 228.
Titheables, clerks paid for furnishing lists of, 7, 12, 19, 27, 31, 38, 46, 49, 52, 59, 65, 72, 75, 77, 80, 84[2], 87[2], 91, 96[2], 99[2], 102[2], 105[2], 110, 114, 117[2], 121[2], 126[2], 131[2], 134[2], 138[2], 141, 142, 145, 148[2], 152[2], 155[2], 160[2], 164[2], 167[2], 170[2], 173[2], 177[2], 180[2], 183[2], 187[2], 190, 194, 199, 202; have option of paying levy in cash or tobacco, 225; in Blisland Parish, 1; number of, and amount taxed, 3, 6, 8, 13, 20, 28, 31, 36, 38, 39, 47, 50, 53, 57, 60, 63, 69, 75, 77, 81, 85, 88, 92, 96, 100, 103, 107, 111, 115, 118, 123, 127, 132, 136, 140, 143, 145, 149, 153, 157, 162, 165, 168, 171, 174, 178, 181, 182, 183, 185, 186, 188, 189, 192, 196, 197, 198, 200, 201, 203, 207, 211, 214, 218, 222, 225, 228, 230.

Tithes, supernumerary, 77.
Tobacco, xli; act for improving the staple of, mentioned, 9, 15; given toward building a dwelling house, 45, 46, 49; levied for an addition to the Upper Church, 123, 127; levied for parish charges, 3, 6, 9, 13, 22, 24, 28, 32, 36, 39, 48, 50, 53, 58, 60, 61, 70, 73, 76, 78, 82, 86, 89, 93, 97, 100, 103, 108, 112, 116, 119, 124, 128, 133, 137, 155, 158; levied for repairing church, to be sold, 94, 95, 125; levied toward building a glebe house, 62, 63, 66, 69; levied toward building a new church, 47, 50, 51, 53; levy payable in cash or, 225; low price of, xlviii; sold for the use of the parish, 43, 48, 72; taken in execution of an estate, to be returned, 127; to be reprized, 95.
Tobacco casks, allowed, $2^3$, $5^2$, 13, 19, 20, 26, 27, $34^3$, 39, 52, 57, 62, 65, $70^2$, $71^4$, 72, 74, 76, $80^2$, $84^3$, 87, $90^2$, $91^3$, 95, $98^5$, $101^4$, $105^3$, 113, 117, 120, 125, 130, 137, $138^2$, 141, $144^5$, 147, 148, $152^4$, $155^5$, $160^6$, $164^5$, $166^2$, $167^3$, $170^5$, $173^5$, $176^5$, 179, $180^4$, 182, 186, 201, 205; allowed minister in lieu of glebe, 1, 4, 7, 12, 18, 26, 30, 34, 38.
Tobacco collectors, appointed, 3, 9, 13, 22, 23, 28, 32, 36, 61, 64, 67, 70, 73, 76, 78, 82, 85, 86, 88, 89, 93, 97, 100, 103, 107, 111, 112, 115, 116, 119, 123, 128, 136, 137, 140, 143, 147, 151, 154, 157, 163, 165, 169, 176, 179, 182.

Tobacco house, to be built on glebe, 85.
Tobacco plants, xlv (note), xlix; a justice of the peace suspended from office for failure to check cutters of, xlix; destroyed, xlviii; parish divided into precincts in order to number, xvii, 9, 10.
Tobacco riots, xlvii, xlviii$^2$, xlix, l.
Tobacco viewers and tellers, appointed, $10^2$, $11^2$, $15^2$, 25, 26, $33^3$, $34^2$, $37^2$.
Toby, a Negro, $22^2$.
Toner, Joseph Meredith, lvii.
Toney, a Negro, 169.
Townes, ———, 31.
Townes, John, 190, $191^3$; churchwarden, 185, 187, $188^2$, 189, 190; successor to, appointed, 197; vestryman, 185.
Towns, feoffees of counties to establish, xlviii.
Townsend Creek, xii (note).
Treasurer, report of the parish, 182.
Tree, maple, xi.
Trees, marked, xi; planted at the Lower Church, 69.
Turner, Henry, xlvi, xlvi (note).
Twin, Thomas, 149, 153, 156, 161, 165, 171.
Tyler, John, 110.
Tyree (Tirey, Tyre), Benjamin, 39, 41, 44, 47, 96, 99, 102, 114, 131, 134, 138, 172.
Tyree, Isaac, 126.
Tyree, James, $150^2$, 165.
Tyree, Lucy, 153, $168^2$, 172, $175^2$, 178, 181, 184, 187, 191, 195.
Tyree, Roger, 153.

# INDEX 273

Tyree (Tirey), Sarah, 88, 96, 99, 102, 105, 110, 114.
Tyree, William, 191, 192, 195, 206, 209, 212.

Underwood, James, 190.
Upper Church, lviii, lix$^2$; addition to, 94, 122, 123, 127, 129$^2$, 136; benches for, 142, 191; clerk of, 59, 62, 65, 68, 71, 74, 76, 79, 84, 87, 91, 95, 98, 101, 104, 109, 113, 117, 120, 125, 130, 134, 138, 141, 144, 148, 152, 155, 160, 164, 166, 170, 173, 176, 180, 183, 186, 190, 193, 198, 202, 205, 232; communions for, 126, 131, 134, 138, 148, 152, 156, 161, 164, 167, 170, 173, 176, 180, 183, 187, 190, 194, 198, 202, 205, 206; dial post repaired, 158; horseblocks for, 31, 142, 191; materials for, 150$^2$, 191; minister engaged for, 39; repaired, 90, 147, 150$^2$, 168, 171, 191; sashwindow for, 206; sexton at, 2, 12, 19, 26, 30, 34, 38, 46, 59, 63, 65, 68, 71, 74, 79, 82, 84, 87, 91, 94, 95, 97, 98, 101, 105, 110, 114, 117, 120, 123, 125, 131, 134, 138, 141, 143, 144, 148, 152, 155, 160, 164, 167, 170, 173, 176, 180, 183, 187, 190, 194, 198, 202, 205; to be painted, 93; vestry for Blisland Parish held at, 56, 61, 62, 67, 68, 82, 86, 89, 93, 95, 100, 101, 108, 116, 124, 125, 133, 137, 144, 151, 155, 158, 159, 163, 170, 176, 182, 189, 197, 204, 208, 226, 229, 231, 232.
Upper Church, of Wilmington Parish, plate belonging to, to be demanded, 53, 58.

Vadin, Julius, processioner, 192.
Vadin, William, 143.
Valentine, Edward, 107, 150.
Valentine, James, 177.
Valentine, John, 202, 209.
Valentine, Nicholas, 94, 99, 134$^2$.
Valentine, Nicholas, sr., 107, 110, 114, 117, 121, 126, 131, 138, 141, 145.
Valentine, Sarah, 171$^2$, 174, 177, 180, 183, 187.
Vaughan, John, xlvi, xlvi (note), li.
Vestry, agree that an addition be made to the Upper Church, 94; agreement with minister regarding glebe, 1; agreement with contractors to build church, 55; agreement with contractors to be enforced, 67; clerk of, 2, 4, 6, 7, 9, 11, 12, 14, 18, 19, 23, 25, 26$^2$, 29, 30, 33, 34$^2$, 36, 37$^2$, 38, 39$^2$, 40, 41, 44, 45$^2$, 46, 48, 49, 51$^2$, 52, 54, 55, 56, 57, 59, 62, 64, 67, 68, 74, 79, 82$^2$, 83, 86$^2$, 89$^2$, 90, 91, 93$^2$, 94, 95$^2$, 98$^2$, 100$^2$, 101$^2$, 104$^2$, 108$^2$, 109$^2$, 112$^2$, 113, 116$^2$, 117, 119, 120$^2$, 123, 124, 125$^2$, 128$^2$, 129, 130, 133$^2$, 136, 137, 138, 140, 141, 144$^2$, 147, 148, 151, 152, 154, 155, 157, 158$^2$, 159, 160, 163, 164, 166$^2$, 169$^2$, 170, 172, 173, 176$^2$, 179, 180, 182, 183, 185$^2$, 186, 188, 190, 193$^2$, 197, 198, 201, 202, 203, 204, 205, 208, 211, 212, 214, 215, 217, 218, 220, 222, 223, 224, 226, 228$^2$, 229, 230$^2$, 231, 232$^3$; clerk of, member of committee to proportion the parish levy, 220; clerk of, to keep register books,

158; committee to have vestry house built, 107; delegate to Richmond convention appointed, 231; dissolved and a new one chosen, 208; elect minister, 159; examine addition to Lower Church, 204; fix date for settling parish accounts, 67; glebe tenant allowed to make repairs in lieu of paying rent, 73, 85; indigent persons aided by, 49, 67, 73, 75, 83, 92; lay out parish into precincts, 9; list of the clerks of, 234; meeting of, postponed, 217; order board of workmen to be paid, 42; order churchyard to be laid off, 83; order indigent boy bound out, 44; orders made by, before taking oaths to be in force, 67; processioners appointed, 173, 186, 201, 203; processioners returns recorded and examined, 166, 169, 179, 189, 192; repairs and additions to glebe house made by, 42; to build dairy for minister, 45; to build glebe house, 58; to build Negro quarters on glebe, 44; to levy tobacco for building a glebe house, 62.

Vestry book, letters recorded in, 66, 97; processioners returns recorded in, 166, 169.

*The Vestry Book of Christ Church Parish, Middlesex County, Virginia, 1663-1767,* xxvi (note), lii (note).

*Vestry Book of Petsworth Parish, Gloucester C o u n t y, Virginia, 1677-1793,* li (note), lii (note).

Vestry book of St. Peter's Parish, xviii (note), xix (note), xx, xxxii, xxxiii (note), xliv (note)[4], xlv (note)[6], xlvi (note)[5], xlvii (note)[5], 1 (note), lii (note).

Vestry house, to be built, 107, 112.

Vestrymen, 1, 4, 7, 9, 12, 14, 15, 18, 23, 25, 26, 30, 33, 34, 36, 37, 38, 41, 42, 45, 46, 48, 49, 51, 52, 54, 55, 56, 59, 61, 62, 64, 67, 68, 71, 74, 76, 79, 83, 87, 89, 90, 93, 95, 98, 101, 104, 106, 108, 109, 112, 113, 116, 120, 124, 125, 128, 130, 133, 137, 141, 144, 147, 151, 155, 158, 159, 163, 166, 170, 172, 173, 176, 179, 182, 186, 189, 193, 198, 201, 204, 205, 208, 212, 213, 215, 217, 218, 221, 223, 225, 226, 229, 231, 232; appointed, 1, 14, 15, 41, 42[2], 50, 58, 61, 62, 64, 73, 75, 83[3], 88[2], 89[2], 90[2], 93, 94, 97, 100, 103, 109, 112, 140, 143, 154, 157, 159, 172, 179, 185, 197, 203, 207, 208, 213, 225, 231, 232; governor's opinion regarding the taking of oaths by, 65; letter of resignation to be recorded, 97; of Wilmington Parish, xxxi, liii (note); resignations, 50, 73, 97, 179; sworn, 1, 14, 15, 41, 42[2], 50, 58, 61, 62, 64, 73, 75, 83[2], 88, 89[2], 93, 94, 100, 103, 104, 137, 140.

Virginia, v, ix, xxii, xxxii, xxxvii; Commissioners for the Affairs of, xxxvii, xxxix, xl, xli, xlii; counties in, co-terminous with parishes, xxvi; Diocese of, lix[2]; Diocese of Southern, xvii, lix[2]; dividing line between counties and parishes in, xxi; historiographer of the Diocese of,

lxi; parish record books of colonial, x; parishes established in, during the period from 1643 to 1655, xxvi; parishes of, xxvii; Protestant Episcopal Church in, x; schedule of parishes in, xx; secretary of, xlviii; surrender of the colony of, xv; tobacco riots in, xlvii.
Virginia cloth, 191, 195.
Virginia Land Office, *Patent Book* no. 2, xii, xiii; no. 3, xi (note), xii (note), xiii, xxi (note), xxiv (note); no. 6, xxi (note), xxiii (note), xlv (note), xlvi (note).
*Virginia Magazine of History and Biography*, xxvi (note).
Virginia State Library, lxi, lxii; vestry books in custody of, x.
Virginian, appointed minister of Blisland Parish, 40.
Viewers of tobacco plants. *See* Tobacco viewers and tellers.

Waddell, John, xlvii, xlvii (note)².
Wade, James, 105², 107, 150, 224.
Wade, Jeremiah, 209.
Wainscot pews, 56.
Wainscot shutters, 56.
Wakefeild, John, xlvi.
Walker, Charles, 227.
Walker, Edmd., 66.
Walker, James Norvel, 227.
Walker, John, 227, 229².
Wall, Benja., 195.
Wall, Eliza., 148.
Wall, John, 110, 165, 168, 171, 174, 177, 195², 200.
Wall, Rachel, 195, 200².
Wall, Reba., 122.
Wall, Thos., 195.

Wall of churchyard, lengthened, 129.
Waller, Benjamin, 77, 80, 84, 87, 91, 96, 99, 102, 105, 110, 114, 117, 121, 126, 131, 134, 138, 141, 145, 148, 152, 155, 160, 164, 167, 170, 173, 177, 180, 183, 187, 190, 194, 199, 202, 206.
Waller, Benjamin C., 228.
Wallingford Parish, xxvi.
Wallis, Susa., 92.
Walton, Edward, xlvii.
Walton, Elizabeth, 12.
Ware Creek, xiv⁵, xv, xvii², xxxi, liv, 10².
Warehouse, at Taskanask, liv; established at Brick-house, lv; petition for repealing at Taskanask, lv.
Warrany Creek, xiv⁸.
Warrascoyack Bay, xxxvi.
Warren, Edward, processioner, 192.
Warren (Waren, Waring), Richard, 5, 8; petitioner, 22; sexton, 12, 19, 26, 30, 34, 38, 46, 52, 57, 59, 63, 64, 65, 68², 71², 74, 76, 79; successor to, appointed, 82.
Washer, John, 7.
Washer, Kirby, 146, 194, 199, 207.
Washington, George, lvi², lvii, lviii².
Washington, Martha (Dandridge Custis), lvi, lvii.
Water table, 55.
Watkins, Jos., 131.
Weave, an apprentice taught to, 39.
Weldey, Mrs. ———, 54.
Weldy, George, xxx, 5.

West, John, xxi (note)², xxiv (note)².
West Point, xxxv, xxxvi, lv (note), lxi.
Westmoreland County, 199.
Westover Parish, xxvi, xxix, xxx, xxxi².
Weyanoke Parish, xxvi.
Whaley, ———, xxxv², xxxvi.
Wheat, for indigent person, 122; for Upper Church, 150.
White, Rebecca, 121, 126, 131, 134, 138, 142, 145, 148, 152, 156.
*White House* plantation, lvi.
White lead, 56.
Whitehead, Charles, 75.
Whitehead, Mary, 39.
Wilks, Obadiah, 227.
Wilks, Thomas, 202, 206, 209.
*William and Mary College Quarterly Historical Magazine*, second series, xxiv (note).
Williams, Bartlett, deputy sheriff and collector of parish levy, 179, 180, 182, 184, 185, 186, 188, 189², 196.
Williams, David, successor to, appointed, 33, 90; tobacco viewer and teller, 25; vestryman, 88.
Williams, David, 187, 192, 196, 224.
Williams, Dudley, 115, 130, 168; clerk of the church and vestry, 82; clerk of the Lower Church and vestry, 113, 117, 120, 125, 130; clerk of the Upper Church, 84; clerk of the Upper Church and vestry, 87, 91, 95, 98, 101, 104, 109, 134, 138, 141, 144, 148, 152, 155, 160, 164, 166, 170, 173, 176, 180, 183, 186, 190, 193, 198, 202, 205; clerk of the vestry, 82², 83, 86², 89², 90, 91, 93², 94, 95, 98, 100², 101, 104, 108², 109, 112, 113, 116², 117, 119, 120, 123, 124, 125, 128², 129, 130, 133², 136, 137, 138, 140, 141, 144, 147, 148, 151, 152, 155, 157, 158², 159, 160, 163, 164, 166, 169², 170, 172, 173, 176, 179, 180, 183, 185², 186, 188, 190, 193, 197, 198, 201, 202, 203, 204, 205, 208, 211, 212, 214, 215, 217, 218, 220, 222, 223, 224, 226, 228², 234; collector of parish levy, 203, 207, 208, 211, 214, 218, 220, 222; member of the committee to proportion the parish levy, 119, 157, 158, 220.
Williams, Eliza., 121, 126, 131², 134, 138, 141, 145, 148, 152, 155, 160, 164, 167, 174.
Williams, John, 48, 77, 80, 81, 84.
Williams, Lewis, xliv.
Williams, Randal, 77, 80², 81, 84.
Williams, Rebekah, 135, 139, 187.
Williams, Roger, 10, 16², 17², 20, 25, 132, 140.
Williams, Thomas, 45, 49, 50, 52, 64; tobacco viewer and teller, 15, 34, 37; vestryman, 15², 23, 25, 26, 33, 34, 37, 42, 49, 61.
Williams' Ferry, lviii.
Williamsburg, xxxii, li, lvi, lxi, 40², 235.
Williamson, Eliza., 188, 191, 195, 199.
Williamson, Joseph, xxxv (note).
Williamson, Macoy, 99.
Willis, ———, liv.
Willis, Joel, 138, 149, 153, 156, 161, 165, 171, 191, 199.
Willis, Mrs. Joel, 199.
Willis, Joseph, 138.

INDEX                                                          277

Willis, Stephen, processioner, 192.
Willsford, Charles. *See* Millsford, Charles.
Wilmington Parish, xxvi, liii (note), 20[4], 54; act for dissolving, xxix, xxx, liii, 15[2]; area and population of, lii; minister of, lii; part of added to Blisland Parish, 15; petition of some of the inhabitants of, liii; plate belonging to Upper Church in, to be demanded, 53, 58; register books of, 85; vestrymen of, xxxi.
Window lead, 190.
Windows, arched with sashes, 56; frames primed with Spanish brown, 56; glazed, 191; in church gallery, 66; mended, 31.
Winifride, Henry, xlvii.
Witnesses, paid for services, 2[5], 5.
Wood, Walter, sexton, 2, 4, 7.
Wood, William, 135.
Woodington, John, xlix.
Woodward, George, vestryman, 15[2], 18, 25, 26, 30, 33, 34, 36, 37, 38, 41, 42, 45, 46, 48, 49, 52, 61, 62, 64, 67, 68, 71, 73.
Woodward, Jeremiah, 131.
Woodward, John, 214.
Woodward, John, jr., 80, 84.
Woodward, Lancelott, 80, 81, 84, 85, 109; churchwarden, 78[2], 81, 82; member of the committee to run dividing line, 85; successor to, appointed, 85; tobacco viewer and teller, 15, 34, 37; vestryman, 15[2], 18, 25, 26, 30, 33, 34, 36, 38, 41, 42, 45, 46, 48, 49, 54, 55, 56, 58, 61, 62, 64, 67, 68, 71, 74, 76, 79[2], 82, 83[3], 87, 89, 93, 95, 101.
Woodward, Lancelott, 174.
Woodward, Philemon, processioner, 192.
Woodward, Randolph, 192, 219[2], 221.
Woodward, Samuel, 102, 105, 110, 139.
Woodward, Warwick, 216, 224.
Workhouse, 147, 154, 196, 197.
Wright, Arth., xlvi (note).
Wrighte, Sam., xlvii, xlvii (note).
Wrighte, Will, xlvi, xlvi (note), xlvii (note).

Yard, to be laid off at Lower Church, 83.
Yates, John, 121, 138, 139, 142, 145, 154, 156, 225; sexton, 167, 170, 173, 176, 180, 183, 187, 190, 194, 198, 202, 205.
Yates, Lucy, 210, 214.
Yates, Mary, 195.
Yates, Sarah, 21.
York County, x, xi, xv, xxvii, xxxv, xlv (note); parishes in, xii (note), xvi (note), xvii; patents to land in, xi, xii, xiii, xiv; sheriff of, xlix.
York Parish, xvi (note), xvii[2].
York River, xi, xii, xiii[4], xiv, xiv (note), xvi[2], xvii, xviii[5], xx[3], xxi[2], xxii[2], xxvi, xxvii, xxviii, xxxi, xxxii[2], xxxvi[2], liv.
York-Hampton (Yorkhampton) Parish, xvii[2].
Yorktown Creek, xii (note).

www.ingramcontent.com/pod-product-compliance
Lightning Source LLC
Chambersburg PA
CBHW050333230426
43663CB00010B/1841